D1213096

MAZZINI: PROPHET OF MODERN EUROPE

Mazzini: Prophet of Modern Europe

BY GWILYM O. GRIFFITH

HOWARD FERTIG

NEW YORK · 1970

WILLIAM MADISON RANDALL LIBRARY UNC AT WILMINGTON

First published in 1932

HOWARD FERTIG, INC. EDITION 1970
Published by arrangement with Hodder and Stoughton Ltd.

All rights reserved.

Library of Congress Catalog Card Number: 78-80552

PRINTED IN THE UNITED STATES OF AMERICA
BY NOBLE OFFSET PRINTERS, INC.

DG552
8
.M3
.G7
1970

ACKNOWLEDGMENTS

THE author desires to acknowledge his special indebtedness (in addition to the principal Mazzinian sources) to the following works: *The Birth of Modern Italy*, by Jessie W. Mario (Fisher Unwin, 1909); *New Letters and Memorials of Jane Welsh Carlyle*, edited by Alexander Carlyle (John Lane, 1903); *Memories of Two Cities* (Agostino Ruffini), by David Masson, LL.D. (Oliphant, Anderson and Ferrier, 1911); *Letters of Swinburne*, edited by T. Hake and A. Compton-Rickett (John Murray, 1918); *Memoirs of Alexander Herzen* (" My Past and Thoughts "), translated by Constance Garnett (Chatto and Windus, 1927); *Palmerston*, by Philip Guedalla (Benn, 1926); and to the Italian studies mentioned in the Foreword and the Supplementary Bibliography. His grateful thanks are due to Mrs. E. F. Richards for permission to make free use of the material contained in *Mazzini's Letters to an English Family* (John Lane, 1920), and to Dr. Leonard Huxley and Mr. Murray for a like favour in respect of Mrs. Carlyle's letters: *Jane Welsh Carlyle: Letters to Her Family, 1839-1863*, edited by Leonard Huxley, LL.D. (John Murray, 1924). It is right to add that Mrs. Richards does not entirely endorse the author's portrayal of Mazzini, as she considers that the moral elevation of Mazzini's character and his prophetic consecration are inadequately presented.

81989

FOREWORD

MANY biographies and biographical studies of Mazzini have appeared since his death in 1872. Among English publications Émilie Ashurst Venturi's brief memoir, brought out in 1875, occupies a place of its own, while Mr. Bolton King's *Life of Mazzini* (1902) has established itself as a standard and authoritative study. Since, however, the appearance of Mr. King's work, thirty years of Italian research in the oceanic welter of Risorgimento documents has brought new material to the surface, and not only so, but old material also has passed through the process of specialising study. Thus we have had, besides Donaver's compact biography, such contributions as those of Codignola, Cozzolino, Levi, Luzio, Mondolfo, Salvemini, Rosselli and Salucci. Among English publications, too, there have been contributions of value, notably the posthumous papers of Mme. Jessie White Mario, Mrs. Hamilton King's *Recollections of Mazzini,* Mrs. Hinkler's study, the admirable selection of *Mazzini's Letters,* translated by Miss Alice De Rosen Jervis, and such memoirs as those of Alexander Herzen. Above all we have had the three volumes of *Mazzini's Letters to an English Family,* edited by Mrs. E. F. Richards, an incomparable collection, carefully edited and linked together with historical and biographical notes. With such an added accumulation of material a new attempt to interpret Mazzini's life and thought may not be without justification.

As for the present study, what has been attempted in the main is the setting forth of the development of Mazzini's inner life. This aim has dictated the chronological method of dealing with Mazzini's writings, and this method in turn has necessitated the interruption of the narrative, especially in the first half of the book. Incidentally it may be said that Mazzini's thought developed very little after 1836. By that time he had arrived at fixed principles in religion and political philosophy and from these he never deviated. For the rest, an attempt has been made to re-interpret Mazzini's influence in the later and much criticised phases of his agitation, an influ-

9

ence which was more decisive and more constructive than some
are inclined to suppose. This must be the excuse for the space
given in these pages to the tortuous policies and confused events
of the later years of the Italian struggle—events which in their
Garibaldian setting have been brilliantly and finally chronicled
by Trevelyan, and policies which, in their Cavourian orientation, have been expounded by Thayer.

*   *   *   *   *

One question inevitably arises out of any study of Mazzini's
life. He stands or falls as prophet, or, as Francesco De
Sanctis prefers to say, as *precursor,* of the new age. How
has time dealt with his reputation? " The future," he wrote,
" will declare whether I have foreseen or have merely
dreamed." Does it appear now that he is discredited? Certainly in 1914 it seemed as if the reputation of no European
statesman, from Metternich onward, had worn so well. The
Great War found all the liberal thinkers of Europe and
America hastening to subscribe to the Mazzinian creed, and
President Woodrow Wilson's gesture of homage at the grave
of the great Italian was appropriate and representative. Comes
now, too, the recollection of a Mazzinian gathering in London
(it was after the Genoa Conference) with Mr. Lloyd George
as the chief speaker (and Mr. Bernard Shaw in the audience).
Perhaps the memory of the (then) Prime Minister's eloquent
eulogy is now a little indistinct, but who that was present will
forget its refrain: " *How right he was!*"?

But what of these later years? One thinks of the long and
strenuous debates at Cheyne Row between Mazzini and Carlyle.
Is it not Carlyle who has been vindicated? In Italy itself, for
example? Sixty odd years ago the Chelsea oracle gave Democracy sixty more years in which to play itself out. . . . Yet
to suppose that this argues Mazzini's discreditment is to betray
a curious misreading of his thought. The present condition in
Europe is precisely what he predicted would be the consequence of a half-hearted democratic régime captured by the
middle-classes and governed by *bourgeois* interests and the
egoism of rival States. Shock and counter-shock, the clash of
classes, the menace of materialistic communism on the one
hand offset by the rise of dictatorships on the other—these
things he foresaw; these things, indeed, he regarded as inevit-

able so long as Europe remained in moral anarchy, preoccupied
with class safeguards and the desire to halt the Revolution
before it reached the stage of economic as well as political en-
franchisement.

As for his prescription—that is another matter. It may be
true, for example, that his faith in modern humanity was
rather too hopeful and idealising—that, for all his enthusiasm
for Dante, he lacked Dante's sense of sin. But on the whole
would not the modern mind (supposing it gave attention to
the matter at all) find his formula not too hopeful but too
serious, too drastic and too difficult? Thus, a sovereign remedy
that goes, as his does, so far beyond Tariff adjustments, Empire
Free Trade and recurrent International Conferences on Debts
and Disarmament, may be regarded as curiously extravagant.
And indeed it may be admitted that not even a League of
Nations, operating amid existing confusions, would have met
his mind, though he projected some such league, eighty years
ago, as a practical necessity (see p. 241): at least he would have
viewed it as little more than a solemn witness, set up in the
midst of the peoples, to a Duty and a Law beyond its power
to enforce, the focal point of the moral failure of the world.
He had, in fact, little hope of any permanent and fruitful
agreement in Europe apart from a common currency of conscience, a common standard of values, a common Authority.
Like any gospeller or distressed Archbishop, he propounded
his alternative—the Kingdom of God or Chaos: only he did
not interpret the Kingdom of God in terms of the Council of
Trent or the Thirty-nine Articles or the Westminster Standards.
He looked, it seems, for a League of Faith to provide the basis
for a League of Nations—looked, in fact, for a new religious
unity ("synthesis" was his own rather overworked term)
to proceed from a reformed Catholicism, delivered from the
absolutism and immobility of the Papal system. And he
thought it would come when the flag of the Republic should
float above the Vatican and the Capitol. What is to be made
of a dreamer whose dreams, fashioned in the ethereal Un-
apparent, are so remote from present realities? Yet they
strangely haunt the mind. "Just as in the days of his flesh
he passed along the by-ways of Europe, an exile from every
land but our own, ever conspiring and ever eluding the

authorities, so his subsequent influence has been fugitive, secret, noiseless, but none the less real, deep, persistent. His best compositions have had little vogue, but they are treasured by the musicians who know."* And what are our own more realistic alternatives to European chaos? Fascism, Hitlerism, Sovietism. . . ? One sobering lesson, at least, we have learnt from Russia—namely, that not even the most thorough-going of proletarian revolutions has cancelled the necessity for an absolute discipline, a lean and strenuous life, an iron code. The popular gospel of an easy liberty and happy idleness has passed, and Mazzini's insistent emphasis upon the Duties of Man has been confirmed. Meanwhile other aspects of the Mazzinian doctrine have touched reality disturbingly enough —in India, for example. It must be remembered, however, that an ebullient, self-centred national*ism*, as such, was alien to Mazzini's thought and spirit. He believed in Nationality as he believed in Individuality; he hated ego-centric national*ism* as he hated individual*ism*.

One other word may be added. Mazzini was in a sense the Mahatma of nineteenth-century Europe, but what of his ethical standard? He was committed to methods of violent revolutionism. It would have been strange, indeed, if in Italy in his day he had escaped that commitment. It may be questioned if even Mr. Gandhi, dealing with the Austrian régime of the nineteenth century, and living beneath the moral firmament of Southern Europe at that time, would have seen so clearly the lode-star whose white radiance has guided his own remarkable career. But it remains true that Mazzini's idealism was embarrassed by its entanglement in measures and methods which future generations must regard as morally obsolete. If we do not feel that this fact calls for exposition in the case, say, of Lincoln or John Brown or Kossuth or Gordon, it is because their reputation never stood, as Mazzini's does stand, in an idealism, deliberately set forth as an anticipation of future standards of faith and action. Yet when this has been admitted, the fact remains that Mazzini advocates a policy whose effect would have been to build out war from Europe as it is now built out from the American Union. Peace (which

* Thomas Jones: Introduction to Mazzini's *Duties of Man* (Everyman's Library series).

for him never meant simply " no more war " but active, harmonious co-operation in one sovereign aim)—peace as he understood it would come through Union, and Union through the voluntary autonomous association of the free peoples. He would have agreed with Kant's dictum that the existence of every isolated and independent State signified a potential war. But, unlike Mr. H. G. Wells, he did not propose to " kill patriotism," nor did he regard nationhood as a fungoid growth. The way to a sound internationalism, as he saw it, lay through the recognition, not the repudiation, of the principle of Nationality; the solidarity of Europe must, he insisted, rest upon the pact of the national units associated in a common purpose and destiny, and no nation could be regarded as an effective unit so long as it was organised into rival classes with conflicting interests and aims. Hence economic democracy must keep pace with political democracy and the basis must be laid for religious, political and economic unity. In this connection he preferred the term " social government," since " democracy " had become too exclusively political in its significance.

* * * * *

Special and grateful acknowledgments are due to Dr. Gaetano Salvemini, who, in the midst of his many labours, has found time to offer valuable corrections and criticisms. Unfortunately, owing to pressure of time, not as many of these have been incorporated in the text as the author could have wished. This should be made clear in fairness to Dr. Salvemini.

To Professor Carlo Rosselli for his unfailing interest and courtesy; to Mlle. Elis Béguin, Neuchâtel, and Miss Megan Griffith for their assistance; to the Rev. A. Charlton, Bradford, for kindly contributing biographical material and the Rev. F. W. Merlin, St. Anne's-on-Sea, for valuable suggestions; to Miss Probyn, Stamford Hill, and Mr. G. F. Pullen, Oxford, for their kind assistance; and not least of all to Mr. Whalley P. Morgan, Classical master, Newtown County School, Mont., for his generous help and criticism, particularly in the Italian section, the author desires to express his indebtedness.

GWILYM O. GRIFFITH.

WYLDE GREEN,
 BIRMINGHAM.
  January, 1932.

CONTENTS

BOOK ONE: 1805–1830

TWILIGHT

BOOK TWO: 1830–1837

RED DAWN

BOOK THREE: 1837–1848

GREY MORNING

BOOK FOUR: 1848–1849

NOON

BOOK FIVE: 1850–1857

AFTER NOON

BOOK SIX: 1858–1866

EVENING STAR

BOOK SEVEN: 1867–1872

CURFEW DEFIED

TWILIGHT

CHAPTER I   THE MAZZINIS

THOMAS HARDY'S *Dynasts* begins with a panorama of Europe as seen from the Overworld, and the year is 1805. The nether sky opens and the Continent is disclosed in the form of a prone and wasted figure, the Alps shaping like a backbone and Spain the head. The view then focuses upon " the surface of the perturbed countries, where the peoples, distressed by events which they did not cause, are seen writhing, crawling, heaving and vibrating in their various cities and nationalities."

For our present purpose we may let the point of view, sinking further downward, focus upon the city of Genoa and upon a narrow street, the Via Lomellini, lying off the main thoroughfare and climbing the hillside from the port. This street was mainly composed of middle-class houses, and in an upper room in one of these, its green casements shut against the blaze of the June sunshine, a dark-eyed mother, Maria Mazzini, held to her breast her newborn son. A century later that house, that birth-room, would be visited by pilgrims of all nationalities; even the old nut-wood, canopied cradle would be piously preserved.

And as for that particular time, 1805 was, in truth, a year to invite the imagination of the historical dramatist. The world was under arms. Nelson was sweeping the seas in pursuit of Villeneuve. Pitt, prematurely aged, was organising the third Coalition. Bonaparte had renounced the Channel for the Rhine and the Danube, for Ulm and Austerlitz, and presently at Milan, before the high altar of the Cathedral, had assumed the iron crown of the Lombards and the title of King of Italy.

17

Nor was there any city in Italy where these events were debated more keenly than in Genoa—annexed to France in that same year. Eight years earlier the city had passed, through riot and saturnalia, to a revolution on its own account and had proclaimed the Ligurian Republic; and in 1800 the presence of Masséna and his garrison had involved it in the rigours of an Anglo-Austrian siege. Provisions had been reduced from horse-flesh to mice and worms, and, while plague followed in the track of famine, noble matrons and maids, basket in hand, wandered " over the green slopes behind the town, eagerly digging up some few roots and herbs."[1]

Thus in Genoa the political discussion of European events was no mere academic exercise, and debate ran high among the educated classes who had abetted the late revolution. It ran high in the Via Lomellini, in the parlour of Dr. Giacomo Mazzini, where ardent and public-spirited young liberals like Andrea Gambini and Bernardo Ruffini would drop in for regular discussion of the gazettes. But in this month of June— the month following the coronation at Milan—the domestic event took place which temporarily eclipsed, for the Mazzinis, all political happenings, and which, as future developments were to prove, held the secret of very considerable political happenings in itself. For it was on the 22nd of June that the young Signora Mazzini presented her husband with a son— Giuseppe.

As for Europe, viewed from Hardy's Overworld or elsewhere, it was certainly forlorn and afflicted enough. Yet there were less depressing considerations. Throughout the Continent there was a ferment of new ideas. The vinous fountains of the French Revolution were still active. Mr. William Wordsworth, having drunk at these fountains a little earlier, had found it bliss to be alive and very heaven to be young. On the Continent he had contemporaries by the million who knew that high intoxication long after he himself had repented of it. Bonaparte may have sadly mixed the vintage, but at least there was no lack of stimulation. Bonapartism itself served to excite and challenge the imagination of men : " the gigantic entered into our very habits of thought."

Nowhere was this more true than in Italy, where centuries of foreign domination had starved and demoralised the national spirit. The country had long been a crazy patchwork of kingdoms and petty states, and Foscolo could lament that Italians, set apart by arbitrary boundaries, regarded each other as foreigners. One institution had indeed remained—the Church, capable of conserving and directing the common aspirations of the people. But the Church was not dreaming the Italian dream, and while the Pope governed his own dominions in the style of a mediæval prince, his Jesuit emissaries cooperated with the Austrian Court to preserve the foreign régime on the peninsula.

To the Italians, then, the vintage of the Revolution came as the nectar of the gods. Liberty, Equality, Fraternity—the Age of Reason—the Rights of Man—what could be more exhilarating to the ill-nourished but now eager and stimulated mind of young Italy? And the victor of Lodi and Marengo knew his Italians. History inspired him, the history of Italy most of all, and his manifestos were steeped in the poetry of nationalism. "*Peoples of Italy, the Army of France comes to break your chains.*" "*We are the friends of the offspring of Brutus and Scipio. . . . To re-establish the Capitol, to set up there the statues of the heroes, to awaken the Roman people which for centuries has been paralysed by servitude*" —this, it seemed, was to be the mission of the heaven-sent Liberator.

This, then, was the new spirit in Italy. In literature it had found early expression in the writings of Alfieri and of Foscolo. Before the end of the eighteenth century Foscolo and others, in the *Monitore Italiano,* were openly advocating Italian union. After Marengo Count Melzi d'Eril, a Milanese and Vice-President of the Republic of Italy, openly advertised that as Bonaparte was of Italian blood he should be persuaded to renounce all connection with France and give himself to the building of a United Italy.[2] And now in this year of 1805 Bonaparte had returned from the East and once more the Bourbons and Habsburgs were scurrying before him. Austria was banished from Lombardy and Venetia, Ferdinand from Naples, and the Kingdom of Italy was proclaimed with a revival of Carolingian pomp. It was union by instalments, promising a federation of client kingdoms under a Corsican dynasty; but it was union.

In some degree there were sections of the Church itself that responded to the new spirit; among them, for example, the Jansenists. Jansenism as a puritan-evangelical movement within the Papacy had long ago earned the hostility of the Jesuits and declined; now it revived, and here and there a Jansenist group discovered a new zeal. The priest who acted as tutor to Dr. Mazzini's family was a Jansenist. And beyond this many a young novice, many a friar and parish priest, innocent of Jansenius' heresies, responded secretly to the new doctrine of liberty and progress.

Among the earliest of these clerical converts had been Dr. Mazzini himself.

*   *   *   *   *

In Mazzinian annals Maria Mazzini's husband is apt to appear as a blurred and slightly forbidding figure in the shadowy background—"the dour Dr. Mazzini." Who would have supposed that the dour doctor had himself been a revolutionary? Who would have supposed that he it was who had helped to sow, or at least to nourish, the seeds of Jacobinism in his young wife's mind?

He was a native of Chiavari—the home, before they moved to Nice, of the Garibaldis. His family was poor. He himself was set apart for the priesthood. But the world was young, and in secret he read French philosophy, dreamed dreams of liberty and universal reform, and finally broke his novitiate to study medicine at the University of Pavia. It was still a young world when, with his friends De Albertis (about to enter the French service) and Count Bartolomeo Alberti, he came to Genoa. He spent his evenings in the home of a middle-class Genoese family of the name of Drago where there were three sisters, Rosa, Antonietta and Maria; and while Count Bartolomeo and De Albertis wooed Rosa and Antonietta Dr. Giacomo duly fell in love with the dark-eyed Maria. In due time also he brought his young bride (for Maria was many years his junior) to his house in the Via Lomellini and settled down to mix medicine and politics with great content.

Viewed from the windows of the Via Lomellini home it was now, in very truth, a young and hopeful world, with the oriflamme of a new dawn in the sky; and the Doctor joined a group of young bloods (Andrea Gambini and Bernardo Ruffini were among them) out to revolutionise Genoa. Liberty, Equality, the Rights of Man, the Sovereignty of Reason—the young ex-cleric swallowed them all. With his colleagues he helped to found a Jacobin anti-clerical journal, the *Censore Italiano,* and hovered (he was by nature prudent) on the edge of a secret society or two. By 1796 the new propaganda had succeeded so well that the Doctor and his friends may well have been alarmed. For a while mob violence reigned in the city, and while a petrified Senate sat impotent in its Council Chamber a vociferous populace stormed the forts and prisons and dockyard galleys and decreed the abolition of the aristocracy and of taxes. But by the summer of '97, thanks to the victories of Bonaparte, the reformers were able to stage their milder revolution; the Genovesate was converted into the Ligurian Republic under French protection, and the three friends, Gambini, Ruffini and Dr. Mazzini found themselves with minor appointments under the new Government.

It seems that in his political activities the Doctor was encouraged by his young wife. No more than half-educated, according to modern standards, she was in those days superior in culture to the average of her class. She was fiery, romantic, public-spirited and given, says Donaver, to " expressing judgments not common in a woman "; and one may accept the testimony of her contemporaries that she was beautiful. Dr. Mazzini developed into something of an austere disciplinarian, but he never ruled Maria Drago. In politics she carried his opinions to conclusions of her own; in religion she remained, in spite of his sceptical phase, a devout Jansenist. Perhaps, indeed, it was Maria's magnetism rather than the Doctor's zeal, that turned the Mazzini parlour into a modest political *salon.* Bernardo Ruffini, stormy and erratic, was docile under her glance; Andrea Gambini, shrewd, bluff and matter-of-fact, with a touch of sardonic wit—Andrea rose almost to poetry in his meek and blameless devotion to her society. In 1800 the French reverses at Cassano and Milan drove the apostles of Liberalism to Genoa for sanctuary, and the little *salon* enlarged its circle. Men like Giacomo Breganze, Foscolo's colleague, attached themselves and carried away lively recollections of the Signora Maria's conversation. Breganze's correspondence figures later in the Mazzini annals, but it was to his "estimable friend" the "good Mari(n)a," rather than to the Doctor, that the old jurist wrote.

Up to 1805 two daughters, Rosa and Antonietta, had been born to the Mazzinis, but with the birth of her son Maria's life entered upon a new phase. If ever a mother was son-centred that mother was Maria; and Giuseppe's frail health invited her concentrated devotion. For the first five years of his life the child suffered from spinal weakness and was unable to walk. That he might be under her eye she trundled him in his invalid stretcher from room to room. In the mornings, when the old priest taught Rosa and Antonietta their lessons Giuseppe ("Pippo") liked to be within earshot in an adjoining room. His father, fearing for an over-excitable brain, had prohibited his being taught his letters, but in this way the paternal prohibition was foiled. This was the first but not the last time for mother and son to outwit the Doctor; and at four years of age he was reading fluently. Propped with pillows he would sit up in his book-strewn cot, "looking like a philosopher in Lilliput." Maria watched him with pride. Years later she would write to him: "I have lived and I shall die unrecognised for what I am"—unrecognised the vague dreams and forth-reachings of her inmost being. But he should give expression to it all. She would write to him, too, of her Jansenist-Calvinist faith in the Overworld, in the Immanent Will and its designs. For to Maria—her boy banished and in hiding somewhere among the Alpine solitudes—the Overworld must be something more than a dramatic convenience, and for herself she must affirm her conviction of an actual Immanent-transcendent Will, working through all the sorry welter and maze of things. Poor humankind, "writhing, crawling, heaving"—this tortured Europe! She reports little to be observable on that general level save the working of the two grand passions of self-interest and ambition: "The human species," she declares, "is very wretched."[3] But in her Calvinistic way she sets forth her faith in the Upper Powers in hidden commerce with the Elect. For there are, she affirms, elect souls—"divine emanations" is her word for them—immune from the general corruption; and through them the immanent Purpose throbs up to the surface of events. As she sees it, these Word-bearers or prophet-souls are the true makers and martyrs of history, enabling the mass of mankind to heave foward to some new and higher level of being. Attached to this conviction was mother-faith, more secret and personal. She believed that one such Word-bearer had been quickened in her own womb, nursed at her own breast. Spiritually, too, he had drawn something of his life from her. In her own soul also she had felt something of the stirrings of a new Word, vague and inarticulable. But to watch over her son, to train him, to prepare him for his high calling —this was now her life.

And even in the earlier years there were happenings which encouraged her private and almost messianic faith. One of these (worn threadbare this long while by repetition in all Mazzinian chronicles) was what Maria liked to call the " symbolical " incident at the Church of the Annunciation. For it fell out that sometime in 1811 she took Pippo for his first walk beyond the bounds of his own home and must needs pass the great church on the corner of the main street, hard by the Via Lomellini. On the church steps sat an old beggarman, long-bearded and ragged, drumming noisily with his staff to attract the notice of passers-by. Whereupon Pippo (she says) came to a standstill with eyes for nothing but old Misery. Supposing the child to be frightened, for it was his first sight of human wretchedness, she took him in her arms, but he broke away from her, ran forward to the steps, and flung himself upon the old man's neck, kissing him and crying "Give him something, mother! Give him something!" At which, continues Maria, old Misery suddenly became transfigured as by the kindling within him of some hidden nobleness; did, in fact, most tenderly return the child's caresses, not without tears of his own, then rose with venerable dignity and said " in pure Roman accents ": " Love him dearly, signora. He is one who will love the people."[4] A " symbolical " incident, thinks Maria, set, as it was, against the background of the great Church of the Annunciation.

But more to the point was the " prophetic letter " of good cousin Colonel Patrone, of the Artillery school at Pavia. The gallant Colonel, returned to Pavia from a visit to the Mazzinis, writes to his " most distinguished Cousin " Maria (August 20, 1812) and offers suggestions regarding the education of her "adorable son." He would emphasise, among other things, "a compendium of Italian history," the elements of world-history and modern languages. As for these last—French, English, German—the admirable Patrone would have them taught by conversation, leaving rules of grammar to follow in natural course. And as for advanced studies, let his parents be not too forward in putting into Pippo's hands books of *opinion* and *theory*; "a genius such as his, in its own good time, will appropriate the best or will create it." Let Pippo learn music, and, now that health permits, dancing; and for the rest, let his parents be assured that with his retentive memory and unbounded capacity of apprehension, he will pass easily from subject to subject without any risk of his impressions being confused or his mind overburdened.

But for Maria the jewel of the letter was the prophecy with which it began:

" Believe me, signora cousin, he is a star of the first magnitude, shining with a true light, and destined to be admired one day by all the culture of Europe. Thus it behoves all to regard him as belonging to themselves and to concern themselves to see to it that the extraordinary gifts lavished upon him by Nature should be turned to the best advantage. The great geniuses who, in distant epochs, have bestowed lustre upon their age, have usually in their infancy displayed just such powers as are observable in him."*

These portents, with much else, Maria in later days related to Emilie Ashurst. Indeed, the records of his youth conform to the opening chapters in those " Lives of the Great " upon which a past generation was customarily edified. Pippo, it seems, was " unusually thoughtful and serious " and indisposed to bestow himself upon the ordinary diversions of childhood; all the same, he had a fund of drollery and would laugh "almost convulsively " at such stories as were comic, but unlike most children could never endure to hear the same story twice. In due time he learnt his Latin grammar and read Livy with the old Jansenist priest, Don Luca; in the summer he would ramble

* See Cozzolino: *Maria Mazzini ed il suo ult⁰ carteggio.* After Maria Mazzini's death the letter was copied and various versions were circulated. The original passed into the hands of Aurelio Saffi, ex-Triumvir of the Roman Republic. It is still preserved with date and seal and the endorsement "*Lettera profetica* " in Maria's hand.

among the uplands of Bavari, in the Bisagno valley; and through the long winter evenings he would pore over his father's books and old Girondist papers.

Meanwhile for Dr. Mazzini it was no longer a young world. There was, for one thing, the sobering responsibility of a family. There were now four children, Rosa, Antonietta, Giuseppe and Francesca, and three of them were delicate. Rosa was threatened with phthisis; Pippo had been bedridden for the first five years; Francesca, if not crippled, was infirm and frail. Moreover, the Doctor's experience of public office had left him disillusioned. He found that a republican administration was not in itself a guarantee against political corruption or a sure remedy for the vices of mankind. Years later he wrote that he could have got rich quickly during his period of office. He resisted; others were less scrupulous; and he began to reflect that there might be more in the Church's doctrine of Man than was dreamed of in French philosophy. Was not the Revolution collapsing because it started with an inadequate conception of human nature? Mankind in general, and the Genoese in particular, did not really want to be reformed; they wanted to eat, drink, make money and cultivate their pet vices. Avarice and hyprocrisy were rife, and with a humanity of this type, he declared, even Christ and His apostles, if they returned, would be "doomed to a solemn *fiasco*." Europe, he prophesied, might become Cossack but not Republican, Russian but not Red. So it was an old world, after all, and with the Corsican out of the way the petty tyrants slipped back and resumed their administration of the decrees of Providence.

There was one flicker of rejuvenation. Over in Elba Napoleon, wearying of a toy court and toy army, was meditating a new descent upon Europe. The liberals, secretly advised, organised promptly in Turin and Genoa, drew up a new programme of reform, and invited the exile to put his fate to the touch. "Say like God to Light, *Let there be Italy,* and Italy shall be." Discussion ran high in the Mazzini *salon,* as elsewhere; the bankers of Genoa voted a large sum for the enterprise and liberal citizens secretly prepared warlike equipment. But Napoleon, turning from Italy, elected to bestow himself once more upon France.

This seems to have been Dr. Mazzini's final disenchantment. Henceforth he regarded national politics with disgust. Retiring behind a mask of Genoese taciturnity, he witnessed unmoved the return of the Absolutists and observed the Holy Alliance, having duly said grace before meat, proceeding once more to the carving up of Italy. The Roman States were served to the Pope, Lombardy and Venetia were piled on Austria's plate, Naples and Sicily went to Ferdinand, Tuscany to a scion of the Habsburgs, while Parma, Lucca and Modena were offered for the appeasement of the territorial appetites of the Grand Dukes and Genoa was annexed by Piedmont. The Doctor, against the outraged sentiment of the Genoese, supported the annexation. It was his last political gesture. His action has been curiously attributed to his belief in a piecemeal unification of Italy. He himself testified otherwise. He did what he could, he declared, to further the union under the Piedmont (Sardinian) crown because he had no faith that either the Genoese aristocracy or the citizenry could restore stability and tranquillity. " Aristocracy would be persecutive, democracy would be complete anarchy."⁵

Henceforth Dr. Mazzini concentrated upon his profession. He had moved in 1810 from the Via Lomellini to a more ambitious residence. Through his friend Armfelt, who belonged to the *entourage* of the King of Sweden, he had already made excursions into the upper circles of society, and of this he was proud. He had once or twice dined even with that ornament of the English nobility, the Duke of Kent, come South " with a lady whom he wished to marry." Now he cultivated advancement in his profession, and in 1816 accepted a post on the Medical Faculty of the University of Genoa and became Professor of Anatomy and Physiology. Clearly, Italy was not ripe for reform; therefore it was enough that an honest man should look to his own affairs, laying the foundations of a " virtuous independence," an " honourable security." These were the expressions which, in lieu of the old Jacobin watchwords, henceforth governed his paternal admonitions. " Security!" " Sicurezza!"

Also he returned to communion with the Church. Outward conformity was required by the University, but his return was not merely formal. He was persuaded that " the secret of tranquillity and felicity" was contained in the essential truths of Christianity, and politics had little to do with it. "Jesus Christ and His apostles," he reminded his son, "spoke neither of a republic nor of government." He professed a liberal creed and avoided the Jesuits and the extremists "who run to Church to pray and then hate and kill whoever is not of their way of thinking"; but the Philippini Fathers, installed in the neighbourhood, were congenial. He found them "true and virtuous," edifying in their conversation and able, on the lighter side, to play a good game of bowls or billiards; also their *ravioli* suppers were excellent. For the rest, while he was justly gratified to find his practice and reputation extending to the upper classes, he was rigidly conscientious in his charitable attendance upon the poor. Thus did Professor Mazzini, most methodical of men, find and follow his groove. The French philosophy books were left to accumulate dust on their neglected shelves, the old Girondist journals were hidden away behind them; and henceforth, to the day of his death in 1848, his way of life did not alter by a hair's breadth. His neighbours might have regulated their watches by his punctual movements.

It was otherwise with Maria, his wife. In her splenetic moods, which were not infrequent, she might despise her own generation and lampoon the Genoese, but it was not in her to forsake her political interests and principles. It was not in her to retreat from any position which she had once taken up, and she had a defensive and offensive armoury of pointed epigram and knife-edged satire. To argue with the Professor was useless, but she watched his political defection with displeasure. She was a loyal wife, but perhaps her affection was now, in the main, a resolute and dutiful fidelity. He was weak, poor man; so—politically—was Gambini; and Bernardo Ruffini was nothing more than a loud, excitable, overgrown boy, not to be taken seriously or trusted with important affairs. So Maria developed a secret maternal pity for most of her men-folk (always excepting Colonel Patrone and Judge Breganze and her Jansenist priests) and concentrated her hopes upon Pippo, the idol of her heart. Perhaps the Professor was conscious of the change. His wife had dethroned him from her inner heart, and to offset his annulment he became more and more a martinet, close-fisted in money-matters, methodising the family *ménage* with military precision.

*   *   *   *   *

Meanwhile, with the Professor proceeding with his lectures on morbid anatomy, and the hotheads of '97 now appreciably cooler, the Piedmont (Sardinian) Government improved its opportunities. No parleying henceforth with liberty, citizenry, reform and the Rights of Man! The French Terror had exposed all that. The French Terror had shown that such euphemisms meant only the taxation of wealth, confiscation of estates, guillotine-massacres and general saturnalia—with a new, upstart, illegitimate Absolutism emergent at the end. The only answer to this heresy of popular sovereignty was the divine right of legitimate despotism. "Here," says Governor Thaon de Reval to his Genoese—"here we are not ' citizens ' but only a King who commands and a people who obey." Old Victor Emmanuel I., "King who commands," was himself no fire-breathing tyrant; his people, who beheld him munching his bread-sticks in the royal box and ogling the girls of the ballet, understood as much; but there were minor tyrants— military governors, Jesuit clerics, Jacks-in-office—who supplied the royal deficiency, and Genoa as a garrison town of doubtful loyalty was treated to edifying military displays. For the small boys of the town these constant parades with bands and banners were exciting enough, though by one of them at least—a fair-haired, freckled, blue-eyed Nizzard—they were regarded with repugnance. He avoided them "with pain and horror," not because they represented a despotic government, but because he recoiled from the idea " that one portion of mankind should be set aside to have for their profession the business of destroying others." So at least he assured Mr. Gladstone in later years, when he had become the most illustrious captain of his time.[6] For the Little Nizzard, Pippo's junior by two years, and come to Genoa to school, was Giuseppe Garibaldi.

As for Pippo himself, the military parades as such excited in him no repugnance. By nature he had in him something of the aristocrat and cavalier; something, too, that responded to the theatrical, the spectacular; and he thrilled to the roll of drums, the blare of bands, the sight of armed battalions on the march.

Also there were stories of bygone days in Genoa, well calculated to kindle his ardour. For example, there were still old
men in the city who remembered the immortal days of 1746.
From Bedin his nurse, or from Maria or the old priest, he would
hear how sixty odd years ago the hated Austrians had ruled
and plundered Genoa, and how, when the nobles and the
Council sat still and did nothing, the people rose and attacked
the oppressors from roofs and windows. He would hear how
women and children joined in the struggle, and how, after eight
days of street-fighting, the Genoese had fought the white-coats
back, foot by foot, inch by inch, through the S. Tommaso gate,
and cleared them, bag and baggage, out of their coasts. And
was it not a boy, Berasco, who had led the first onslaught?
And had not another boy, Pittamuli, eleven years old, snatched
up a pistol and attacked fifty Austrian soldiers carousing in a
Bisagno inn? These were the tales, decked out with many a
heroic embellishment, with which old men in Genoa renewed
their youth. They were tales which remained to confirm Pippo
in his later faith that, given sufficient resolution, a people could
achieve its liberty against the best-drilled armies of oppression
in the world. It was the faith of Wordsworth:

> " The power of Armies is a visible thing,
> Formal, and circumscribed in time and space;
> But who the limits of that power shall trace
> Which a brave People into light can bring
> . . . —for freedom combating,
> By just revenge inflamed?"

THE Reverend Father-Rector (Principal) of the Royal College of Genoa remains an engaging figure in the shadowy background of those early days. We are given a glimpse of him as a quaint old cleric in knee-breeches, with a red wig and a blue-veined nose usually crammed with snuff. He was of noble family and his erudition was believed to be prodigious. At the desk (says Giovanni Ruffini) he was a Moses, in the chamber of correction a Torquemada, and in the sick-room the gentlest of nurses and most delightful of playfellows. There is no proof, it is true, that Pippo ever wore the cocked hat and brass-buttoned dress-coat of a Royal College schoolboy; at most his connection with the school must have been brief: but Donaver, who had good opportunity for verifying his facts in the Genoa of his day, is clear that he studied there. And are there not Genoese citizens still living who can recall their grandsires' recollections of Pippo's prowess among the Collegians? Thus Sig. Giov. Novella, an alumnus of the College, was fond of describing to his grandson, now Sig. Avv. G. S. Bianchi, how young Pippo's class-recitations were apt to win commendation from his teachers, and how sometimes the Fathers Somaschi, moved to tears, would embrace him.*

The curious fact to observe, however, is that under the direction of the remarkable Father-Rector, and under the nose of the College's royal patron, Victor Emmanuel I., the institution was run very much as a republican and revolutionary seminary. Greek and Roman history was the only secular subject taught with any care, and this, says Ruffini, the Fathers Somaschi taught in the form of a constant libel upon monarchy. When did Athens flourish, and Sparta, and Rome? When they were republics. When did they decline? When the government passed into single hands. The boys were encouraged to " hurl

---

* The author is indebted for this reminiscence to a conversation with Avv. Bianchi some few years ago. Certainly the Ruffinis were Royal Collegians.

the thunder of their Latin eloquence" against Cæsar, about
to cross the Rubicon, or to prove, "in an oration of three
parts," that Cæsar's suppression of the republic was by way
of being the act of an unnatural son who strangled his mother.
But on the other hand, how noble was Brutus, how admirable
Mucius Scævola and Cato! "Our indignation against tyrants
and our enthusiasm even for their assassins," says Ruffini,
"seemed even to be purposely excited."[1] Perhaps the recollections of Giovanni Novella and others permit us to picture
young Pippo hurling the thunder of his Latin eloquence in
some such wise, and being embraced by the Fathers.

Withal the Collegians staged their own revolutions. From
time to time the school was systematically oppressed by bullies
in the upper forms, who levied tribute and terrorised their
"fags." Against these tyrants the boys formed their secret societies, laid their plots and carried out their *coups de surprise.*
They formed themselves into "republics" and referred to their
school, in tremendous proclamations, as "the nation." There
were elaborate Constitutions, elections (by universal suffrage),
programmes of reform (abolition of corporal punishment, etc.)
and state processions. "The active bustle of our little republic
. . . can only be compared to that of a hive of bees. . . . Who
can estimate the enormous quantity of wood, paste, paste-board,
grey, red, yellow, gold and silver paper consumed?" And
while the demonstrators marched round the quadrangle
(to the strains of Rossini's *Tanti palpiti*) with fasces, banners
and canopies and such devices as "*Union is Strength*" and
"*Republic-Fraternity,*" the Father-Rector would smile over his
snuffbox and say nothing. Doubtless he reflected that there
were more ways than one of teaching school under a repressive Government. "It was affecting, also, to see the good old
man on a Sacrament day, his countenance radiant, shedding
tears of tenderness as he prayed for his beloved children, whom
he believed to be in a state of grace." But when young Lorenzo
is caught reading a translation of *Paradise Lost* he is remitted
to the cells for solitary confinement on bread and water.

For the rest, Donaver is pleased to show us a little manual,
Maxims of St. Paul, inscribed in a priestly hand: *Josepho
Jacobi Mazzinio optimo spei adolescentulo pietatis et studiorum
incitamentum;*[2] and we have a letter to Maria Mazzini dated

December 8, 1814, from Judge Breganze. The learned Judge
had gathered Pippo was of sanguine temperament with a tendency to melancholy (he was nine at the time), that his physique
was fragile, and that whatever he felt he felt intensely; and
—with a gesture of deference to the professional opinion of Dr.
Mazzini—Maria was warned that her son's blood must be encouraged to circulate in his stomach as well as his head.[3] We
get a glimpse of him later in a Jansenist school, and at thirteen,
according to Jessie White Mario,* he was reading Shakespeare
and Byron in English, translating Schiller (but his knowledge
of German must have been slight) and impressing his class-
mates with his austere aspect.

Then in 1819 we find him at the University, turning from
Law to Medicine and back to Law, and turning withal to a
more active way of life—the vital stream now circulating more
in accordance with the Breganzian formula. There were fenc-
ing lessons, chapel " cuts," clandestine visits to the theatre, and
regrettable scenes of disorder in the Philosophy class; he was
arrested after a " rag " (directed against the Royal Collegians)
and released only upon the intervention of the Father-Rector;
and Maria writes to Judge Breganze of a certain perturbing
satirical tendency now developing in Pippo (exercised occasionally upon the Professors), and the Judge replies with an erudite
epistle on Satire, its Use and Abuse. Also in their secret reports
to the Government the University authorities are regretfully
obliged to refer to undergraduate Mazzini as a youth of singular
talent whose conduct is "extremely wild," since on various
occasions he had violated regulations and disturbed the good
order of the classes.[4] Withal he learns the guitar and falls in love.

The Zoaglis, a family belonging to the old Ligurian aristocracy, were near neighbours of the Mazzinis; so were the
Thomases, who hailed from Great Britain. Adele Zoagli was
a charming girl. Surely they were meant for each other!
Adele, too, seemed disposed to agree; and when, later, the
young Marchesina bestowed her hand upon the dashing
Cavalier Mameli, what was Pippo to do but believe himself
mortified and inconsolable—and turn to " Marianne " Thomas?

---

* An uncertain authority in these matters. But see *Benoni*, ch. xvii. He
was reading Scott in English in 1828 (v. *Indicat. Genov.*, No. 10), and was
composing in English by 1829 (Luzio: *Maz. Carb.*, 204).—G. O. G.

"Marianne's" admittedly unclassical figure was atoned for—or nearly so—by a face of singular beauty. The attachment was transitory, but she quickened his devotion to the tongue of Shakespeare, and inspired him to compose (but not in English) a love-lorn sonnet or two:

"That your sweet face for such as I
Bedew'd with tears should be—
Not this, my love, I crave of thee,
But only supplicate a sigh."[5]

When, in 1824, she returned to England, he fell into "an ardent fever" and apostrophised the Moon. Before her departure "Marianne" promised to write to him, and fulfilled the promise at her leisure twenty years later. But then he was an exile in London and she a widow in straitened circumstances, with a son in the English Church,[6] who desired to be satisfied concerning Mr. Mazzini's religious opinions before consenting to an interview. (The satisfaction, it appears, was not given. "Imagine," Mazzini writes to his mother, "my confessing to an Anglican priest!") Adele, too, crosses his path in the later years—as mother of the soldier-poet Goffredo Mameli. It was young Goffredo who joyously summoned him to Rome in '49 and died defending the Mazzinian Republic.

But now, in 1820-21, Mazzini's preoccupations were to be transferred from love to rumours of war.

* * * * *

For in truth the Restoration which had brought back the Habsburgs and Bourbons and their cadets could not cancel the spiritual effects of the Revolution. Bonaparte's legions had been rolled back, but the ideas which he had exploited in his flaming manifestos—Liberty, Nationality, the Rights of the Peoples—these ideas remained. They were indeed the real Army of the Revolution, impalpable but potent, marching on viewless tracks. Foreign absolutism might return, but only as fact, not as truth, and this despite the rhapsodic homilies of a mystical Czar and the evangelism of the Holy Alliance. And even as Fact it was not unchallengeable, and persecution served only to drive the movements of protest below the surface. There was still the hum of mighty conspiratorial workings. And if, over the mountain passes and vine-terraced slopes and dusty highways of the north, the white-coated Austrian columns lumbered and clattered on their errands of repression, these workings did not cease. In Piedmont and Lombardy men badged with knotted straw-coloured cords began to greet each other with secret passwords. In the South the order of the Charcoal-burners (Carbonari) spread secretly northward. Even in Greece, blotted out of all official recognition, the *Philike Hetaireia,* with its watchwords of liberty and independence, began to muster under the spell of Hypsilanti. In 1820, in Spain, Ferdinand VII. was suddenly presented with excellent reasons for avowing his meek adhesion to constitutional government. His namesake of Naples, disturbed a little later by joyous popular hubbub, and informed it was due to certain pleasing intelligence from Spain, promptly followed suit and took the constitutional oath. In Turin, old Victor Emmanuel, hearing similar hubbub (agreeably provided by his Genoese troops) under his own windows, promptly abdicated in favour of his brother Charles Felix; while from a Turin balcony Charles Albert, a pale, tall young prince "with a charming expression," impulsively promised the desiderated Constitution, amid "immense acclamations."

These were great days. Maria and her circle, and many another circle in Genoa, met often to exchange rumours from everywhere. At the quayside, in ships' fo'c'sles and lamp-lit cabins, and in the back parlours of seamen's taverns hidden away in the winding alleys around the Piazza Banchi, men foregathered in groups for secret conference. In the Royal College little boys declaimed their falsetto eulogies of Brutus, their shrill invectives against Cæsar; and in the University the students were uproarious. But Austrian columns, 80,000 strong, rolled out the Naples rising to adequate flatness, and, returning, crushed Lombardy, risen in their rear; and France, on the pretext that Yellow Fever (following the Red) had broken out in Spain, dispatched 100,000 soldiers to the frontier, to overawe the aggressive bacilli with a *cordon sanitaire.* Europe was once more safe for autocracy.

*   *   *   *   *

It was at this time that an incident happened which had a direct bearing upon young Mazzini's career. Externally, the

incident was trivial. It was on an April Sunday in '21, following the collapse of the northern rising. The outskirts of Genoa
around S. Pier d'Arena were crowded with proscripts of the
revolution, awaiting a chance to embark for Spain. Maria and
Pippo, walking along the Strada Nuova with devoted friend
Gambini, after Mass, were accosted by one of the leaders, a
certain Rini of the National Guard. He held out a kerchief
in the form of a purse and asked aid "for the proscripts of
Italy"; then, having received their offerings, went on his way.

This was the entire incident, and yet for the boy it was an
Event. Something in Rini's flashing glance, something in the
lingering cadence of the word *Italia* smote him. The idea of
country, the sense of the wrongs of Italy, the feeling that to
struggle against these wrongs was a duty, the presentiment that
in that struggle he must play his part—these things, he declares, flashed in upon him. He had heard them before, and in
a vague impersonal way had accepted them. Now they were
within him, settling into his innermost being and fashioning,
so to say, a new inner world in the depths of it. For the
present, however, the new world was fire-mist, a vague, tormenting ardour. "The remembrance of these refugees . . .
pursued me wherever I went by day and mingled with my
dreams by night. I could have given I know not what to
follow them. I began collecting names and facts and studied,
as best I could, the records of that heroic struggle."[7] One
wonders if among those collected names and facts was included
the record of the young Lombard girl of noble family, Giuditta
Bellerio, who at fifteen married a wealthy young Reggian
named Sidoli and risked life and fortune with him in this
rising of '21? Perhaps not. This girl with the "dark velvet
eyes" and the wreathed flame of golden hair was as yet no
more than a dim figure in that procession of the exiles and
martyrs of Italy. Meanwhile that procession which led to the
gallows, the galleys, the reeking dungeons of the Spielberg
and the Neapolitan prisons or to exile had begun in earnest.
In Genoa itself, always suspected of disloyalty, the restrictions
were galling, and the University, as a natural hot-bed of sedi-
tion, was singled out for repressive measures. For a while it
was closed; for a further period classes met only in the private
houses of the professors ("where," says Ruffini, "we were

stowed together like negroes in a slave-ship "). Professors and
students alike were under espionage, and informers, meeting
openly at the Piazza Nuova like brokers on 'change, drove
a brisk trade in hush-money transactions.[8] Nor was the solicitude of the Government for the spiritual welfare of the student-
body limited to the requirement of monthly certificates of
Confession and of secret reports from the Faculty concerning
the private habits and tendencies of individual students; with
almost an excess of paternal vigilance the Authorities required
that the chins of the undergraduates should be examined for
signs of any untoward growth. Beards were a symptom of
incipient republicanism.

As for Mazzini, undoubtedly the thing most observable in
these University years was the early development of the " fire,
sensibility and volume " of his own nature. Before he graduated the strength of his innate and dominant characteristics—
his isolation of spirit, his austerity, his persistent force of will,
and on the other hand his vivacity, his wealth of affection, his
lavish generosity, his power of fascination—all these were
clearly marked. Just now what was uppermost was the sense
of isolation. He was sixteen, and older than his years; his sensibilities had been newly aroused, and, in his own confession
at the time, he was " full of repressed furor." The atmosphere
of his home was that of strict and fervent piety—strict on the
paternal side, fervent and mystical on his mother's. In 1822
his sister Rosa took the veil.* But now the first consequence
of his own inner awakening was a revolt into scepticism. How
could one believe in a God who allowed tyranny to be perpetuated, and perpetuated in His name? How could faith grow
in the shadow of the scaffolds where the patriots of Italy suffered, and where their persecutors claimed the sanctions of
Holy Church and were decorated with the Order of the Holy
Annunciation? For if the polished rationalism of the French
schools had little to offer him that was to his taste, the Church
had still less. And what was Christianity in its visible embodiment but this same Church, whose dogma was an obsolete

* She took the veil January 23, 1822, died (of phthisis) December 30, 1823,
and was buried in the crypt of the Church of the Madri Pia Franzionane,
S. Pier d'Arena. (See Salucci: *Amori Maz.*, p. 44.) Mazzini's elder surviving
sister, Antonietta, married Francesco Massuccone, August 20, 1829. She survived her brother.

mediævalism, whose sacred emblems were the painted, passive, self-commiserating Christs of the wayside crucifixes, whose authority was the militant absolutism of the Pope, and whose emissaries were the Jesuits who cancelled individual, domestic and political liberty and ruled Genoa from the confessional? In his Italy there seemed no middle way between submission to the Roman obedience and the rejection of Christianity. He accepted the alternative. When he broods upon it all (he writes at this period to his friend Elia Benza) he lies awake at times all night, invoking " Him who will not hear " or reviling " the Chance, the Power, whatever it is, that has cast us here with this unavailing passion, this immense yearning, for a Country, and which gives us tyrants instead."[9] He proposes an essay entitled " Doubts on the Existence of God," and in his commonplace-book sketches suggestions for poems, crude and juvenile enough but significant of the same mood.[10]

Thus in the midst of the general ferment he withdrew into himself. It was easy to avoid Confession; there was always a good-humoured priest ready to sign the required certificate; it was not so easy to avoid inquisition at home. Professor Mazzini was brusque and methodical, expected a due attendance upon religious duties and lectured him upon the importance of preparing for a successful career and achieving an honourable independence in the world. Without this, the Professor insisted, virtue itself was precarious and without solid foundation. Politics he would not discuss, and " Italy " was not a subject for boys to bother their heads about. Let them eat their own polenta—mind their own affairs. There can be no true communion of feeling (writes his son to friend Benza) between youth and age. For one thing, disparity of years demands of the younger a certain respect which destroys equality, and for another, age chills the heat of enthusiasm and affection and makes men slaves of what they adorn with the name of prudence. Even his mother, too, was now a stranger to his mood. Her religious faith was simple and unwavering. She went to Mass, she burnt candles on Saints' days, she found rest of mind and soul in her Calvinistic Jansenism. He could not expect her to understand. She could only lavish affection on him and look at him with troubled and anxious eyes. Moreover, fiercely liberal in politics though she was, she had no liking for secret revolutionary societies, at least, if there was any danger of her son's being attracted to them. After all, she was his mother, and she feared this mood of rebellion and its consequences. So he felt himself alone. On the benches of the University he sat (he says) moody and absorbed, turned to French rationalism and read *Jacopo Ortis*.

It is curious, indeed, that in his frugal Autobiographical Notes, written nearly forty years later, he should pause to relate this early reading of Foscolo's now forgotten book. To moderns with other affectations than the cult of despair, this poor Ortis, inviting the universe to groan with him, and rhetorically invoking the desert or the tomb—to moderns this Ortis is alien enough. But in Foscolo's age, with its Hamlet-Werther complex, it was otherwise. Did not Napoleon read *Werther* seven times over? And Foscolo's morbid hero, in fact, exercised a fascination hardly less potent upon successive generations of young Europe, winning even from that least Ortis-like of Englishmen, Mr. Matthew Arnold, a chaste poetic tribute.[11] And presently (so infectious is the cult of misery) even the youthful Cavour, despite his romping good spirits, would be reflecting upon suicide in the true Ortisian style, and praying, as an alternative (one had to consider one's family), for a galloping disease to carry him off.

Foscolo's hero is, in fact, a proscribed Venetian patriot who unfolds his tragic story in a series of letters to his friend Lorenzo. From the beginning the hero is draped in melancholy and weeps on every page. Inevitably he adds to his sorrows by a hopeless passion for a divine Teresa, pledged in loveless troth to another, and finally he ends all with a poniard. "The wound was extremely wide and deep; and although he had not hit the heart, his death was accelerated by the loss of blood, which ran in streams over the room."

Young Mazzini learned the book by heart. The thing, he admits, became a passion with him. It would, perhaps, be difficult to understand this but for the fact that, in spite of its erotic spasms, the underlying motive of the book is an intense though half-despairing patriotism. "We are strangers in Italy," laments poor Ortis, "abandoned by our fellow-countrymen who look upon those Italians as barbarians who do not belong to their own province, and upon whose limbs the same chains are not clanking." And there are occasions when he strikes a bolder note: "Raise your voices in the name of all. . . . Write! Persecute your persecutors with Truth. Pronounce judgment upon your oppressors. . . . Amid the abasement of prisons and punishments you will raise yourselves high above the man of power." The thing was irresistible. It was an expression of all the "repressed furor" of Pippo's heart. He could only brood over it all, sitting solitary "like one suddenly grown old." "I childishly determined to dress always in black, fancying myself in mourning for my country. . . . Matters went so far that my poor mother became terrified lest I should commit suicide." Had not one* of those highly-strung sons of Bernardo Ruffini already done so, moved, perhaps, by this same dreadful *Ortis* mania? The Professor, too, was alarmed, and packed Pippo off to Tuscany for a holiday.[12]

The danger was not altogether remote, and to the end of his life he was subject to fits of black depression which at times threatened to cloud his reason. On the other hand, his was a nature made for endurance. Few can have surpassed him in power of recuperation and resiliency; and just now his melancholy was a passing phase of adolescence. He soon recovered; and meanwhile, so far as he was concerned, *Ortis* served to break the brief and meagre spell of French rationalism. No form of materialism, indeed, could have appealed successfully to such a nature as his: an Overworld of some sort he had to have, even though its presiding genius were the Spirit Ironic. He was, in fact, haunted by religion and confessed himself tormented by vague yearnings which anything, a poem, a book, a word, a glance, might excite. And just now he preferred to the French cult of happiness a mystical worship of Sorrow, which did, after all, afford some recognition of the deeper instincts of the heart. "I know not," says Ortis, whether Heaven pay attention to earth, but if ever it did regard us, I believe it wrote in the books of eternity: MAN SHALL BE UNHAPPY." Mazzini found this saying rather more believable than the popular gospel of natural happiness. It was something of a relief, in any case, to observe this worship of Sorrow, and, for the rest, to exalt patriotism to a religious elevation. Thus,

* The eldest son; later Jacopo Ruffini also.

in his Overworld, broods the Spirit of Italy—of Rome—mother
of glory and of grief. He writes of it in his boyish scrap-books,
weaving grandiloquent sentences. Italia's mournful smile re-
illumines with a soft memorial light the splendour that was
Rome, and that light "shines through the mist of ages to
touch with enchantment thy fallen City, O Italy, like a ray of
sunshine on the face of a wan but beautiful woman."

And then there were the Ruffinis. Bernardo Ruffini was
an old friend, the families were near neighbours, and Jacopo
Ruffini was with Pippo at the University. Bernardo's portrait
is unsympathetically drawn in *Lorenzo Benoni*, where he
figures as an irascible tyrant, but in Maria Mazzini's letters,
where his temperamental storms are described with indulgent
amusement, he cuts a better figure. But it was to Bernardo
Ruffini's wife that Pippo now turned for counsel. She was his
saint, his oracle, his "second mother." And Eleonora Curlo
Ruffini was in fact a remarkable woman. Her health was frail,
and she had been chastened by domestic sorrows and the
vagaries of an erratic husband, but her nature was idealistic
and ardent, and in general culture she was Maria's superior.
She had brought up five highly strung and temperamental
boys of her own and she was sympathetic toward the dreams
and insurgencies of youth. Better, perhaps, than Maria, she
was able to follow Pippo in his intellectual conflicts, and to
her he unburdened himself. She was his mother-confessor.

During the long summer vacations the two families saw
more of each other. The Mazzinis' summer-cottage, a white
house on the cypressed slopes of Bavari, was within sight of
the Ruffinis' villa. Pippo would call at early dawn, and
together the boys would saunter up the slopes of Mount Fasce,
Eleonora accompanying them. They would halt on the uplands, make her a seat of moss and fern, and watch the sunrise,
the morning air sprinkled with the tinkling of the cow-bells in
the upland pastures, the Mediterranean, brilliant with a
thousand varying reflections from sun and sky, stretching out
far below: "Why," Pippo would murmur, "should there be
bad governments in a world like this?" There were pleasant
evenings, too, with the patriarchal old rector of San Secondo,
half-peasant, half-priest and a stout liberal withal. How

delightful to lead the good old soul on into heretical fulminations over the wine and cigars! And then there was the neighbouring priest who liked to drop in on such occasions and
share what was going; an ex-monk of enormous girth and
great heartiness who took pleasure in condensing his political
philosophy into a simple formula—"*Hang all monks!*"

These things, together with the inseparable companionship
of Pippo and Jacopo, Giovanni Ruffini recalls at length in
his enchanting autobiographical romance, *Lorenzo Benoni*;
and Mazzini, as a grey-haired man, in due time paid his own
tribute to those far-off days. Particularly he dwells upon his
friendship with Jacopo. "He had an intellect massive and
alert and a capacity for the greatest ideas; for the greatest
spring from the heart." "We grew into an intimacy unique in
my experience, then and since. I do not believe I have ever
known a soul more completely, more profoundly, and—I
affirm it with sadness and with comfort—I never saw one
single blemish in it." In truth, the Ruffinis at this critical
time helped to save him from himself and from his morbid
Ortisism.

And now that he was free to do so, he turned again to his
philosophical studies. The German thinkers of the Enlightenment began to attract him—Kant, Fichte, Herder, Hegel,
Lessing.* It was Herder who stimulated him supremely. The
tendency of Rousseau and the French school had been to deny
the progress of mankind and society. Rousseau defined history
as the record of human deterioration. Man was perfectible,
but his hope lay in a break with the past (through the Revolution) and an idyllic return to Nature and primitive com-
monalty (through the Social Contract). But Herder attacked
Rousseau at the centre. History from the beginning onward
was the record of a development decreed by God and involved
in the nature of things. The task of the future was not to
destroy the past but to fulfil it; and the destiny of man on
earth lay not in any return to a primitive felicity but in an
advance to moral and social perfection. This involved, according to Herder, the unfoldment of the true genius of the various

* I may have overstated his German studies at this period. The evidence is
definite for *Herder*, *Schiller* and *Goethe*.—G. O. G.

races of mankind; and the voices of the Peoples must unite at last to form the one vast music of Humanity. Thus the Divine Law of Progress and the Idea of Humanity were the clue to universal history.

More and more, it was this German doctrine that now gripped him, and what he found in Kant and Herder and Lessing and Schiller he rediscovered in Vico and, implicitly, in Dante, whose *De Monarchia* fascinated him. His Germans had, in fact, presented him with a clue with which he could explore his world and relate his facts in harmony with his own spirit. History, Politics, Art, Commerce, Nationality—everything could be unified in terms of God, Progress and Humanity. Christianity itself, effete in its mediæval orthodoxy, became interpretable now as an unfoldment of the divine Idea, a stage in the progress of faith through symbol to reality. "I must write to Torre or Benza," he enters in his diary, ". . . about working out a comparison between the first centuries and this present time." It is his earliest reference to a theme which, for the rest of his life, was to have for him a potent fascination. The decay of traditional faiths in the pre-Christian world, the break-up of philosophies, the decline of moral authority, the swarming of new sects and superstitions, the *malaise* of Pagan society—and then the incarnation of the new Word, the rise of the new Christian world: this was the parallel in his mind, to be developed some years later in his first book, *Faith and the Future,* and re-expounded in 1860 in his manifesto *To the Youth of Italy.*[13] What, then, if in these present times, with the old order once more declining, a new divine impulse should re-animate the souls of men? The world was not meant for happiness; so far Foscolo was right; but what if it were meant for something diviner? What if it were the school-ground of Humanity, the place of its education in truth and love? What if the law of the universe were a law of progress in which mystery, pain and sacrifice subserved the supreme all-justifying Purpose? In that Purpose there was unchallengeable sovereignty, and the soul of man must respond to it. Thus in his solitary walks, "in secret moon-beholden ways," he pondered it all—discussed it with Jacopo and the Donna Eleonora in daybreak vigils on Mount Fasce, or in quiet saunterings over the white roads of San Secondo under the green canopy of the olive trees—until presently it burst upon him with the authority of truth, baptising his faculties. . . .

And thus the summer days passed. Dr. Mazzini, dozing over his favourite religious books, tending the peasant folk, and spending his evenings in edifying conversation with a congenial priest, wore only his mildest moods; the womenfolk devised pleasant excursions for the united families; and on Sundays bluff old Andrea Gambini would come over and enliven everybody with his shrewd raillery. As for the boys, " sometimes," says Giovanni Ruffini, " it was our turn to go over early with our guns to Fantasio [Mazzini] and then to wander among the vineyards on the hillside in pursuit of game." But "Fantasio," remorseful over the convulsive flutterings of a bird he had brought down, gave up the sport. It was better to go on botanising rambles with Jacopo over the Bavari uplands, and there to lie on the mossy slopes discussing Herder and Schiller and Dante, the Resurrection of Italy and the Perfectibility of Man. Vague, tidal hopes, alluring and heaven-reflecting as the blue waters of the Mediterranean that stretched out below them, fading into the infinite!

A SELECT group of University men*—chiefly Old Boys of the pious Fathers Somaschi's select academy—gathered regularly on the vine-trellised balcony of Mazzini's room, overlooking the Acquaverde. At Mazzini's instigation they had formed themselves into a more or less secret brotherhood. Their mild excitement was (with the connivance of a liberal bookseller named Doria) the smuggling of contraband books into Genoa. They gathered on the Mazzini balcony to discuss them over coffee and cigars. It was pleasant and even exhilarating. Under their cloaks, as they assembled, their pockets were stuffed with the precious "contraband of the intellect" —the lectures of Guizot, odd numbers of poor Pellico's suppressed *Conciliatore*, something of Cousin's, the Florence *Antologia*—their heads equally stuffed with projects and ideas.

Some stray echoes of these balcony-colloquies have come down to us. For example, there were the discussions of the heaven-shaking issue of Romanticism *versus* Classicism. (The brotherhood of the balcony were Romanticist to a man.) But also the debates went further afield. For did not the contraband association presently succeed in smuggling in an engaging History of the Regeneration of Modern Greece?[1] And what could be more fascinating than the record of that Homeric struggle which had fired the soul of Byron and drawn him from Genoa to Missolonghi? What could be more exciting, or more to the point, than the story of Adamantios Korais and his labours to resurrect the old Greek spirit through a revival of national literature? And what could be more inspiring than the exploits of Hypsilanti? But above all, what could be more timely, more appropriate, more thrilling, than the history of the *Hetaireia*, the great secret brotherhood of Greek patriots? The comrades of the Hetæria met secretly in churches at dead

* Federico Campanella, Napoleone Ferrari, Federico Rosazza, G. B. Noceti, Elia Benza, the Marchese Imperiale, Jacopo and Giovanni Ruffini, and others.

44

of night, knelt together at the altar, exchanged weapons in ancient token of fraternity, joined hands and vowed in unison: *" Thy life is my life; thy soul is my soul "*; and thus fortified by sacred pledge and mystic empowerment, they went forth to achieve a nation. Sublime spectacle! Something finer here than the theorists of modern France had yet offered—something finer than any doctrine of Rights and material interests—something that appealed to the immortal part of man, arousing and commanding the loyalties of the soul! And had not Italy a cause as sacred as Hypsilanti's? Had not Italians a past as glorious as the Greeks? What was wanting was an Italian Hetæria. . . . So (records the Chronicler) the coffee would be left to grow cold and the cigars would go out and the voices of the brotherhood sink into awed whispers. And in the gathering dark the figures on the trellised balcony were blurred into still shadows, and the Overworld with its myriad eyes became a brooding presence behind the purple night, above the city and the sea. . . . And Giovanni Ruffini, with a few of the more reckless spirits, affected Hypsilanti trousers—slightly balloon-like and laced round the ankles.

Later there were other enterprises. There was, for instance, the taking over, by the brotherhood, of Sig. Ponthenier's modest little four-page sheet, the *Indicatore Genovese*, and its conversion into a Romanticist journal. Then, before that (sometime in 1827), there had been Mazzini's first serious essay in literature. It was in fact an essay on The Patriotism of Dante — lengthy, erudite, idealistic and glittering, like Macaulay's *Milton*, with an opulence of allusion. (Dante, declared the essayist, was the prophet of Italian unity, in whom poetry returned to its ancient authority in the service of the fatherland. His love needed a larger idiom than that of Tuscany and embraced " all the fair land from the Alps to the sea.") But the only journal in the country at all likely to publish an article which declared that the fatherland of an Italian was all Italy, was the Florence *Antologia*, then directed by Niccolò Tommaseo. And Tommaseo, with the absolutism of a liberal editor, had reserved the manuscript without acknowledgment and published it in another journal, eleven years later. Curious, however (remarks the Chronicler), that Mazzini's first essay should have been on Dante, and Cavour's on—Model Farms! Curiously suggestive, the one of the poet and pedagogue in politics who wore his gown now as prophet's mantle, now as conspirator's cloak; the other of the statesman with a shrewd eye for the weather, the rotation of political crops and the uses of diplomatic fertilisers.

And in any case, if the *Antologia* was unaccommodating there was now the little *Indicatore Genovese* (alas! presently to be suppressed); and while young Dr. Jacopo Ruffini, Elia Benza and the rest of the brotherhood fleshed their literary swords, Pippo was indefatigable with reviews of such new publications as Scott's *Fair Maid of Perth,* Schlegel's *History of Literature,* Manzoni's *Promessi Sposi* and the early works of Guerrazzi. And did not the exclusive *Antologia* presently open its arms to Sig. Mazzini's valuable (and extremely lengthy) dissertations *On a European Literature* and *The Historical Drama?* And was not the *Indicatore Livornese* (directed by Guerrazzi) enriched by the same pen? Editor Guerrazzi was certainly appreciative. "Do not abandon me," he wrote. "Do not forsake Italy which has such hopes of you." There was, indeed, no sign of abandonment. Mazzinian contributions poured in— on Goethe's *Faust,* on Foscolo, on *Some Tendencies of European Literature* and much else. The style may occasionally have been staccato, but there was no denying the power of the new voice. And always (and in spite of the circumnavigation of a world of erudition) the general thrust and burden of his writings were the same. It was the idea of Progress, the impulsion of the universal spirit, "translated by religion into conscience, by philosophy into concepts, by history into facts, by art into imagery." Italians must understand that Progress was on the point of a new unfoldment. A European consciousness was emerging, nations were being brought to a point from which they could advance only as they were united; and in this movement toward international association Italy had her mission to fulfil. This, indeed, was the function of nationhood, not to oppose internationality but to achieve it. On the whole it was novel doctrine, and Maria Mazzini, watching over the sure outworking of good Colonel Patrone's prophecy, read and re-read all Pippo's writings, educating herself on his infallible ideas.

Only Professor Mazzini and Andrea Gambini were disturbed. From the Professor's letters and from "Uncle John's" discourses in *Benoni* it is easy to reconstruct their protests. Why (asks the Professor) this hymning of "Italy"? There is no Italy. There are no Italians. There are Genoese, Lombards, Tuscans, Neapolitans. . . . It was all very well for Pippo to demonstrate apocalyptic possibilities on paper: to achieve them was quite another matter; and he needn't think of converting with a stroke of the pen a generation of hypocrites, egoists and unprincipled money-grubbers into a Messianic nation. What did the King of Naples say (the Professor had his stock-anecdotes) when Gustave of Sweden declared that with the Kingdom of Naples for his own he would overrun the peninsula and achieve the Kingdom of Italy in a year? "My brother, you don't know my *lazzaroni*!" *Ecco!* What was the use of chasing clouds with a butterfly-net? Let Pippo attend to his legal profession and build up a position of Security, the first concern of every honourable man. And what (asks Gambini) was all this talk about Progress? Progress was excellent, but it was not in our keeping. It was a mysterious principle, like the law of gravitation. It operated in ways unknown to us, without us, in spite of us. Idealistic political systems, conjured up and rushed through on a riotous afternoon, were not Progress. Its first necessity was the reform of human nature, which was not to be done in a day. Society couldn't be turned like a pancake. But a pack of boys with their heads stuffed with Latin and Greek, with historical romances, German fol-de-rol, Dante, Byron, what not, must imagine they had the formula which could change everything.—Thus did these old revolutionaries, with '97 far behind them, admonish Youth and 1829.

But the brotherhood of the balcony were undissuadable, Pippo most of all. In his Autobiographical Notes he writes of it characteristically. "A little nucleus of chosen friends, men of independent mind, and aspiring after better things, began to group themselves around me." They were "chosen" and they gathered "around him." This assumption of centrality was naïve, unforced and accepted by himself, no less than by the "Pleiads," as belonging to the nature of things. And he could be exacting in his choice. Thus he rejects a promising nominee on the score that the candidate reasons much but feels nothing. "Now with such I will never hold friendship. I

have always felt an invincible repugnance for these calculators."
He adds pontifically: "My mind is made up." It always
appeared to be. Giovanni Ruffini contributes another of Mazzini's aversions. "If any of the companions he gathered round
him occasionally indulged in some wanton jest . . . [Maz-
zini] would put an immediate stop to it by some one word
which never failed of its effect." It was an authority due
(Giovanni explains) to his force of character and his incontest-
able superiority. In fact, the group of Pleiads—it was his own
name for them—were at an age when hero-worship is natural
and spontaneous; and even after the bitter estrangements of the
after years, Giovanni falls under the old spell when, looking
back upon this youthful period, he paints "Fantasio's"
portrait.

"He had a finely shaped head, the forehead spacious and prominent
and eyes black as jet, at times darting lightning. His complexion was
a pale olive and his features, remarkably striking altogether, were set,
so to speak, in a profusion of flowing black hair, which he wore rather
long. The expression of his countenance, grave and almost severe, was
softened by a smile of great sweetness, mingled with a certain shrewd-
ness, betraying a rich comic vein. . . . When he warmed upon a subject
there was a fascinating power in his eyes, his gestures, his voice, his
whole bearing, that was quite irresistible."[2]

His habits were abstemious; he seldom touched wine; coffee
and cigars were his only indulgences; his purse was usually
well supplied, but he gave away all he had, sometimes the
cloak off his back. His books, his guitar, a game of chess,
a turn with the foils, and solitary nocturnal rambles were his
diversions. And for the rest, the group were prepared to
admire even his foibles—his slight theatricality, his affectation
of sombre dress, his exaggerated abhorrence (in spite of Byron)
of white collars, even his tendency in debate to overwhelm
opposition with impetuous monologue delivered in Olympian
tone.

It is plain, in short, that Mazzini's ascendancy was as absolute as it was unforced. Like the unnamed hero of Robert
Louis Stevenson's college days in Edinburgh,[3] power seemed
to "reside in him exhaustless"; his friends held him marked
for higher destinies; they loved his notice; they "loved the
thing he was for some shadow of what he was to be"; and

like the unnamed hero, he walked among them, "both hands
full of gifts, carrying the seeds of a most influential life."
Only, unlike his Edinburgh counterpart, he did not carry them
with nonchalance. He was committed to his course, and he
knew it. With the gravity of youth, which may be so much
keener in sensibility than the solemnity of age, he felt himself
under the shadow and power of destiny. Thus if the adulation
and submission of his friends did not spoil him, reducing him
to vanity, it was because his powers were already guarded by
a purpose which wore an authority higher than his own ambition. He was, in the strictest sense, preoccupied.

And, for that matter, it is curious to note that already he
had looked Metternich in the face. For in the summer of
1825 the Austrian Kaiser and his Chancellor had paid a state
visit to Genoa. According, indeed, to the informer Doria,
Mazzini and a fellow-student had planned to interrupt the
civic welcome with a salute to the Emperor not provided on
the official programme; but the informer's evidence, given
eight years later, is unsupported. Certainly the Kaiser and his
Chancellor passed through Genoa without untoward incident,
and Mazzini slept that night in his white bedroom with green
blinds at Bavari, undisturbed by *poliziotti*. Thus if Metternich's
glance ever fell that day upon a pale-faced law student with
melancholy eyes, nothing happened to fix the impression. The
duel between the two was to be fought out later, and in other
ways. Yet in a sense the strange unequal struggle had already
begun. And unequal it was, in a sense other than that of the outward show of things, for after all, the imponderable odds were
with the pale-faced youth; and it was his incalculable advantage
that he firmly believed it. "Faith and the future! The victory
is ours!" All that was needed now was an Italian Hetæria.

*   *   *   *   *

Meanwhile into the political atmosphere of Turin and Genoa
came occasional wafts of metaphorical charcoal fumes, rising
mysteriously in the South and blown about on the winds of
rumour and persecution.

The secret Order of Charcoal-burners or *Carbonari*, it was
believed, was so called because, hiding among the fastnesses
of the Abruzzi, its first and fugitive leaders made charcoal* for

* This legend is not supported by modern research.—G. O. G.

a living. It was, in fact, a Neapolitan development of Bonapartist Freemasonry, and for a while the ill-starred Lucien
Bonaparte was its leading light. After the revolutionary con-
flagration of 1820-21 the glowing embers of *Carboneria* were
carried far and wide—into Northern Italy, France, Spain, even
Ireland. Thus Carbonarism became a cosmopolitan agitation
with some vague project of a revolutionary Latin League.

But it belonged to the very nature of the sect that its apostolate did not burn with a clear flame; it smouldered. It was,
in fact, not a pure idea but a confusion of combustible elements.
It was anti-Bourbon, anti-Habsburg, anti-clerical, but it was
neither republican nor royalist, or it was either, according to
the circumstances of the moment. Its incendiary principle was
hate, hate from whatever motive, of the existing régime. Thus,
if it was served, as it was, by a few able minds, there was much
in it that appealed directly to the baser sort. There were the
subtle appeals of secrecy, of mystery, the puerilities, attractive
to the ignorant and the superstitious, of a ritual and a ritual-
jargon half-Catholic, half-cabalistic, and, not least of all, the
promise of the perpetuation, in one form or another, of the
old fierce feudist tradition of the South. Thus the Order revealed an extraordinary vitality and propagating power.
Church and State had combined to stamp it out, but police-
vigilance, trials, courts-martial, the galleys and the gallows
all alike had failed. Persecution had only fanned and scattered
the smouldering flame. In its power of endurance and propa-
gation it was almost like a religion, proscribed, occult, mysterious, but appealing to some deep instinct in the masses of
the oppressed.

To the band of brothers at Genoa, ignorant of the inner
character of the Order, and full of dreams of an Italian Hetæria,
the elusive glow of these metaphorical Carbonarist braziers
was as the swinging of hieratic censers. Here, it seemed, was a
movement of the utmost sweep and potency, and rumour had
it that the secret signal of the sect had been known to be exchanged between captives and their warders in gaol, between
judge and prisoner in court, even between statesmen in council,
always with magical effect; in short, these metaphorical
braziers were as potent as Aladdin's lamp. Even in Naples and
Sicily alone the initiates ("Good Cousins") were numbered,

it was said, by the hundred thousand; Italy, France and Spain were involved in the invisible meshes of the Society's designs, and it needed only a signal from the Supreme Lodge (" High Vendita ") in Paris for armies to rise as if out of the earth. Nevertheless, such was the disciplined secrecy of the Order that it was easily possible to live in the midst of an entire colony of " Cousins " without evei suspecting it.

Such was the legend. " A halo of poetry," says Ruffini, " surrounded these exceptional beings, whom the popular imagination pictured as holding their assemblies in woods and caverns at the midnight hour, and continuing their mysterious work, nothing daunted by the thunders of the Vatican or the prospect of the scaffold." Here, then, it seemed, was the *Eteria Italiana* all ready to hand. The only thing wanting was its discovery—to track it to earth. "I watched, questioned, searched on every side," says Mazzini—but in vain. It seemed as if the Order must be as invisible as it was ubiquitous.

But in '27 two events of importance occurred. Mazzini graduated Doctor of Law, with the right to plead in the lower courts, and he and Jacopo Ruffini became Carbonari.

Perhaps Mazzini's initiation into the mysteries of Good Cousinship was a trifle disappointing. He mentions Raimondo Doria as his initiator, but the " elderly man of forbidding aspect " who actually administered the oath, at " the house near S. Giorgio," was more likely to have been one who bore the title of Marchese Da Passano di Bonifacio. Than this seasoned old Carbonaro no one was better versed in the mechanics and mumbo-jumbo of the Order, no one happier in its mysteries, no one more ready to oblige in the matter of initiation. Indeed, initiations of every variety, including those of obsolete brands of Bonapartist Freemasonry and their like, were Passano's speciality, and it was his way to explain that though a particular Order unfortunately no longer existed, it was as well to belong to it. It was this Passano who was at the head of the local *Speranza* lodge of the Carbonari. But the young advocate Mazzini, thrilling to the august event, and ascending the stairway of the appointed house as if it were a Jacob's Ladder with a rainbowed Hetærian Effulgence awaiting him at the summit—the young Mazzini was a thought crestfallen to find the ineffable contracted into this elderly forbidding presence with its stuffy mumblings, hocus-pocus incantations and naked dagger by-play. To have to kneel to *that* and vow oneself away was somewhat below expectation. Moreover " I reflected with surprise (he declares) that the oath administered to me was a mere formula of obedience "—of loyalty to the sect itself without any hint of an ulterior aim, any passing reference to Italy, Unity, or Independence, not to mention Progress and the Perfectibility of Man.

Yet, after all, these things must be implicit, and it was splendid to be a Good Cousin. Even a touch of melodrama could be stimulating, as when, of a moonless midnight, one must needs steal forth, cloak-enveloped to the eyes, and join other mute and muffled figures, all proceeding in groups, and led by the guiding-signals of the Order—the distant, long-drawn notes of an accordion; and Passano's melodramatic brain was always arranging such things. " So at last," soliloquises Giovanni Ruffini, upon his own initiation—" at last I have reached Archimedes' resting-point. The wish that has tantalised me so long is at length realised! I am one of the free men— I have brethren throughout the whole world—my life has now an aim! With what profound pity do I look down upon the mass of my *profane* companions! I dream of dangers, of sacrifice, of success bought by a noble death. . . ."[4]

With sad fidelity, too, Giovanni describes the emotional reaction when, after tense expectation and long waiting, nothing happened—when it seemed as if, after all, the solemn initiation had terminated upon itself—when it appeared that, in spite of everything, the tremulous preparation, the self-examination, the reduction of smoking, the saving of pocket-money, the thousand little self-denials, had all led nowhither and gone for nothing. The " plethora of enthusiasm " and " exuberance of living power," he must record, began to waste away for want of appropriate employment. No upspringing of youthful armies over-night, no grand overthrow of governments, no marching to the Acquasola with colours flying and shouts of " Italy for ever!" " I felt a sort of void in my life never experienced before." Young souls! They were like converts experiencing the first reaction of an emotional revival. It was a difficult world.

Only Pippo set his teeth and would confess to no disenchantment. There was always that tenacity, that sanguine confidence about Pippo. "Patience!" he counselled. "The time will come!" And with the advent upon the scene of the Marchese Raimondo Doria, Grand Master of the Spanish Carbonari, affairs took on a new complexion. Doria (the D'Orias had long been famous, and occasionally infamous, in Italian history) had, in fact, all the prestige of an ancient name and title* and of a personal reputation appropriate to it. He was a soldier; he had fought in the Spanish wars; he stood high in the inner circles of the Order; he was believed to be in touch with the mysterious and all-but-unapproachable Supreme Lodge in Paris. It was understood by the local Cousins that his presence at Genoa was a portent. It was.

* His right to the title, or to any association with the ancient family, is, however, disputed.—G. O. G.

THE truth was that if the poor Da Passano di Bonifacio illustrated the ceremonial senilities of the Carbonarist Order,
Raimondo Doria embodied its more malign characteristics.
If, indeed, malignancy was the Carbonic principle, Doria personified the Order's fundamental quality. But though the
man was vain and morose and affected the aloofness of a
master-conspirator meditating vast designs, at the moment
(apart from embarrassing the cousinly amenities of the local
lodge by an illicit intrigue with the girl-wife of an affiliate)
he had little personal intercourse with the group.

But in truth the intrusion of the arch-conspirator Doria was
sinister to the point of melodrama. As Signor Luzio[1] says,
no one could imagine a more bizarre emergence with which
to accentuate the contrast between the genius of light and
darkness in the Mazzinian annals. For with this scion of a
decayed aristocracy,* this Marchese Raimondo Doria, the lust
for conspiracy had reached the pitch of dementia and was
feeding, so to say, upon its own substance. He was still a
young man, not yet out of his thirties. His zeal was beyond
question. He had helped to organise the sect in Spain; he
had risen step by step to high and responsible rank; he had
seen the entire peninsula honeycombed with secret lodges; he
had proved the effectiveness of the Order's terrorism by employing its emissaries, with gratifying success, in his own
private and personal vendettas. And while, for his military
services, he was receiving a generous pension from his grateful sovereign, he superintended the weaving of conspiracies
which aimed at enmeshing in its web all, or almost all, the
royal governments of Europe. But now, though continuing
his Carbonarist activities, he proceeded to conspire against his
own conspiracies.

At what precise point, or from what cause of disappointed
ambition or wounded vanity, he entered upon this final phase,

* But see foot-note, p. 53.

it is useless to inquire. It was not the sixteenth century and he was no luckless Ruy Lopez, whirled helplessly around in the eddies of general conspiracy and treachery: what he did was done deliberately. And it is clear, at all events, that he had come to hate Carboneria with an insane hatred, and to pursue his vendetta with the obsession of a fanatic. By the time Mazzini crossed his path he was already deep in his counter-plot and communicating secretly with Venanson, the Governor of Genoa. Venanson's gratitude to the informer was in proportion to his alarm at the information disclosed; he received the Grand Master with almost lover-like affection. Also his paramour, Maria Davino, whose movements excited no suspicion, was a peculiarly appropriate *liaison* agent. Through her every important detail of the lodge's activities was at the disposal of the authorities.

It was certainly a hazardous game. Every day Doria was putting his fate to the touch, and he had every reason to appreciate the jeopardy. The vengeance of the Order was apt to be swift, and in any case it was relentless. Thus, at best, detection meant for him the life of a vagabond and a fugitive; it meant, in fact, that Carboneria would become for him a dagger whose heft was in Paris and whose point was everywhere. But Doria's was the confidence of a fanatic, the courage of a madman. He was sure of success, and if he forbore to strike, it was because a mere local *coup* would only have jeopardised the greater project. In his dreams he beheld himself in Paris, banqueting the mysterious potentates of the Supreme Lodge, the "High Vendita," and at a clap securing their arrest and thus the collapse of the entire European organisation. It was on this account, too, that the instinctive repugnance between himself and Mazzini was heightened on Doria's side by a certain fear. There was something incalculable about the young advocate; he would, as Doria remarked, "stop at nothing," and by forcing a local crisis he might spoil the entire, grandiose scheme.

As for Mazzini himself, his confidence in man, says Ruffini, was great, and in himself unlimited. He suspected no treachery, but it was clear that the Hetæria would not come through the Dorias and Passanos of the Order. By this the members of the balcony brotherhood were affiliates, and he

called them into secret conference. His plan was simple. It
was to recruit new *nuclei* among the students and liberal youth
of Piedmont and Tuscany, and, with these for a beginning,
to link up a chain of new-model lodges or, alternatively, of
free groups of unaffiliated *federati,* pledged to the Hetæria-
ideal. It was a hazardous project, for it cut across the rule
and method of the Carbonarist hierarchy; but it was worth
the risk. All that mattered was the Hetæria. Meanwhile (he
was now Secretary of the *Speranza* lodge), it was interesting
to be employed by Doria in the drafting of letters and manifestos. There was, for example, a grandiloquent Open Letter
to Charles X., and (in happier vein and Mazzinian English)
an appeal to Dan O'Connell and the Irish patriots. Occasionally, perhaps, the full-sailed eloquence of the appeal grates its
keel on a treacherous idiom ("Would you have destruction?
Divide yourselves. But if existence and freedom are dear to
you, embrace yourselves like brothers"), but at least he will
have all Irish comrades reflect that "time is fecund with
events," and that there are those who, inflamed with love for
Humanity, have entered upon "a great thought" to unite all
oppressed peoples around a common centre "for generous
and noble ends."[2] Unhappily, Dan O'Connell and his
patriots were denied the stimulus of the appeal. The letter,
committed to the charge of a shipmaster, was seized in an
Austrian port.

*   *   *   *   *

Meanwhile the political tremors that had fitfully passed over
Europe were changing into something more convulsive. In
Paris, in the July sunshine of 1830, excited mobs stormed the
Louvre and the Tuileries, seized the Hôtel de Ville and cheered
for Thiers and the Revolution. In Hanover, Brunswick,
Saxony, Hesse-Cassel the cedars of monarchy bowed before
a sudden gale of liberalism. There were disorders in Switzerland, outbreaks in Warsaw, Home Rule riots in Brussels and
Louvain. Even England, scarcely recovered from Catholic
Emancipation, found the revolutionary flag displayed on the
streets. Brougham, in resounding speeches, hailed the kindling
of the new fires of liberty—"Be it mine to fan the flame"—
and while a London mob smashed the Iron Duke's windows

enthusiastic labourers in the provinces burned the ricks and mills of their masters. In the circumstances it was hardly to be expected that Italy should remain quiescent. There were, in fact, smouldering conflagrations at Bologna and Ancona; in Tuscany a paternal Government assisted Guerrazzi (after a rhetorical indiscretion) to the pastoral seclusion of Montepulciano; and at Genoa a young lieutenant of Engineers named Camillo Benso di Cavour earned his transference to the remote fortress of Bard by shouting (after dinner), in the pavilion of the Porta d' Arco, a *Viva la rivoluzione!* " We daily expected," says Giovanni, " to be called to arms "; and at Bavari Pippo and the young Ruffinis secretly employed themselves in casting bullets.

But Doria sounded no tocsin. Instead, he staged an ugly farce, convoking the Mazzinian affiliates to a midnight parade at the old Carignano bridge,* and bidding them pray for the soul of a certain Cousin at Cadiz sentenced to death for treason to the Order, and at that appointed hour paying the penalty of his crime. With this significant threat, he dispatched Mazzini on a mission to Tuscany. It was to be his last journey on Italian soil, as a free man, until 1848, and it was memorable for his meeting Guerrazzi at Montepulciano.

The meeting was perhaps a trifle disappointing. Mazzini was in high spirits. At Leghorn he had met young Carlo Bini of the *Indicatore* and together (dismissing Doria's threat and the awful example at Cadiz) they had recruited a band of promising young Tuscans. What could be more hopeful? The Hetæria was taking shape at last. But Guerrazzi was at work on the unfinished manuscript of his *Assedio di Firenze*, and the irruption of the Genoese emissary was a trifle disturbing. " I spoke to him," says Mazzini, " with warmth and enthusiasm of the philosophical lectures of Guizot and Cousin "— and then, it appears, passed into an engaging monologue on the law of Progress and the Perfectibility of Man. It was doubtless an attractive scene—the young apostle in his sombre but not unbecoming garb of black Genoa velvet, with his flowing black hair, animated gestures and " eyes of extra-

* In *Lorenzo Benoni*, where this incident is vividly described, the time of the episode is inaccurately given. As a romance, *Benoni* takes liberties with chronology.—G. O. G.

ordinary brilliance," discoursing with warmth and enthusiasm upon his

"land of dreams,
So various, so beautiful, so new ";

but Guerrazzi thus besieged and stormed in the midst of his *Assedio* listened without fervour, though with Tuscan courtesy. "I sought in vain in Guerrazzi for a glimpse of that loving nature which shone in the eyes of Carlo Bini." Instead, as the discourse proceeded, the Guerrazzian countenance wore a smile "half sad, half epigrammatic" (*sic*), and the apostle, at sight of it, checked himself. "It impressed me at the moment as painfully as if I had even then foreseen all the dangers which menaced that privileged intelligence." So it would always be. Always there would be something strangely amiss if his own absolute dogma were questioned; and the privileged intelligence that resisted his conclusions would leave him murmuring sadly, "Lo, what a noble mind is here o'erthrown." Intercourse became freer when Guerrazzi was invited to read aloud from His *Assedio* manuscript ("The blood rushed to his face as he read, and he bathed his head with water to calm himself"), and they parted with cordial pledges of esteem. The next time they were to meet, Leghorn would be astir in the early dawn of a winter morning of '49, with guards of honour assembled, civic procession, "a hundred banners waving," windows "all hung with tapestry" and church bells pealing a triumph; and Chief Minister Guerrazzi would hasten from Florence to join in the public welcome to Giuseppe Mazzini.

And for the present Carlo Bini, at all events, had been gained, and with him a hopeful band of like-minded recruits. Why not a chain of associations, binding together the patriotic youth of Tuscany, Piedmont, Liguria, and stretching gradually across the peninsula? Jacopo and Giovanni Ruffini met the diligence by which he returned. "I shall never forget," says Giovanni, "the accent of triumph with which he said as he got out of the carriage, 'The Italian Hetæria is found!'"

Three weeks later (it was in November, 1830, and Maria was at Bavari) he was marched off to the Sarzano barracks under arrest (see Appendix). Without knowing it, he had forced Doria's hand. The Grand Master had fed the authorities with too much information and now Mazzini's activities had alarmed them. Governor Venanson had, indeed, been alarmed since the July Revolution. "The city is full of spies," wrote young Lieut. Cavour; "lists of suspects are drawn up . . . all our words and, I think, all our thoughts, are taken down."[3] Doria could do no other now than make a virtue of necessity and jeopardise his grandiose plot by conniving at Mazzini's arrest. He more than jeopardised it. For from the Sarzano barracks Mazzini contrived to transmit a lightning warning to the Good Cousins to have Doria watched; which warning introduced that worthy to his deserved iliad, including flight, vendetta, an attempt at his slow poisoning by paramour Maria Davino, duels, escapes, imprisonments and general vagabondage.

Then one night in this month of November the prisoner at the barracks was aroused from his sleep, hustled into a sedan chair, and conveyed through the deserted streets to a waiting horse-carriage at the gates of S. Andrea prison; whence emerged, between armed guards, and cloaked up to the eyes, the melancholy but still melodramatic figure of old Da Passano di Bonifacia. At which halt, also, and out of the darkness, came the sound of a familiar, untuneful voice bidding Pippo be of good courage. "I know not how my father had heard of my departure, nor learned the hour and the place. But I still recall with indignation the brutal behaviour of the *carabinieri* who sought to drive him away . . . and their rushing furiously up to identify a youth who was smoking a few paces off, and who had nodded to me. He was Agostino Ruffini."

Then off between armed guards along the wind-swept rocky coast road, with dawn reddening in the sky and with old Genoa, wrapped in bodeful shadows, left far behind. The Chronicler supplies a pathetic detail gleaned from the Mazzinian letters. In the Mazzini house, year after year, Maria's devotion would preserve his room as he had left it, with his favourite flowers, the climbing campanula, the thyme, the verbena, carefully tended on the trellised balcony—in vain. He would see Genoa again, but never again as a free man until 1870.

BOOK TWO: 1830–1837

RED DAWN

CHAPTER I   SAVONA

MAZZINI and Passano, driven under guard along the
coast road on that November night in 1830, found themselves at dawn within the gates of the fortress of Savona, on
the Western Riviera. The fortress stood, and still stands, on a
bluff commanding the sea. It bears to-day an inscription in
honour of the young prisoner who, that morning, shed angry
tears as he waited in its gloomy corridors for the turnkey to
conduct him to his cell.

Yet the three* months of more or less solitary confinement
to which he was fated were not unendurable, and seven years
later, from the drab gentility of Euston Square, he wrote to
his mother that his thoughts turned with strange wistfulness
to Savona. " I recall every trivial circumstance—for instance,
the walk on the ramparts which the Commandant Fontana
made me take for exercise, and the magnificent view that
stretched out before me, with Genoa in the distance."[1] And
did not Cavalier Fontana so far succumb to the magnetism of
his prisoner as to break regulations and invite him to his own
quarters for coffee and cigars? Fontana and his wife (" a
gracious little woman related—I forget in what degree—to
Alexander Manzoni ") possessed good Italian hearts and a not
unjustifiable prejudice against Carbonarism. Young Signor

* " I was in solitary confinement at Savona," says Mazzini, " in the fortress
for five months." (See B. King: *Life*, Append. I.) Here again Mazzini,
always unreliable in chronology, is out of his reckoning. Arrested November 13 and detained for some days at the Sarzano barracks, he entered Savona
probably the third week in November. His release was signed January 9, 1831.
It took effect within that month, possibly about the 28th. (See Luzio: *Mazzini
Carbonaro*, p. 250.)

Mazzini must not be led away by these Charcoal-burners. What were they after? Let him listen to an old soldier who knew. What they wanted was another '93—plunder in the name of Liberty—abolition of religion—the guillotine *chop, chop* in the public square! Young Signor Mazzini would do well to wash his hands of Carbonarism once and for all.

Young Signor Mazzini, as it happened, was about to do so. And perhaps it is curious to reflect that he was brought at last and decisively to that pass, not by any twinge of conscience effected by Fontana's homilies, but by a sudden titillation of the *comic* nerve. For it fell out that one day, while his cell was being swept out, he met fellow-prisoner Passano in the corridor. To him he managed to whisper, *"I have means of correspondence. Give me some names."* Whereupon the melodramatic Passano responded by tapping him solemnly and rhythmically on the head, " in order to confer upon me I know not what 'indispensable' Masonic dignity." Thus did those ridiculous ritualistic *taps* of Passano's finally dislodge in Mazzini's head the slowly crumbling fabric of his Carbonarist faith. For here, as he saw the case, were they two, " Good Cousins " and fellow-sufferers for the Cause—here were they, brought together for a propitious moment, and in urgent need of swift and practical co-operation. And the good Passano must say in dumb show : " Behold! There are resources in our excellent and ever-to-be-admired Order which exactly meet the emergency. A moment, and the thing shall be done. I will give you a new Initiation." And in sober truth the poor *farceur* could think of nothing better than to administer these ridiculous rhythmic taps.

And this, reflected Mazzini, was Carbonarism to date! Old Da Passano di Bonifacio was its now normal product. Carbonarism was plainly going the decadent way of all ritualistic movements that mistake " initiations " for initiative. No hope, then, for the regeneration of Italy from that quarter any more! This mystic Carboneria, which he had once idealised and beheld as the angel of the Risorgimento, now appeared witch-like and futile, stirring its mixed broth over its charcoal fires and muttering its curious incantations.

Thus he went back to his swept and garnished cell, his own mind at last swept clean of Carbonarism.

*   *   *   *   *

It would have been strange if at this stage there had been no new and vital emergence. In a sense, all the conditions were favourable. If the confinement was strict, at least it was not the duress of the Spielberg. He had the sea air, exercise on the ramparts, and as much of Riviera sunshine as could reach him through his grated window. " It was at the top of the fortress and looked upon the sea, which was a comfort to me. The sea and sky—two symbols of the infinite, and except the Alps, the sublimest things in Nature—were before me." When the wind was favourable he could hear the voices and songs of the fishermen: and, besides the society of the genial Fontanas, there were daily human contacts that relieved the solitude. Thus " Caterina " who regularly brings his dinner, survives as a pleasant memory, thirty years later; and gruff, kindly old Sergeant Antonietti, quickly captivated, stages a burlesque which he repeats diurnally with a fine gusto for his own wit. " Invariably every evening he would inquire with imperturbable gravity ' *if I had any orders* '; to which I would as invariably reply ' *A coach for Genoa.* ' " Thanks to Fontana, he was allowed, also, the solace of books. He chose a Bible, a Tacitus and a Byron—a selection, religious, Roman and romantic, which fairly reflected his mind. Perhaps the linnet which he tamed and petted (" a little bird full of pretty ways and capable of affection ") symbolised a fourth affinity, as with something elusive and lyrical. Moreover, into his letters home he contrived to work an ingenious Latin code which the Ruffini brothers were prompt to decipher and, through the Signora Maria's correspondence, to answer. It was an engaging pastime and kept him in touch with the outside world. And for the rest, his mood was hopeful. He was free from interruption and flung upon his own resources. The Tuscan mission had inflamed him with projects for the Italian Hetæria, his imprisonment had sealed his political dedication, the Passano farce had liberated him from the last entanglements of Carbonarism. It was time for a new emergence.

What actually did emerge was " Young Italy " (*La Giovine Italia*). That is to say, in that Savona cell, sometime between November, 1830, and the end of January, 1831, an apostolate was conceived which, in the fulness of time, and for a brief but eternal hour, was to engage the absolutist Powers of Europe in the name of the Ideal, and bring the impossible to pass.

Concerning all of which we note that what he now elaborated was for him something beyond argument. It was something which he *saw*. The thing was there before him, indisputable, compelling. A thousand influences, known and unknown, had contributed to his mental preparation: Jansenism, Bonapartism, the Fathers Somaschi, Rousseau, Foscolo, Dante, Byron, Romanticism, German philosophy, the Greek Hetæria, Guizot, Cousin—even Carbonarism itself; but it was now no mere matter of analysis. The thing had slowly worked upward through "repressed *furori*," through subconscious struggle and an agony of concentrated purpose; and now it *was*. It announced itself. It was the rising of a world out of the deep.

Thus at a time when the projects of the boldest terminated upon a piecemeal and partial liberation, he sees Italy "one, indivisible, free." Thirty years later, the patriot Pallavicini would confess that in those earlier days his own wildest dream had been a Kingdom of Upper Italy. Manzoni would declare that, as late as 1848, though he was a partisan of Unity, he said nothing about it for fear of passing for a maniac. In the 'fifties, Cavour would write of Manin: "He is a very good man, but he keeps talking about the Unity of Italy and suchlike absurdities." In '47 Richard Cobden, as the oracle of Progress and European enlightenment, would pronounce Italian Unity "a child's dream." But in that *celletta* at Savona, in 1830, Italy was beheld as queen-mother, already arrayed "in Alpine white and Tuscan green" and the red garlandry of the South. For the young seer nothing was more sure, and he would never swerve from it. *"Italy One and Independent, with Rome for her capital"* formulated for him not simply a programme but a faith. It was absolute dogma. It was the stuff of dreams, but then the dream was more real and more luminous than anything the garish light of day could reveal.

> "For who sleeps once, and sees the secret light
>   Whereby sleep shows the soul a fairer way,
> Between the rise and rest of day and night,
>   Shall care no more to fare as all men may,
> But, be his place of pain or of delight,
>   There shall he dwell, beholding night as day."[2]

It was the same with his dogma of Rome. "I had within myself the cult, the worship of Rome." It was "in him," deeper than argument, this "worship of Rome." It might be illusion, but if so, so was he. He would not argue with those who would project a loose federation of States centring around Florence or Turin or Milan, and who would call it Italy. He would not argue; he would denounce them. They did not know, they had not seen, they would not understand. "Come with me," he writes to the youth of his country when his hair is grey, "and I will show you where beats the heart of Italy." And in imagination he conveys them over the Tuscan road to the Campagna and points them forward: "Bow the knee and worship. Yonder beats the heart of Italy; yonder, eternally majestic, is ROME."[3]

Nor was it simply that Rome was ideally the moral centre of Italy: it was the centre of Europe, of the world. Twice had the Great Unity, the One Life of the world, been proclaimed from within her walls. The First Rome, concluded by the Cæsars, had carried on eagle-wings across the world the idea of Right, of Justice, the source of Liberty. The Second Rome, governed by the great Popes, and centre of the next Unity, had "elevated the Law from earth to heaven" and super-posed upon the idea of Right the idea of Duty—of Duty common to all, the germ of Equality. The Third Rome, the Rome of the Italian People, should proclaim a vaster Unity, linking earth with heaven, and bringing Right and Duty into harmony; it should utter, not to individuals only but to nations, a message of Association, and instruct the free and equal peoples in their united mission here below.[4]

This he saw—the Third Rome, Rome of the People, Rome of the new unfoldment of the eternal Faith, uniter of the nations of the world. Ask of him the basis of his assurance, bid him analyse the stuff of his dream and the prophet can only smile and sadly shake his head. It has "flashed before his spirit like a star." How should he explain? "The future will declare whether I have *foreseen* or only dreamed." Eight years later he wrote to Melegari: "I desired to lead Italy back to Rome, but I desired more. I wished to lead Europe and Humanity thither—to make Rome the soul of the world, God's Word in the midst of the nations."[5]

So that the distinctive genius of the Savona conception was neither political nor nationalist but (in the broader sense) mystical. For here he repudiated once and for all the materialism of the Continental schools of revolution. As he saw it, no pantheon of deified expediencies and interests could nourish anything better than a sterile idolatry, a *bourgeois,* prudential morality. The progress of the world must mean a goal beyond the world. Politics, Art, Commerce must have an Overworld, a Heaven. Thus, in his eyes, the fundamental trouble with modern Europe was that it was un-heavened—living and moving beneath a seeming void. " I felt that Authority—true, righteous, holy Authority—the search after which, whether conscious or not, is in fact the secret of our human life . . . had vanished and become extinct in Europe, and that for this reason no power of *initiative* existed." A new creative Word alone could restore faith to the peoples and, through faith, effect a return to sovereign order; and for this he looked to a reformed and re-illumined Rome. Fore-echoes of her voice, resonant again and world-reverberant, he heard—beheld her proclaiming the new Word which should restore moral unity to Europe— beheld the people, then painfully gathering the crumbs of the banquet of wealth, rise to a new future, " ungoaded by wretchedness, unspoilt by luxury " and " awed by a consciousness of their rights and duties." All of which, no doubt, as Frederick Myers[6] suggests, was nearer to the dreams of Huss and Savonarola—nearer even to the theocratic Utopias of the Munster Anabaptists—than to the theories of Robespierre and Mirabeau. As the Hebrew prophets hymned Zion, so young Mazzini must hymn Rome.

But it was not all rhapsody. It was now sufficiently clear to him that Revolution was not the all-sufficing word. Revolution itself was not extraordinarily difficult. A disaffected regiment or two, cheers for " a Constitution," a popular demonstration under the palace windows—these were usually sufficient to induce in Grand Dukes and petty kings a convenient passion for democracy or foreign travel. The trouble was apt to begin the day after. Then elated revolutionaries began to discover that their preparations extended only to the barricades. Faced with the need for developing a constructive

policy they fell out over extemporised and conflicting programmes; political direction passed in the confusion into the
hands of provincial politicians, ready to adopt and exploit the
revolution once it had succeeded; and what had begun with
some promise of being a national movement degenerated into
a medley of separate revolts inviting easy suppression.

What was necessary, therefore, was that every local rising
should be carried out in the name and under the direction
of the national movement. What was necessary was that the
organisers of the revolution should retain the initiative with a
political programme consistent with the revolutionary idea.
And finally what was necessary was that this should be prepared for by an educative apostolate, principled in the faith.
And for this the secret hierarchical societies with their negative formulas of hate and destruction and blind obedience were
of no avail: "the era of sects was concluded." Of no avail,
either, was a movement dominated by the greybeards of bygone revolutions, tethered to old traditions or tamed by time.
Youth, rich in enthusiasm and thriving upon movement, upon
action, was the true architect and artisan of revolution. Arose,
then—"Young Italy"—an Association simple in organisation,
positive in faith, direct in aim, open in purpose, to be recruited
from the youth of the country.*

One other consideration was so clear to him that he would
rarely debate it. War was the inevitable instrument of national
emancipation. For the overthrow of the provincial despotisms
but little violence might, indeed, be necessary; the ramshackle
governments would easily collapse: but Austria must be
reckoned with, and Austria could be dislodged only by a
national war. Later, when he settled in England, this would
be challenged by pacifist Radicals as the one grave error in
his national idealism. "I ventured to say," writes Thomas
Cooper the Chartist, "that I felt doubtful whether it was consistent for some of us who were lamenting the physical force
folly of some in our own country, and were often and deeply
protesting against it, to conspire for aiding another people
with arms." And "young Peter Taylor" followed up in the
same strain. Why could not Italian nationhood be gradually
developed though internal reforms, until, in the long run,

* The age limit was 40.

through sheer moral expansion, Italy should outgrow the Austrian tyranny?

But Mazzini, as Cooper vividly remembers, was up in a flash. " Mr. Cooper, you are right about your own country. You have had your grand, decisive struggle against Tyrannous Power. Your fathers brought it to the block: and you have now a Representation, and you have Charters and Written Rights to appeal to. You need no physical force. Your country-men only need a will and union to express it, and you can have all you need."[7] But what hope was there of that in Italy? What hope of " peaceful expansion " when Tyranny, with its triple army of spies, Customs officers and police, guarded its impenetrable defences at every frontier? What hope of " gradual progress " in countries without a free Press, without a Parliament, and whose universities were either closed or enslaved? What hope of internal reforms when every move-ment aiming at freedom was sooner or later quelled by Habs-burg or Bourbon or Papal intervention; when every reformer within reach was sent to the scaffold or the galleys, or boarded on bread and tallow in the Spielberg dungeons; and when even the testimony of suffering, the witness of martyrdom, was muted or perverted by an official Press? " Intelligence perishes in infancy for lack of nourishment. Young men sell their faith for self-indulgence, or waste their strength in fits of barren cynicism, oscillating between Don Juan and Timon. . . . How may we introduce . . . the undefined but sacred thought invoked by all . . . if we dare not, with arms in our hands, like the smugglers of the Pyrenees, defend the con-traband of the intellect?"[8] In some such fashion he defended himself, developing an argument which, it may be, proved too much; but Cooper adds, " we were all subdued."

Thus the conception of passive resistance, of *Ahimse,* found no place in the Savona philosophy, and occasionally this em-barrasses his idealism. " There is a voice that cries to us," he declares, " ' The religion of Humanity is Love,' " but " love demands equality of esteem " and " forgiveness is the virtue of victory." " You cannot *pray* Austria out of Italy." And so he dismisses the subject. When his violentism leads him, as in the case of the Milan attempt of '53, to dubious methods, he defends them with that strain of antinomianism which was

always in reserve. " If you don't like our daggers," he replies
to Manin, " give us guns." Peace was fraternal co-operation,
active harmony, and was the fruit of Law—of Law whose
roots were in liberty and justice. Tyranny was moral outlawry
and war was its eternal answer. Perhaps even his asceticism,
the repressions of a volcanic ardour, heightened his martialism.
A " holy war " of liberation became the supreme romance, the
ultimate passion.

Thus always in his complex Italian nature there will be this
strife of contradictory elements. He " abhors bloodshed," and
risks his life, when in hiding, to cry out against a boy who
is torturing a grasshopper; but he condones the assassination
of Rossi and names Felice Orsini with William Tell.[9] To
Emilie Ashurst he writes (in English) after the fall of Rome
in '49: " I feel from time to time emotions of rage at this
triumph of brutal force thoughout the world. We shall be
better than they (the tyrants) are; we shall be such to the end.
But suppose we should react—suppose I should make myself
what they assert me to be—suppose we should appeal to the
dagger and organise a vast League of Avengers—who could
justly declare us to be in the wrong? Depend upon it, it is
owing to my love of God, of mother and sisters, that I do not
put myself at the head of such a League. As to *their* life, in
spite of all idle talk in Congresses of Peace, I would care much
less than of [for] the life of a dog. Still to have to struggle
against feelings of hatred for which we have not been born, is
very sad."[10] The outburst was eloquent of the two voices
which were Mazzini. He was, in the words of Carducci, " the
man who sacrificed everything, who loved much, who pitied
much, and who hated never "; but in order to expel the
Austrians he would readily have revived the Sicilian Vespers
and have hymned the new Procidas as heroes of Italy. Thus
an alarmed Austrian spy who presently (1831) wins his confidence at Marseilles reads him with some penetration: " The
character of this young enthusiast is most dangerous. Devoid
of the last vestige of self-interest, and breathing only for the
regeneration of Italy, he is ready, in order to secure it, to face
any peril, to sacrifice everything, even life itself, not scrupling
even at assassination provided it make for Italy's advantage."[11]
And at that time, at least, the inference was probably true.

But thus, at all events, and with all its limitations and enswathements, the Mazzinian *idea* had now taken definite form : A new religious synthesis—the " religion of Humanity "; a new political synthesis—the democratic union of the nations; a new social synthesis—the gradual fusion of the classes into one inclusive class, the People; and for the Messianic incarnation and proclamation of the new Word, a regenerate Rome indwelling a United Italy.

By the end of January he had taken leave of the Fontanas and old Antonietti, and of the home-folk at Genoa, and was coaching over the ice-bound Alpine roads toward Switzerland and exile. He would have no glimpse of Genoa again for eighteen years, and his beard would be grey before he would set foot in the city. And then the balcony-room with its flower-embroidered trellis would no longer be kept for his welcome. Genoa would have nothing left for him but graves.

His travelling companion was Uncle De Albertis (last observed by us as a suitor in the Drago home). On Mt. Cenis the exile beheld his first Alpine sunrise, " the first ray of light trembling over the horizon, vague and pale, like a timid, uncertain hope, then the long line of fire cutting the blue heaven, firm and decided as a promise." Perhaps the scene reflected his own mood. Hopes that had been dim and tremulous were now flaming into certitude and kindling the far-off, unscaled heights of the ideal.

THE spring of the year found him at Marseilles, in the midst of burgeoning schemes and enterprises. Between Savona and the French port his route had followed a wide course. There had been a sojourn at Geneva, an adventure at Lyons, a flight to Marseilles and Toulon, an interlude in Corsica, and now a return to Marseilles. The experience had been educative.

For one thing, there had been the test of disillusionment and opposition. Was not Geneva a sanctuary of exiles and a centre of "progressive intellects"? He had looked forward to meeting in Geneva worthy representatives of the hidden heart of Italy and of Continental liberalism. Pellegrino Rossi was there, whose violent death was later to precipitate the crisis which led to the founding of the Mazzinian Republic. Sismondi the historian was there, also, and such European *savants* as Pictet, Charbuliez and De Candolle. Young Cavour, visiting the city two years later, was to find it agreeable and stimulating enough. He would savour the mild excitements of a ploughing match, attend an agricultural dinner, discuss politics with American and European publicists, and inquire of Sismondi concerning the personal qualities of Advocate Mazzini. But just now the Advocate himself felt like a revivalist among correct and tepid churchmen. Sismondi and his Scottish wife, Jessie Mackintosh, made him welcome and introduced him to their distinguished circle. He was courteously received. The young, lithe-figured Genoese certainly had an air. But cordial hand-shakings passed into sad head-shakings as he expounded his new gospel. "I felt," he declares, "an indescribable sense of discouragement steal over me. . . . There was not a man of them who would admit even the desirability of Italian Unity." It seemed incredible, but it was too true. Even Sismondi (treated to a glowing monologue on Progress, the Italian Mission, and Human Perfectibility) was non-committal. There was almost the suggestion of the Guerrazzian " epigrammatic smile." It was certainly discouraging, and the only possible conclusion was that, like Guerrazzi, Sismondi and the rest of them had allowed their judgment to be clouded. Sadly he recorded the verdict. What never occurred to him was to question the validity of his own dogma. Never. It was not these men who passed judgment upon the faith; it was the faith which passed judgment upon them. They might shake their own heads; they could not shake his.

At Lyons, whither his Paris-ward journey had been deflected by rumours of hopeful conspiracy, the atmosphere was more stimulating. In the *Café Fenice* he had seen, through clouds of tobacco-smoke, and effulgent as a rainbow of promise, the intertwined tricolours of France and Italy, and, amid general Italian hubbub at the tables, he gathered the news. Modena, Parma, Bologna, the Romagna, were "up"; Genoa was expected to rise at any moment. The men at the tables were of military bearing. He recognised among them some of the stern, gloomy visages that, in '21, had haunted the San Pier d' Arena and his boyhood dreams. They told him they were concentrating for an invasion of Savoy. Behind them was an Albertist-Constitutionalist committee at Turin—Brofferio, Durando, Cadorna and others. They had funds, depôts, arms. The Prefect of Lyons was well-disposed. There were French volunteers. Would he join? Assuredly he would! . . . At which point, however, the walls of Lyons were placarded over-night with official prohibitory proclamations, the *Café Fenice* was dismantled of its decorative regalia, and many expeditionaries were seized and conducted handcuffed to Calais for transportation overseas. There was nothing for it, then, but flight. With a group of fugitives he left by diligence for Marseilles and Toulon and thence " across the most temptestuous sea I ever beheld " to Bastia on the Corsican coast. And while a distressed Signora Maria and an exasperated Uncle De Albertis had temporarily lost track of him, Austrian espionage had duly advised the royal governments of his movements. By the end of March it was able to report that a De Albertis (" Genoese ex-commissary of war in the French service, age about 60 ") was at Marseilles awaiting the return from Corsica of " Avvocato Masini," who, since the collapse of the risings in Central Italy, had lost hope of a Corsican expedition.[1]

The information was accurate. The fugitive insurgents of the Centre were flocking by the hundred to Marseilles. By the beginning of April " Avv. Masini " had joined them. The hour of Young Italy had struck.

*   *   *   *   *

For at Marseilles, among the Modenese and other refugees, he found men of his own temper. It is still pleasant to tell over their names—names not to be wholly forgotten so long as the Risorgimento is a history to be read—Nicola Fabrizi, lion-headed and lion-hearted, fresh from his attempted relief of Ancona; Celeste Menotti, whose brother Ciro had raised the first Italian tricolour of the revolution and perished on the scaffold; Luigi Amedeo Melegari, student-patriot, lately imprisoned in the fortress of Massa; young Giuseppe Lamberti, frail, high-spirited, gentle-hearted; Angelo Usiglio, a young Modenese writer; Gustavo Modena, marked for celebrity as a tragedian and for richer fame as a patriot of Italy; many more. Arriving later from Geneva there was also, as the fates ordained, the fair-haired Lombard Judith (we last noted her as a girl-refugee in '21) who had risked her life in the recent Reggian rising—Giuditta Bellerio Sidoli. They formed a community of their own, meeting for conference in a back-street room, and later in Giuditta Sidoli's house, 57, Rue Saint Ferreol. A few local liberals like Démosthène Ollivier were in their confidence. Most of the exiles were *Carbonari* stung with a sense of defeat and humiliation. For in the important hour the Order had somehow failed to produce the desired miracle; and certainly it had failed to influence the policy of France. They were discouraged, but they were still young.

In this exile-colony the rumour of Mazzini had preceded him. As we picture the figure which they beheld a century ago, it is hard to escape the impression of the stage-hero with all the *bizarrerie* of an idol of romance. They saw him as a cloaked figure in black velvet attire, wearing a black stock in lieu of a collar, and carrying a cane and a broad-brimmed " republican " hat. His black hair fell almost to his shoulders; his stature was slightly above medium height; his bearing was graceful and charged with decision and energy; he wore a slight moustache, and the strong curve of his chin was accentuated at the base by a black line of close-cropped beard; above it his chin was shaven. His voice was sonorous and singularly musical, his speech rapid and animated, his gestures swift and dramatic. And with all his frankness and spontaneity there was about him the suggestion of involuntary reserve, not the reticence of the conspirator but the aloofness of the mystic, as of one who intently waited and listened. "Altogether" (so wrote one who belonged to the Marseilles circle), "he was the most beautiful being, male or female, that I had ever seen, and I have not since seen his equal."[2]

As for the newcomer himself, he was consciously facing a crisis, and facing it with decision. The hour had come to fashion into fact the dreams of the Castelletto balcony and of Savona. He acted promptly. The month of April saw him founder and president of the republican society of "Young Italy" (*Giovine Italia*).* At one stroke he had supplanted Carbonarism and assumed the moral leadership of the Italian movement. Over in Genoa young Dr. Jacopo Ruffini summoned the balcony brotherhood to co-operate—Campanella, Rosazza, Elia Benza, brother Giovanni, a few others. "Here are we, a few young, very young, men, without illustrious names, without financial resources; and we are called upon to overthrow an established order. . . . So let it be, then, and so God help us!"[3]

*   *   *   *   *

"God help us!" in very truth. And yet, in spite of local reverses, the times were propitious. European liberalism and nationalism were gaining strength. Belgium had wrenched herself free from the Dutch. Poland was in arms. In France the Citizen-King was expressing (with a slightly American accent) a discreet passion for democracy. In Great Britain the Reform Bill was launched upon a flowing tide; Palmerston at the Foreign Office was weaving the tough and lengthy strands of his protocols into an obstructive boom against Metternichian diplomacy; and Lord John Russell, having presented an uproarious House with the alternative, "Reform

* Another society formed in Southern Italy about this time was called "The Sons of Young Italy." There was no connection between the two associations. (See Salvemini: *Mazzini*.) Perhaps April is too early a date for the *G.I.*—G. O. G.

or perish," presented the Continent with a piquant interrogatory: "When I am asked if such or such a nation is fit to be free I ask in return, 'Is any man fit to be a despot?'"

And in Italy itself a new hope was above the horizon. In April Charles Albert succeeded to the throne of Piedmont. He was a soldier who had proved his mettle. He was no friend of Austria. In his youth, it was said, he had taken the Carbonarist oath. In 1820, as regent, he had impulsively promised a Constitution. One of the first acts of his accession had been to quash the charges against the Turin liberals concerned in the Lyons-Savoy conspiracy.

Thus liberal hopes ran high, and at Genoa Jacopo Ruffini burnt the midnight oil composing an Open Letter (never delivered) to the King. At Marseilles Mazzini did likewise—a letter cogent and level-toned in the main, with occasional Olympian inflections. And though the tight little world of Piedmont wagged on as before, the letter was an event. It was read by the few, discussed by the many, and earned for its author a further sentence of indefinite banishment.

For Charles Albert, invoked in the name of Napoleon, Washington and Kosciuszko, was not of their kin. He was not even a Faust, caught in the conflict of two irreconcilable forces. His line had given a Pope to the Church and many a fighting Duke to the army; he himself might have made a conscientious friar or a good soldier; as a ruler he was debilitated by contradictory reactions—by an inward struggle that was not a duel but a mêlée. A mixed ancestry had given him a strain of the Stuart kings, of Teuton princes and of the Dukes of Savoy; a mixed education had given him a training part Jacobin and part Jesuit; and now a mixed fate had placed him between Austrian protocols and Papal encyclicals, between " the dagger of the Republicans and the *chocolat* of the Jesuits." It was well to exhort him to proclaim " the sanctity of ideas," but a king invited by implication to be a Luther as well as a Napoleon, a Washington, a Kosciuszko, and a constitutional monarch in a despotic succession may well have had sinkings of heart.

The apostle, however, was not to be deterred. Let the King understand that Europe was divided into two camps—that the battle was joined between the old world and the

new. Let him understand that it was a conflict not of individuals nor dynasties but of principles, and therefore inexorable. It was in fact a struggle between Right and Force,
between movement and inertia, between liberty and despotism.
In this struggle Italy had a nation's part to play and awaited
only the bold leadership that would liberate her for her mission. Let the King, then, dare greatly, for the times were
propitious. The French nation was favourable; Prussia was
preoccupied; Russia, engaged in a sanguinary struggle, was discredited in the eyes of Europe; England was condemned to
inertia until she had settled her own controversy between
feudalism and the people. And what of Austria? Austria was
a composite of heterogeneous parts, threatened already in
Galicia, Hungary, Bohemia, the Tyrol, Germany. Austria was
powerful only in her immobility and in the weak fears of her
victims. Let the King, then, put himself at the head of the
Italian nation and unfurl the banner of unity and independence.
Let him give his name to a century. " Take the crown. It is
yours if you will it. . . . Choose."

There are things that monarchs love more than being exhorted in public, and Charles Albert was not a second Victor
Emmanuel but only his father. Yet if the impossible had
happened and he had actually, in that hour, put his fate to
the touch in the spirit of the Mazzinian appeal, it is conceivable
that Italy would have kindled round him, and that local
opposition, the timidity of governments, the jealousy of princes,
would have shrivelled like tow at the touch of flame.

But at least the apostle was not abashed by the royal refusal.
He had expected as much, as he confessed to Palmieri at the
time.[4] " By publicly declaring to the King all that his own
heart should have taught him of his duty toward Italy, my
object was to prove to my countrymen his absolute lack of
those qualities which alone could have rendered the performance of that duty possible." So he wrote in his Autobiographical
Notes. The next move was with Young Italy.

*   *   *   *   *

Thus at last Mazzini had found his element.

Years later he would write of his abandonment of a literary
career for politics as the first great sacrifice of his life. But it

was a sacrifice which did no violence to his nature. He needed the stimulus of action no less than the retirement of study, and it was precisely this combination that was to make him dangerous. Men might be amused at his soaring idealisations; what was disturbing was that, henceforth, his flights were apt to end in a swoop. Within six months of his appeal to the King he had Piedmont honeycombed with republican societies. And there was genius in the movement's simplicity. The absurd hocus-pocus of Carbonarist ritual and secrecy was swept aside together with the old Order's terrorist methods: the aim of the Association was clearly stated and a simple oath of allegiance was the sole initiation. Young Italy was " a brotherhood of Italians who believe in a law of Progress and Duty " and who dedicated both thought and action " to the great aim of reconstituting Italy as one independent sovereign nation of free men and equals." It was republican because " all true sovereignty resides essentially in the nation " and because " every nation is destined by the law of God and Humanity to form a free and equal community of brothers, and the republican is the only form of government that insures this future." The movement was directed by the Marseilles executive with a central committee at Genoa, provincial committees in all the cities, and agents in the smaller towns. The organisation was secret, the apostolate open, supported by a steady flood of Mazzinian tracts. " In six months of incessant labour," says Ruffini, " we had obtained results at which we ourselves were astonished. Not a single town of any importance in the [Piedmont] kingdom but had its committee at work, not a considerable village that lacked its propagandist leader. We had succeeded in establishing regular and sure means of communication . . . and we corresponded abroad, through affiliated travellers, with Tuscany and Rome, through Leghorn and Civita Vecchia, and so on to Naples. . . . People of all classes joined us—nobles, commoners, lawyers, men employed under Government, merchant captains, sailors, artisans, priests and monks."[5] No emissaries more useful than these blue-jacketed, glazed-hatted sailors with their cork-screw curls and bronzed faces—quick-witted, hardy, passionate! Hardly a sailing vessel or steamboat plying between Marseilles and Italy but had its agent entrusted with bales of Mazzinian tracts—sometimes concealed in barrels of pitch or pumice. The band of brothers, mingling with the crews at the quayside or in the taverns, picked out their likely men; a smile, a hand-grasp, a word from the Chief, and they were illuminated. "There arose in my mind," says one of them (his name was Garibaldi), "strange glimmerings by the light of which I saw in a ship no longer a vehicle charged with the exchange of the products of one country for those of another, but a winged messenger bearing the word of the Lord and the sword of the Archangel."[6]

By 1832 a little yellow-back Review, *Giovine Italia*, emerged, with Mazzini as editor and chief contributor. So great was the demand that secret presses had to be set up in Italy to cope with it. Gioberti read it and contributed a hymn (*" All hail to you, precursors of the New Law!"*); young Louis Napoleon read it, and offered an essay on Military Honour; Metternich read it, and was moved to obtain back numbers and fuller information. Also Alarmed Reaction read it, and began an apostolate for the countering of the dangerous heresy. (It was as absurd, said Alarmed Reaction, for all persons born in Italy to conceive the notion of a particular bond or relationship as for all smokers to do so, or all persons named Bartholomew.)[7]

By the early months of '32 the Chief was writing to friend Giglioli that, what with journalism, infinite correspondence and endless interviews, he was tired at heart and sapped of energy; moreover, for weeks together, rooming in miserable quarters he had slept in his chair because his bed was infested with vermin. Still, the work went on and his vitality, nourished upon its own essence, revived. The indefatigables rigged up a private printing-press in a back-street room; La Cecilia (recruited in Corsica) acted as type-setter, Lamberti as proof-reader, others as packers and porters. "We lived together, true equals and brothers in one sole thought, one sole hope, one sole worship of the ideal. Very often we were reduced to the extremity of poverty, but we were always cheerful "; and manifestos, tracts, articles poured from the Chief's pen. Thus there were "Thoughts Addressed to the Poets of the Nineteenth Century," an apocalyptic essay on "The Brotherhood of the Peoples," an "Appeal to the Catholic Clergy" and much else. (Wonderful, he declares to the clergy, that in the land of Arnold of Brescia and Savonarola no priest dares to take up the heritage

of the Pistoian Synod and restore to the clergy that right of
suffrage which made the Apostolic Church a true republic!
It was not a question of destroying the Church but of re-
establishing a supremacy over the Pope: it was a question of
saving alike Church, Christianity and religion.)[8] But whatever the immediate theme, the message was always the same:
The world of Individualism was at an end; the world of
Association was begun; dynasties were crumbling, nations were
rising from the dust; poetry and faith were forsaking throne
and temple alike, for the prison of the reformer, the scaffold
of the martyr. Thus the old order was passing, the new faith
was emerging, a faith whose centre was the New Rome and
whose circumference embraced the world.

So did a handful of penniless youths enter into solemn covenant to found a nation and refashion Europe. Over against
them were the massed forces of inertia, tradition, prejudice,
and the organised immobility of governments. Over against
them were all the persecutive resources of Power—spies, informers, police; the dungeons, the galleys, the scaffold. Over
against them were the wealth, the prestige, the armies and
navies, the diplomacy of the Absolutists. To so grotesque a
challenge history could provide but few parallels.

Yet these youths did in fact bring to the struggle an impalpable element with which their adversaries could not easily
cope. It was not simply that Young Italy's assault was the
assault of ideas; not simply that it was the first in the field to
expound the principle of Nationality in relation to the collective life of the world; nor yet that it was the first to " endeavour
to comprehend all the various manifestations of national
life in one sole conception." It represented, in fact, a new
psychic element in Revolution. Pride of race, hatred of the
foreigner, the spirit of vendetta, the lust of " liberty " as an
end in itself—these had been the motive-forces of the past;
these and doctrinaire formulations of human rights and interests. " Young Italy," in spite of its limitations, sought a
revolution " governed from the height of a religious principle,"
motived not by hate but by faith, by duty, even by love. What
was life, the world, but a God-given possibility? What was
the sovereign aim but progress toward perfection, individual

and social—" progress in truth and love "?   Apathy, brutality,
egoism, materialism—these were the forces that opposed it;
and these were organised around despotic institutions. Therefore the despots must be overthrown, that the people might
be free to advance toward their divinely appointed destiny.
If you would elevate men, says the Chief, give them responsibility. If you would make a people great, teach them great
principles. Preach faith. Tell the whole truth. Put your trust
not in numbers but in unity. Avoid compromises, which are
almost always immoral. Counter diplomacy with publicity.
Climb the hills; sit at the farmer's table; visit the workshop.
Repeat incessantly that the salvation of Italy depends not upon
foreign intervention but upon the Italian people. "Accept
as members only those whose convictions are our own. We are
not merely conspirators; we are believers." This was the new
note. Withal the apostle passed easily from high dogma to
discussions of guerrilla warfare, "principles of musketry,"
"essential weapons." And at his side was Giuditta Sidoli.

＊　　　＊　　　＊　　　＊　　　＊

Since Adele Zoagli no woman had attracted him so much
as this young Lombard.[9]   Moreover, in Genoa, amid the preoccupations of Carbonarist conspiracy and literary and legal
work he had avoided romantic attachments. His prime objects
had been his one passion. And now at Marseilles there were still
preoccupations enough, in all conscience, but somehow it was
different. He had no home-life and no Eleonora Ruffini to
serve as mother-confessor, and he was living at a high pitch
of mental and moral excitement. To adapt Lowell's familiar
passage on Keats, his intellect was satisfied and absorbed by
his work, but he had excessive sensibility, "electrical nerves,"
and whatever he did was a sacrifice of vitality. He needed
the restorative of feminine sympathy. And anyway Giuditta
Sidoli was extraordinarily fascinating. She had not the classic
and ravishing beauty of a Cristina Belgiojoso, perhaps not the
intellectual brilliancy of that strange enchantress; but she had
a grace and charm and a warmth of womanly nature which
the Belgiojoso never knew. A few months his senior, she was
born at Milan in 1804. Her father, Andrea Bellerio, a wealthy
Milanese, had been created Baron by Napoleon. At sixteen,

as we have noted, she had married a Reggian patriot, Giovanni Sidoli, and had shared in his Carbonarist conspiracies. A year later he was condemned to death for complicity in the rising of '21. With his girl-wife he fled to Geneva and thence to France, where he died at Montpellier in the winter of '28. Returning to Italy with her four young children, Giuditta flung herself into the ill-starred insurrectionary movement of '31. After the collapse of the rising she escaped once more to Geneva and thence to Marseilles. Meanwhile the care of her children had been wrested from her by an anti-liberal father-in-law who took advantage of her banishment to enforce the separation.

Such had been her history up to now. Her appearance, we find sketched in blurred and uncertain outline in the prosaic lines of her passport of 1833. "Age 29; stature, rather tall; hair, blond; forehead, high; eyebrows, fair; eyes, large and dark; nose, rather large; mouth, large; chin, regular; face, oval; colour, rather pale; complexion, fair; figure, lithe." In Barbiera's more poetic description she is a woman of fascinating *aura*, a graceful blonde with large and expressive brown eyes and fair hair reddening around brow and temples "like a wreath of flame." Private dispatches of the Secret Service describe her as "beautiful" and "extremely dangerous." And extremely dangerous in a sense she was. For it was no mere sense of physical attraction that drew men to her—not simply the lithe beauty and flame of a leopardess, of which Keats was conscious when Fanny entered the room. For this Italian blonde had all the qualities of a political emissary—resourcefulness, courage, intelligence, magnetism and a fierce constancy.

But Giuditta was no mere revolutionary zealot or fiery Carbonarist *giardiniera*; she had a cultivated mind, a rich personality and depths of womanly feeling. To him her presence brought a touch of refinement, of poetry, into the squalid surroundings of his existence. She was suffering much, but she could still be gay, and her conversation was vivacious and deft. There was a subtle charm even in the slightly exotic quality of her speech—in her French idiom, acquired in the years of her exile in Provence—in her Lombàrdisms. And she deeply understood him. In his occasional black fits of moroseness she was not, like the others, afraid to approach him, and her presence was tranquillising. Moreover, unlike so many revolutionaries brought up on Continental ideas, she was no sceptic: she had genuine religious feeling; she could share his faith.

Friendships can ripen quickly in an exile community, and soon their attachment was an open secret. His love for Adele Zoagli and for the " fair Marianna " had been a boyish passion, but this was different; he was a man now, with a man's seriousness and responsibility, and he was proud to call her " my Giuditta." To him she was the symbol of his Italy—lovely, tragic, persecuted, robbed of her children. His love for her— so he liked to tell her—would never come between him and his mission; it would inspire it, for he would mingle all his dreams of Italy with her image; and soon, in his letters home, she was enclosing daughter-like notes to Maria. Yet there were times when he doubted, not his heart but his conscience. What right had he to invite her love, to dally with individual happiness? What had he to offer? How could he protect her and her children? Thus he would violently reproach himself, and vent his black moods in outbursts that would make her weep. But then he would be filled with remorse and renew his vows of eternal affection.

That their love was ever passionate has indeed been questioned by the most authoritative of Mazzini's English biographers;* but two years after Giuditta's return to Italy Mazzini was declaring that his heart was a volcano. " I love you with passion. I have always loved you with passion. Of you I dream and dream through days of paradise and of hell . . . you in the daytime, you at night, always you. . . . I have crowned you with roses, covered you with flowers . . . I have been intoxicated with love."[10] " Oh! this little note will be in your hands . . . and I—not. I cannot fling my arms around you, cannot gather you to myself, kiss your face, your eyes, your cheeks, your brow—cannot feel your arms around me, your lips upon mine." The style is not Platonic. She gave him a lock of her hair; he wore it in a locket over his heart.

Did they not presently regard themselves as united? For a while, when the police-hunt was persistent, Giuditta seems to have concealed him in her apartments. Maria urged them to

* Bolton King.

marry, but the disasters of '33 forbade it. With one of them in hiding, a fugitive from country to country, and the other torn from her children, with a battle to fight for their possession, marriage in the sense of any domestic life was impossible. Yet years later, when Melegari urges him to marry "Madeleine" (Marie) Mandrot, he answers: "Can I have any intentions? Am I free? God knows I am not. I am free in the eyes of Society . . . but before my own heart and God who watches over promises, I am not."[11] There was always Giuditta.

At Marseilles, after the catastrophe of '33 it was she who stood beside him and nursed him back to sanity. "Pippo is better. He still has need of great care. He will recover. The *singulti* [fits of convulsive sobbing] are growing rather less." So she reassured his mother. But already in June of that year she had left Marseilles for Switzerland, without informing her friends, and then had made her way to Montpellier. About the same time Mazzini also departed. Next month, rejoining the group at Geneva, he would explain nothing. To the aggrieved Melegari he wrote: "If I have concealed anything . . . it has been not for my own sake but for others . . . because of definite obligations and through a certain delicacy." Angelo Usiglio wrote to Melegari in the same strain. "If you knew where Pippo was concealed you would understand that the secret was not his own and that honour and delicacy forbade his confiding in anyone." Giuditta herself wrote to the same friend: "I cannot justify myself. Appearances condemn me, and I am ready to suffer the consequences." Writing some seventy years after the event, ex-Premier Emile Ollivier, son of Démosthène Ollivier of Marseilles, recalls that about this period "*une dame Modenaise,*" "*une belle Italienne de Reggio,*" left in the care of his (Ollivier's) parents an infant son of whom Mazzini was supposed to be the father, and who died a year or two later. There are passages in the Mazzini-Sidoli correspondence which seem to confirm Ollivier's recollection.[12] The "mystery," such as it is, may rest there.

And at all events, before the end of that fateful summer a new emergency intervened—the news from Italy of the serious illness of Giuditta's son, Achille. The tidings crystallised her resolution. By the end of August, through resourceful friend

Démosthène Ollivier, she obtained a false passport and, under the name of "Pauline Gerard," set out for Italy. It may have been, as Mazzini declared, an act of sheer madness, but it was mother-madness, and beyond even his dissuasion. By September she was haunting the gates of Modena and beginning her long, maternal struggle. "I will pass the gates. I will see my children. Let them arrest me if they will." Achille recovered, and lived to fight, in due time, in defence of the Mazzinian Republic on the ramparts of Rome. But the local authorities, duly warned of the arrival of a "most dangerous emissary," "young, beautiful, of extreme republican principles and an intimate friend of Mazzini," took action. Giuditta was placed under arrest, but released through the intervention of the British Consul. She made her way to Naples, then to Rome (where the police raided her rooms in search of Mazzini), and later to Parma. Once she outwitted the authorities and for one half-day had her children to herself: but Achille was promptly removed to a Jesuit academy and his sisters to a convent: and finally postal espionage cut her off from correspondence with Mazzini. The poor Giuditta, her "faint feet stumbling through yearlong days," was in truth become a symbol of her suffering country—a *mater dolorosa*.

*   *   *   *   *

But now, in this year of 1832, the hour of crisis was to be hastened. The "Young Italy" programme was simple. First a *coup*, swift, and, if possible, bloodless, bringing the governments of the strategic centres under Mazzinian control: then a national war to drive the Austrians back across the Brenner. No sporadic sectarian mêlées this time, but the uprising of a people!

By midsummer the Prefect of Marseilles, alarmed by certain urgent representations, was ordering Advocate Mazzini's expulsion. He promptly went into hiding; first, as it seems, in Giuditta's house and then in the house of the Olliviers (little boy Emile, future Prime Minister of France, being then seven years old or so, and caring little about the dark stranger). Aware of the continuance of mischief, the lynx-eyed police raided Angelo Usiglio's rooms (in vain), ransacked the Italian quarter at Lyons, and in Paris pounced upon a luckless

M. Masini (composer of music, Rue de Choiseul). When, with happier inspiration, they searched the house of M. Démosthène Ollivier, Advocate Mazzini (in the uniform of the National Guard) passed through the midst of them, and returned when the search was over. For a year he remained indoors, save for two nocturnal outings, once in the old disguise, once in bonnet, skirt and shawl; but his hold upon the threads of his design never slackened, and at the Olliviers' there were always ways and means of seeing an experienced and unfailing emissary—Giuditta. By February, 1833, he convoked a conference of Young Italy delegates at Locarno, and a date in June was fixed for a Genoa *coup*.

At which point two Genoese artillery men, quarrelling about a woman, noisily pursued their dispute into other fields of recrimination, including certain barrack-room activities of a secret and seditious character. . . . And was not a box, consigned from Marseilles to innocent Andrea Gambini (to be called for by Dr. Jacopo) secretly opened in Customs and duly resealed and delivered—after its contents of cipher-code and key had been copied? Thus a secret guarded by thousands is like gunpowder guarded by fire, and a plot once tampered with is lost.

And in due time, at Genoa, Turin, Nice, Alessandria and elsewhere, Officialdom staged and brought off its own dramatic *coup*, with wholesale arrests, *processi*, imprisonments and shootings at dawn. And at Genoa, while Giovanni Ruffini escaped across the sea, Dr. Jacopo, imprisoned in the tower of the Ducal Palace, died by his own hand.

BY the autumn of '34 Mazzini was writing to Giuditta that he was settled in a patch of country between the Alps and the Jura. Even his description of the scenery suggests that his mind was still shaken and haunted. "As night falls, the Alps, which are so sublime so long as the sun shines upon them, become terrible in their aspect, taking on a hue so pallid, so livid, that a dreadful something about them recalls dark thoughts to my mind."[1]

There had been plenty of occasion for dark thoughts. For a while, indeed, he had refused to leave Marseilles. With the police-hunt once more in full cry he had contrived to elude the authorities long enough to reknit the broken strands of the Association and plunge into new and desperate activity. The *Giovine Italia* review was still on his hands; he collaborated in the founding of another—*L'Europe Centrale*, and spent his spare moments enlisting recruits, among them a tawny-headed, blue-eyed Nizzard sailor named Garibaldi. But he had, in fact, passed the limit of endurance; he was a mere shadow of his former self and was prostrated by convulsive seizures and fits of delirium. Then he had bidden Giuditta farewell and faced a new ordeal. He had met Eleonora Ruffini, arrived at Marseilles with her fugitive sons, Giovanni and Agostino. How could he face her? After all, was it not he who was the cause of these new sorrows that had overtaken her? Step by step, against the warnings of his elders, he had led her boys into ever more inextricable entanglement in his schemes, and now how many mothers had he caused to mourn? Yet Eleonora, come straight from Jacopo's grave, had brought neither reproach nor an accusing pardon; he was still her "figlio dell' amor mio." Four years later she would write to him: "By the everlasting memory of my beloved Jacopo I swear to you that from that time . . . my affection for you became so supremely sacred, I could not live and not love you." And at the Navigation hotel, Pâquis, Geneva, they had pieced together the tidings of disaster slowly reaching them from various sources.

Charles Albert, indeed, had struck at the revolution with a panic-ferocity. Official calumnies accused " Young Italy " of every crime in the calendar, from atheism to poison-plots and a conspiracy to burn down the city of Turin. Mazzini's death-sentence was ordered to be proclaimed in " high and intelligible voice," with preliminary trumpetry outside his parents' house. In order to reduce the moral resistance of prisoners and obtain confessions, enervating drugs were introduced into the prison fare: for the same purpose incessant noises were made outside their cells, and the names of executed comrades read out beneath the prison windows. Andrea Vocchieri, a young lawyer of Alessandria, was made to pass to his execution by a route which led him under the windows of his own home, in sight of his wife, then pregnant, and his young children. Galatieri, the local Governor, having first kicked his prisoner in the stomach, presided at the execution, bestraddling a cannon—and for exemplary zeal was awarded the decoration of the Order of the Holy Annunciation.* Jacopo Ruffini's fate had been hardly less cruel. To extort disclosures the authorities had shown him a forged confession in which the names of his comrades were given in full, together with the key of the last cipher. It was this evidence of apparent betrayal that had driven him to suicide in his cell, and to leave on the wall a message written in blood: " *Behold my answer. To the brothers my vendetta.*" It was this that inflicted upon Mazzini a mental wound which tortured him at every successive crisis. Thirty years later, after the disaster of Aspromonte, Jessie White Mario and her husband would hear him pacing his tiny room at Lugano and repeating through a sleepless night, " *Jacopo! Jacopo! I did not betray!*"[2]

But " Young Italy " had at least exposed the hollowness of liberal hopes in the new King. Events had shown him to be a despot with all a despot's disposition to rule by force and terror. He was once more " the execrated Carignano." And was it not at this time that the melancholy little group in the Navigation hotel was joined by a figure whose elongated and rather ridiculous shadow was to haunt Mazzini's path in the later years? For it was at this point that young Antonio

* Some of the details of Galatieri's brutality are disputed.—G. O. G.

("Mariotti") Gallenga had announced himself, to beg money and a passport for a certain great Act of Expiation to be performed somewhere in the region of the Turin palace. The necessity for the deed, it seems, had grown upon him during solitary musings amid the fastnesses of Corsica, and had at length become gigantic and compulsive and had thrust him forth. Also, according to Gallenga (contradicted by Mazzini), the pale-faced Donna Eleonora Ruffini had approved his inspiration and urged him to hold to his purpose. The devout Melegari, too, had commended him to the Chief.

There is no reason to doubt Mazzini's recollection that he himself discouraged the project. Such things were no part of Young Italy's apostolate. But perhaps he offered his dissuasions in a tone faintly suggestive of an Abbot analysing a difficult case of conscience with a promising but perhaps overzealous novice. "*I discussed the project, setting before him everything that could possibly dissuade him.* I said that I considered Charles Albert deserving of death, but that his death would not save Italy. I said that in order to assume a ministry of expiation it was necessary to know oneself pure of every feeling of ignoble vengeance."[3] He added other considerations. But perhaps the tone was still slightly unconvincing. Perhaps mysterious echoes of the "Latin thunder" of the Fathers Somaschi's pious academy were reverberating fitfully around the Pâquis hotel. And what if this young Gallenga were after all "one of those beings whom Providence, from the days of Harmodius onward, has sent to teach tyrants that their fate is in the hands of a single man?" Sacred, the sword of Judith; sacred, the arrow of Tell! And the dagger of the tyrannicide was never more terrible than when whetted upon the tombstones of the martyrs. . . . The Illuminated, at all events, was undissuadable, and presently departed (with passport and money), prostrating himself *en route* before the high, flaming altars of the St. Gothard, and renewing his "vow to Italy." A little later he sent an emissary to Pâquis. By a curious oversight he had forgotten a *weapon*. He was accommodated (ironically by this) with a paper-knife, taken from the Chief's writing-table. It was never used.

Thus had passed, then, in morbid revulsions and "repressed

furor," the sultry summer of '33. In later years Mazzini annotated the episode: "I abhor, and all those who know me well know that I abhor, bloodshed and every species of terror erected into a system, as remedies equally ferocious, unjust, and inefficacious against evils that can only be cured by the diffusion of liberal ideas. I believe that all ideas of vengeance or expiation, as the basis of a penal code, are immoral and useless, whether applied by individuals or society."[4] He added that his own practice had been uniformly consistent with this attitude, "except in one sole instance"—the Pâquis affair.

And now, with Eleonora Ruffini returned to Genoa, and with a general descent upon the Navigation hotel of Marseilles comrades and new refugees—Melegari, the brothers Fabrizi, Scipione Pistrucci, Angelo Usiglio, Federico Campanella, Lamberti, Antonio Ghiglione, Fanti—he had flogged his energies into new activity. It was indeed his only escape from mental torment. Only action, victorious action, could vindicate "Young Italy" and give it a national impetus. Only action and victory could lift from his own mind the crushing burden of the June tragedy. To lay the Italian tricolour upon Jacopo's grave and the graves of all the victims—to proclaim above them that their sacrifice had not been in vain—this was the one thing left to live for. Withal there were diehards in Piedmont who were writing hopefully of a new prospective attempt at Genoa with some prospect of concerted risings in Naples, the Duchies and the Papal States. He resolved to lead an expedition into Savoy, raise the country and join forces with the insurgents of Piedmont. It was a mad project. Popular sentiment in Savoy was only tepidly Italian; it was certainly not republican. But he had persuaded himself, and he was always able to persuade others; moreover, the Piedmont Committee approved, stipulating only that an experienced soldier should lead the expedition. They had found, in fact, the very man. Girolamo Ramorino had the advantage of being a Savoyard by birth; he was a veteran of the Grand Army, had been a Major in the Piedmont army of '21, and a Corps Commander in the Polish insurrection of '31. And Ramorino, generously agreeing to bestow his talents and prestige upon the enterprise, and to recruit an additional battalion, had appropriated (in advance) 40,000 francs for its equipment, and departed for a recreative interval at the gaming-tables of Paris. Mazzini was displeased; he had wished to take command; but the Committee were firm; they desired no amateur *capitano*, and Ramorino was indispensable; but certainly the " Young Italy " Chief should prepare the expedition. He did so. Once more he was a miracle of energy, amassing arms (smuggled in from Belgium), collecting funds, organising depôts, enrolling recruits and billeting them in outlying villages. For the moment the dogma of the sufficiency of Italian arms for Italian liberation was set aside, and Swiss, German, Polish and French volunteers were enthusiastically enlisted. " I rejoiced in the idea of thus linking the cause of Italy with other oppressed nationalities and raising the banner of European fraternity upon our Alps."

Thus the winter (January) of '34, viewed from the windows of the Navigation hotel, had opened upon a white world with new and flaming horizons. The suspense indeed (for Ramorino was procrastinative) was trying, and young Agostino Ruffini, homesick and ill-content, sounded a petulant note about " late rising, smoking, coffee, endless chatter "; but at least the Chief, labouring night and day, and sleeping only in snatches over his work, was feverishly hopeful. And though Ramorino, when he ultimately presented himself, was without the promised battalion and the greater part of the funds, he had at least brought two Generals (one Grabski and another) and a surgeon. Moreover, the Generalissimo's final instructions breathed an admirable resolution. " As you advance upon the bridge of La Caille [the immediate objective was the village of St. Julien], the enemy will open fire. March on. He will fire again : you are wounded. March on. He will fire a third time : you are killed. March on."[5]

But, thanks to Ramorino, the expedition miserably failed. From the first, indeed, there had been frustrations, and while, at Nyon, the Polish column under the intrepid Grabski was rounded up by Swiss steamboat patrols, large bodies of German students, marching from Berne with oak-leaves in their hats and cockades in their coats, were dispersed before they could reach the frontier. A third company, pressing forward from Grenoble, was repulsed by a detachment of Piedmont troops, leaving prisoners who were conveyed to Chambéry and shot.

The main body, under Ramorino, was marched aimlessly about
for twenty-four hours as if with the fixed intention of avoiding
the objective. On the second night, in the camp at Carra,
Mazzini had swooned after a stormy encounter with the
General. When he recovered consciousness he found himself
in a Swiss barracks. Ramorino had disbanded the column.

Once more, then, the horror of great darkness had descended.
Blame, ridicule, utter failure, the accusing spectres of the dead
. . . what was there left to live for? He fancied he detected
scorn and hostility in the eyes even of his friends. Were they
not regarding him as a mad Quixote, a futile Hamlet, or worse?
He was persuaded of their secret persecution, and in his letters
he took refuge either in over-strained self-reproach for not
" dying in Savoy " or else in a feverish Messianism. He and
his followers had " snatched a spark from the Eternal " and
placed themselves between God and the nations. They were
suffering for all and their sacrifice was accepted.[6] " I am
morally ill," he confessed in a letter to Giuditta; " I have
moral convulsions." There were times, he added, when he
could not endure to look into human eyes, times when he
would lie writhing on the ground. He was plagued with
neuralgia, but almost welcomed it. " Don't be troubled about
my toothache," he wrote to his sister Francesca; " it is nothing.
Besides . . . a little of it serves as a diversion." But the one
thing he could not do was to relax his purpose; to do that,
to abandon the Idea, would have meant, not death, but the
second death, the disintegration of his innermost being. And
for the rest there was his mother, there was Eleonora Ruffini,
there was Giuditta. " Even now," he wrote to Giuditta, " you,
you stand before my eyes, beautiful, loving, holy. . . ." He
would fight on. It was, in fact, precisely this tenacity, this
tensity of will, which would characterise him to the last, so
that again and again he would leap defiant out of hopeless
defeat.

From the reports of the spy Santarini, indeed, we catch
some reflections of him at this time. Spy Santarini had got
himself enrolled among the Savoy expeditionaries, had been
promptly promoted for his excellent spirit, and was just now
shadowing Mazzini with exemplary diligence and reporting to
his Austrian masters.

Berne, March 8.—"Yesterday I spoke with Mazzini, who received me with every mark of friendship."

March 11.—"A great storm is raging around Mazzini from every quarter. Letters of reproach pour down upon him from far and near, accusing him of being dictatorial, obstinate, arrogant. . . . He has wasted to a shadow."

April.—"Mazzini continues visibly to waste away. One can see the pallor of death in his face. All the same, he speaks always of hope and work."[7]

Spy Santarini, continuing his hopeful reports of Mazzini's rapid and perceptible dissolution, continued also to marvel at the dæmonic energy of this living, fire-breathing corpse. Was he not deserted by Belgiojoso and practically all the wealthier of his supporters—his "bankers"? Was he not heavily in debt? Was he not all the things already faithfully reported? Yet, in less than a fortnight after the Savoy fiasco, he must issue (with Melegari and the Ruffinis) a declaration, broadcast to the universe, that "Young Italy" was indissoluble. "*We have sought to found a nation, to create a people. What is defeat to men with such an aim?*" He would even draw encouragement from defeat itself. Why (he inquires) all this European hubbub against us, and shower thick as hail of protocols and notes? Why this cordon of scaffolds stretching from frontier to frontier? Why all this over an abortive raid by two or three hundred mothers' sons? Why? Because the Powers have made a strange discovery; because they have discovered that Something is abroad, an idea, a faith, potent even on the scaffold. Most potent there, perhaps; with invisible artillery sweeping a wider zone than cannon can command. "*I die in peace,*" says Vocchieri, "*as a true son of Young Italy*"; and on the scaffold he implores, "with utmost expansion of heart and soul," the divine benediction upon his judges. And the litany lengthens as the martyrs increase.

And at Berne in this month of April, as the astonished Santarini duly reports, something new had emerged. For did not this strange being with his wasted body, deathly pallor, and sunken, martyr-eyes, assemble his "nationals"—his little circle of Polish, German and Italian exiles—and propound his new "covenant of international fraternity"? To the poet Giannone in Paris (poets would understand) he had presently outlined the project, with safeguarding admission of present practical difficulties. What he desired to see was, among other things, a "college of intellects," detached from the material work of revolution, and endowed with adequate funds for travel, research and the issue of a monthly organ of enlightenment. Its *savants* should occupy themselves in the study of social and economic problems in relation to the general European movement; they should devote "deep and concentrated research" to national origins, language and history, seeking in these for indications of the various national vocations; and in short they should seek to deduce the future European order and forecast the political and economic map of the Europe of the Peoples. "I desire at least to sow the seed of this idea in other minds. Will it germinate? I don't know. Certainly not as I could wish."

For the rest, facing his nucleus of nationals in his room in Berne, the pale apostle was lucid and expansive. They must beware of mere pithless cosmopolitanism—the individual sprawling in vague humanitary welter. There must be, for effective action, a middle term between the individual and the race; the Pact of Humanity could be signed only by free and equal Nations. They must beware, too, of the mere materialistic Rights-and-Interests propagandism now being elevated to the level of a universal gospel, a propagandism that took account only of this world and was therefore powerless to transform it. For to what did this Materialism *plus* Cosmopolitanism lead in the end but to some new tyranny of a Super-system imposing itself by force—to the emergence of some "chosen people," confiscating every other people's freedom in the interest of its own order? And they must beware no less of the toy nationalism of kings, with its false, egoistic, rival "patriotisms" defiant of the one true principle of progress —the association of the free peoples in the family of mankind. And alas! they must have done, too, with waiting for the Pope to move. The Pope would not move. Immobility was his principle.

For what or whom, then, must they wait? Had the Word quickened within their own souls? Then, for nothing and for no one! They, therefore, being such as they were (eighteen souls, at the moment, all told), and with such faith, resolution and means as they could command, must covenant together* as a society ("Young Europe") organised to support the movement to constitute Humanity "in such wise as to enable it throughout a continuous progress to discover and apply the Divine Law, sole source of good, by which it should be governed." And so covenanted, they must subscribe to their common faith: One God, One Law, One Aim, One Fellowship of Humanity, One Future of free, harmonious development, One Means—Association, One Principle of Representation—Nationality . . . and so onward in expansive detail.

Truly, must we not smile at these Eighteen assembling thus, in that unidentified room in Berne, to give a new charter to mankind and propound the "constitution of Humanity"? To us whose enlightened realism has achieved a policy, or absence of policy, so much more consistent with the *rationale* of an evolving universe, such bizarre fantastications can hardly be other than grotesque. And even at that time Mr. Thackeray, writing from Paris of a prevalent Continental apocalyptic, was trusting in Heaven that a fund of English roast beef (and a National Church) would save England from any such humbug. For what with divine Monsieur de Balzac, and divine Victor Hugo, and divine Madame Sand, there was scarce a beggarly, beardless Continental scribbler who was not discoursing of the *sainteté* of the *sacerdoce littéraire,* nor a poor student who (with his grisette from the *chaumière*) would not descant over his beer and tobacco upon the newest Messianism.[8] Yet these Eighteen, assembled at Berne in the shadow of their so sublime and precarious tower of Futurity, may not have been sinners nor mad above the rest of the new Galileans. It is even arguable that, after all, the pathetic mad delusion lay with the Europe which believed with Metternich that imperial coalitions and the syndicated absolutism of the dynasts were the one guarantee of "*le premier des bienfaits pour toute société humaine—le repos.*"

But also there were more practical enterprises. There was Switzerland itself for a field. The Swiss republican flag, floating above the Alps, was something unique and challenging in dynastic Europe: but thanks to the jerrymandered Pact of 1815, a loose Cantonal system, lacking in co-ordination, had

* The date of this "Pact of Fraternity" was April 15, 1834.

thwarted a proper national development. In many of the cantons local government was in the hands of an oligarchy, and in general the lack of direct representation weakened the authority of the Diet and left the Confederation a prey to foreign intrigue. Thus it was not long before Mazzini had got into touch with Swiss reformers. Swiss liberals like Druey and De Mandrot and Professor Weingart welcomed his ideas and urged him to turn his pen to the advocacy of Swiss reform; funds were provided and yet another Mazzinian journal was launched—*La Jeune Suisse*. The sheet was brought out at Bienne, twice a week, in French and German. Principally it carried Mazzini's own articles, expounding the liberal faith, advocating specific reforms, and discussing the European Question.

The success of the venture was gratifying. The little paper found a select public in all the cantons and was soon the organ of a sort of mystical-political revival. Young men, "tired of mere rebellious scepticism," wrote to the anonymous editor for spiritual counsel; matrons who had hitherto discouraged their sons from entering the "barren strife of party politics" professed conversion to "a duty of love and truth": and while Protestant pastors were writing to inquire into the precise religious implications of the doctrine of Progress, "Young Switzerland" societies were springing up in Berne, Vaud, Vallais, Geneva, and Neuchâtel. Presently, through German exiles and groups of Tyrolese artisans employed at Zurich, the movement passed even beyond the Swiss borders. It was heartening to observe all this, and the letters of the exiles took on a more cheerful tone. Even Giovanni Ruffini, who liked to affect a slightly sardonic reserve, turned for the moment from his favourite Balzac to the study of Lamennais, and permitted in his letters a faint exhalation of mystical enthusiasm.

*   *   *   *   *

And now, to avoid the undesirable attentions of the Jesuits and the Swiss police, he had moved to the canton of Solothern. The patch of country which he had described in his letter to Giuditta was Grenchen, which was then (and still remains) a modest cluster of dwellings and country stores, set in idyllic surroundings within easy reach of Bienne. He lodged on the outskirts of the village in an establishment which served as a combined tavern and bath-house and which was managed by a Dr. Girard and his brothers. The change was in every way salutary. The air was bracing, the seclusion restful, and the isolation was relieved by the society of the Ruffini brothers and the young Genoese, Antonio Ghiglione, who had joined them at Geneva. The editing of *La Jeune Suisse* and other literary work employed his time, and, thanks to his mother, he was able to stock his room with " half a library " of books.

Grenchen, in short, was a new and much-needed Savona, without Savona's duress, and gave him opportunity to compose his spirit. The black depressions and accusing voices, indeed, were by no means overcome, and perhaps his description (in Giuditta's letter) of the Alpine landscape reflected his own changing moods. His thoughts now exalted, now terrified him; he beheld his ideals now as radiant sublimities, now as pallid, phantasmal projections whose fascination drew the mind into an unillumined void. Yet instinctively he was fighting back toward physical and mental health, and the external conditions were favourable. On the whole, too, the society of his fellow-exiles was congenial. Young, dark-eyed, snub-nosed Agostino, at least, remained in the mood of hero-worship, sure that Pippo had no equal among moderns, save perhaps for Lamennais and Chateaubriand; and if the lank and somewhat bilious Giovanni could be irritating with his pose of Balzacian realism, his attitude, though touched with disillusionment, was not unfriendly, and his sojourn at Grenchen was intermittent. As for Antonio Ghiglione (see Appendix C), always half-mad, he was just now employed (in the intervals of amorous escapades) upon the creation of dramatic masterpieces, and too preoccupied to be troublesome.

And for the rest, he had the solace of Maria's and Francesca's letters by every courier, and, from the Professor, an occasional affectionate, admonitory epistle, sprinkled over with prudential maxims. Maria's letters (meticulously transcribed by Government agents who opened them in the Post*) were full of glancing reflections of the Genoa circle. Now it is Andrea Gambini, sick of a fever and tormented because in his delirium he sees Pippo at his bedside and cannot hide him from the police; now,

* These official copies were discovered by Signor Luzio in the Turin archives and form the material of his book *La Madre di Gius. Mazzini*.

Bernardo Ruffini pacing up and down the Mazzini parlour, imprecating novel and ingenious maledictions upon a wicked Government or energetically apostrophising Maria's framed *Ecce Homo* on the wall, and needing to be called to order; or again it is some good Jansenist priest dropping in with a word of Scriptural encouragement—as that the Thousand Years is surely at hand, when the Devil will be put in chains.[9] And always it is the same maternal faith, love, devotion. The cause is the Lord's, and the cunning of wicked men shall not prevail against His elect: and Pippo must beware of the night air; and when he is in need of this or that he had better append a *detachable* list of his wants, for she is the first to read his letters, and the Professor need not be disturbed. And let Pippo remember the Scriptures, " They that sow in tears shall reap in joy," and let him be sure to get his bills properly receipted; and she is glad to hear that that rascal of a Ramorino has found the inside of a Spanish gaol; and Pietro Torre has married for money. . . . So she writes, careless of grammar, careful of little except Pippo and his needs: but for him she will accomplish miracles, " improvising erudition," interesting herself in the subjects of his study—Paolo Sarpi, Giordano Bruno, anything —ferreting out books for him, employing her Jansenists to burrow for him in libraries and archives, organising a sort of volunteer clerical staff for him among her friends, and transcribing for him long extracts with her own hand. Religiously she reads every line of his own writings, and when one day he sends her De Vigny's *Chatterton* she weeps over it: only she is thinking not of Chatterton but of Pippo.

Just now, too, Maria's letters, for the first (and last) time thrill with a genuine admiration for her husband: " The heroic Professor " is her word for him, and she finds it impossible to do justice to his bravery and zeal. For she must report that Genoa, in the grip of the cholera plague, is in a state of panic and takes the air in mid-August enswathed, cocoon-like, in winter furs and with nostrils stuffed with garlic and wool; amid which general demoralisation the entire Medical Faculty of the University—except the heroic Professor—makes hurried and ignominious exodus. But staunch old Dr. Mazzini stands his ground ("with the courage of a giant," says Maria), and devotes himself day and night to the care of the sick; until the entire city rings with his praise, the poor bless him through their tears, the Gazette eulogises him, and a grateful monarch recognises his services. As for himself, the good Professor remains in the best of health "sustained by a consciousness of virtue."

It almost seemed as if the clouds were slowly lifting.

THE clouds were slowly lifting. In cheerful surroundings Mazzini revived, and if the haunting memories were not to be exorcised, at least he could thrust them into the background. For his solace there were cheering visits from comrades like Lamberti, Angelo Usiglio and Gustave Modena; Tommaseo of the defunct *Antologia* dropped in to discuss Catholic theology, and Dr. John Bowring to discuss Byron. It was especially gratifying to meet Bowring, whose *Anthology of Bohemian Folk-Songs* had already excited in the exile new visions of a coming era of Slavonic nationalism and the disintegration of the Austrian Empire. Also, the Ruffinis were musical, and there were evenings when he sang and strummed his guitar with them (to the imense delight of the Girards); and now and again there was a stolen visit to the Courvoisiers on the lake-side—good " Fritz " Courvoisier and frail Anna, his wife, soon to bid farewell to them all, but just now the goddess of young Agostino's hopeless adoration. And not least of all there was the society of the Swiss family Girard themselves. Giovanni, indeed, was not to be disarmed by the Girards' cordiality: " This entire family," he admitted, " composed of three brothers, three sisters and their aged parents, diffuses a fragrance of patriarchal simplicity that is refreshing; but I, an observer *à la* Balzac, am not to be deceived."[1] These verdant simplicities, he was convinced, concealed volcanic elements of jealousy, antipathy and petty tyranny. But in spite of the depressing influence of the indeceptible Giovanni, the Girards were excellent hosts, and the three sisters, Marianne, Madeleine and Francesca, were especially delightful. Francesca in particular, as namesake of Pippo's own sister, was prepared to take far-off " Chichina's " place in all sisterly ways, while Madeleine was similarly disposed to be a sister to Agostino (and slipped into his portfolio a pleasing picture of cooing doves). It was all very pleasant and restorative; in addition to which there was

the attachment of the Girard cat, a singularly sagacious
creature who knocked at his door every morning, and
the diversion of feeding the birds that presented themselves regularly on his window-sill. Soon he was confessing to his parents that he found himself a born Northerner; in
spite of its individualism he was, he declared, drawn to the
Northern type of character, to Northern society, and in general
to Northern Literature, Northern music, Northern scenery.
Among the Teutonic youth, more than in France and Italy,
he believed he found a native appreciation of *principles,* and
the frank freedom of social intercourse between the sexes in the
North impressed him more favourably than the formal reserve
of the South. "We Southerners (he declares to his mother) are
immoral—*ecco tutto.*" For natural scenery he had the symbolic rather than the purely æsthetic sense; it was not the scene
in itself that moved him but the scene as parable, symbol,
drama. Even so the Northern snows and Alpine sunsets and
mountain storms were stimulating enough. (How like Byron,
yonder falcon, floating proudly in the zone of the Alpine storm
and bounding defiantly aloft at every thunderclap! And
yonder stork in the Girard garden, turning his head toward
the warring elements with half-indifferent curiosity and then
drawing up a long sinewy leg and composing himself—how
like Goethe!)

Withal there was the solace of regular correspondence with
Giuditta. "Your portrait grows more precious every day. . . .
Then there are your letters, your lock of hair, the rose-petals,
your ribbon, the little purse—I have fashioned them all into a
little world, the world of my Giuditta and me." When she
suggests half-jestingly that he ought to write a romance and
weave their story into it, he replies: "I have thought of it a
thousand times," but it could not be done: their love had too
sacred a history. Years later, in London he would attempt
something of the sort, but would get little further than the
title, *Benoni,* which Giovanni would presently appropriate for
an autobiographical romance of his own.

And for the rest, Giovanni just now provokes an outburst by
writing to him from Bienne that the time has come to set
"poetry" aside and be practical. He relieves his outraged feelings in a Vesuvian epistle to Giuditta. What, he would know,

would the world become on Giovanni's terms? A mud-heap
on which insect-creatures swarmed and battened! Take away
the enthusiasms of the heart and he would spurn the earth with
rage and loathing. Would Giovanni have him a book-keeper?
He beheld around him, indeed, crowds of frigid beings supposed to be shrewd and expert calculators; they seemed to him
vile, abject, stupid. It was precisely these men of prose who
had oppressed the world, destroyed everything sacred, made
matrimony a traffic, patriotism a career, poverty a crime.
They had dubbed the poets mad and driven them mad—
Tasso, Chatterton, thousands more. No! he would suffer, but
he would be himself to the last. He would not, to please
Giovanni or anyone else, perjure his soul and turn himself
into a living lie.

*   *   *   *   *

Now was the time, then, for him to annotate Savona; now
was the time for him to re-examine his attitude and clear his
mind. And, in fact, for intellectual output, this Grenchen
interval of eighteen months, concluded as it was by the supreme
crisis of his inner life, was relatively the most prolific period of
his career. Thus he writes some sixty articles for *La Jeune
Suisse,* collaborates in the translation of De Vigny's *Chatterton*
and Werner's *Der vierunzwanzigste Februar,* with introduc-
tions from his own pen; projects a *Foreign Review* to be published at Genoa (quashed by the censorship), attempts a *Review
of European Literature* to be brought out at Lugano (also in
vain); collaborates successfully with Tommaseo and Accursi
in the founding of an Italian journal published in Paris; contributes elaborate and extensive essays on the *Philosophy of
Music,* on *Fatality as a Dramatic Element,* and on Victor Hugo;
and collects materials for an edition of Foscolo and for essays
on Bruno and Sarpi. In addition, after cordial correspondence
with Lamennais and Gioberti (and influenced perhaps by
Lamennais' newly published *Words of a Believer*) he produces
his first work, *Faith and the Future.* He writes it in French,
publishes it at his own expense at Bienne, and loses in the
enterprise some 600 fr., ill to be spared. All the same, the little
book confiscated on the French frontier and, circulating in
Switzerland only in a few pallid copies, left miserably to die

of neglect—the little book was a confession of faith written out of his own heart, and would presently (1849) be revived. For us it is too significant to be passed over.

*   *   *   *   *

As he saw it, the new world could not be evoked with obsolete formulas: every age had its own distinctive faith. Just now, however, European liberalism was in bondage to the past—not so much to its errors as to its achievements. Thus, unless they were careful, the French Revolution would be their undoing. It fascinated, dazzled, dazed the modern liberal mind, and its formulas were recited as the final wisdom. Yet the French Revolution was not so much an initiation as a conclusion, summing up the epoch of the Reformation. To-day they must advance further. Liberty was not enough, nor Equality, which was the liberty of all, nor Fraternity, which was the brotherhood of all. The Liberty of all without a sovereign Law above it must lead to the war of all—to shock and counter-shock and endless dissipation of social energies. Even Fraternity fell short. Brotherhood, " the word which the Revolution disinterred from the foot of the cross of Christ," yielded the first condition of social progress, but it did not define the aim. The principle of brotherhood was compatible with movement in a circle: it denoted a relationship between individuals, the ethical link between individual liberty and equality. It needed to be carried forward to its fulfilment in the conception of Humanity, the One Life of the world, and to the idea of progress through association. There was, however, little sign of this. In France, the home of the Revolution, the liberal faith, denied expansion, was shrinking into unfaith —either into an opportunism which said "We will use Monarchy for our own ends"—and which had no ends beyond its diurnal improvisations, or else into a negativism which ranted of " flinging Monarchy into the abyss," and was innocent of any positive policy beyond that performance. Where was the constructive faith which would fill in the abyss and build upon it? And what was the thing to be built? The Republic? But what was the value of a republic without corresponding ideas, principles, beliefs? What was the value of republican forms with a monarchical, *bourgeois* spirit? True democracy was not a quantified mass of voters but a qualified society of believers. But alas for modern liberalism, which attempted the reconstruction of society without a faith, a moral centre; which played with the word "Humanity," but first emptied it of all its spiritual content; which talked largely of "harmonising the human faculties," but neglected the most potent element of human nature; which dreamed of a material unity of Europe, but ignored its fundaments—moral unity, uniformity of sanctions, community of faith and of aim! The task of the future, then, was like that which challenged the first Christian believers in the age which witnessed the dissolution of ancient Paganism. The ideas which governed the past age were no longer sufficient. Only a living faith could put an end to the confusions of the present. The task of the future was to found the Catholicism of Humanity, of which the Christian Gospel was the germ, as man was the germ of mankind. The task of the future was to build upon the ruins of the old world with its divisive dynasties and classes the altar of reconciliation, of unity. "Are these illusions? Do I presume too far in asking such prodigies of faith in an age still undermined by scepticism; among men still slaves of the *ego,* who love little and forget soon, who bear about discouragement in their hearts and are earnest in nothing save in the calculations of egotism, and the passing pleasures of the hour? No. . . . It is necessary that these things should be, and they will be. I have faith in God, in the power of truth, and in the historic logic of things. I feel in my inmost heart that the delay is not for long. The principle which was the soul of the old world is exhausted. It is our part to clear the way for the new principle."

The general criticism was obvious. It was the criticism levelled against all his idealistic propaganda, the first murmur of the protest which was to increase in volume in the later years. Let M. Mazzini come down from the clouds. Instead of dissertating on "principles" and a nebulous "religion of Humanity," let him descend to the actual economic situation, instruct the proletariat in its true interests, and proclaim the revolt of the wage-slaves. The criticism nettled him and he retorted upon its authors. Who (he inquired) were these men of fact and utility who chose to assail him? What had they achieved? The facts which they deplored had long existed—

social injustice, the sweat and tears of the oppressed—why had these men of fact, of practical reform, failed to dispose of them? They had failed for lack of the very thing which they affected to despise. Riots, class-vendettas, might be carried through by hate, by passion; revolutions might be wrought in the intoxication of a brief enthusiasm, stimulated by initial successes; but enduring transformations were wrought only through the immortal part of man, through faith, love, self-sacrifice: and, to a people who had no stimulus outside material self-interest, martyrdom was a folly: "to their intelligence Christ has lost all meaning." For by what theory of self-interest could men be persuaded to sacrifice their all? Moreover, what was the effect of a doctrine of mere rights and interests in a class-divided society where rival rights and interests were constantly clashing? To what did it lead but a ceaseless eddying in a whirlpool, an endless making and unmaking, a confused cycle of crises returning upon themselves? Where in all the medley and jostle of things was the centre around which chaos could be organised into harmony? To have a centre for all the divergent interests of society they must first find that which was sovereign over them all.

And so onward in tireless iteration. . . . One day Maria will write to tell him of a young preacher who has taken Genoa by storm—a Barnabite friar named Ugo Bassi. He answers that he would like to be a preacher himself, and perhaps the *Times* obituary which described his essays as sermons was on the mark.

For the rest, with the Northern aurora still attracting him, he composed his essays on Music and on the Drama, the portents of whose renaissance he believed he discerned in the North. The contemporary music of Italy, indeed, "lyrical almost to delirium, passionate to intoxication, volcanic as the land of its birth, brilliant as its sunshine," celebrated unbridled egoism—"man without God." So also most modern composers, victims of the prevailing moral anarchy, were concerned with effects rather than effect, their work a mere whirl of *motifs,* given with a rush, leading nowhither, and vacuously applauded by audiences interested in the individual performances of their favourites rather than in the production as a whole. But in German music there was a mystic element, however tentative, "cradling you upon a wave of chords, elevating and awaking the heart to the consciousness of another world, revealed afar off, not bestowed—to the sense of having approached the first mysteries of a great initiation, never begun." A barren mysticism as yet—"God without Man." But in Meyerbeer, behold the promise of the new synthesis.

And so with the Drama. "Nowadays we have no Drama because we have no Heaven." Fatality, the dramatic principle of the Greeks, was extinct as the ancient gods: a limited Necessity—the retributive dooms that descend upon the individual ego as it stands in its brief and puny freedom over against the Infinite—found its supreme interpretation in Shakespeare: and no new principle had taken its place. The mind of the modern playwright wandered hesitant in the void, without central direction, without supreme sanctions, without any unitive conception to give measure and value to human action. But German Schiller had re-discovered the Overworld—the Heaven not of Fate nor of Necessity but of a sovereign Providence whose designs comprehended both the individual and the race.

"In Schiller man is presented to us as free, and possessed of a fulness and power of faith of which neither the ancients nor Shakespeare had any conception. The guiding star of his destiny burns . . . in his own breast; and you feel at the same time that . . . should he prove unworthy and grovel in the dust . . . rebellious to that social idea and to the law of the universe . . . [even so] the idea is immortal, and Providence, watching over its fulfilment from on high, will cause even his action against it, and the brief triumph of the power he abused, to bring forth some element of social progress and aid in the development of the design of God. . . ."

His interpretation of Schiller reflected his own faith and agreed with the Calvinism of his Jansenist upbringing. In its broad lines it was novel criticism, but a century later its primary contention was to be maintained and expounded with singular fidelity by Mr. Bernard Shaw.[2]

Withal he confesses to Giuditta that with him Papal Catholicism is dead, and Christianity, as a system, moribund. When Niccolò Tommaseo calls at Grenchen, it is on that issue that they draw apart. It was annoying to find Tommaseo becloud-

ing an able intellect with vapourings about a Papalist revival
and a future Liberator-Pope—as if the new wine could be
put into the old bottles! Tommaseo irritatingly challenges
him to produce the formula for the new wine; Paolo Pallia
("Corso") objects (on the ground of the Gospel miracles and
the Resurrection) that the old wine and the old bottles are
alike certified as final; Melegari accuses him of Pantheism
and warns him against intellectual and spiritual pride. But
he is obdurate. With Melegari and Pallia, indeed, he expos-
tulates. He pleads guilty to the charge of Pantheism, but
shows that his use of the term is very much his own. "Certainly I am a pantheist—why should I deny it? But is there
only one form of pantheism in the world? Between that of
Spinoza, of Bruno, of St. Paul, and of the Germans, is there
no difference? . . . I believe in God, in a causative intelligence superior to the created world . . . and because I believe
the Divine Unity is fundamental, and reproduces itself in all
creation, and necessarily involves *one* law, *one* design, *one*
continuous development . . . *one* purpose, *one* Humanity;
and hence *one* Art, *one* Philosophy, *one* Polity, *one* Religion,
of which all arts, philosophies, epochs of civilisation, religions,
are no more than evolutionary phases, progressive and transitory manifestations, divine at one time, human at all times
—because I so believe, you excommunicate me. . . . I begin
to despair of you."[3] And why cannot Pallia see that the
eternal spirit of religion cannot be forever contained within
one set of fixed and dated symbols? Primitive Christianity,
supreme and unsurpassable on the individual side, concentrated upon religion in the soul; mediæval Christianity was
its attempted extension to society as a whole: the Reformation
fell back upon the primitive emphasis, limiting itself to the
sphere of individual salvation, and to that extent was cynical
in its omissions. The dogma of the future must be humanitary,
looking toward a social Incarnation—"the expansion of Christ
the Man into Christ the People"—"an initiator-Messiah
people, great and free, associated in one sole Thought, one
sole Love."

"And now see what is the outcome of the idea. Christianity is a
[fixed] eternal religion, an unique religious synthesis. And what of
mankind prior to Christianity? Oh, in what sense do you understand

God . . . and the unity of the mind of God?   A progressive law at the
beginning and an eternal synthesis later on! . . .   Believing as I do,
with yourself, in continuous progression, there ought to be between us
only a question of time, but never a denial of the new synthesis when
the time comes.   Christianity is the formula of the individual, and as
such is eternal and perfect to my thinking—for that formula is what no
one can nullify. . . .   Only behind it one seeks for another—the social.
Where is the contradiction?   Tell me, my Corso, with your hand on
your heart: to the arguments which I scatter in my letters, hurried,
unconnected, and almost sportive . . . and which you (permit me to
say) shirk a little in your replies, have you anything to oppose?   Do not
some of the things which I say, if you think them over seriously, cast
some doubts on your mind?   As to what you cite to me regarding
miracles and the resurrection of Christ, etc., I will not discuss them
to-day; but I confess to you it seems to me strange that you should
regard these as being irrevocably proved in history."

And for the rest:

" I say it seriously, someone will come to furbish up my ideas without
knowing I advocated them.   I am more than likely to die without
doing this, because I am conscious of my mission, and I know the
duration of it—and I know that it is not I who will wage the war.
Truth means to run her course and she will do it . . . but I have no
future.   I have discerned, but it is not given to me to do more: therefore I still devote my days to a work very inferior to that which my
longings would have sought for—the actual production of the instrument.   I am neither more nor less than a political revolutionist, and to
that I resign myself."[4]

For the political revolution must precede the religious reformation.   First the Third Rome, then the New Catholicism.
Withal he adds: " I have moments of *spleen,* of individualism,
which rebels.   But these are moments of irritation arising out
of what I have myself been suffering these three years, and
this is more than you suppose.   Then I return to myself, and
where I can see any little advantage, any symptom of duty,
I submit."

    *   *   *   *   *

Further reflections were rudely interrupted.   For sometime
toward the end of May, 1836, Agostino looks out of window
after dinner and beholds descending upon the Girard establishment the combined military forces of the Canton—a
storming-party of Carbineers "armed to the teeth," a supporting force surrounding the house, and reserves posted on

the Solothern road. "Nothing more was needed except cavalry and artillery."[5]

Agostino describes the arrest—the two dangerous prisoners (himself and Pippo) "perfectly calm," the Girards raging and vociferous, old father Girard rating the commanding officer with extreme and personal allusions to his high hat, his antecedents and his relations, and Marianne, Madeleine, Francesca and their mother loudly weeping. Amid which general confusion the prisoners (now including Danish Harro Harring, arrived in the nick of time) were marched off to Solothern gaol. At Solothern, however, Officialdom was further embarrassed, the town being in an uproar, with young women running through the streets and rallying the citizenry in true revolutionary style. So that next day (Sunday) alarmed Officialdom, fearing an attack on the gaol, released the dangerous prisoners and gave them twenty-four hours to be gone from the canton. "Then," says Agostino, "the ovation began"—with impromptu civic welcome at the prison gates, invitation to public banquet (regretfully declined), and carriages of escort back to Grenchen: where, down the tree-shaded avenue to the Girard grounds, comes the local Philharmonic in tuneful chorus, followed by immense crowd, with maidens and matrons laughing and weeping; then in due time a generous flow of speeches and Swiss wine. All of which, indeed, is now commemorated in an historical inscription adorning Grenchen's municipal hall. But all of which, none the less, failed to cancel the official eviction, and next day saw a long, sad adieu to Grenchen and the Girards—poor red-eyed Francesca so bereft and sorrowful that she "wished to die."

"WERE I to live for a century," says Mazzini in his Autobiographical Notes, "I could never forget the close of that year [of 1836] nor the moral tempest that passed over me." The eviction from Grenchen, in fact, had happened in May, and the close of the year found them still on the Solothern borders, at Langenau and elsewhere, eluding the police by sheltering in untenanted houses and mountain cabins. But as Mazzini goes on to describe the circumstances of the struggle it is clear that it began, not toward the close of '36 but in the former winter, before the departure from the Girards. Three years later he writes of the experience to Elia Benza: "[It was] in Switzerland, in the midst of the snow, in a solitude almost absolute, in the room of a hostel round which the wind howled dismally. . . . Jacopo's mother and another woman whom I greatly esteemed, and who is now [1839] dead, helped me, without knowing of my actual condition." The general description suggests the Gerard establishment, and the "other woman" was almost certainly Anna Courvoisier, who died before the winter of '36.

In any case it was inevitable that the crisis should come. Since '33 he had evaded it, repressing the insistent questionings and accusings, first provoked by the death of Jacopo and his fellow-victims. But evasions and repressions could not go on forever; and indeed there were times when he seemed to have faced his nameless dreads and gained the victory. As early as the beginning of 1835 he was writing to his mother, in almost evangelical vein, that, after four years of thought and suffering, he had found his gospel. "Woe (he writes) to him who does not know himself sinful! Woe to him who is ignorant of the pride of his own heart! Infallibly his evil tendencies will victimise him." For the wicked may overcome his wickedness, but what can save the unknowing, the self-complacent? But for himself, he knows well enough that he has it in him to be "an atheist, a libertine, a rogue, a Don Juan, a Timon, or worse." All the same, in these last four years his gospel, he declares, has rooted itself in his heart. *Life is a mission; Sacrifice is the supreme virtue:* this has become his faith— the faith "that Christ taught in words and deeds."[1] To Anna Courvoisier he wrote in the same strain.

But by the autumn of '35 he was in the slough again and writing to Giuditta of the return of the night-terrors and the *singulti*—the old fits of convulsive sobbing. Moreover, toward the end of the Grenchen sojourn his former avenues of activity were beginning to close against him; one by one every door of escape was being shut. Thanks to Jesuit influence and general political opposition his connection with *La Jeune Suisse* had to be abandoned; his book, which might have opened up new opportunities, had miserably failed; his offers to serve as correspondent for local journals (at five centimes per line) were declined; and, owing to responsibilities undertaken for the expenses of the Savoy expedition, he was burdened with a dead-weight of debt. And as if this were not enough, he found himself obliged to resign the leadership of Young Italy and watch the labours and hopes of the crowded years since Savona dissolve into dust.

There was another harassment. Eleonora Ruffini confided to her sons that she was financially embarrassed. To appeal to her husband was worse than useless; in such matters Bernardo was apt to be either adamant or dynamite; she knew not where to turn. But the boys knew. The Ruffinis always cherished a cheerful belief in the unlimited wealth of the Mazzinis, and it seemed natural to turn to Pippo. And because the plea involved Eleonora, his "second mother" and the mother of Jacopo, its appeal was irresistible. To Maria, however, he could not turn for the necessary funds; her scanty store had already been too heavily drained on his own account; and to state the facts to the Professor would be useless, and a betrayal of confidence. He solved the problem by writing to his father for an advance of 7,000 fr. "for the purchase of shares" in an iron and timber business founded by the Milanese exile, Rosales. It was a sorry ruse, and to Rosales he was obliged to write a precautionary explanation in case the Professor should make inquiries ("It is one of my hallucinations, one of my dreams, and means nothing "). The Professor took the bait. He was gratified by Pippo's hopeful turn toward practical affairs, and trusted the investment would be a step toward placing Pippo on a firm, solid and honourable footing—" the first concern of a good man." " I want to know nothing more. See that you make good use of the money." He added that he was feeling the approach of his three-score years and ten. " My only trouble is the fear of not being able to embrace you before I go. I love you and shall love you to the last moment of my life."

The Professor's money was duly disbursed. Agostino communicated the news to his mother with a " Hallelujah!" Eleonora was equally lyrical, and Giovanni felt obliged to assure her that Pippo was embarrassed and mortified by " so great an acknowledgment of so slight a service."

Pippo was in truth embarrassed and mortified. Everything had gone wrong, everything had become twisted, perverted as in a distortive mirror. " I wished," he wrote, " to do good and I have always done harm . . . and the thought grows and grows upon me till I think I shall go mad." " I looked upon everyone," he declared to Benza, " with anger and antipathy, and upon myself with that terror which is begotten of a sense of crime." No one, indeed, guessed his secret. If he was silent and self-absorbed, his companions exercised a charitable tolerance. There was, they explained, a great deal of the child, perhaps the spoilt child, about Pippo; he was moodish and wilful and only happy when he was conspiring. He himself strove to banish the spectres of the mind by refurbishing his neglected Latin,[2] but it was of no avail. The accusing ghosts returned; there were voices in the night winds that moaned and sighed around the Girard house; " it seemed to me," he told Benza, " that Jacopo arose from his grave to curse me "; and he wrote to Giuditta of a " Faustian region of gnawing worms." In the autumn of '36, with poor Anna Courvoisier in her grave, and with a growing, morbid sense of persecution and estrangement, he appealed pathetically to Eleonora Ruffini to certify him, if, in good conscience, she could, that his faith was not a false belief. " Do not mention what I ask of you to a living soul; but if, without contradicting your conscience, you can give me an encouraging word, do; if not, I shall know that I am wrong . . . for I believe in you as in an oracle."

For now the supreme moral crisis was upon him. Loneliness, defeat, self-accusation, doubt—all the dreads hitherto evaded, all the voices, mournful, reproachful, Satanic, hitherto smothered into half-silence—all these had now to be met.

And this moral isolation was reflected in his surroundings and was heightened by them. For with the Ruffinis he was now thrust out and wandering in solitary places. They lived as it were by stealth, sheltering in forsaken habitations and succoured only by the charity of kindly Protestant pastors or by peasants and goat-herds in their hillside hovels. And as the winter drew on and the valleys lay under drifts of snow, the enveloping silence and the darkness of the nights invaded his soul, torturing his imagination and deepening his sense of dereliction. "I felt myself not only supremely wretched; I felt as one condemned, conscious of guilt and incapable of expiation."[3] "You lack faith," wrote his mother. "I have it absolutely. . . . Your name is destined to shine among the benefactors of mankind. It is decreed."[4] "Among the benefactors of mankind!" The words seemed to mock him.

When deliverance came it was not through laborious thought nor supreme effort of the will; rather it was through a mystic opening or occult shift and resettling of the mind. Thus one morning he awoke to find himself strangely calm, as one conscious of having come safely through some extreme danger. Even Nature, he recalled (it was a morning of bright sunshine), seemed to smile reassuringly upon him. It seemed to him as if a message had been inscribed upon his mind, and with returning consciousness he was able to read it: "*This* [ordeal] *of thine is a temptation of egoism; thou misconceivest the meaning of life.*"

Thus, now that calmness had come, he was able to interrogate his mind afresh; and taking up his pen he wrote out his conclusions: for writing had now become a sort of mental necessity with him. And perhaps the noteworthy fact is that the new emergence was not at all in the sphere of belief. As to that, in every detail and altogether, his conclusions reaffirmed his former faith: what emerged was in the sphere of self-discovery. He had combated egoism in others, not sufficiently in himself. He had cast off "every baser stamp of material desires," but egoism had only retired to the citadel of the affections. He was still pursuing happiness in the form of reciprocated love. He had regarded the esteem of his friends as a right, as the wages of the heart, the condition for the fulfilment of the appointed task. Thus he had written to his mother: "God, conscience, conduct governed by duty, resignation—these are the cardinal principles . . . but a little love is necessary to us, and through whom can that priceless thing come to us if not through the few beings whom we ourselves deeply love?"[5] When he had fancied he detected the "estrangement of fraternal souls," he had rebelled and despaired. "I had unknowingly worshipped, not love, but the happiness, the joys of love." He had not yet made terms with life on the basis of the true irreducible minimum. But now it seemed to him that he must strip himself, not, indeed, of the affections, but of all their selfward demands and earthly rewards, of every claim to love as a condition for the fulfilment of duty.

"Having reached that point, I swore to myself that nothing in this world should again make me doubt or forsake it. It was as Dante says, a passing through martyrdom to peace; a peace violent and desperate, I do not deny: for I fraternised with sorrow and wrapped myself round in it as a wayfarer in his cloak; yet peace it was, for by it I learned to suffer without rebellion, and from that hour to live calmly and in harmony with my own spirit."

He adds that he noted down at that time a record of the struggle. Later he expanded the notes into a book which he intended to publish anonymously under the title *Reliquie d'un Ignoto* ("Records of an Unknown"). In 1843 he writes of it to his mother;[6] it was to be a little book of the *Jacopo Ortis* type, "but with an entirely different moral aim," describing "a youth who passes through all the saddest disillusionments of life," but who, instead of despairing like Ortis, "attains to the peace and comfort of faith." Five years later he took the manuscript with him to Italy. "I carried it with me, written in minute characters upon very thin paper, to Rome [1849] and lost it in passing through France on my return." So at last he records, years later, in his Autobiographical Notes. But at the time of the loss he writes to Emilie Ashurst that, most deplorably, he had left the manuscript " in a trunk in Rome " itself, together with numerous other papers, including an essay on Jansenism and " thoughts on history, politics and religion "; " the best part of myself was there."[7] Strange if these heretical bundles of " very thin paper," written over in that well-known, microscopic hand, should yet be reposing *somewhere* in Rome— duly collected, trunk and all, from the Triumviral office in the Quirinal, or from the Triumvir's private lodgings, after the Papal restoration!

In any case, the crisis was over. He had " found peace." " Be the sky radiant with the blue serenity of a cloudless Italian morning or leaden and deathly grey, as in the winters of the North, yet . . . our duty remains the same. Above the earthly firmament is God, and in our souls shine the holy stars of faith and the future, even when their light consumes itself unreflected as the sepulchral lamp."

In London in 1860 the Russian exile, Alexander Herzen, will spend such time as he may in the fascinating company of a frail, grey-haired, dark-eyed gentleman who dresses always in black and goes by the name of " Mr. Flower." He has another name, and Herzen knows it—and goes home to enter in his diary his impressions. For it appears that this elderly stranger is a person of some European importance; and just now he is being anathematised by all political parties and vilified by all the Continental Press, in Italy especially. Into the bargain he is loaded with the abuse of *The Times*, of Disraelian Mr. Urquhart and the English petty *bourgeoisie*. But what Herzen must note is the victim's superb indifference.

"For Mazzini nothing exists but the cause. . . . However many flowers and pheasants the king might send him, he would not be touched. . . . Mazzini is an ascetic, the Calvin of Italian emancipation. One-sided, forever absorbed by one idea, forever ready and on his guard, he keeps his vigil with the same obstinacy and patience with which he created a compact party out of scattered individuals and vague yearnings, and after a dozen failures . . . preserved the living, infallible hope. . . . Day and night, catching fish and going out hunting, lying down and getting up, Garibaldi and his followers see the thin, melancholy hand of Mazzini pointing to Rome, and they will still march thither."[8]

The final stamp of that character was sealed in Solothern in the winter of '36.

    *   *   *   *   *

So ended a fateful year. Nor had it all been dolorous. The Ruffinis, for example, had risen to the occasion and shown a proper spirit—young Agostino especially. After the Grenchen eviction Agostino, indeed, had kindled to a fine Mazzinian ardour. " God is our defence," he wrote to his mother. " He increases our courage and resolution in direct proportion to the malevolence of our enemies . . . . We say with Luther "[9]— and so forth, in valiant style.

And did not good Pastor Stueli, of Langenau, write (in *Greek*, for greater safety) to his local brethren to have them prepare secret aid for the evicted ones—himself dismantling his own manse in order to furnish some garret or other for their comfort, and " translating some lines of Psalm 37 " for their confirmation in the faith? " Blessings upon that saintly pastor," exclaims Maria, " for his so prophetic psalm! I read it and re-read it and take refuge in it!"[10]

All the same, how remote, now, was the Savona dream! Observable from the Hardeian Overworld was a still prostrate Europe, its peoples still " writhing, crawling, heaving "—in Italy, perhaps, worst of all. Little hope of the " Third Rome " with Gregory XVI. in the Papal chair! Little hope for a Piedmontese initiative with Charles Albert as " King Wobble "! Little hope from Naples with Ferdinand in control! Little hope from Modena with Duke Francis avowing his Sanfedist creed: *" God has made Hell, and the godliest prince is he who makes the hangman his Prime Minister "*! Little hope of any movement anywhere, with Austria holding the passes of the North, and Metternich ready to enforce the blessings of tranquillity at the point of half a million bayonets!

And to Metternich, before leaving Switzerland, Mazzini pays his tribute. " On the monarchist side there exists but one man in Europe. This man—the only one to comprehend the present European situation and its inherent dangers—is Metternich; and Metternich is Immobility personified, the Chinese principle in its highest expression, the *Status Quo* incarnate. . . . Metternich is a great man. He has penetrated and grasped the nature of the principle he represents, and from all his study he has derived an axiom which is the *résumé* of his entire political science: *Movement is fatal*."[11]

And yet, in spite of all contrary experiences, Young Italy had become the one living thing in a land of death. It had attained to a life that was already independent of its body. It was a breath, a spirit. It was a viewless presence overtaking men on the wayside, surprising them at their daily tasks, whispering to them in their dreams, and breathing into them a new hope, a new purpose. Its republican dogma might make little impression, its political argument might fall into confusion; but its word of faith and hope, its call to Italians to hold their Italianity as a solemn trust, not for themselves but for Humanity—these things touched the spirits of men with an electric flame.

Thus through the long years of reaction its influence would break out at unexpected times and in unlooked-for ways; not only in the satires of Giusti, the romances of Guerrazzi, the recitals of Gustavo Modena, the political mysticism of Gioberti, the fiery preachments of Ugo Bassi and Gavazzi, but also in the talk of the workshops, the cafés, the barracks, the ships' cabins and fo'c'sles. Everywhere the new spirit was abroad, mysterious, elusive, but waiting to manifest itself in the fulness of time.

And as for the founder of "Young Italy," he now intimated to the authorities his readiness to leave for England. What could be more commendable? Relieved Officialdom promptly supplied passports and safe-conducts for M. Mazzini and his friends.

Thus, on the second day of the New Year of 1837 they return to Grenchen to bid hurried farewell to the Girards. And do not the mayor and councillors of Grenchen accompany them (with flags flying) through Langenau to Nidau? (Something almost triumphal in this departure—to be able to emerge at last and look every gendarme in the eye!) And at Nidau, as Agostino reports, they all dine together—those warmhearted Switzers "brushing their hands across their eyes" now and then. As for the high disdain of the men of State, says Agostino, those brushed-away tears outweigh it all. And now—to London, "where every man is under the protection of common rights," where we can wear our own names, assume our own personalities and live like free men!

At Troyes they pick up Angelo Usiglio; at 3 o'clock on the morning of the 12th they board ship at Calais, and at 4 in the afternoon, after a wretched passage, four cloaked and weather-drenched foreigners drive through London mud and rain to the Hotel Sablonnière. Eleven years were to go by before the chief exile should leave England and cross once more to the Continent at the call of Italy.

GREY MORNING

CHAPTER I   LONDON

THE London which Mazzini and his fellow-exiles entered was the London of Dickens and Thackeray, of Carlyle and John Stuart Mill, of Wellington and Melbourne and Peel. Cruikshank originals walked abroad, stage coaches clattered over ill-paved streets, and top-hatted "Peelers" kept the peace. It was the year when the Girl-Queen ascended the throne and when young Mr. Disraeli (in bottle-green frock-coat and fancy-pattern pantaloons) burst upon the House of Commons. Patrons of "the Fancy" still foregathered at Seven Dials, young bloods still sent their cartels for the settlement of affairs of honour (at twelve paces) in the neighbourhood of Chalk Farm, and old magnificoes still dined occasionally on truffled swan and deplored the decline of Almack's. At Gore House the Countess Guiccioli was contributing her mature and slightly *prononcé* charms and a flavour of Byronic reminiscence to the unfailing piquancy of Lady Blessington's receptions: and at Broadlands Palmerston was entertaining foreign diplomats with a bluff and occasionally disconcerting *bonhomie*. As for Mazzini, it was persistently rumoured in Genoa that he had been appointed Lord Palmerston's secretary, and Francesca wrote that the Professor was greatly gratified by the report, though he knew it to be untrue.

Nothing, in fact, could have been further from the truth. Two years earlier Cavour had visited London with letters of introduction which had admitted him to the best literary and political circles. He had met De Tocqueville, dined at John Murray's, heard Peel in the House of Commons, spoken at the annual dinner of the Royal Geographical Society, and

inspected everything from Almack's to the Thames Tunnel—
and had returned to Italy to organise railways in Piedmont,
a steamboat company for Lake Maggiore, a Bank at Genoa,
and a whist club at Turin. Mazzini with his three companions
had slipped into London unheeded, passed from the Hotel
Sablonnière to modest lodgings at 24, Goodge Street, Totten-
ham Court Road, and limited his patronage (ready money
being chronically scarce) to the local pawnshops. His father
and Andrea Gambini, it is true, had provided him with letters
of introduction to London Italians, and of these there was
a prosperous circle—the Pepolis, Panizzis, Rossettis, Rolandis:
but they were not of his republican faith and he would not
be beholden to them. Before approaching them he would,
in his father's favourite phrase, "establish himself in an
honourable independence."

It was, however, more easily said than done. He wrote
to his mother of the oceanic vastness and tumultuous life of
the city, in which he and his friends were as unheeded flot-
sam. Citizens showed no yearning desire to engage a group
of young foreigners to whom spoken English was unintelligible and who themselves lapsed into French on the smallest
provocation; and literary hack-work was difficult when one
had to compose in French and have one's articles done into
English, at a high rate of charges, before they could be considered. Dr. John Bowring might have been helpful, but he
was abroad. His place was taken by a kindly Quaker physician,
apparently of the Toynbee connection, who drilled them in
English (with the Bible for a primer), and somehow humor-
ously reminded them of the old Father-Rector.

On the whole, conditions were discouraging, and Mazzini
adjusted himself slowly. "In this country," he told his mother,
"modesty, like religion in Italy, centres in outward observ-
ances. One is forbidden to speak of shirts or trousers in a
lady's presence, or to mention the thigh of a chicken at table ";
all the same, "one cannot walk out at night without being
accosted by prostitutes, of whom there are here at least fifty
thousand." Moreover, all bearded foreigners were apt, he
complains, to be mistaken for Frenchmen and insulted by
tipsy patriots. Gin-drinking was a universal pest, and "the
English people, when they are in liquor, are beastly, and at

the slightest provocation assume the attitude of a boxer—that is, of combatants." For the rest, he made an early visit to the House of Commons and was mildly scandalised, preferring the Zoological Gardens, which he visited repeatedly and with enthusiasm.

Nevertheless, English political life at once impressed him, and in his letters to his parents he paints the contrast between British and Continental standards. "In England (he remarks to his father) there was once a Walpole, and he was called by his right name; in France there are whole generations of Walpoles." "Over there they fight for office, for money, or from other low motives; here they fight for convictions—mistaken, as I believe, but convictions all the same. Thiers is the most unprincipled man in the whole of France; Lord Melbourne is a man of austere probity."[1]

Within three months of his arrival in London he was summing up the British political situation. The real issue (he wrote to his parents) was not Whig *versus* Tory; it was Labour *versus* Privilege. After all, and apart from the High Church question, what were the Whigs doing but attacking an aristocracy of blood, dating from the Conquest, in the interests, chiefly, of a more numerous aristocracy of wealth, "and, sometimes, intelligence," dating from the new industrialism? Labour, he prophesied, would reject both and press its own claims. As yet the movement was in its infancy, but "in England, when a desire begins to be expressed by a section of the people, you may be sure it will triumph in the long run." The English working classes had good sense and a grasp of politics. They had a greater respect for law and legality than the French, and would conduct their struggle accordingly. But the issue was joined; the conflict would be long and increasingly grave; and in the end the limited liberalism of the Whigs, driven to perpetual shifts and evasions, would be unable to cope with it.[2] It was a shrewd and long-sighted forecast for a foreigner to make in 1837.

For the rest, anticipating Whistler, he found poetic stimulus and inspiration in London fog and penned lyrical descriptions of it to his Swiss friends, the Mandrots of Lausanne. The eye (he declares) lost itself in a reddish abyss that suggested the sombre, sulphurous glow of Dante's Inferno. The whole

city was laid under a magic spell. One thought of the first
scene in Macbeth, of the Brockenberg, of Endor. The passers-
by in the streets looked like spectres; one felt spectral oneself.
Cupolas, columns, buildings emerged and faded, and all was
vague, shadowy, Ossianesque, exciting to reverie and appealing
to the mystical side of one's nature. How much better this,
he exclaims, than the finite geometrical completeness of cities
where the vision can embrace everything by the four corners
and nothing is left to the imagination! "You will smile at
all this, but I assure you that in me these impressions have
a serious source. They are a reaction against the positive, the
prosaic, the utilitarian—a word which continues more and
more to invade our age, stifling all those powers of enthusiasm
necessary for creative work and turning everybody . . . into
a pettifogging arithmetician in everything."[3]

But it was not possible to live upon mystical reactions to
London fog. Lodgings in Goodge Street were expensive (ten
shillings a week per room), and even a staple diet of fried
hogs' brains and beer (varied with bread crumbled in a dish
of coffee) demanded an outlay, while cigars—an indispensable
item—cost not less than the appalling sum of threepence each
(the happy discovery of Cubas at ten for a shilling came later).
Moreover, the Ruffinis were usually penniless, and though
Angelo Usiglio was working upon a literary masterpiece (in
eight parts), his earnings were mainly prospective.
With unusual worldly wisdom Mazzini determined to retain
at least the appearance of genteel independence. "We need
a sort of *salon*," he wrote to his mother; "certainly nothing
luxurious, which I should detest, but something that would
afford a polite appearance, a suggestion of well-being."[4] For,
in England (he explains to his father) money talks, and if
one allows oneself to appear in urgent need of employment,
he only weights his chances of not obtaining it. Accordingly,
at the end of March, and with his little retinue increased by
the addition of young Giambattista Ruffini, of Modena, and
a Newfoundland dog of healthy appetite (adopted by Usiglio),
he moved into a ten-roomed house at 9, George Street, Euston
Square. The Ruffini brothers were amiably disposed to the
venture. They had previously, with great good humour,

appointed Maria Mazzini "Minister for Foreign Affairs," and forwarded to Genoa a joint list of their larder-requirements, in bulk (barrels of oil, casks of vinegar and unlimited supplies of sausages, macaroni and cheese). The house was furnished with funds provided by the combined families, but chiefly by the Mazzinis, and Pippo was left to arrange the domestic *ménage*.

He wrote cheerfully to his mother of the arrangements. "We employ an English servant (Mary) and a boy of fourteen named David." But the vagaries of Mary and her successors developed into a domestic iliad. Mary objected to rising before nine or ten; her successor, after engagement, was found to be *minus* one arm; a third was deaf; a fourth—to the alarm of the neighbourhood, who carried the house by assault—accidentally set the kitchen ablaze; a fifth left without notice; a sixth was dismissed for theft but reinstated. ("She has confessed, wept, etc.; and if we can rescue her and teach her better ways it will be one soul saved.")

Meanwhile, save for contributions to Lamennais' short-lived journal and later to the *Helvétia,* his work was unremunerative. And no doubt his temperamental *fierté* imposed its own limitations. Nothing would induce him to hire himself out as private tutor. He would not accept fees "from individuals," and when, presently, Lady Harriet Baring invited him to read Italian with her, he procrastinated. He would call as a guest but not as a paid instructor. He was equally unadaptable in his literary contributions. "The other day," he tells his mother, "I met a certain [John Stuart] Mill. He is the editor of a Radical review, and he has asked me for articles, especially on the political situation in Italy." This was a hopeful opening, but Robertson, who directed the *Westminster,* found the articles "too mystical, too soaring," and urged Signor Mazzini to "write things to amuse people," —for example, on Italian manners, foods, fashions and *banditi.* "Why should I," he exclaims to his parents, "for the sake of a few sovereigns, write silly articles to make strangers *laugh* at Italy while I *weep* for her?" An article on Byron was rejected because the poet was immoral, another on Thiers because "it contained too many Continental ideas." "God knows," he comments, "what is meant by Continental ideas. I know only two kinds—the good and the bad." "I cannot and will not do violence to myself by changing my style, my ideas," he declares to Giglioli. "I write *spiritualistically,* synthetically, theoretically, educatively; here they are materialism incarnate—pure analysis, practicality, bare facts."

But Robertson was obdurate. Signor Mazzini must confine himself to names and dates, "with brief biographical notices, dwelling less on the author's views and aims, and with fewer criticisms of his failure to transform art into a patriotic mission." It was distressing. "My ideas and style terrify," he complains to Melegari. "I dare not speak of a mission of Humanity, of continual progress, of collectivism." Kemble of the *British and Foreign* was more encouraging, accepting and praising an article on Hugo's *Voix intérieures*; but apart from two contributions to the *National* on "The Present State of Literature and Art," this was his solitary success. He was driven by sheer necessity to hack-work, "writing on subjects that bore me, collecting anecdotes of famous men, and what not."

And, in truth, the necessity was urgent. "I have pawned my cloak," he confessed to Melegari, "in order to be able to smoke—the one thing which seems to me impossible to do without." Before the summer was out his mother's signet-ring, his watch, his maps, even his books, had gone the way of the cloak, and one Saturday evening found him "obliged to pledge an old coat and a pair of boots in order to obtain food for the Sunday." Reluctant visits to the poet Campbell and one or two members of Parliament yielded no more than polite assurances of good-will, and an expensive journey to Edinburgh, where friend Giglioli was studying medicine, was fruitless.

Financial difficulties, it is true, weighed upon him lightly: "I did not suffer from these things more than they were worth, nor did I feel either degraded or cast down by them." Nor was there ever any question of utter destitution: for though he endeavoured to conceal the pawnshop exploits from his parents, the Ruffini brothers circumvented him, and his mother promptly increased her remittances. Withal, his embarrassments were due to the helplessness and improvidence of his companions and his own spendthrift generosity. Even

Agostino, borrowing his brother's cynicism, could complain
with some point that Pippo's "chimera of human brotherhood" was attracting a daily procession of beggars to Euston
Square; and street-singers were apt to mark the house where
a slim, dark gentleman would reward their performances with
silver, flung (with slightly erratic aim) from an upstairs window. And one snowy morning does not the same dark gentleman, departing as usual for the Museum, return unexpectedly
with a bundle in his arms?—which bundle (found huddled, as
it seems, not far from the door-step, like many similar bundles
similarly dropped or self-deposited in those bitter days in
London) develops animation before the parlour fire; and waif
Susan is duly adopted, to grow into a massive Mazzinian institution. The Ruffinis may have felt justified in their general
protest against an "absurd Quixotry." But also the Ruffinis
themselves, unknown to their parents, borrowed money from
the senior Mazzinis; poor Angelo Usiglio, too, burning the
midnight oil and straining his weak eyes over his masterpiece
(in eight parts), blinked amiably behind his blue spectacles
but could contribute little; and Giambattista Ruffini of
Modena, whose "wolfish appetite" at table stirred his name-
sakes to secret wrath, would have Pippo assist in the matter
of a £60 loan.

A worse affliction was the growing estrangement between
himself and the two brothers. For while Giovanni, after a
brief interval of Lamennaisian fervour, returned to his strong,
silent rôle of sardonic observer, and maintained a studied
aloofness, Agostino became petulant, argumentative and
quarrelsome. No doubt they felt stifled under the unconscious
tyranny of Pippo's moral and intellectual mentorship. "For
two years," they confessed to their mother, "our ideas [and
Pippo's] have been in complete disharmony";[5] and for those
in disharmony with his ideas Mazzini was an unideal companion. Pippo, they said, lived in a world of his own, "as
solid as a spider's web," and added that, without knowing it,
he was a slave to himself. Probably there was a measure of
truth in their complaints. Perhaps he was too apt to treat
them as wards and expect conformity to his own fixed
standards. On their side they could not forget that it was
Pippo's headlong enthusiasm which, from the death of Jacopo

onward, had led them into disaster. So long as they shared
his faith and hero-worshipped him as the heaven-anointed
apostle, all was endurable; but now the spell was broken;
they had seen the cause pass from failure to failure;
they had seen the dissolution of "Young Italy," the decline
of "Young Europe"; and if it was galling to be dependent
upon a leader whom they had ceased to follow, it was intolerable to live, as lapsed believers, in the shadow of his moral
rebuke.

Only this can excuse the amazing bitterness of some of their
letters at this period. "The Signora [Mazzini] may well
wonder if you still love her son," they wrote to their mother.
"Truly you have done so little for him and received so beautiful a recompense!" "You may tell her," they added, "that if
she thinks we are living upon him, she had better send someone to London for fuller information." Thus, while they paid
their debts with punctilious honour, they writhed at being
obligated to the Mazzinis, and disliked them the more for
every favour received: and because an open rupture was out
of the question, their hostility found vent in oblique opposition and petty disputes. Especially they enjoyed baiting Pippo
in arguments over his pet subjects and in cleverly satirising
his enthusiasms. Because Victor Hugo had made a heroine of
a courtesan, lo, Pippo would regard all drabs as Madonnas;
because some women were virtuous and admirable, Pippo must
worship all women as martyrs and angels; because the Germans fantasticated philosophical systems which nobody could
understand, behold, says Pippo, a spiritual people predestined
to found one knows not what stupendous religious Synthesis
over their pipes and beer! Satire, indeed, was a dangerous
weapon to turn against one who was more dexterous and
better armed for that sword-play than themselves; but always
between him and the brothers stood the ghost of Jacopo. With
others he could be merciless in turning defence into attack;
never with them. So they plied him with continued raillery;
and occasionally, over trifling disagreements, there were more
violent scenes in which Agostino would fume and rage and
Pippo would bow the head and weep.

The soul of young Agostino was, in fact, in revolution. For

the time he was out of equilibrium, and one looks in vain in his letters for any reflection of that "reserved and gentle" Ruffini who lives in David Masson's noble memoir—the Agostino of the later days in Edinburgh:

"No average refugee was he, but one of Italy's best, finest and gentlest —a man to be known on and on, ever more subtly and intimately, and yet never to be exhausted or known enough: to be found wise, true, honourable and good by even the most delicate tests that could be applied."[6]

The events of the past five years had, in truth, denied him a normal youthful development; he was emotionally starved and willing to persuade himself that the death of Anna Courvoisier had left him without spiritual kinship in a sordid world. Above all, perhaps, he was in rebellion against the unconscious tyranny of Mazzini's dogmatism, and even against his watchful and slightly domineering affection. He found relief in privately documenting his criticisms. He would forsake (he vowed) the forbidden fields of Pippo's theosophisings and return to the true faith. There was no religion, no philosophy so true to the fundaments of life as Christianity. True, it promised nothing on this earth, but pointed to the vision of God in Paradise: but under its influence the soul, even here, could attain to a hope that was able to transmute the sorrows of existence and make of them an offering to the Eternal Father. But where was there any sure foundation in modern theories, humanitarian and civilisational? Man and his "perfectibility"! Generation after generation, age after age of "progress"! What solid edifice could one build upon so unstable a thing as human nature? What was "progress" but a theory, now fashionable, of historical interpretation? "Show me (he writes) a historian who looks at things from another point of view, and it may be he will set about to prove just as cogently that humanity has all the time been going backward." It was possible, for example, to argue that man had progressed in science and gone backward in art. Science was empirical, art inspirational, and while experience grew with age, inspiration belonged to the youth of the world. . . . It was somehow a satisfaction to record these protests if only in secret; and so in his private papers and his letters home he pours out his rebellions. "Everyone, from Giovanni down," he tells his mother, "disapproves of my new ideas, and it is a relief to unburden myself a little to your divine heart."

But he could find no peace. In the atmosphere of the house in Devonshire Square his soul, he felt, was stifled, fretted, ulcered. "Pippo is very good to me, but the opposite tendencies of our natures and certain fatal memories mar our affection." "If I had a living faith," he records in his private journal, "a faith truly Christian, my life to that degree would be tolerable. But mine is more a philosophy than a faith." Why, he asks, could Anna give no sign from the other world? If the soul was immortal and the spiritual affections survived death, why should not communication be possible? "And if I lack faith, yet ardently desire it, why does not God help me?"

So in depths or shallows, and always in miseries, the poor Agostino floundered on, becoming irritable and petulant and yielding (like his father) to neurotic storms. "What demon is it," he asks himself in his journal, "that makes me argue about everything?" "The rest must think me a tormentor of Pippo. . . . He himself believes I indulge in systematic opposition. Poor Pippo! if only he could know how indifferent I am to all. . .!" "This sort of life must stop," he adds. "We are sufficiently unhappy without adding to our wretchedness with continual, bitter, mad disputes;" and he registers twelve pathetic Resolutions " to be read and pondered at least three times a week," beginning: "I swear by my mother and the memory of my beloved dead to avoid as much as in me lies all disputation with anybody, but particularly and above all with Pippo."[7] But the Resolutions were not kept.

*   *   *   *   *

It was small wonder, perhaps, that when, in those early months, Mrs. Archibald Fletcher, widow of the Scottish jurist, met Mazzini, she was impressed and even alarmed by the sadness of his face. "I found in the drawing-room a young, slim, dark Italian gentleman of very prepossessing appearance. He could not then speak English and I very imperfect French: but it was impossible not to be favourably impressed at once by his truth and sadness. He told me he was an exile, and without endeavouring to excite my compassion, or dwelling at all on his wrongs and circumstances . . . he looked so profoundly unhappy . . . that I foolishly took it into my head, after he had left me, that he meditated suicide "[8]—particularly as his conversation had turned upon Chatterton. "I am alone," he writes to Giglioli; "I use the word in its fullest significance": and he confesses pathetically to Melegari that when he returns from the Museum library, after a day's miserable compilation of names and dates and anecdotes of famous men, he has the sensation of entering a strange house, "a room that does not belong to me, desolate and empty as the tomb."[9]

There were other trials. He was plagued with neuralgia and a painful inflammation of the eyes; and news that his poverty was being discussed by sympathisers in Italy and that a private subscription was being raised for him in Turin, stung him with a sense of disgrace. He promptly forbade the subscription ("my mother would have died of shame"), but was obliged to raise a new personal loan.

Meanwhile his father plied him with well-meant exhortations.[10] He had had the consolation, he declared, of being able continually to respond to Pippo's requests, but he must soon retire and forfeit his professional income, and at best his allotted days must be few. Let Pippo reflect upon this and upon the necessity of his establishing himself in an honourable independency, so as to be in a position to support his mother and Chichina (Francesca). Let him renounce politics and his monomania of Italian Unity and make a name for himself, like Foscolo, in literature. Let him write, for example, light comedy of the Pantaloon-and-Harlequin sort. There was money in that. And what a proud day it would be when Pippo would send home a gift of, say, £2,000! Then his parents could drive about in a carriage-and-pair, and say, "It is a present from our son!" What an answer that would be to Pippo's enemies! And, by the way, what about that 7,000 francs invested in the timber and iron business in Switzerland? Pippo had not mentioned it recently.—And so forth with affectionate cruelty, which Maria, with maternal annotations, sought to mollify. "Your father has an intense affection for you, but everyone has his own way of showing it."

Meanwhile, too, Melegari—primed, perhaps, with Tommaseo's new book on a Catholic revival in Europe—returned to the attack with reproaches for Pippo's spiritual pride in forsaking the true faith. "God forgive you!" Mazzini flashes back. "You understand neither history, nor the times, nor Humanity, nor Christ." He was more distressed when the same candid friend told him that a daughter of the Mandrots of Lausanne had conceived an infatuation for him and was seriously ill in consequence.[11] What, inquired Melegari, did he propose to do for this unfortunate girl?—He had in fact met her but twice, once when she was a child of thirteen, once three years later. He had met her on each occasion in the Mandrot home, in the presence of her parents and the family, and had never corresponded with her nor had any private conversation. "Why inflict useless tortures upon me?" he exclaims to his tormentor. "You ask me if my intentions are in accordance with the only possible ending. . . . My God! Can I have any intentions? Am I free?" To his mother he unburdens himself. He had no more thought of inspiring affection, he declares, than of claiming the throne of the Indies; and he registers a vain resolution henceforth to be "brusque and severe with all women."[12]   But the image of the Mandrot child haunts his mind, and he hints to his mother that only the thought of Giuditta deters him from that "only possible ending" which Melegari would have dictated. As for Giuditta herself, direct correspondence between them was now involving her in police-raids and prejudicing her chances in her fight for the possession of her children. Occasionally Maria served as intermediary, and in October he was thanking her for a "very precious" transcript of Giuditta's letter: "After the long silence I needed it. Tell her how dear it is." But Maria's transcripts likewise received police-attention; and a romance so starved and restricted had already lost its first ardour.

The new year, 1838, brought a fresh sorrow. In January Francesca died. Three days before her death she had written to him blithely, concealing a mortal pain. Afterward, for a month, Maria had withheld the news from him. "Where does Francesca sleep?" he inquires, a fortnight after her death. In his room, he hopes—the room with the balcony with its flower-embroidered trellis and its climbing *campanule,* whose flower-bells, he remembers, were so beautiful on a sunny morning after a night of gentle rain. When the news is finally broken

Maria sends him Francesca's little volume of à Kempis, with the bookmark in the place of her last reading. "Think of father and me," she writes, "and remember that we live in and for you, that you and your good are the one aim of our every thought and act." And the old Professor writes that he can find no other comfort than the life of Jesus Christ; but "this bears me up in every adversity, and without it, when our Chichina left us, I should have taken means to follow her out of the world."

So the struggle continued. There was an increasing pressure of debt, with desperate resorts to London money-lenders, whose weekly interest had to be paid at gin-shops "at certain fixed hours, among crowds of the drunken and dissolute." Once, with the Ruffinis, he embarked upon an Olive Oil and Cheese enterprise in the City, but a discriminating English public demanded the oil of Lucca and not the Ligurian product imported by the new agents, and the venture went the way of all other Mazzinian dreams. "For the last year," he wrote to Melegari, "I have suffered in a way that makes me feel I must be immortal, else I should have died"; and he sighed for the peace and seclusion of Grenchen and the little room looking out upon the Alps. City life was well enough for those who wished to enjoy themselves, running into society and living an *outward* life: "for my part I do not wish to live other than an *interior* life."

For his own relief, in the intervals of hack-writing, he set himself to build up a little book of religious reflections," entering his thoughts as they flashed in upon him in his "best moments, when it seemed to me I was fullest of love and conviction." Three years later he wrote of it to Elia Benza: "One day, before I die, or after, you shall see that little book, which to-day I would not show to a living soul, because . . . I need more time to make sure that these thoughts proceed from the intuitions of the heart and not from excited fantasy." With the mood of isolation now upon him the alternative possibility was real enough, but it belonged to his fundamental sanity that he was aware of it. To Eleonora Ruffini he confessed that, in a life like his own, concentrated within itself, the danger of violent mental reactions was extreme. He had watched himself, he added, and was alarmed at his powers of fantastication. As for the "little book," with the *Relics of an Unknown* it was finally lost—left behind in that "trunk in Rome" in '49.

* * * * *

Gradually the clouds began to lift. By 1839 he was slowly becoming known among English liberals, and his more serious literary work was gaining acceptance. Even the reclusive Wordsworth was discussing him at Rydal Mount,[13] and was telling his friends a pleasant story of Maria Mazzini. When Enrico Mayer, a friend of the poet, had called upon the Signora at Genoa, before leaving for England, he had found her too ill to leave her room. For a moment she had wept, then asked his pardon and said: "Do not tell Pippo that you found me ill. Tell him that not a day of my life passes that I do not thank God for giving me such a son." It was worthy, as Wordsworth agreed, of a Spartan mother.

And from Italy itself came reviving rumours of new and hopeful portents. Thus Maria's letters were presently full of a new preacher, come to town to "preach a mission" at S. Lorenzo. Something truly remarkable about this friar! Maria, who cannot get near him for the crowds, is assured that he is the image of Pippo—dark hair, oval face, dark flashing eyes—and does he not preach a discourse on Hell and put there all bad priests, cardinals and Popes? He preaches much else, too, of most daring sort, until the whisper goes round, "*It is the voice of Young Italy!*" and at certain passages in his discourses even the priests whisper "*Giovine Italia!*" to one another, behind their hands. Almost one could believe it was Pippo in monk's disguise! ("Oh, what a lovely thing it would be if you yourself should mount a pulpit like this preacher! Yesterday a priest who loves you devotedly exclaimed, 'If only *he* might preach just for one hour from a pulpit in the Piazza what miracles would be wrought for the truth!'") As it is, the whole countryside flocks to hear this second Pippo—the piazza crowded before dawn—the church full by 4 o'clock, with four hours to wait—all eager to hear this Young Italy voice; and the University students meeting the friar by chance in the street line up on the instant and give him the salute. His name is Ugo Bassi: his portrait sells by the thousand; women rave about him; and in private—like Pippo—he sings and plays the guitar and smokes! Truly the city is swept by a "Young Italy" revival and the Jesuits are enraged and persecuting the local Jansenists. . . .

And for Mazzini himself a new era was beginning; for, not without misgiving, he was about to make the acquaintance of the Carlyles.

A T Cheyne Row in after years, and in rare moments of mellow recollection, Carlyle liked to recall how Mazzini had " sat for the first time on the seat there," for the most part " rather silent " and trusting himself chiefly to French when he spoke. " A more beautiful person," he would add, " I never beheld "; a graceful Ligurian figure with " soft, flashing eyes."

This first visit took place as early as November, 1837, the introduction having been arranged through Mr. Taylor of the Carlyle circle.[1] There for two years the matter had ended. Then in '39 Mazzini writes amusingly to his mother of his embarrassment at finding that he must meet the Carlyles at the house of a friend. He had, he felt, treated them discourteously by not calling since '37. It was an example, he confessed, of his " grave social defect " due to procrastination and physical inertia. Also the village of Chelsea was five miles away, and it cost too much to hire a conveyance. He had " wasted a lot of time saying ' I will go to-morrow ' until, as usual with me, after some months had gone by in this way, another feeling slipped in : I thought, ' How can I go after so many months?' "

And now there was an embarrassing complication. He had been commissioned by the *Monthly Chronicle* to review Carlyle's *French Revolution*, " and because, as I see it, the work contains views that are radically wrong, and because, moreover, it lacks *aim*—to me a grave defect—I am writing very critically—much more so than he will like." It would be awkward to dine with an author one day and publicly castigate him the next. But before the month was out he was informing his mother that " Carlyle is one whose acquaintance I mean to cultivate, for he is a man of heart, of conscience and of genius "; and the Editor of the *Monthly Chronicle* was persuaded to insert a slightly mollifying paragraph in the critical review.*

* The review appeared in the *Monthly Chronicle* for January, 1840, not 1843, as stated in M.'s *Works* (English edn.)—G. O. G.

The friendship quickly ripened. By December he was "dining, and gossiping and smoking" at Cheyne Row; on New Year's Day Mrs. Carlyle gave him a bottle of Eau de Cologne ("I don't know why"), and by February he was beginning to fear that the social amenities of Chelsea were interfering with his work. "Carlyle invites me to dinner. He is good, his wife is good. We dine, the three of us, without the least ceremony"; but "Carlyle has got it in his head that I must meet this, that and the other person," which meant "compliments, invitations and promises to pay calls," which was diabolical.

From this time forward for the next eight years he dined at Cheyne Row every week, and by August, 1840, after a brief intermediate sojourn in Clarendon Square, his new friends had induced him to remove with the Ruffinis to a house in King's Road (4, York Buildings). The change was salutary. "Waif" Susan, now married to a ne'er-do-weel exile, Pio Tancioni, was installed as housekeeper, and the principal tenant was soon writing delightedly to his parents of the orchards, fields and rural quiet of the neighbourhood. "I think of our terror of cows [at Bavari]; and here they are just outside the gate; yet there is not the least danger." English cows, in fact, were "very picturesque" creatures, "susceptible of affection," and might be seen any day in Arcadian Chelsea "lovingly following their master." Maria, pacified respecting the cows, was still perturbed. York Buildings, she gathered, was near, too near, the great English river, the Thames; there might be floods, and Pippo was not a strong swimmer. . . . But the Thames (she was reassured), like the cows, was picturesque and meek, and York Buildings was in no danger of being swept away. Withal he must report that Mrs. Carlyle has made him walk more in six weeks than he has walked before in two years. "Our nearness means that, often when I least expect it, either Carlyle turns up to invite me for a stroll, or a note comes from his wife asking me to accompany her to town." There was also the delightful privilege of sitting beside Mrs. Carlyle at the *Heroes* lectures of 1840. "Carlyle speaks, not reads," he tells his parents, "and utters the most audacious things imaginable, but clothes them in such fine language that his English audience listens respectfully." The more critical Gio-

vanni observes that the lecturer is apt to be nervous and confused at the outset, hesitates a good deal, and is visibly
embarrassed by his *hands*; then gets going, speaks with freedom
and is " greatly applauded " at the close.

This sudden transition into the Carlyle world was, in short,
welcome and invigorating. It was like the mountains, the
sea, and the clean winds, after long confinement in a stuffy
atmosphere; albeit the Carlyle weather was occasionally violent
enough. The Sage was now forty-five—by ten years Mazzini's
senior. He was not the Carlyle made familiar to us by Whistler
and the photographic art of the later decades; the blue eyes were
not yet pouched and puckered, the thick thatch of unkempt
hair was still dark and ungrizzled, the firm-set, deeply lined
mouth, the massive chin, were not yet muffled by moustache
and beard. But the complexion was already slightly bilious.

At this period, indeed, Carlyle was perhaps more than
ordinarily difficult. With Oliver Cromwell and Abbot Samson
contending in his mental womb, and the *Heroes* needing to be
made presentable for recurrent exhibition at the Edward Street
lecture-hall, he was, on his own admission, " in the vilest welter
of confusions and repugnancies." Margaret Fuller, visiting
England in the 'forties, has described his conversation in a
quotable passage. " He sings rather than talks. He pours
upon you a kind of heroical, critical poem, with regular
cadences, and generally, near the beginning, hits upon some
singular epithet, which serves as a *refrain* when his song is full,
or with which, as with a knitting-needle, he catches up the
stitches, if he has chanced now and then to let fall a row."
" You cannot interrupt him . . . he raises his voice and bears
you down."[2] The Ruffinis, who admired his genius, listened
to these monologues with bewilderment and a faint suggestion
of alarm. " Signor Carlyle " (they wrote to their mother) " has
a horror of Lamennais. And why? Because Lamennais has
somewhere written these words: ' *Jeune soldat, où vas tu?* '
Carlyle must keep on repeating this sentence and crying, ' It is
too much—too much ! ' "[3] Or does someone mention Napoleon?
Carlyle pounces at once. He recalls that the Emperor once
said, " *Je me trouve dans une fausse position* "—and improvises
upon it for half an hour on end. What can be done, asks
Giovanni, with such an artist in *capriccio*?

Mazzini, of course, bore the brunt of the attacks. The two had common ground in their admiration of Dante and of the Germans, their detestation of utilitarianism, materialism and the popular gospel of happiness, in their belief, also, in a religion of Worship, Duty and Work, and in their distrust of most modern political tendencies. But was not the Italian an admirer of "George Sand and that sort of cattle," and "hopelessly given up to his 'republicanisms,' his 'Progress' and other Rousseau-fanaticisms"?

One may still picture the scene: the sombre-garbed, frock-coated exile sitting on the edge of his chair, his doe-skin boots oozing mud on the Carlyle carpet, a black cigar between his lean fingers; and, standing before him in lengthy smoke-coloured dressing-gown, churchwarden clay pipe in hand, the gaunt figure of the apostle of Silence. Nor is it difficult, with the aid of Margaret Fuller and Jessie White Mario,[4] to reconstruct the harangue—"thunder following upon lightning" in sultry torrent of invective, with now and then a sudden gust and broad outshining of mirth, as if to signify, "Not too seriously is all this to be taken." "'The People'?" (quoth the oracle) "the ignorant, blind, vicious People? Chiels and fools! If they will not behave, put collars round their necks! Let the few Wise take charge of the innumerable Foolish. As for 'Italian democracies' and Young Italy chimeras and all such paper-formulas, they are fitter for little Byronic *histrios* than for serious men, and will avail for no Man's Work in a quack-ridden, devil-ridden world. Have done, in Heaven's name, with little lyrical Revolutionism and rose-water imbecilities of 'Progress' and 'Perfectibility of the species,' as if this huge imposthume of lies and cant could be cured by the like! Alas! our speech-making, 'Divine Law of Progress' felicitations, little Byronic insurgencies and tar-barrel illuminations will cure nothing. Have you not *talked too much*, Mazzini? Patience and Silence! God is great. . . ."

And while Mrs. Carlyle accompanies the departing guest to the hall, the monologue-become-soliloquy goes booming on through the open door.

*　　　*　　　*　　　*　　　*

After a battering at Cheyne Row it was always a relief to

pass an evening at Burton Crescent, off the New Road, with guileless, devoted, learned and absent-minded Worcell—the more so as the Carlylean tirades were just now being reinforced from Genoa.

For, as if conscious of his British ally, Professor Mazzini had returned to the attack. What (he inquired) was the use of Pippo's crying for the moon and projecting impossible Utopias for whole generations of muck-rakers? Pippo's ideas were veritable ulcers and needed to be cut out: " I write as a medical man and know what I am talking about." As for himself, the Professor had had the satisfaction of being able, through his own efforts, to support his father, brother and sister in their time of need. What sorrow for Pippo if he should presently find that his own dear parents were in need, and himself unable to succour them! " Caro, it is well to reflect upon all this." And if Pippo could send £2,000 the Professor would retire to Posalunga to-morrow. And by the way, let Pippo see to it that it be known in the proper quarter that his father attended the Queen's father, the Duke of Kent, years ago at Pisa.[5] . . . Yes, it was a relief to pass an evening with Worcell.

Stanislas Worcell, Polish exile, mathematician, linguist, philosopher, Count of Volhynia, and one-time brilliant figure in Warsaw society, was five years Mazzini's senior. In the rising of 1830 he had put aside his philosophical and mathematical studies in order to raise an insurgent troop on his own estate and fight his way to Warsaw. After the collapse of the insurrection he had come to England, a penniless proscript. His confiscated lands were in part restored to his wife, who denounced her husband and trained her children to forget their father. In London he set himself to earn his bread in order to continue the struggle. But London could offer little to a foreign philosopher-mathematician who read in six languages but could never remember his own street number, and Count Worcell kept body and soul together by trudging from one end of the town to the other, giving lessons in French at half a crown a visit. Privation told its tale, and City smoke and fog affected his lungs: but he lived in his dream. Herzen records indulgently that the eccentric philosopher (it was his foible) believed in a spiritual world. Was not Poland a Messiah-nation whose age-long sufferings were ordained of God to further

Europe's redemption? . . . All his spare time he gave to revolutionary organisation, wheezing laboriously up back stairs in Soho and coughing in the tobacco-laden atmosphere of dingy committee-rooms—often gasping in spirit also, half-stifled by the malhumours of the exile-cliques. " A man to revere and love," wrote Linton; " a saintly martyr, a true hero, a wise philosopher and a man whose knowledge seemed to be unbounded."[6]

Strange souls, these mystical revolutionaries! But it was comforting, after a Carlylean typhoon, to pass a quiet evening in edifying conversation with friend Worcell.

* * * * *

"We soon tired of each other, Mazzini and I," declared Carlyle. As was indeed inevitable, and for a reason which Mrs. Carlyle once clearly expressed to " Babbie " : " Carlyle was contradicting everything and neither taking the good of Mazzini nor letting me get the good of him "; and again to Margaret Fuller : " These are only opinions to Carlyle, but to Mazzini, who has given his all, and helped bring his friends to the scaffold, it is a matter of life and death." " The conclusion is," Mazzini confided to his parents, " that Sig. Carlyle is one of the best of men and a powerful genius, but that two-thirds of our opinions differ without there being any hope that either of us will convert the other." Which was also true.

And for the rest, an apostle must deliver his soul. In the *British and Foreign Review* (Carlyle couldn't talk one down in a Review) he faithfully exposed the fatal Carlylean errors : This noble genius (he wrote) was after all in schism within himself. He was forever weaving and unweaving like Penelope : he alternated between hope and despair, faith and unfaith, heaven and hell. And why? Because on one side his view of life and the world was curiously limited; because for him *men* existed but not Man; because in his philosophy there was no conception of any collective life and purpose, no echo of St. Paul's *The whole creation groaneth*; no hint that Religion was more than a simple relation of the individual soul to God— no suggestion that it involved a collective ideal, a common aim. With this limitation it was small wonder that Carlyle's seerhood sometimes suffered, that in him occasionally the artist rose above the prophet. Thus his *History of the French Revolution* was properly no history at all but phantasmagoric *Walpurgis Nacht* reflections—gigantic spectacles, sad or infuriate, flung out in bewildering pageant, appearing, vanishing, signifying nothing. The prophet, left without a clue, and lost in the artist, was content to transmit the image of external events that had fascinated and bewildered him. Small wonder, too, that, without a social criterion or sense of anything greater on earth than the individual, Carlyle should tend to estimate a man's achievement by its *energy,* and to extol success and victorious force, or, lapsing into discouragement, should contemplate the puniness and futility of man, isolated in the presence of the Immensities. For in truth human life, regarded from a merely individual standpoint, was deeply sad. But there was that which was greater than all the great men of the earth—the earth which bore them, the human race which included them, the Thought of God which stirred within them, and which mankind collectively alone could accomplish. Duty lay in the perfecting of a colective labour, the conquest of the medium through which mankind should co-operate unitedly.

But what hope was there that Carlyle would see this and be saved? He would read the review, to be sure—then fasten upon a convenient phrase and improvise his newest monologue! The Catholic-collectivist bias in Mazzini, the Protestant-individualist bias in the Scot were swinging them off into divergent curves of progression, to meet only at some remote, incalculable point of infinitude.

So "we soon tired of each other,* Mazzini and I, and he fell mainly to *her* share, off and on, for a good many years, yielding her the charm of a sincere mutual esteem." And clearly there was no question about either the charm or the esteem. Mrs. Carlyle might declare that Mazzini in his conspiratorial excitements forcibly reminded her of Frank Dickenson's goose with an addled egg; she might obtain

* But let no one speak a word in Carlyle's presence in disparagement of his friend! Once does the Sardinian Minister attempt as much. Carlyle turns upon him with Johnsonian ire: "Sir, you do not know Mazzini at all—not at all—not at all "—and abruptly strides out of the room. (See Bolton King: *Life.*)

infinite amusement from his guileless fantasy of dirigible
balloons for revolutionary operations; she might poke cruel
fun, in her letters, at the Savoy expedition, "turned back at
the first toll-bar "; she might tell him—with indisputable truth
and the prerogative of four years' seniority—that a Harrow or
Eton schoolboy who meditated such nonsensical escapades
would be whipped for a mischievous blockhead: but even so,
it was no more than a reassuring demonstration that having,
within limits, lost her heart to the charmer, she had at least
not lost her head.

But how pleasant it was to be able, for example, to report to
"Babbie "[7] that Mazzini and Erasmus Darwin had called,
and "the three of us sat with our feet on the fender—the
folding doors being closed "—and had "the most confidential
fireside party " imaginable! And was it not on that occasion
that Mazzini spoke of Sismondi's being at one time nearly
lapidated? "'Nonsense,' said I; 'you should say *stoned*.' . . .
'Let him alone,' said Darwin, 'he is quite right; *lapidated* is
an excellent word.' 'Do not mind him,' said I to M. 'He
only wants to lead you into making a mistake.' 'But are you
sure?' asked M. with the greatest simplicity. 'In the Bible,
for instance, does not She call it lapidated in speaking of
St. Stephen?'"[8] And how pleasant it was thereafter for Mrs.
Carlyle to spice her letters with Mazzini's "modes of locu-
tion "—his "Upon *my* honour," his exclamatory "Thanks
God!" his "here down " (*quaggiù*), his interjectional "What
shall I say?" his use of the feminine for the neuter, his pro-
nunciation of "heart " as "hort," of "cough " as "cuff," his
habit of addressing his friends as "my dear "! All the same,
"Is it not almost a desecration, a crime, ever to *jest* with that
man? He lives, moves and has his being in *truth*, and take
him out of that, he is as credulous and ignorant as a two-year-
old child."

So she must try to advise him in his sadly tangled financial
affairs, translate an essay of his for *Tait's*, to save him trans-
lator's charges, slip over occasionally to York Buildings with
hot pies of her own baking (Susan's cooking was execrable),
and take him from his books and papers for compulsory con-
stitutionals. Thus there was an adventurous sight-seeing trip
to St. Paul's (three-quarters of an hour up in the dome, he tells

his mother, in the teeth of a diabolical wind, with London tiles and chimneys looking like a petrified *Inferno*), followed by many other excursions—now to see Macready in *Mary Stuart,* now to hear Cobden (or was it Fox?) on the Corn Laws, now—with Carlyle in the party—to the Waxworks Exhibition.

And soon she is corresponding with Maria in schoolgirl Italian, and Maria sends her a keepsake ring and a posy of *immortelles,* and bids her "love Italy's martyr." And she replies: "'Love Italy's martyr'? No need to bid me do so. I can do no other. Oh, if only you could know how much I love him!"—and sends her *cara madre* the gift of a locket with locks of her own black hair and Pippo's (intertwined) and "Young Italy's" motto *"Now and Forever"* worked upon the clasp. And Pippo must explain that in England such keepsakes signified nothing more than friendship and that Mrs. Carlyle's affection, though perhaps a little demonstrative, was no more than sisterly. And the *cara madre* is enchanted with the precious locket, but the Professor, inexpert in the higher symbolism of intertwined tresses, needs to be reassured concerning "Madama Carlyle," and even Maria betrays a certain curiosity about the Signora's appearance. Her son satisfies her as well as he can. "Mrs. Carlyle is still young: she is neither beautiful nor plain; her eyes are dark and, as you will have seen, her hair is as dark as mine. She is tall, slender, vivacious, but of very delicate health." And for the rest, father needn't jump at wrong conclusions. An entanglement was quite out of the question. Besides, there was always Giuditta; and just now (1840) they were able once more to exchange letters. "I have given my heart to my poor, good Giuditta, and have never dreamed of recalling it."

Always it would be the same. Circumstances, Giuditta, and a rigid asceticism precluded romantic attachments, but the half-romantic provocation of feminine sympathy he could not deny himself. To borrow a distinction of M. Maurois', he needed the friendship of women, not, like Byron, because women appeased him, but, like Shelley (but with a more puritan reserve), because they brought to him a discerning sympathy and a certain exaltation. And it would matter little whether the understanding affection came from Jane Welsh

Carlyle, or George Sand, or Mary the kitchenmaid at the Tancionis', or Margaret Fuller Ossoli, or Caroline Stansfield, or Mary Coralli, whom probably he never met, or Francesca Girard, or Emilie Hawkes, he would gather the subtle magnetic *stimuli* and transmute them into idealistic schemes or mad conspiracies.

There was another perpetual solace, less idealistic. In an outburst of confidence to his parents he expressed surprise that Mrs. Carlyle, or indeed any other woman, should tolerate his society; and that not simply because he was ill-dressed, apt to upset things, and destitute of " small talk," but also because he was incessantly smoking. It was true. In London his abstemiousness and monastic austerity came to be proverbial, and Holyoake in his *Bygones* quotes a once-popular squib :

> " A cheaper world no one can know
> Where he who laughs grows fat;
> Man wants but little here below—
> Mazzini less than that."

But even in the days when he pawned his cloak or boots for his dinner, cigars were a luxury he could not do without. Put upon his defence by his English friends, he could be eloquent and ingenious :

" To compare smoking—generally speaking—with eating-enjoyment is to compare moonlight with the fire of a baker's shop, the appearance of a forget-me-not with that of an onion, aspiration with animal-downward-posture . . . and so forth. To compare *my* smoking . . . with repast-enjoyment is *à peu près* to compare me with one of those venerable Old-England specimens of the race who—after having enjoyed their dinner—sit in the corner in a chop-house, light a pipe, and go a-dozing for want of a better occupation. I smoke whilst reading or writing : never dominated but dominating; transforming, not assimilating substances; producing, not consuming : perhaps looking unconsciously for a symbol, alas ! to my thoughts and schemes, ending in smoke. Milton used to take a tobacco-pipe and a glass of water when going to bed : compare him to Charles Lamb's ' enjoyments ' on roasted pigs !"[9]

And so the months passed. And when in the summer of '43 he came nigh to death through overwork and self-neglect, and developed a painful and disfiguring facial tumour, Mrs. Carlyle railed at " the mess in which those wretched Tancionis keep him " and the " accursed conventionalities " which forbade her nursing him: for in reality "he has nobody but poor helpless me." And withal how heart-breakingly indifferent he was—the one side of his face "looking so sweet and placid as if nothing ailed the other." ("Little inconveniences"—*piccoli incomodi*—he calls his troubles.) "Oh dear me, Babbie, I am very anxious and sorrowful about Mazzini. . . . God knows whether it is not too late."[10]

Behind his back she called in good Dr. Toynbee, who, as a last recourse, carried him off to the chief surgeon at St. George's. It was found, after severe probing, that the tumour had reached the bone, and Dr. John Carlyle warned her that nothing could now prevent a cancer. Even so, the victim was unperturbed ("'Well but, my dear, there can still, you know, be an operation'—as if he were speaking of a hole in his coat"). He had a tooth extracted from the affected jaw, and next day walked from Queen Square to Chelsea to report improvement, looking "so emaciated and so calm" that she could not keep the tears back.

But by autumn the Cheyne Row bulletins became more hopeful, only "heaven knows when his face will look as it did—but what cares *he* how it looks?" By the New Year he was well enough to be the Carlyle's "first foot," and a few days later Mrs. Carlyle was delightedly reporting that the strange being was brighter than ever. "I saw one sunny flash in his eyes which might have been the first waking to life of Pygmalion's statue."

MEANWHILE there had been changes and developments. Thanks to Mrs. Carlyle, the unquiet Agostino had removed to Edinburgh (1840) and was earning a modest living as a private tutor, and an enviable reputation as the oracle and father-confessor of a widening circle of University men. Was he not, indeed, by way of becoming one of the minor notables of the city? There were youths and elder folk who nudged their friends and pointed out the trim, rather diminutive frock-coated figure, cane in hand, walking down Princes Street. How perfect his courtesy and modesty, how admirable his mastery of the English language and English conventions, how touching his secret anxiety to prune away all foreignisms! (Students, glancing over his shoulder, had read "*Ruffini, don't gesticulate!*" inscribed across the margins of their tutor's classbooks.) Above all, how illuminating were his discourses upon Dante and Vico, upon Shakespeare and Byron, upon French literature and German philosophy! And how wise and penetrating, how austere and yet tender, his counsel on the more personal problems of youth! This reserved and retiring stranger, so reticent concerning his past, but evidently a political exile and fugitive from his youth—from what *maestro* had he derived a culture so broad and distinctive? and through what vicissitudes had he attained to a wisdom so experienced in the more private problems of domestic disagreements, of personal estrangements and of individual conduct in general? If a certain undertone of despondency—a broken sentence—a sigh —intimated that the exile had resigned all hope of the deliverance of his country, the subject was not dwelt upon, and his sympathisers respected his reticence. "We might, as a fraternity, have been called Ruffinians," confesses Masson. "It was strange to see how, in a Scottish city, so many persons, the circumstances of whose lives were different enough from anything native to Italy, were drawn to this Italian, this alien, and found in him, far more than in each other, a confidant to whom they could entrust what was of deepest and most private interest to them."

It was strange, too, when the nightly clinic was over and the little attic-room in George Street was deserted of its guests, how the exhausted oracle would sit in his dressing-gown beside his midnight lamp, composing epistles of sad and relentless bitterness against the mentor to whom he owed so much of the wisdom he dispensed. For somehow Pippo was now an exasperation, a ghost not to be laid, a habit not to be shaken off, a memory not to be recalled without compunctions and resentments.

Giovanni, too, had left London for Paris (1841), charged with the same antipathy. "If Pippo goes east," he declared, "I go west"; only thus could any show of friendship between them be maintained. "I could wish he would cease correspondence . . . there is in his letters a tincture of reproach which galls one in proportion to its being undeserved."[1] In Paris, also, he had caught sight of his idolised Balzac and shed another illusion: "How could such lovely creations have come out of that pot-bellied barrel!" Later, Agostino, re-visiting London, had reported to his mother upon Pippo's strange case. "Giovanni and I have grown into men: Pippo has remained a child. We possess mediocre talent and plenty of good sense; Pippo has great talent (much less, though, than you used to think) and next to no judgment at all." Pippo had remained, in short, an obstinate fantasticator, butting against the evidence of hard fact and seeking to pivot the universe upon his own will. Eleonora must beware of his too plausible fulminations: "as a woman, and as my mother, it behoves you to maintain a certain cautious reserve."

Eleonora was troubled. She was now alone. The tempestuous Bernardo, having bidden final adieu to a preposterous world, had left his widow to languish in genteel poverty. She had leaned for support upon the Mazzinis, but Maria, with her maternal egotism, had become very trying of late, and Eleonora yearned more and more for her sons. Why must she be bereaved of the living as well as the dead? Could not something be done? Could not an undertaking be given that would satisfy Charles Albert? She herself was prepared to make the necessary overtures, even to the limit of suggesting that the

Government had possibly confused the activities of her innocent sons with those of G. B. Ruffini of Modena. Agostino, to his credit, had promptly vetoed the petition with a peremptory "No, by God!" and Giovanni had been only less decided: but Maria Mazzini, suspecting apostasy of some sort, had excommunicated Eleonora from her confidences. The fissure had become a chasm.

*   *   *   *   *

In the meantime the fantasticator's activities in London were entering upon a new phase. The departure of the Ruffinis had relieved him of domestic friction and left him with the more congenial society of his canaries and his Newfoundland dog. It had also simplified the financial situation, and though money-troubles, his own and other people's, were a constant besetment, Carlyle's interest had opened up new opportunities for more or less remunerative writing. To the *Westminster,* the *Monthly Chronicle, Tait's Magazine* and the *British and Foreign Review* he was now a recognised contributor and from '38 to '40 his writings had covered a wide field. There had been essays on English Chartism, on Italian and French Literature, on Italian Art, and lengthy critical studies of Victor Hugo, Sismondi, Paolo Sarpi, Louis Napoleon, Lamennais, Carlyle, Thiers, Guizot, Lamartine, George Sand, Byron and Goethe. In addition there had been a new effort to complete the *Records of an Unknown* and an attempt to act at last upon Giuditta's suggestion and compose an autobiographical romance. It was to be entitled *Benoni* ("Son of my Sorrow"). Only the title survived. It was appropriated by Giovanni Ruffini for his own Risorgimento romance, *Lorenzo Benoni,** published in Edinburgh in 1853. By 1842, also, he had paid his debt to the memory of Ugo Foscolo by unearthing and editing the manuscript of his unpublished commentary on Dante's *Divine Comedy.* He had unearthed it from dusty heaps of discarded literary lumber in Pickering's bookshop and edited it (in four volumes, published by Rolandi) with a liberal interpretation of the editorial prerogative. For Foscolo, in fact, had not carried his work beyond the text of the *Inferno.* "It appeared to me a sacred duty, both toward Foscolo and the

* See Append. A.

study of Dante, not to allow the work . . . to be lost; and I believed myself able to complete it . . . by identifying myself with Foscolo's method." He had paid his debt to the memory of the author of *Jacopo Ortis*; but exhaustive lists of Mazzini's literary works seldom include the erudite commentaries on the *Purgatorio* and *Paradiso*.

*   *   *   *   *

But what, after all, was literary activity except an *interim* occupation? Already in 1840 he was dreaming of new Italian ventures and renewing, on an ambitious scale, his political correspondence. "I have decided," he wrote, "to begin anew the work for which Jacopo died, and God knows what sorrows are in store for me." By the end of the year he had gathered the Italian artisans of London into an Italian Working Men's Association and founded yet another propagandist journal, the *Apostolato Popolare*. Its title-page was embellished with the familiar Young Italy mottoes and with a new and significant one—"*Labour and its Proportionate Reward*": and while its irregular numbers circulated near and far—in Paris, Marseilles, Malta, Corsica, New York, Montevideo—and were smuggled, as of old, in contraband bundles into Italy, its preachments proclaimed with the old insistence the articles of the Savona faith. Italy must be One and Independent with Rome for her capital, and a United Italy must pronounce the creative word which should give to the peoples a new era of democratic solidarity.

And after all, too, what was the writing of edited and emasculated essays for the eunuch-journals of English Liberalism compared to this pouring of one's soul into the uncensored columns of the *Apostolato*? It was true that the English review-articles were occasionally remunerative and a £20 cheque was always acceptable; the *Apostolato*, on the other hand, was distinctly an expensive enterprise. But even so, the English cheques could be dispensed with at a pinch. Maria's remittances were unfailing and sufficient for his personal needs: and for philanthropic emergencies the London money-lenders were always available. With them, as he explained to Mrs. Carlyle, his credit was always good. And it was so much better to expound the Duties of Man in the columns of the

Apostolato than to discuss the vagaries of celebrities in the British reviews.

Withal he read widely in the British Museum Library, filling his note-books with curious jottings ranging from the newest geological theories to Chinese Buddhism and the Lamas of Tibet, and returning in his correspondence to the discussion of religious dogma. Upon the fundaments, God, the soul, human freedom and immortality, he disliked to argue. " Call it God or what you please, there is Life which we have not created but which is given "; and as for Determinism, " no sophistry can cancel the testimony of remorse and of martyrdom." Personal immortality was equally clear, and Jacopo and Francesca were spiritual presences in his life. " I feel," he writes to Lamberti, " that in love there is an immortal principle, that our love constitutes our individual life as our service of others constitutes our social life. I feel that this soul-life is absolutely immortal or it is nothing."[2] " Above all beliefs," he declares to Melegari, " is God, the consciousness of an immortal soul, and the faith in other worlds nearer Him, in a necessary progress of ours towards God, in a virtue which must resist all temptations, in a constant sacrifice, in a love of the Humanity in which He has placed us, in a worship of prayer, of affection, of sacred poetry."[3] Occasionally he passes into an esoteric strain: " The sorrows of this present life *may* be for the purging of evil wrought in some previous existence, veiled from us now, but later to be remembered and understood." What was certain was that we were " set here for initiation into a new stage of life in the future, better, purer, and nearer the ideal which God has put in our hearts." So he writes to Eleonora before the estrangement.

But from orthodox Christianity he definitely breaks away. " I love Jesus as the man who, of all mankind, has loved the most—servants and masters, rich and poor, Brahmin and pariah "; but " if by religious belief you mean the Roman Catholic faith exclusively, then I am neither a Christian nor a Roman Catholic " (*sic*). Orthodox Protestantism with its individualist emphasis and literal authoritarianism was no more acceptable than Catholicism. " All those who make books and discourses on Revelation anatomise a corpse "; they do not see that Revelation must be treated as one and continuous.

The Jansenism of old priest Luca and his kind, with its hope of the restoration of primitive Christianity, wins his respect but not his adhesion. The primitive, he declared, could never be restored; its conceptions were obsolete, its world was beyond reconstruction, its firmament had waxed old and passed away. " Observe," he writes to Elia Benza, " that if you interrogate your own heart you will find that what you believe in is the Christian *morality*, not the Christian creed, in the precepts of Christianity, not its dogma; and observe further that the world is not changed by a morality; it must have a religion." There must be new heavens before there could be a new earth.

Lastly, to his conception of the pontifical primacy of Humanity as the supreme revelator he is always returning. It seems as if he comes to speak of Humanity not simply as the totality of mankind upon earth, but as an ever-developing collective Being (" essere ") whose progress, though not infinite, is toward a perfection beyond our defining, and whose life, while it is involved in the terrestrial struggles of the passing generations, transcends mortal limitations. It is this humanitary Over Soul which, in his view, is brooded by the Divine Spirit and is the progressive repository of Truth. The function of individual revelators is simply to bring to birth truths already communicated to the soul of Humanity, and with which the collective consciousness, or subconsciousness, of the peoples, vaguely aware of its throes but ignorant of the cause, is travailing. Truth is committed to the Peoples, its definition to the seers, its confirmation to the conscience of mankind. The movement begins with the *malaise* of the masses and is consummated when its banner is at last recognised and accepted by them as their own.

Thus his " Holy Alliance of the Peoples " is his equivalent to the Catholic *consensus mundi*. There must be a world-fellowship through which the universal conscience may realise and express itself. And this fellowship or world-union cannot be imposed. It must be moral and therefore voluntary. In other words, it must come through a spiritual Theo-democracy. " The People, as we understand the term, are not an aggregation of folk enjoying certain rights, but the union of all in one faith, one aim, one common law."

So he proceeds from dogma to dogma, diffident in personal

discussion to the point of humility, yet pained, a little incredulous and occasionally irritated if his friends fall short of his faith; occasionally, too, asserting an esoteric authority: " my beliefs spring from an inward inspiration which is of God." If Benza is hesitant he is bidden interrogate his heart more deeply; if " Corso " is unconvinced it is because, good man though he is, he shirks conclusions; if Melegari is definitely in opposition, it is because, God forgive him! he is blind to the truth. Yet the apostle is no censorious bigot or self-conscious Mahatma. In a sense, Agostino was right. In some respects Mazzini had remained a child, with a child's naïveté, a child's eagerness and positiveness and impatience. Something like the light of pure innocence played around his dogmatism and softened it: there was also the lamp of sacrifice. And certainly he was conscious that his beliefs isolated him, and he hungered for communion in the faith. Thus, just now he turns pathetically to Lamennais. It is time, he suggests, to pass from philosophy to religion and organise a fellowship of like-minded believers, " submitting to all possible persecutions." Alas! replies Lamennais, Christ was free to speak to the multitudes openly on the lake-shore, but to-day in France four men may not meet in a field to speak of the things of God and the people without running the risk of being haled before the magistrates.—It was an unsatisfactory reply.

Even Maria sometimes gasps in the too rarefied atmosphere of this enthusiasm of Humanity. Her Jansenists, as well as her husband, believe in human depravity in general and in Genoese, Piedmontese, Neapolitan and Roman depravity in particular. " If it were not for fear of the Devil and the hangman," she quotes, " man would be the most ferocious animal on earth." He is at pains to correct her. Man by nature is neither ferocious nor evil. He is born for the good, in the image of God, and called to the knowledge and execution of the divine law. Therefore he has been endowed with the necessary powers and faculties. What is needed is to develop and guide those powers —to administer human society so that it will help and stimulate them toward the good and not toward evil. And it can be done.—If only father could see this! And if only he could understand that we have not taken up politics as others might take up business—that ours is a work of regeneration and

education or nothing! "For me republic, laws, popular suffrage are nothing but the *means*."—And his mother dutifully
marks the correction. All the same, how can one hope (she
must reflect) for even a shadow of virtue when, nowadays, one
sees shameless men going around with *busts* and *waists* like
women and *beards* like Capuchins? Moustaches, whiskers and
bosoms! It is a crooked and perverse generation, and Maria
herself has a growing sense of isolation in Genoa: "If only
(she exclaims) I had my Giuditta with me . . . !" By this,
indeed, they had met, for Giuditta had visited Genoa.

And now, by a strange ordering of events, the "work of
regeneration and education" was taken up intensively.

*   *   *   *   *

For some time in 1841 the obstinate fantasticator, stopping to
converse with tousley organ-grinder boys and vendors of white
mice and plaster images, butted into the evidence of certain
things which called for further inquiry. He found himself, in
fact, on the track of a curious slave-traffic of which these waifs
(they were mainly Sicilians) were the victims. Taken from
their too credulous parents by glittering promises of English
gold, they were being exploited by a vicious ring of London-
Italian *padroni,* who herded them in vile dens, kept them half-
starved, and appropriated their earnings. He assured himself
of the facts, raided, at some personal risk, the Whitechapel
haunts of the ring, appeared against some of the culprits in
the English courts, and communicated to the rest a salutary
incentive to immediate reform. Thus aroused, he continued
his explorations and came upon "whole streets full of Italians
from all parts," but chiefly from Northern Italy. They were,
he found, "living in absolute barbarism." "I don't say merely
that they could not read; they could not even speak," save in
an almost unintelligible jargon, half-*Comasco,* half-Cockney.
So he described them to the Signora Quirina Maggiotti. His
mind was quickly made up. How should a man preach the
redemption of Italy and neglect the unredeemed Little Italy at
his door? Along with his Working Men's Association he would
found a free Italian Night School.

Perhaps there was a slight suggestion of disingenuousness
about his public appeal for funds, an appeal in which the

Founder's connection with the enterprise was screened behind
an attractive list of non-partisan patrons. "We open," he wrote
to Lamberti, "on November 10. . . . Most of the subscribers
belong to a class of people who tremble at the bare mention of
our name. Among others, I believe, the Sardinian Consul has
subscribed. However, the leaders are all our own men, so we
shall have the school in our own hands." But once the school
was in being (first at 5, Hatton Garden, later at 5, Greville
Street) he stood his ground. Solicitous patrons were naturally
concerned when they found in the school's curriculum subjects
so dangerous as history and geography. The moral perils
attendant upon such a course were alarming, and they trembled
for the welfare of the objects of their charity. But the Founder
was undissuadable. He had no intention (he declared) of turning the school into a revolutionary seminary for young conspirators, but neither would he consent to Italian classes in
the free City of London being limited to the curriculum imposed by Austria upon the schools of Lombardy. History and
geography would continue to be taught, and if it was an
offence to teach Italian children that Italy was the country of
a people called Italians, who also possessed a history of their
own, then he and his voluntary staff must continue to offend.
After all, the school had been founded to impart not mere
dead instruction but "a word of life."

He had his way, and sympathisers rallied to his aid. There
were fashionable Italian bazaars in West End drawing-rooms
and charity concerts at which Italian and Jewish operatic stars
gave their services. The school's supporters included com-
patriots like Gabriele Rossetti, Carlo Pepoli and Pietro Rolandi,
and British liberals like Joseph Toynbee, the Bullers, the
Barings, the Milner-Gibsons, John Stuart Mill, Lord Ashley,
W. J. Linton and Lady Byron. ("I saw Lady Byron twice,
and she looked to me a good, sharp, positive, somewhat dry,
puritanical woman, sad from the past, conscious of having
been not altogether right, and doing good half for good-doing's
sake, half for forgetfulness' sake. . . . But I am so thoroughly
Byronian . . . that my impression cannot be trusted."*) And
now, in order to be nearer the scene of his new duties, the
Founder forsook Chelsea for the less attractive venue of Queen

* Bolton King: *Life*, Append. VIII.

Square (47, Devonshire Street) and later for the New North Road (19, Cropley Street). On Sunday evenings he lectured to his Italians on History, Morals and Astronomy, and yet another Mazzinian journal, the *Pellegrino,* afterward the *Educatore,* gave a wider circulation to his discourses. Timorous supporters, indeed, fell away, Carlyle indulged in private tirades against "Mazzini's nest of conspirators" (but supported the enterprise), and there was bitter opposition from the priests of the Sardinian Chapel. There were occasional bouts, too, with hired gangsters who threatened the lives of the staff, and one Sunday night did not the intrepid Founder himself seize a ruffian in the act of cutting off the gas? There was punctual competition, also, from rapidly organised rival schools, Catholic and Protestant, French, English and Italian, and a neglected neighbourhood suddenly became a centre of impassioned educational enterprise.

The experiment, in fact, had justified itself, the attendance of scholars swelled to imposing proportions, and the anniversaries (celebrated with public speeches, suppers of fish, macaroni and ale, the declamation—in unison—of lengthy odes by Gabriele Rossetti and old Pistrucci, and the presentation of bouquets and sonnets to the embarrassed Founder) were famous events. "Carlyle will not go, I fear," writes Mrs. Carlyle, "but if I am well enough and can front all the black, black eyes that will flash out on me if I present myself along with the 'Capitano,' I will go and put my sovereign into the 'bason or box, what shall I say?' at the door." And who could resist the enthusiasm of the occasion, with its flag-draped walls and platform, its steaming windows, its lusty Italian choruses, its deafening cheers for everybody, its two hundred pairs of "black, black eyes," set in faces once rough and brutalised but kindled now "with a gleam of human nature, of Italian nature"? One such evening, declared the Founder, was equal in moral effect to a whole year of mere instruction. It was indeed, as he could claim, a "holy work," for seven years "holily fulfilled"; and it was soon emulated by Italian colleagues in New York, Boston and Montevideo. At last a "Mazzinian dream" had materialised.

*   *   *   *   *

In such an atmosphere his spirits revived. The school had gained him new friends; and the Memoirs of one Gisquet of the French police, in which the old story of the " Young Italy " chief's complicity in the Rhodez assassinations was dished up afresh, served only to bring his name before the public. The *Athenæum* had spread the libel in a lengthy notice of the Memoirs; Dr. Mazzini had promptly supplied funds for legal action against Gisquet; Carlyle, Dr. Bowring, and faithful old priest Luca had contributed eloquent letters, which were read in the French Court; the plaintiff's reputation had been cleared; and Advocate Benoit (a kinsman of Lamennais) had handsomely returned his fees to Dr. Mazzini. What could have been happier?

Moreover, was it not now rather piquant to be able to claim acquaintance with this distinguished revolutionary, accused (unsuccessfully) of nefarious plots, and said to be so noble and charming in private life? Mrs. Carlyle, who took to calling him " the murderer," roundly declared that, even if the charges had been proved six times over, she would continue to welcome him at number 5, Cheyne Row—and was secretly envied for her daring. There were, indeed, exclusive circles who were now prepared to recognise, even to pet, him, and an English patroness visited Greville Street to call the Deity to witness that Mr. Mazzini was the Prophet of the Age. Even Lady Harriet Baring, momentarily diverted from Carlyle, cast a favouring eye upon the hero and arranged (Mrs. Carlyle notes as much with a perceptible sniff) to " bring divers persons in authority to meet him " at the Grange. Mrs. Carlyle found it delightful, too, to record the sequel. Mazzini would not be caught by " that syren." " The insensible man that he is—he did not come! ! ! It must be strange for the Lady Harriet to have found *one* man that can resist her fascinations."[4] To his mother, however, the insensible man explained the reason—he had no evening clothes. " I want to be able to say to any lord or lady who asks me my opinions, ' I am republican,' but without parading republicanism in the cut of my clothes. So I must get a new suit, and then I will make my plunge into Aristocracy, and father will be pleased."[5]

His spirits, indeed, might well revive. The days of isolation were over. Years later, in a moment of genial reminiscence,

Carlyle recalled the change: "Mazzini was much sought for, invited to dinners and all that. But he did not want their dinners." Yet it was pleasant to be invited. Above all, he was doing good and surrounded with affection. When serious illness—the tumorous inflammation of the jaw—had overtaken him and he had obstinately continued to haunt the School, how his organ-grinder boys and his working men had rallied round him and with loving vehemence censured his self-neglect! Did not his Working Men's Association submit a drastic resolution (carried with resolute enthusiasm) that Mr. Mazzini be laid under obligation to take care of himself, and that *constraint* be exercised if necessary? Did they not wait upon Dr. Toynbee to inquire what particulars of treatment he wished to have *enforced*—and even take steps to post a guard at his door? His life, they decided, was not his own property; it belonged to Italy—the world.

Yes; his School and his Working Men's Association, his *Apostolato* and his *Educatore*, his increasing correspondence with exile-congregations abroad, and the stirring news from South America, where Colonel Garibaldi and his rough-riders were winning dazzling honours on the battle-fields of liberty— all these things helped to justify his faith and revive his hopes. Mrs. Carlyle observed the effect and dashed off a lyrical paragraph to "Babbie." "Some 'change has come over the spirit of his dream'—I know not what it is—I know only that he looked almost dazzlingly beautiful yesterday, and that this beauty was plainly the expression of some inward new-found joy."[6]

Even of the causes of the new illumination she might have learned a little, if Elizabeth Pepoli had not chosen that day and hour for one of her surprise visits. As it was, Mazzini had barely time to slip the wine-glasses and ginger-bread into the writing-desk before Elizabeth had walked in. Of course it was absurdly discomposing, and Elizabeth (whose mind, as Mazzini put it, was "always running on—what shall I say?—strange things, upon *my* honour") was pleased to observe that Mrs. Carlyle was QUITE well again now. For a virtuous woman, Mrs. Carlyle complained, Elizabeth was always singularly suspicious. "She would not sit down, but having quite *looked us thro' and thro'* (as she thought) went home 'to write letters.'"

A BOUT the time when Mrs. Carlyle was wondering what could be the cause of the exile's mystic illumination, he was writing to his parents: " If I believed in presentiment I might say that I never felt so strongly the hope of seeing you again as I have felt it at the beginning of this year " (1844). To his father he added: " I have grieved you, impoverished you, tormented you with my insistence upon certain things which you believe should be left to God and the course of human events: but at least I have not forsaken those principles of good living which you instilled into me. Thank God you are in no danger of having to blush at the mention of my name. . . . And suppose (not that it is at all likely) that I should fall into the enemy's hands, you could always say ' He died through being faithful to his convictions.' These, dear ones mine, are real consolations."[1]

Plainly he was anticipating a crisis. To read through his immense correspondence from 1840 to '44 and onward to the actual crisis itself is, indeed, to feel something of the dæmonic energy and sublime arrogance of the man who, alone and exiled, yet thought and acted as if the word had been entrusted to him which should command the forces of chaos. " Prepare," he writes to Fabrizi at Malta—" prepare the field for my influence." The man whose irresistible magnetism was due, according to Lloyd Garrison, to his utter self-effacement, and whose childlike helplessness in his own worldly affairs aroused the mothering compassion of his women friends, was yet, in all that concerned Italy, the unbending Chief, a master always, a disciple never—" the sultan of liberty." Thus he had always his key-men who were his to devotion, and he treated them now as brothers, now as wayward children, now as a revivalist his lay-helpers, now as aides-de-camp; but he got his way. Had Fabrizi identified himself with another organisation—the *Italian Legion*? He was taken to task. (" Whenever you tell me that in such-or-such a month the Legion will initiate the Italian movement, you must allow me to laugh at, or I had better say mourn, one more abortion.") Over in Paris had Lamberti and Giannone made up to a new group under Ricciardi? They were warned. (" We are an association of years' standing. Why, when half a dozen individuals accost us, must we put everything into their hands? If I could believe that they were capable . . . I should willingly serve in their ranks, but I do not believe it.") Emphatically he did not, and never would. For him no organisation was capable of leading the revolution but his own. And after all, if the Savona ideals and aims were true, it was the only possible conclusion. No other Party gave the least promise of representing them.

And now there was much to arouse him. Affairs in Italy were by no means stagnant. The warlike Romagnuols were continually in insurrection, the old Carbonaro spirit was reviving in the South, in Piedmont there was a slow ferment of new ideas. For while Cavour was renewing his acquaintance with London and Paris and savouring the pleasures of the Jockey Club and the *salons* of Princess Belgiojoso and Madame de Castellane, Gioberti, the Turin priest, exiled in Brussels, was coming into fame with a two-volumed essay on *The Civil and Moral Primacy of Italy*. Following Niccolò Tommaseo's less popular work on the same theme, it argued grandiloquently for a reformed and idealised Papacy as the dynamic centre of an Italian-European initiative. All nations formed a cosmopolitan society as all the tribes of Israel formed a single nation. The Italians were the Levites of Christian civilisation, chosen by Providence to keep the Christian Pontificate and protect the ark of the new covenant, the Papacy, if necessary by force of arms. Italy, then, should be encouraged to claim her independence, not through a democratic revolution, but through a princely federation of kingdoms and duchies under the presidency of the Pope; and Piedmont, as the military arm of Italy, should co-operate with Rome to that end. Such was the Giobertian thesis. It was exasperating. Gioberti was once a eulogist of Young Italy. He had contributed a glowing rhapsody to *Giovine Italia*, full of democracy, the republic, the people; and now he had taken the Young Italy wine-skins and mixed the wine. He had retained the religio-political appeal of Young Italy but perverted it into something *bourgeois* and reactionary. "I am furious," Mazzini wrote to his mother.[2] The book, he found, was full of "ultra-Roman Catholicism, eulogies of Charles Albert and all possible stupidities." Yet it was setting the fashion and selling by the thousand.

Besides Gioberti there was Cesare Balbo of Turin. Balbo, solid and erudite, turned aside alike from the Giobertian and the Mazzinian dream, and in his *Hopes of Italy* built up a plodding argument for an Italy gradually enclosed and fortified within a wall of secular reforms, initiated by Turin. For the rest, he counselled a patient waiting behind that wall for the inevitable development of political events. For with the downfall of the Turkish Empire imminent, Austria must be drawn more and more toward a policy of Eastward expansion, leaving the Italian hegemony to Piedmont.

Such were the new ideas, the tares sown among the wheat. Moreover, there was danger even from the Communistic quarter. He watched with distrust the propaganda of Étienne Cabet and his school, which, working southward from Paris, was threatening to draw away the Italian artisans and to prejudice liberal opinion against any democratic revolution. It was, he declared to his father, an absurd, impracticable apostolate, destructive of every stimulus to activity, substituting the idea of material well-being for any idea of moral progress, and reducing civilisation to a society of bees and beavers.[3] But it was seductive. And on the other hand he had already developed his own social and economic theories. The social and political power of the working classes would be, he prophesied, the "principal new element" of history, and as early as 1837 he had foretold the political emergence of Labour in England and its ultimate victory over the old Parties, Tory and Whig alike. And in this year of 1844, as Dr. Salvemini has pointed out, he was outlining his own Labour programme for the Italian revolution.

"There exist in Italy . . . two classes of people, the one the possessors exclusively of all the elements of industry—land, credit, capital, the other deprived of all except their own hands. The first, fettered in the exercise of their faculties . . . (and) governed by stupid and pernicious principles, has need chiefly of a political revolution; the second, crushed by poverty, tormented by the precariousness of labour and by the insufficiency of wages, chiefly needs a social constitution. . . . When the workers, well organised, strong in uniform convictions, bound together in singleness of purpose, take their stand as a National Association, not only as citizens but as working men, they need no longer have the fear of being deluded in their rightful hopes or of seeing the revolutions consuming themselves away upon questions of purely political reforms for the benefit of one single section of society. . . . The workers have special needs. . . . Merely political remedies are inadequate. Nevertheless revolutions will always be merely political so long as they are committed only to the [revolutionary] impulse supplied by the other classes. The conditions of these classes are radically different: how should they labour to provide for needs which they have not felt and which lack any collective expression from those who do feel them? And who can express those needs effectively if not those who do actually experience them?"[4]

His remedy was the formation of groups of Working Men's Associations (Friendly Societies), federated into a national organisation, working on the voluntary principle, and gradually emancipating the workers through their own co-operative effort, with the help of State credits.

But the first necessity was the democratic liberation of Italy and the saving of the national movement from the spoilers. His own policy was clear. A loose Federation of Italian States under the various Princes was not to be thought of; it would be " the Protestantism of politics " and would divide Italy into provincial " sects." " We must stand for Political Catholicism —One nation, One national association, One faith." And what folly, he exclaims, to talk of unity through the Princes! Already were they not conspiring in Bologna for the Grand Duke of Tuscany, in Sicily for the Prince of Capua, in Piedmont for a constitutional monarchy? What hope was there of concord and co-ordination under such a system? And a Papal initiative? Gregory XVI. as champion of national liberty? Could even Gioberti conjure up that vision? Presently he publishes a bitter indictment of the Papacy and negotiates a working agreement with Dr. Lyman Beecher's (American) Christian Alliance—" an undertaking difficult to manage," he confesses to Lamberti, " but there is common ground between us "—the desire for the free development of the religious idea, unchecked by Papal absolutism.

And as always his argument sweeps the entire European field. He denounces European statesmanship as opportunist, planning for two or three years ahead but blind to the tremendous future. The imperialist balance-of-power régime with its imaginary equalities, calculated by ciphers rather than by human tendencies and ideas, must pass, and the principle of Nationality as the means for the regrouping of Europe in homogeneous units must inevitably come to the fore. But here again he is no mere zealot with a pet obsession. He makes an admission often overlooked by the critics of his philosophy : " Distinctions of country, sacred now, may possibly disappear " in the future evolution of world society; what he holds as beyond dispute is that in the present epoch the principle of Nationality must be recognised as the appointed means to international union; and, be the struggle short and sharp or long and exhausting, opposing forces must yield before it. A race of eighty millions, including Poles and Russian Slavs spreading from the Elbe to Kamchatka—five million Czechs in Bohemia —two million Moravians scattered through Silesia and Hungary —two million Croats and Slovenes—the Serbs, the Bulgars, the Bosnians, the Greeks—these were the stuff of the new era. " In Austria there is a Slav movement which no one troubles about, but which, one day . . . will wipe Austria off the map of Europe." But as yet there was no such thing as Public Law in Europe. There existed, indeed, among the despots a league to enforce tyranny and thus to accomplish evil; there was no League for the protection of national boundaries, the defence of the weak, the peaceful development of progressive tendencies —no league to accomplish good. Instead hate reigned—hate and force. " In the heart of Humanity which calls itself Christian there is absolutely nothing *collective* to represent the consolidation of the families of Humanity." Would this gauntlet of brutal defiance be taken up? It would " without doubt, in an hour more or less remote."

And as for Italy, there was no time to be lost. He proposes to " resolve the present Italian confusion into a fundamental dualism." " I desire that the present generation of Italians shall be divided into two main sections: the people of action, who, sooner or later, will rally to us—and all the rest, who voluntarily condemn themselves to inertia." So he confesses in private, and so he proceeds, organising, preaching, expostulating, coaxing, chiding and reknitting with infinite industry the severed strands of his associations. In Paris he establishes a " Central Congregation " under Lamberti and a few others, at Marseilles another group under Campanella; through Fabrizi he organises the Malta exiles, through Cuneo the *émigrés* in South America. A glance at a single page of his notebook suffices to show how close he had woven his net, how wide he had cast it. His list of trans-Atlantic agents takes in New York, Boston, Montreal, New Haven (Conn.), Philadelphia, Richmond (Va.), Charleston (S.C.), New Orleans, and passes on to Venezuela, Cuba, Havana and the West Indies.[5] Everywhere he has his key-men.

So in these fateful years, while Bismarck was giving himself to Junker love-making among the oaks and limes of Schönhausen, and Louis Napoleon was studying gunnery in his prison at Ham or savouring the delights of liberty and Miss Howard at Jermyn Street and St. John's Wood—in these years the prophet of Queen Square and Cropley Street was proclaiming his visions and launching his dooms with few to believe his report. " Who is this M. Mazzini? " inquires Lord Brougham. " I hear he keeps a gaming-house somewhere in the East End."

*   *   *   *   *

By a curious turn of events Lord Brougham was soon to be better informed. In a secret missive Mazzini advised his principals that he had " prepared a scheme." It was at once simple, explicit and extensive. Risings were to take place in Romagna and the Papal States, spreading to Parma and Modena, with Piedmont, Lombardy and Naples to follow. Volunteers were to be shipped from Corsica and elsewhere, and Colonel Garibaldi with a force of Montevidean Italians was to land near Genoa. A rising in Poland could be counted upon, and revolutionary ferment among the Austrian Slavs would spread to the imperial army. Russia would be preoccupied with Turkey, Hungary would revolt, Switzerland would dissolve the Federal Pact, and there would be insurrections in the German States. The machinations of monarchical France would be neutralised by its liberal elements, Great Britain would observe a benevolent neutrality, and Protestant sympathy in the United States would be nourished by Dr. Lyman Beecher and the Christian Alliance. The estimated cost in immediate outlay would be 150,000 francs.

Such was the " Scheme of 1844."[6] To the unbelieving the secret missive might have suggested a disquieting resemblance to the lucubrations of Old Moore's *vox stellarum*; and even the modest outlay of 150,000 francs presented practical difficulties. The chief conspirator, indeed, complained of this. One could liberate a nation, he told Maria, on the money that changed hands at an Oxford and Cambridge boat-race. Yet in truth the missive, with almost uncanny accuracy, outlined the actual events of '48.

'Forty-four, however, produced only the tragic fiasco of the Bandiera expedition. The sorry enterprise, it is true, was no fault of Mazzini and his Executive. Attilio and Emilio Bandiera were brothers. They were of noble Venetian birth and they served as officers in the Austrian navy, in which their father was an admiral. But the lads were high-mettled patriots of the *Ortis* type. With a comrade, Moro, they deserted their ships and put themselves in communication with the exile. " I am an Italian," wrote Attilio. " My profession is that of arms. I believe in God, in a future life and in the progress of Humanity. I school myself to direct my thoughts, first to the welfare of Humanity, then to my country, then my family and my own individual life. . . . Do not disdain my offer." Here was the pure milk of the Mazzinian word, and the appeal was irresistible. Mazzini commended the brothers to Fabrizi; Fabrizi designated them for the projected rising in the Centre.

But events moved too slowly for the impetuosity of youth. " We are not vegetables," they complained, " that we should have to wait for the Spring ": and it was their impatience in forestalling regular instructions that was their undoing. Dogged incessantly by spies and preyed upon by informers, they knew no caution, and finally they were lured to their fate. Their inveiglers were Austrian agents who, masquerading as a revolutionary " Committee of Paris," instructed them to proceed to Calabria to assist in a (fictitious) rising. They were only too eager to obey. Assembling a prodigious expeditionary force of eighteen souls, they set sail and landed near Cotrone, to find themselves trapped. They put up a brave resistance and routed an urban guard, but their plight was hopeless, and at their trial their defence was unconvincing. They had sought, they declared, to give the King of Naples the opportunity of leading an Italian war of liberation. With seven of their party they were sentenced to death. On the way to their execution they sang the chorus, "*Chi per la patria muore,*" and were shot by a weeping firing-squad. It was a strange world.

And the volley of the Calabrian firing-party had strange repercussions. For one thing, the foreign governments were once more thoroughly alarmed, and Mazzinian apparitions were afflicting the nerves of their secret service. Mazzini had been "seen" in Malta, Naples, Rome and Paris; he had, it seemed, haunted Bavari (disguised as a girl), and there were rumours of a "woman" of striking appearance and hypnotic eyes who appeared (and disappeared) in the region of Grenchen. But undoubtedly his headquarters were in England and at the moment (secret information was specific) he was in hiding at Portsmouth. The reports were baseless,* but Mazzini was content to encourage them. "You see," he wrote, "I am everywhere, like the Deity."

The Powers were now aroused. It was infamous that Great Britain should afford sanctuary to a conspirator who took advantage of her protection to organise insurrections against friendly governments. Strong representations followed, and on the strength of British assurances the Vienna and Milan gazettes were able to announce that in future Mazzini would cease to be a person unknown to the London police. The announcement may have put the offender on his guard; and, by a coincidence, W. J. Linton, the engraver, carrying in his pocket a letter from Mazzini, observed that the top layer of the private seal had fallen off, revealing the original seal beneath. Thus the upper seal was counterfeit. A few ingenious experiments, and the disclosures of a postal clerk, confirmed the suspicion. The Government was secretly opening Mazzini's correspondence.

It was an engaging situation. Peel was in power, Lord Aberdeen was at the Foreign Office, Sir James Graham was

---

* Baseless, also, is Cagnacci's supposition, supported by Donaver, that in this year of '44 Mazzini visited Genoa disguised as a Capuchin. The "Capuchin" in question was Antonio Ghiglione. (See Append. C.)

Home Secretary. The ethics of conspiracy were difficult, but the ethics of tampering with private correspondence and of forging private seals were hardly less so, and Peel's Government, caught unawares in an embarrassing predicament, sought a convenient, if unoriginal, way of escape. It lied—roundly, hopefully and explicitly. Emphatically it had not opened, and would not think of opening, Mr. Mazzini's letters.

Its resources, however, were inadequate. From the Commons Gallery Mazzini listened to the tortured evasions of Sir James Graham, and, on the opposite side of the debate, to the shrill and penetrating invective of Sheil, the fluent elaborations of Macaulay and Monckton-Milnes, the circumstantial charges of Duncombe, the attacks of Bowring. The controversy became heated. There were angry Front Bench malignings of Mazzini as an assassin and hirer of assassins (withdrawn), and renewed explicit charges against the honour of the Queen's Government (not withdrawn). Select committees of inquiry were appointed in both Houses, and amid a *crescendo* of public wrath it was disclosed that Mr. Mazzini's correspondence (unfortunate official statements to the contrary notwithstanding) had been opened; that, in fact, for the past forty years or more, the governments of the day had, in urgent cases, issued orders for the discreet opening of private letters in the post and the subsequent resealing and prompt delivery of same in a manner calculated to save the parties concerned any unnecessary inconvenience.

The revelation was, in fact, as exciting as it was unexpected. The British public might know very little about the Italian question, but it had a general contempt for foreign despots, an abhorrence of official espionage and a jealous regard for the privacy of the Post. The storm became nation-wide, discharging itself in roaring indignation-meetings; and while *Punch* hit off the public mind with a caricature of Sir James Graham as Paul Pry at the Post Office, and irate citizens took to marking their letters " *Not to be Grahamed*," Carlyle took up the challenge and wrote to *The Times*. As to Italian democracies, extraneous Austrian Emperors in Milan and chimerical old Popes in Bologna, Mr. Carlyle knew nothing and desired to know nothing. But he must hold it a question vital to every Englishman that, except in cases of the very last extremity, the opening of men's letters—a practice near of kin to picking their pockets and other and fataller forms of scoundrelism—should not be resorted to in England, certainly not for Austrian Kaisers and their like. And as to Mr. Mazzini, he would certify the Editor that that gentleman was not unknown to various competent persons, and he himself had had the honour to know him for a series of years. And whatever he might think of Mr. Mazzini's skill in worldly affairs, he would with great freedom testify to all men that Mr. Mazzini, if he had ever seen one such, was a man of genius and virtue, a man of sterling veracity and nobleness of mind, one of those rare men, numerable, unfortunately, but as units in this world, who were worthy to be called martyr-souls, who in silence, piously in their daily life, understood and practised what was meant by that.—For once Mrs. Carlyle was lyrical in approval. It was "a glorious letter."

Nor were the troubles of the Government over. Carlyle's broadside was followed up by a long and scathing Open Letter from Mazzini himself, addressed "with all due respect" to Sir James Graham. Hitherto the exile's words had reached a liberal remnant; now he had the eye and ear of the nation; and a harassed Ministry (and a delighted public) discovered that in M. Mazzini it had aroused a D'Artagnan whose forensic thrust and parry were out of all character with a reputed keeper of an East End gaming-house. Nor was it enough that he should prick the guilty bureaucrats who had played the spy for the Austrian police; he would drag to light the whole Italian situation. For were not Englishmen being assured that "all was quiet" in Italy? Well, let them know that it was true. "In Italy nothing speaks. Silence is the common law. The people are silent by reason of terror; the masters are silent from policy. One might fancy the very steps of the scaffold were spread with velvet, so little noise do heads make when they fall." Was it not evident that a supremacy reduced to maintaining itself by intimidation and organised violence must be founded upon a vast injustice? And as for the Church, the Holy See was for Italy "the pommel of the sword of which Austria was the point." Who could be ignorant of the fact that the Pope was the creature of ambassadorial intrigue and that the direct or indirect veto of Austria could "throw into conclavial nonentity the so-termed chosen of the Holy Spirit "?[7]

The appeal struck home, and Carlyle in a slightly splenetic relapse affirmed to Gavan Duffy[8] that " the best thing that had ever befallen Mazzini was the opening of his letters." There was some truth in it. It marked the beginning in England of that pro-Italian interest and growing sentiment which Garibaldi's later exploits were to excite to passionate intensity. After all, Attilio and Emilio Bandiera had not died in vain.

* * * * *

So 1845 followed '44 with little to note, save the founding of yet another Mazzinian society (" For the Protection of Italian Organ-grinder Boys "—President, Lord Ashley) and the observation by Mrs. Carlyle—in a letter to " Babbie," and accompanied by a slight epistolary sniff—that Mazzini was " not as solitary as formerly."

Friends, indeed, were increasing. There were the inestimable Nathans and Craufords and Toynbees, and Rabbi Morais and William Shaen and the Mallesons and Dillons and J. C. Hobhouse, and Joe Cowen (whose Blaydon bricks and fire-retorts were useful for the smuggling of contrabrand consignments abroad), and Charles Dickens, and Douglas Jerrold, and many more. Mr. Tennyson, with his " bombastic laudations of insular selfishness," was uncongenial, but there were breakfasts with the poet Rogers (" first Englishman to foretell a Third Italy ") and later so much lionising at a Browning reception that Mrs. Carlyle's sniff was once more in evidence in a letter to dear Babbie. Presently, also, there was Douglas Jerrold's Whittington Club, where Mr. Mazzini became Vice-President and met a number of select gentlemen in close-buttoned frockcoats and strapped trousers, and played chess (developing disconcerting guerrilla tactics and—unsupported—sweeping movements across the board, with great sacrifice of pieces). Occasionally, too, there were box-tickets *gratis* for Covent Garden (they were the days of Grisi and Mario and Taglioni and Jenny Lind), and there was a curious friendship with the Austrian singer, Staudigl. (" Staudigl has been laughing during three minutes and three seconds—I have a watch—at my comparing a Sunflower [Austrian colours] to an omelette with a thought of crime in it.")

There was another attachment, which more seriously exercised Mrs. Carlyle. He formed the habit of walking out on Sundays to the village of Muswell Hill, for political and philosophical conversation with a Radical solicitor of some reputation, named William Ashurst, and his family. Occasionally he took with him his guitar. Mrs. Carlyle, whose information was detailed, was presently reporting the new development (with vigorous underscorings and dashes) to Jeannie Welsh at Auchtertool. Mazzini had "got up to the ears" in a "*good* twaddly family"—who had plenty of money and *toadied* him —till it had rather gone to his head—and the woman painted his portrait and *worked* for his bazaar, etc.—and made verses about him and Heaven knew what all—while the men gave *capital* toward his *Institutions* and imbibed his "new ideas." ... Mrs. Carlyle was perhaps a trifle monopolistic in her affections; but at any rate the weekly visits to Cheyne Row were not discontinued, and Carlyle, at least, approved of Muswell Hill. It "did Mazzini great good—gave him a kind of home-circle."

But now events were moving toward a crisis.

ON June 1, 1846, Pope Gregory XVI. died. On June 15
the Sacred College assembled in conclave for the making
of his successor. On the 16th Gaysbrück, Archbishop of
Milan, was still on his way Rome-ward, bearing the Austrian
veto and making no secret of his intention of settling the election. There was more than ordinary excitement. There were
even wild rumous of a Gunpowder Plot. Half-way to Rome
Gaysbrück received the news that the Cardinals, acting with
unusual celerity, had concluded their work. The Pope had
been made.

The lot, as Gaysbrück learned, had fallen neither upon Lambruschini, the Austrian choice, nor upon Soglia nor Gizzi, the
liberal nominees, but upon Mastai Ferretti, Bishop of Imola.
It was one of those unlooked-for emergences with which, occasionally, Providence seems to upset the calculation of even the
elect. Mastai himself had been one of the conclavial scrutineers.
He had swooned (it was said he was epileptic) as he counted
the ballots which set him on the awful eminence of the Papal
throne.

Next morning, as Pius IX. (Pio Nono), he was presented to
the populace from the loggia of the Quirinal. To the masses of
the people he was unknown. Vaguely they divined that the
fate of Italy was under his hand, that a new Pope might mean
a new national policy, a new era. Their eyes searched his
face as if they would read therein the future. It pleased them
to behold, not an ecclesiastical mask, but an essentially human
countenance, masculine, handsome, genial, the face of an
Italian, a son of the people. Also it seemed hopefully resolute.
It might even have been the face of a soldier. Presently the
story went round that in his youth Mastai had sought the
profession of arms, but, failing through ill-health, had turned
to the Church. He had desired, it was said, to fight for
Italy. . . .

A month later multitudes vaster and more deeply moved poured into the piazza of the Papal Palace. They came with banners and torches and songs of thanksgiving. With all the child-like exuberance of a Roman crowd on holiday, they laughed and wept, they sang and shouted and cheered. And unlike similar assemblies at other times, they knew exactly why they had come. They had come to hail the Holy Father as the long-looked-for deliverer of his country.

For, in the teeth of Lambruschini and the Gregorian Cardinals, Pius had unfurled the liberal banner, and with his first *motu proprio* had proclaimed an amnesty for political offenders. Through the clubs and cafés the news had sped with electric swiftness; it was as if in Rome some strange and occult telegraphy were already in operation. And now, arrayed in white, his robes glistening in the flare of the uplifted flambeaux, the Holy Father blessed his kneeling people, and as he blessed them he wept. He had read their hearts; had not they read his? " *God bless Italy!* " They were Italians all!

That night it seemed as if every window in Rome must be illuminated, and soon Austria-defying beacons were flaming along the Apennines. Indeed, enthusiasm for Pius quickened into a cult and spread into a general *furore*. For while the Jesuits hardly concealed their hostility, and privately reviled him as " the interloper Mastai," the liberals idealised him and the people worshipped him. They worshipped him not less when the bitterness of the reactionaries within the Church became manifest, and when the Sanfedists, threatening a disruption, proclaimed that the religion of Christ was in danger, that Mastai sought to destroy it.[1] Thus when the Pope visited the Jesuit College the crowds, led by the burly Ciceroacchio, shouted their boisterous admonitions: " Holy Father, don't touch their *chocolat* !" Rossini composed a hymn in the Pontiff's honour, women wore dresses adorned with his image, and once the irrepressible Ciceroacchio, clambering on to the Papal carriage, unfurled an enormous flag with the legend, " Holy Father, Trust the People!"[2] From under the folds of this strange banner Pius received the thundering ovations of the populace. In Verdi's opera *Ernani* there is a scene in which Charles V., disguised, discovers a conspiracy in the Church against himself. At the dramatic moment he confronts the dismayed conspirators and cries, "I am Carlo Magno!" The opera was given in Rome. Coletti the baritone took the part of the King. At the important moment he flung back his cloak and pronounced his royal lines; only, instead of "I am Carlo Magno," he declaimed *fortissimo*, "I am Pio Nono!"[3] The setting was too obvious for its significance to be lost, and a crowded house went frantic with enthusiasm. A little later the hostile Cardinals, incensed at seeing their names placarded and vilified on the walls of Rome, made haste to depart.

Nor was it all effervescent emotion. Schemes of reform sprang up in a night and blossomed in a day. There were projects for railways and schools, for scientific congresses and working men's guilds. And while liberalism in Rome breathed and moved in an atmosphere of benign delirium, the world beyond Rome sought to adjust itself to the new miracle. Metternich declared Mastai's election to be the greatest misfortune of the age, and Austria threatened to occupy Romagna in the interest of civilisation. The threat drew from Palmerston an amiable reference to the possibility of a British fleet's anchoring off Trieste, and from Colonel Garibaldi the offer of his Montevidean-Italian warriors for the defence of Rome. Charles Albert declared roundly that if God permitted a war for the freedom of Italy, he would mount his horse and take the field at the head of his army. The people of Tuscany and Lucca took matters into their own hands and mustered a Civic Guard; and Piedmont, with a relaxed censorship, beheld (1847) the phenomenon of a liberal newspaper openly sold on the streets of Turin. The paper bore a title in keeping with the prevalent suggestion of miracle: it was called *The Resurrection* (*Il Risorgimento*). Cesare Balbo was in charge, but the real angel of the *Resurrection* was Cavour—slightly squat and rotund for the part, but in deadly earnest, the trumpet held firmly to his lips. His preliminary fanfares (on the blessings of Constitutional Monarchy) re-echoed from Turin to Vienna.

So the days sped by; and in Edinburgh, surrounded by his circle in the little attic-room in George Street, Agostino broke through his reticence and, with a new freedom and vigour, discoursed upon the Italian situation: "We must fight, fight, fight. If one whole generation of us should have to be swept away in the process, and Italy can then be free, it will be a good bargain."[4] And after a long silence he wrote to Pippo, subscribing three guineas to his Italian Fund. Giovanni, in Paris, also experienced slight relentings. "I wish him well, and I am sure he reciprocates. I even dream about him."

* * * * *

Mazzini himself was now radiating electrical energy. "I cannot tell why," he wrote to his parents, "but I am conscious of a certain spirit of audacity, a certain recovery of energy, quite inexplicable." He was, he said, living in a whirl of work, driven right and left, east and west, in a manner that made him giddy, but every effort was concentrated upon the massing of his own forces for the now inevitable struggle.

Considering, indeed, the general situation his attitude was audacious. For admittedly the developments in Italy were sensational beyond belief; the general enthusiasm had, in fact, already attained the fervour of a religious revival, and, to a degree which, two years ago, would have seemed incredible, the prophesyings of Young Italy were being vindicated. A New Rome (symbolised by a Reformer-Pope)—a growing belief in Italian Union—even Charles Albert himself accepting at last the open challenge of '31 and coming forward as " the Sword of Italy "—was not this sufficient for the moment to satisfy the most exacting of dreamers? It was true there were features and tendencies which approximated rather to the Giobertian travesty than to the Savona original. Thus the new movement had not begun with a democratic revolution; popular suffrage and constitutional reform were not yet inscribed upon its banners; it was possible that the revival would develop toward a princely Federation under a Pope-President, a union of Italian States rather than Italian Unity. But even so, would not the change be an all-but miraculous advance? And in the flood-tide, the full gale of popular enthusiasm, what was to be done but make the most of wind and weather and steer accordingly?

This Mazzini refused to do. There is no hint in his letters of this period that the possibility ever occurred to him. In the matter of the Papal leadership he was willing to temporise, but he never wavered in his assurance that the Young Italy programme was the one and only programme for the nation. He had long ago dropped Charles Albert from his book—" I have no faith in princes," he wrote to his mother—and now when Dr. Mazzini, wavering at last in his unbelief in an Italian revival, wrote to him urging the necessity for " a stable hereditary chief," he dismissed the subject: " First let him show himself, and then we will discuss him." Two years earlier he had written in the same strain: " We have not a Napoleon, and I thank God for it." He permitted the republishing (1847) of his Open Letter to Charles Albert, but insisted upon the inclusion of a stinging preface denying any belief that the salvation of Italy could be achieved " now or at any future time by Prince, Pope or King." To announce as much at this particular stage may have been courageous, but it looked like the courage of madness. It seemed to be a deliberate isolating of his influence at a time when, had he come forward under the general banner, his personal ascendancy in Italy would have been assured. But it did not occur to him to hesitate. He must remain within the beat and rhythm of those ideas which had proclaimed themselves to him. Outside that zone he had nothing to offer; within it he felt himself infallible. Men might believe what they pleased, the real movement would not be an affair of Italian princes, it would be of the people and would mean a European, not a local, revolution. Thomas Cooper has recorded in his Autobiography his recollection of these pronouncements: " Mazzini himself was our great source of inspiration. He assured us—months before it came to pass—that a European Revolution was at hand—a revolution that would hurl Louis Philippe from his throne and endanger the thrones of others. He affirmed this as early as September, 1847, when it seemed so unlikely to some of us."[5] " Never mind," Mazzini himself wrote to the Ashursts, " what they [the Italian Moderates and Giobertians] print or shout; never mind what they act. Depend upon me. . . . Wait a little longer."[6]

The Moderates certainly irritated him. What had they seen that gave them liberty of prophesying? Balbo, D'Azeglio, Cavour, Gioberti—what had they to propose? They were conjuring up old, dispelled illusions and seeking to reconcile incompatibilities. Their policies were gimcrack and opportunist

—monarchical constitutions, princely federations, piecemeal reforms. Not through such measures could the creative idea be enacted which should quicken Italy and transform Europe.

Only concerning the Pope did he hesitate. Of the general excitement over the Papal amnesty he was scornful enough, and when his English friends congratulated him upon the new régime he allowed himself to be playfully sarcastic. The Pope, forsooth, had *forgiven* political liberals and lowered the duties on cotton, so everybody was to go and be happy—as if one could clothe one's soul in cotton and forgiveness—and *that* sort of forgiveness! "Pius IX.," he wrote privately (in a letter which Metternich intercepted), "is a good man, wishful that his subjects should be a little better off than before: *voilà tout*. All the rest is a scaffolding [*échafaudage*] which the so-called Moderates have erected around him, as around Charles Albert." The scaffolding, he declared, would fall away, the illusion gradually but inevitably fade. The hour would come when the people would understand that if they meant to achieve a nation they themselves must do it. On the other hand, with a slightly Cavourian *finesse,* he counselled his friends to avoid attacking the illusion directly; it must be allowed to consume itself away. They must be ready to cry up the Pope in all his liberal measures, and prepare cautiously against the day of reaction. He even toyed with the bizarre possibility of an Italian Pope-President. In this new and strange Italy what might not happen? "I do not grumble much at it—the Pope is a man and not a dynasty"; and he pens a note upon it to the Ashursts, written in curious Carlylese. He considers this "the last agony of Popedom-authority," and for his own part he would not be sorry at a Great Institution's dying in a noble manner, rather than sinking into Crockford or Tuileries mud, like the English aristocracy and the French monarchy. A Moral Power, like a Great Man, ought to die so, the watchword of the future upon its lips.—Then, becoming restless, he addressed to the Pope an Open Letter.

The Letter was pontifical in tone. Also there was no denying its warmth and elevation. He composed it, he told his mother, at a sitting, and in a glow of youthful emotion. It was possible (he reminded the Vatican) for the Holy Father to unite Italy under a government unique in Europe—a democracy based upon spiritual sanctions. It was possible for him to initiate a new era, conserving and fulfilling the principles of Christ while refashioning the forms of faith in correspondence with the progress of knowledge. But there was only one way by which he could fulfil so tremendous a mission: he must dare to make his appeal direct to the Italians. "Do not seek alliances with princes. Achieve the alliance of our people." And for the rest, the Holy Father must remember that the movement, in any case, would go forward. "The unity of Italy is of God. It will be achieved without you, if not with you."

The Letter was privately printed and duly flung into the Papal carriage by a confederate hand. The Holy Father perused it; he did not reply, and his private comments were not published. Inner circles in Rome, however, were presently repeating what Rumour gave out as the Papal pronouncement. "*My God!*" (it was reported he had exclaimed) "*they want me to be a Napoleon, and I am only a poor country parson.*"

Yet the Letter was not to be turned aside with a jest. Extravagant it might be, but its appeal penetrated into the recesses of men's consciences: fantastic it might seem, but it reflected what was in truth a fantastic situation. For by allowing himself, in defiance of Vienna and the despotic Powers, to be hailed as the champion of Italian aspirations, Pius had set his feet in a path which led precisely in the direction which Mazzini indicated. Either he must break with tradition and go forward— against the veto of Catholic Austria, and against Jesuit and conservative opposition in the Church—as the crusader of Liberty and Reform, or he must abandon all pretence to the leadership of the new movement. And it was at least conceivable that he would go forward. Indeed, it needed but one or two more steps or mis-steps, one precipitate lurch in the popular direction, for national enthusiasm to close around him and make retreat all but impossible. Thus in Genoa cheers for the Pope and for Giuseppe Mazzini were already mingling ominously, and the angry Jesuits were with difficulty restrained by their Cardinal from offering public prayers for the Pontiff's conversion. So near, as it seemed, was the Church to something like disruption, and Europe to a new and strange Reformation. And whatever might be thought of its wisdom or timeliness, the Letter defined this situation.

Mazzini was now closely watched, but Palmerston was behaving admirably. Did Metternich communicate a private letter of the Exile's, intercepted in the foreign post, and argue the necessity for maintaining tranquillity in the Papal States—he was reminded of the right which belonged to the sovereign power in every State to make such internal improvements as might be judged by such sovereign power conducive to the general well-being. Did an alarmed King of Naples report that Mazzini's associates were preparing an expedition to be shipped from Malta—Lord Palmerston was satisfied that the specific reports were groundless, but would take the opportunity of intimating the extreme gratification which Her Majesty's Government would derive from learning that the King of Naples intended following the liberal example set him by the Pope.

As for Mazzini himself, he continued in a whirl of activity, teaching in his night-school, lecturing on Sunday evenings, contributing propagandist articles to the *People's Journal,* attending committees of his new International League, superintending the enterprises of his Working Men's Association, writing for the columns of his *Apostolato Popolare,* aiding Worcell in a scheme for a Polish rising, and manipulating the wires of his conspiratorial associations extending to the ends of the earth. His finances continued problematical, and though he was handsomely relieved of anxiety respecting his School funds, hack-writing had still to be done to meet personal necessities, for his mother's regular remittances were usually forespent in the relief of others. " I *must* write things for which I entertain the highest contempt possible, for *Lowe's Magazine* etc.," he complains, and adds that he is giddy with the incessant round of work. All the same, he contrived to contribute to the *People's Journal* a series of studies (" *Thoughts upon Democracy in Europe* "), running into 30,000 words, in which he defined his apostolate as distinct from an extreme unqualified Populism on the one hand and the individualism of the Carlyle-Emerson school on the other.

" Give the suffrage to a people unfitted for it, governed by hateful reactionary passions, they will sell it, or will make a bad use of it; they will introduce instability into every part of the State; they will render impossible those great combined views, those thoughts for the future, which make the life of a nation powerful and progressive. . . . And as for the moralists, the philosophical writers who would begin by transforming the inward man—they forget that the labouring man who works fourteen or sixteen hours a day for a bare subsistence . . . has not time to read and reflect . . . he drinks and sleeps. It is very difficult to find the *ubiconsistat* of the lever of Carlyle, Emerson, and all the noble minds which resemble them, to act on the Glasgow weaver, the *canut* of Lyons, or the Gallician serf."

Communism was no better. The Communist, disgusted with existing society, " but disgusted like the child who breaks his toy because he has knocked his head against it," wished to make a clean sweep of all present institutions. " He has drawn from his brain a model republic of beavers or of bees; he calls upon the human race to come and frame itself therein and remain there for ever." But the true mission of Democracy was neither to create human nature nor to create a fixed immobile society, but to carry human nature forward and to carry society forward. And this could be done only through a religious conception of Life, of Humanity and of the world-purpose.

" You can elevate *men* only by elevating MAN : by raising our conception of life which the spectacle of inequality tends to lower. . . . When all men shall commune together . . . when the arms of Christ, even yet stretched out on the cross, shall be loosened to clasp the whole human race in one embrace—when there shall be no more pariahs nor brahmins, nor servants, nor master, but only *men*—we shall adore the great name of God with much more love and faith than we do now."

This, as he saw it, was Democracy in its essentials, and he defined it in a formula which has since become famous : " *The progress of all through all under the leading of the best and wisest.*" In one characteristic passage the innate Catholicism of his conceptions comes into curious expression :

" I have often dreamed of a state of things in Europe when every loving and devoted soul, convinced of the necessity of a creed of fusion—of a general doctrine that might correspond with the now undeniable movement that is hurrying Europe, and with Europe the world, towards new destinies—should act upon the duties imposed by such a conviction. Instead of all these associations organised for one special branch of teaching, or of activity, and which are now strangers to each other . . . there should be one great philosophical—I might say religious—association to which all these . . . should be united . . . each bringing to the centre the results of its labours, of its discoveries, of its views for the future. Instead of all these academies, universities, lectureships etc., without mission, programme or extended views—and in which, as if to engraft doubt and anarchy upon instruction itself, a materialist professor of medicine jostles a mystic metaphysician, and a course of individualist political economy follows a course of history or public laws based on the principle of association—there should be one real apostolate of knowledge; starting from the small number of fundamental truths henceforth secured to the human race."

The formulation of these fundaments might seem a formidable task: but no. "The balance-sheet of our acquirements would soon be struck; and this balance-sheet being synthetically drawn up, the solution of the programme we are all seeking would not long remain undiscovered." But alas! "at present we are very far from any such Council of the intellects of Europe."

Withal the inner circle of intimate friends was not to be neglected, and his correspondence with them entered into the minute details and small crises of their domestic affairs. To Mrs. Carlyle especially, declining now under chronic invalidism and the tyranny of morbid suspicions, he addressed earnest homilies:

"It is only you who can, by a calm, dispassionate, fair re-examination of the past, send back to nothingness the ghosts and phantoms that you have been conjuring up. It is only you who can teach yourself that, whatever the *present* may be, you must front it with dignity, with a clear perception of all your duties, with a due reverence to your immortal soul, with a religious faith in times yet to come, that are to dawn under the approach of other cloudless suns. I could only point out to you the fulfilment of duties which can make life—not happy—what can? but earnest, sacred and resignated; but I would make you frown or scorn. We have a different conception of life, and are condemned here down to walk on two parallels. Still it is the feeling of those duties that saves me from the atheism of despair, and leads me through a life every day more barren and burdensome, in a sort of calm, composed manner—such, I repeat, as the consciousness of something everlasting within us claims from every living mortal. For I now most coolly and deliberately do declare to you, that partly through what is known to you, partly through things that will never be known, I am carrying a burden even heavier than you, and have undergone even bitterer deceptions than you have. But by dint of repeating to myself that there is no happiness under the moon, that life is a self-sacrifice meant for some higher and happier thing; that to have a few loving beings, or, if none, to have a mother watching you from Italy or from Heaven, it is all the same, ought to be quite enough to preserve us from falling, and by falling, parting, I have mustered up strength to go on, to work at my task as far as I have been able to make it out, till I reach the grave: the grave for which the hour will come, and is fast approaching without my loudly calling for it.

"Awake, arise, dear friend! Beset by pain or not, we must go on with a sad smile and a practical encouragement from one another. We have something of our own to care about, something godlike that we must not yield to any living creature, whoever it be. Your life proves an empty thing, you say. Empty! Do not blaspheme. Have you never done good? Have you never loved? Think of your mother and do good—set the eye to Providence. It is not as a mere piece of irony that God has placed you here: not as a mere piece of irony that He has given us those aspirations, those yearnings after happiness that are now making us both unhappy. Can't you trust Him a little longer? . . ."

To his friends the Ashursts he wrote of his own black depressions:

"I feel since two or three days, without any definite cause, dreadfully annoyed with myself, feeling my life a complete failure, myself . . . a great humbug, and repeating mentally oftener than wanted the forbidden 'Oh, never more—oh, never more on me,'* etc. I cannot give nor receive happiness. This accursed word has come under my pen—do good, I mean. I can feel affection, perhaps inspire it, too; but in *my* affection there is a shadow of everlasting sadness, a consciousness of impotency, as I said, to do any good, very often a fear to do evil. In affection towards me there is no doubt a great deal of charity, which spoils the thing. . . . I feel that the only good thing for me would be to act; to close this useless, wearisome career of mine with a manly protest and fly away. You all would love me in the same way, perhaps more; and I fancy that I would love you all more effectually. But this, too, is idle talk: I cannot act. And after all I think I had better hold my tongue and keep quiet till the 'blue devils' choose to leave me, which will be the case, perhaps, very soon."

*   *   *   *   *

Then in the autumn of '47 the whirlwind of activity suddenly blew him out of London, and the Continental police, pursuing misleading tracks across Switzerland, picked up the scent once more in Paris. "M. Mazzini disguises himself with great care," reports Delessert, Prefect of Police, to Guizot, "and sleeps now at one address, now at another "[7]—in vain attempt, presumably, to elude the lynx-eyed M. Delessert. The industrious Prefect seems, however, to have been shadowing the convenient Mazzinian "double." At that time Grisi and Mario were in the full blaze of their operatic triumphs; during the Paris season they resided in the fashionable part of the city; Mazzini was their guest. Thus it was at the Marios' address

---

* A Byron quotation which the Ashursts, apparently, had forbidden him to apply to himself. (See *M.'s Letters to an English Family*, vol. i., pp. 34, 52.)

that a lank and slightly self-conscious Giovanni paid his respects and reported hopefully to Agostino that Pippo, though little altered in appearance, now gave the impression of being a more practical man and of having profited by experience ("God grant it!"). In discussion with him, even upon matters political, he found Pippo, indeed, commendably sober, calm and reasonable; "only now and then certain Titanic inflexions of the voice, certain minatory shakings of the Olympian head, reveal the man of old. But naturally my presence restrains him."[8] Naturally; and presently the suppers at the Marios' seem to have disturbed the Ruffinian bile. Pippo (he reports) was moving more than ever in the old, vaporous, incense-laden atmosphere. His sojourn in France was in fact developing into a series of little ovations and triumphs, and the great man was being "dragged right and left—yesterday George Sand, to-day Lamennais, to-morrow the editors of the *National*. . . . Whatever he does or says oozes a sort of beatitude of placid self-adoration. I dined with him one day at Mario's, all of us with censers in our hands. My being there, it was clear"— once more—"subdued him."

The poor Giovanni, "mute, austere, unmoved"! What memories of Taggia and Bavari, of S. Cosimo and the Castelletto balcony, of bygone days of hero-worship and covenanted friendship—memories which would yet blossom fragrantly enough in his *Benoni*! And even now he must relax for a mollifying line or two: "The fact is Pippo is an extraordinary man. No one could exercise such fascination unless he possessed great qualities." And a few months later he will write: "Mazzini at this moment is at the apogee of glory. All Italy have their eyes on him. What was yesterday an exaggeration, a dream, a Utopia, is now foresight and wisdom. 'God and the People' becomes the national watchword." He adds: "As I separated myself from him in adverse fortune, I shall not follow him in prosperity, out of pride, if for nothing else." For the Scheme of '44, preposterous as it had seemed, was coming true.

*   *   *   *   *

Viewed now, indeed, from Hardy's Overworld, from any point of view, in fact, Europe was no longer a supine figure but was assuming an aspect of new and vehement activity. For the next time Mazzini crossed from London to Paris—in February, '48—the cannon and the barricades were in the streets and the Hôtel de Ville was guarded by blue-bloused citizen-soldiers of the latest Revolution. At an official reception *Citoyen* Lamartine welcomed the exile and his Italian deputation with appropriate eloquence, punctuated with cries of " *Vivent la République française et l'Italie régenerée!*" At his own house Lamartine was hardly less enthusiastic. " The hour," he declared, " has struck for you "; and he added that he had already advised the Pope that " he ought to be President of the Italian Republic."

The hour had certainly struck, and with a sudden iron clangour which vibrated like a fire-bell throughout Europe. France a republic, Hungary and Bohemia ablaze, liberty-bonfires crackling in the streets of Vienna, Posen in revolt, Bavaria, Baden, Brunswick, Würtemberg—Prussia itself—kindling in the general flame, even the Swiss Alps erupting volcanically against the Sonderbund . . . how was it all to end? A forlorn King of France in Surrey, a shocked and chastened Metternich at Brighton, Guizot renting a house at Brompton, the Prince of Prussia at Lady Palmerston's, Ireland in rebellion, and the Chartists marching on London! "Unprecedented horrors!" exclaims a slightly sardonic Disraeli to sister Sa;[9] and Carlyle to Emerson: " The righteous Gods do yet live and reign! It is long since I have felt such deep-seated, pious satisfaction."[10]

Withal, as Mazzini had foretold, it was from Italy that the revolutionary initiative had proceeded. The cult of a Reformer-Pope had given a new impetus to liberalism, and before the barricades were piled in Paris the Sicilians and Neapolitans, erecting their own, had extorted a constitution from an astonished Ferdinand. And now there was Milan. By the middle of March startled travellers across the northern plains were reporting the city encircled in smoke and flame, with church bells wildly clanging day and night. The infuriated Milanese, driven to desperation with bayonetings and floggings, had, in fact, armed themselves with what they could lay hands on, engaged Radetzky's Austrian garrison of 20,000 whitecoats for five incredible days, and finally had driven them out.

In Venice under Daniele Manin the miracle was repeated in milder but no less effective form; and while the Duchess of Parma and the Duke of Modena (Giuditta's obdurate Duke) fled from their duchies, Leopold of Tuscany conceded a constitution, the Pope summoned an Assembly at Rome and Charles Albert a Parliament in Turin.

Such was the miracle of '48—"the muffled roar of revolutions," and sound of huzzahing multitudes and of citizen-armies on the march; and in Florence, as "all the people shouted in the sun," Mrs. Browning, from her Casa Guidi windows, sought not unhopefully for sign of "God's light organised in some high soul, crowned capable to lead." "Rise up, teacher; here's a crowd to make a nation!"

Time now, at least, for all poor exiles to be packing. Let little Angelo Usiglio lay aside his pen, and Gustavo Modena bid farewell to green-room and footlights, and Scipione Pistrucci to his art-work and classes, and Agostino Ruffini dismantle his George Street attic and bid final *addio* to Edinburgh. Colonel Garibaldi, too, must hasten with his fighting-men from Montevideo; and even "Mariotti" Gallenga, armed now with brand-new English rifle and not with paper-knife (but the new weapon, like the old, will not be used), must take heroic leave of his London admirers. And Giuditta? Giuditta at last has won her long fight and gathered her children about her—children no longer—in Florence. And over in Genoa a retired Professor of Anatomy, grown infirm now, and hard of hearing, is saluted respectfully as he takes his measured and punctual walks along the Strada Nuova and is pointed out as the father of the great exile, Mazzini. As for the Professor's wife, she is already talking with bated breath (for the joy of it is almost frightening) of meeting her son at Milan. Perhaps daughter Antonietta and her husband will accompany her—or, maybe, it will be trusted friend Napoleone Ferrari. For the old Professor it is now too long a journey: faithful Bedin will take care of him at home—or at Nervi. Though, in truth, the Professor must make a much longer journey very soon. Before the year is out he will bid farewell to Genoa and the world.

And now for the Exile himself also the hour of destiny had struck—hour long looked for, discussed in awed undertone on the Castelletto balcony—foreseen, forefelt in Savona betwixt sea and sky. For now was Rome waking from the sleep of centuries; now was Italy rising from the dust and gathering her children around her; now, as it seemed, all the brazen battlements of material Fact, the pride of princes, the pomp of despot-powers, were melting, like walls of wax, before the fervent heat of a flaming idea.

So he turned Southward once more. On foot, and not without danger, he crossed the St. Gothard " amid the everlasting silence that speaks of God." On the southern slopes he picked the first spring flower that greeted him—a *viola dell' Alpi*—and sent it as a token to the Ashursts. He had made the journey under a false passport (was he not Mr. Frank Dillon of London?), but at Chiasso the Customs officers recognised him. The old death sentences still hung over him unrevoked, but the guardians of the frontier greeted him with his own watchwords as, under a fickle April sky, he passed on—into Italy.

CHAPTER I   MILAN

CROSSING the Alps in the early days of April, Mazzini passed from Como to Milan through a Lombardy whose revolutionary besom had already swept the Austrian white-coats into the corners of the Quadrilateral.* In Lombardy itself and Venetia, in Parma, Modena, the Romagna, Tuscany —everywhere—the Italians were rushing to arms; and while General Durando at the head of the Papal troops was pro-claiming a national crusade and threatening to cross into Venetia, Charles Albert, commanding the army of Piedmont, had crossed the Ticino and routed an Austrian force at Monte Chiaro. Nothing could be more promising: Revolt in Feb-ruary, Independence in March, Unity, perhaps, in April, and all by direct Italian initiative without the intervention of any foreign Power. There could hardly have been a more dramatic vindication of the Mazzinian thesis; and if in 1844 Mazzini's detailed forecast—an Italian rising, a European revolution, and the collapse of the Habsburg Empire—if at that time his fore-cast had read like a page of Old Moore, by now it had received the confirmation of something approaching accomplished fact. For with Vienna in the throes of revolution, the Emperor a fugitive, Metternich in exile, and Hungary and Bohemia in revolt, Austria was in ill condition to reinforce her dispirited Italian garrisons. Moreover, these were already depleted, as Mazzini had predicted they would be, by wholesale desertions to the Italian tricolour. Prompt and united action was all that was now needed, either to drive, by a swift offensive, the last white-coat over the Brenner, or else, by sealing up the Trent

* The region defended by the four fortresses of Peschiera, Verona, Mantua and Legnago.

valley and barring the Venetian border, to starve Radetzky into submission. And if at this crucial hour the consummation lagged, it was from a cause which Mazzini had sufficiently exposed. It was because the genius, the spontaneity, of the national movement was already being repressed in the interests of the Princes and of a provincial, *bourgeois* Moderatism.

Mazzini arrived at Milan, unannounced, late on Friday evening, April 7. Already there were liberal stalwarts waiting to welcome him; others—Lombard leaders like Cattaneo and the Princess Belgiojoso, old comrades like Scipione Pistrucci and Rosales, and foreign exiles like Adam Mickiewicz—were hastening to the city. But the Provisional Government betrayed no excessive haste to recognise the Exile's presence. He had come uninvited, and just now, at Milan, the advent of a Radical, Republican Messiah was embarrassing. Milan had risen against the Austrians, but not for a Republic, and the Lombard nobles and leaders who composed the Government were largely Moderate in politics and Charles Albertists in sentiment. All the same, the populace was still to be reckoned with, and Sunday night saw a roaring demonstration of welcome with bands, banners and torches, and crowds that packed the square in front of Mazzini's hotel, the *Bella Venezia*. " They presented me with a flag. I spoke a few words. Then I was led up to the window with torches and the flag. The people were shouting like madmen. I spoke again. Then there came a deputation from the Provisional Government to ask me to go to them. I went. . . . Then at half-past ten . . . another crowd with music. . . . Then . . . some forty or fifty Genoese kissing my face and snatching my hands "[1]—and so onward with vociferous *evvivas,* civic guards of honour, illuminated windows, rhapsodic editorials and infinite flow of public oratory.

Alas, poor prophet! from all this he would have run away if he could. " Torches—cheers—a *diavolerio* " was his brief account of it all to his mother. For how much of the true faith was discernible behind it? Try as he would to interpret it as " a manifestation of the strength of the republican principle," in his heart he knew better. To his English friends he wrote: " Things are not as I could wish." How seldom they ever had been! Thus, though he was deeply moved, and found himself crying like a child when the lads of the Ceccopieri regiment, deserted from the Austrians and happy as schoolboys, marched past his window, singing and cheering, yet he was for the most part, he confessed, "without joy." The people, indeed, were magnificent. They were children, eager, generous, impulsive; but they were children also in their political ignorance, grasping at whatever was dangled glitteringly before them. And for the rest, the heroism and singleness of purpose which had inspired the barricades had not passed over to the Council Chamber. The Provisional Government was a heterogeneous affair, obstructed by divided counsels and conflicting interests. He noted it and was depressed. There was no evidence, he felt, that these men had ever got down to the roots of life: no sign that they had ever *seen* anything. They had not clearly seen even the issues of the National War itself. Beautiful, these newly kindled bivouac-fires of the young armies of Italy, but only so for those who saw them as altar-flames, and saw in them the pledge of the nation-temple that was yet to be reared. For the great work lay ahead, and the sword was not to be its instrument. The sword was for a world of tyrants and slaves; but it could create nothing, build nothing; and in the world of free men, brothers, citizens, there was to be no use for it. *That* was to be a world not for gladiators but for builders. To-morrow they must build Italy. And the next day they must unite with the emancipated peoples of the Continent and build the New Europe. . . . But, so far as he could discover, there was no report of anything of this in the Council Chamber in Milan.

And the confusion at Milan reflected the confusion in the country. "*Un Washington européen*," exclaimed the eloquent *Citoyen* Lamartine; "*voilà le besoin du siècle: le peuple, la paix, la liberté!*" Unfortunately, in lieu of the desiderated Washington, there were (in Italy) a Ferdinand, a Charles Albert, a Duke Leopold and a Pope Pius: the old territorial and dynastic rivalries were still active, and the policies of Rome, Turin, Florence, Milan and Naples were affected accordingly. Charles Albert, for all his Italian impulses, had, at the last, committed himself to action as much to forestall a republican movement in the North as to liberate Italy; and, with the best of patriotic intentions, the professional politicians at Turin were waiting to exploit the King's successes in the field less for the sake of a problematical United Italy than in the immediate interests of the territorial expansion of Piedmont. But the rise of an aggrandised and aggressive Piedmont in the North was not calculated to evoke a *Nunc dimittis* from an ecstatic Ferdinand in the South, nor to appease the territorial and political ambitions of Tuscany and of Rome. Thus, amid a riot of rival interests, the leaders of Italy, as distinct from her partially aroused and more or less eager but ignorant peoples, were blundering dizzily into the supreme crisis.

There was still, it was true, the Pope. More than any other prince, Pius could have assumed the leadership without exciting dynastic jealousies. His spiritual primacy over all the Catholic princes was unchallenged, and the title of Rome to the ideal sovereignty of Italy was beyond dispute. But where a poet-zealot like Friar Ugo Bassi, or a demagogue like Father Gavazzi, might have gone forward, Pius drew back. It was not for him to break every ecclesiastical tie and tradition, flout his Cardinals, brave the ire of the Habsburgs and the vengeance of the Jesuits, and leap into the molten confusions of a world revolution. St. Peter may have essayed to walk on the water; it was not for his successor to walk on fire. Thus the hosannas of the Roman crowds were already losing their fervour and lengthening out into calculated and disingenuous slogans. The myth—the verbal effigy—of a " Liberator Pope " was still being preserved and tricked out by Liberal demagogues; it was " good politics "; but it bore no more relation to the actual Pius than to the Bambino of Ara Celi; and the Pope himself, alarmed by a liberalism whose early impulses he had shared but whose ideas he had never comprehended, was now fulminating against Progress and the Utopists.

Clearly, this was not the Savona dream; and torchlight demonstrations in the public square, floral cascades from the balconies, compliments from the Provisional Government, and *evvivas* from the crowd, were no compensation to the prophet for lack of the true faith. It was in vain that he inveighed in private against the sinuosity of the diplomatic mind, in vain that he protested against the habit of citing the transactions and precedents of 1815, in vain that he cried " We must *create* !" Creation was not on the agenda of the politicians.

In the circumstances it was not unnatural that he should feel that the general situation served only to justify his own original programme. The way to National Unity was not the way of diplomatic huckstering and princely rivalry; rather, it lay along the lines of a popular movement which, sweeping aside the petty sovereigns and their sycophants, should advance under the national republican flag. Nevertheless, the crisis had found some, at least, of the princes *un*swept aside, and it must be met accordingly. Thus, within the limits of a difficult conscience he strove for conciliation and a realist policy. In his quaint English he wrote to his London friends of his intention to " plunge in the midst of all sorts of men, and try to see clearly through the state of things."

What he did see clearly was that everything must be subordinated to Italian Unity. This had been the burden of his correspondence before leaving Paris. He and his colleagues must constitute in the Italian press a democratic propagandist opposition to the provincialism, the *bourgeois* conservatism which the various Constitutions tended to promote : they must dig out convinced and capable Unitarians from every corner of the peninsula; they must combine with them and reconstitute the elements of " Young Italy " into a National Italian Society, dropping the old name because of its distinctively republican associations. All available forces were now to be concentrated upon this one programme—" Unity, not a political crotchet, but the thing upon which every other depends—our power of doing good, our mission in the world . . . the condition in which alone the Word may come to the world again from Italy." " The National Society does not aim at the success of this or the other form of government, but will urge the development of the national idea . . . in accordance with the declared aspirations of the Italian people." So he had written from Paris, and from the balcony of the Council Chamber at Milan he had struck the same note. He was ready " to work with the members of the Provisional Government, reserving till after the day of victory measures that would enable the people to decide upon the form of government."

Beyond this, it is true, he would not go. It was as a confessed republican that he entered Milan, and he promptly registered his adhesion to the local republican group, led by the ex-priest Sirtori, and marched with them, later, in the Corpus Domini procession. In short, it was precisely as a republican, and not as a neutral, that he made his offer of a political truce. And such a truce was in harmony with Charles Albert's own proclamation to the Lombards: "*Italians, my armies, by shortening the struggle, will afford you a security which will enable you, in a calm and unperturbed spirit, to reorganise your internal affairs; the will of the people shall be truly and freely expressed.*" The Mazzinian programme, then, was sane and realist. Even the sardonic Giovanni, watching developments from Paris, could quote, not altogether without sympathy, the tribute of Campanella (of the old, far-off balcony brotherhood): "Mazzini is the one Coryphæus of Democracy who has *ideas*; all the rest do nothing but holler."[2]

But the way of the prophet is hard; and the idealist who, for conscience' sake, and with a " Thus far and no further !" plants his feet in the way of practical expediency, is always urged to use it as a path and not as a terminus. And indeed why should he not now go further? From Genoa came the urgent offer of a seat in the Piedmont Parliament. Why not accept it? A like offer was going to the Ruffini brothers, and they would certainly accept. It involved the support of the monarchy, but along that line lay, perhaps, the one immediate avenue to political opportunity, since to mould the policy of Piedmont would be to direct the Italian movement. Maria seems to have endorsed the urgings of the Genoese liberals. They appealed to him through her to " sacrifice his personal beliefs to the good of Italy." What, then, if the hour had come to subordinate, not truth, but the *pride* of truth, to present practical necessity? Of the existing Piedmont Constitution, and of Piedmont's political importance under a so-called Moderate régime, he had only a contemptuous opinion; but Piedmont under Progressive leadership was another matter. Might it not easily become the banner-State of the national movement? And need he doubt his own powers? Need he shrink from measuring them against those of Balbo and D'Azeglio and Cavour and Gioberti? What if this were the call of destiny?

It was Charles Albert himself who brought the crisis to a head. From the royal camp came an envoy suggesting a *rapprochement personnel* with a view to Signor Mazzini's support of the immediate annexation of Lombardy under the Crown. Perhaps it is true, also, that the royal messenger hinted more or less directly at the offer of the Premiership and the attractive commission of drafting a new Constitution. At all events, a royal proposal was made, the terms were liberal, and the importunity of friends was insistent. "I am assailed," he writes his mother (May 5), "by folk who come to tempt me. I say 'tempt' because the suggestion that I should now re-nounce my beliefs is a real temptation."[3] It was characteristic of him that it was as a temptation and not otherwise that he treated the overture; and by the end of May he was writing privately to his English friends: "I have refused to be a M.P. for Genoa, and for I do not know what place in Piedmont: refused to be more than that with the man Ch. Alb.; refused all the offers of the tempter. . . . Do not believe . . . that it has been owing to pride, reaction or any other narrow feeling; no; I told all tempters the same words that I addressed to Ch. Alb. in my manifesto. . . ." Yet the very asperity of his reference to "the man Ch. Alb." suggests that the King's approach had momentarily shaken him. It was the temptation of power addressing itself to his heart in the form best fitted to move it—the guise of sacrifice for the good of Italy.

But what should he accept in exchange for his inner harmony? He must be free to utter his oracle and follow his dream. "To whomsoever could have assured me of the inde-pendence and prompt unity of Italy I would have sacrificed—not my belief, that was impossible—but all active endeavours for its speedy triumph." But that was the limit of compromise. Let the King understand, then, that the supreme necessity was Independence and Unity. A Piedmont-Lombardy kingdom would be at once too ambitious and too meagre: too ambitious to be easily accepted by the other Italian princes or the inter-ested Powers, too meagre to meet the need of the nation. But did the King really desire to be the architect of the nation? Then let him break with all other Italian potentates, openly declare for Unity and rally to the one national banner all patriots from the Alps to the furthest limits of Sicily. Let him do that, and the republican elements of the country would support him, would flock to him; but they would not sacrifice their flag to a King who refused to commune with the Italian idea.[4]   It was the challenge of the Open Letter once more, and once more an angry monarch turned away.

Yet Mazzini's intuition had hardly been at fault. The hour was critical. Austria was reeling under the first shock of the revolution. The fruits of victory were within Italy's grasp. But if they were to be gathered they must be gathered swiftly, and all the available resources of the nation must be flung into the field. The hour was crying for boldness of conception, audacity and swiftness of action, which would give the Habsburgs and the fugitive Italian princes no time to recover. Above all, the forces of popular enthusiasm must be evoked and directed, not repressed. The leaders must in truth " commune with the Italian idea " and the true genius of the revival, and make direct appeal to the nation.

This was never Charles Albert's mind. He and his counsellors distrusted the popular movement. His appeal for a political truce and a united front meant no more than a coalition of all parties for a Piedmont-Lombardy fusion. Thus while the supreme opportunity for decisive action was passing, while Radetzky and his dispirited Croat troops, in fifteen miles of lumbering columns, were allowed to trail off into the sanctuary of the Quadrilateral, unmolested save by the rains of heaven, the Charles Albertists were rushing through an *impromptu* political plebiscite for the annexation of Lombardy, and announcing the happy union of the two northern States. In Forbes' biting phrase, " while Radetzky was collecting bayonets Charles Albert was collecting votes." Meanwhile, the Pope was angrily repudiating responsibility for a national campaign, and Ferdinand of Naples, succumbing to the Bourbonic plague of perjury, was breaking his Constitutional oath and his patriotic pledges.

At this stage, however, it was still Charles Albert's hour. He had won victories—at Goito and Peschiera—and the North was at his feet. In a bright outburst of loyal enthusiasm at Genoa, Mazzini's writings were burned in the public square, and Garibaldi, arrived from overseas with his fighting-men, was received at the royal headquarters with frigid civility (had he not a Mazzinian past?) and informed that his services were not required. On the other hand, hopes of a pact between Turin and Rome revived, and the priest Gioberti was the man of the moment. The Giobertian programme, no less than the Mazzinian, lent itself to an opulent rhetoric, and the public was invited to contemplate (in advance) the spectacle of an Italian Pope binding the royal brow of the victor of Goito and Peschiera with the iron crown of the Lombards. In Milan (and from the hospitable balcony of the hotel *Bella Venezia*) the philosopher was fêted with due enthusiasm, and at a rousing banquet at Rome he was welcomed by the still irrepressible Ciceroacchio—in a slightly difficult metaphor—as the man who had opened the eyes of Italy with his pen. And while the ecstatic Romans, thronging the Via Borgogne, cheered the inspired ex-cleric on his balcony, the walls of Milan were being chalked with the legend, "*Death to Mazzini!*"

*   *   *   *   *

Careful historians have declared, indeed, that Mazzini gravely blundered by remaining at Milan. He had got on the nerves of the leaders—even of republican leaders like Sirtori; and when the adventurer Urbino made his foolhardy attempt to oust the Provisional Government by mob violence, Mazzini was blamed even for that. At Rome, on the other hand, his intervention would have been welcome and timely. So the argument runs. At Rome, however, the masters of the city showed no yearning desire for his advent. The Pope, his spiritual engagements complicated by a distressing decline in the currency and by certain recurrent embarrassments in respect of a Rothschild loan, was not looking for relief in the form of a Mazzinian diversion. At the end of April Pio Nono had, in fact, been moved pointedly to repudiate "the crafty counsels of those who," in their writings and otherwise, "maintained that the Roman Pontiff should preside over some new Republic of Italy."[5]   On the other hand, Liberalism, for the moment, was under the Giobertian spell. Thus Ciceroacchio, abetted by the journalistic rhapsodies of Dr. Sterbini, continued to delight—and slightly bewilder—the Clubs with assurances of the Holy Father's passionate democracy; and Count Mamiani, as Minister of the Interior, was expounding a scheme of his own for a Constitutional Papal Monarchy. In a persuasive passage the learned Count (he was something of a metaphysician as well as a minor poet) was able to demonstrate that whilst the Prince of the Church was, in the nature of things, incapable of error in deed or in judgment, it belonged to the piety of the State to reserve for purely spiritual affairs the Holy Father's supernatural and beneficent administration.

Rome, then, no more than Milan, was prepared to follow Mazzini. Nor was Florence, where the autocratic Guerrazzi desired no interference. Nor was Genoa, where the founder of Young Italy was still proscribed. Nor Turin, where Balbo, D'Azeglio, Cavour and Gioberti were sufficiently preoccupied. Nor Venice, where the Piedmont-Lombardy Fusionists were now predominant. Nor Naples, where Reaction was once more rearing its breakwater defences behind the abating floods of the revolution. There was not, it is true, a corner of Italy where disciples were not to be found, disciples who were his to uttermost devotion; and, in a vague way, their enthusiasm had penetrated to the masses. After all, it was his ideas, the apostolate of " Young Italy," which had supplied the electric voltage for all the new movements and revival-cults now active in Italy. But for all that, there was bitter truth in his own confession to Lamberti that he was finding himself an exile in his own country. His personal presence, potent, challenging and (almost in spite of himself) dominating—his presence in any given centre was an inconvenience to the men in power, reactionary and liberal alike. " Garibaldi," he wrote to his mother, " is the last illusion; but I am getting hardened to it all."

For it was not one of the least of Italy's misfortunes that already Garibaldi and Mazzini were drifting apart. Nor was it simply that Garibaldi's impulsive action in offering his services to the King without first reporting to the Mazzinian Committee was resented as a breach of faith; the antagonism went deeper. The fact was that the Montevidean chieftain was no longer the docile and eager young enthusiast who in the early days of " Young Italy " had brought to his master a hero-worshipping adoration, and whose devotion had led him to name his first boat the *Mazzini*. Twelve years of hard campaigning in the Uruguayan wilderness had made him, in his turn, a master of men. He was a child of the desert and the sea, self-taught, self-reliant; a natural poet whose stanzas were

deeds, exploits, battles. He was, in short, no longer a Mazzinian; he was a Garibaldian. Perhaps, too, the senior chief,
without intending it, was too proprietary in his attitude.
Perhaps he was apt to regard his junior with something of the
possessive solicitude of a missionary for an early and much-
prized convert, of a tutor for a promising scholar. He it was,
after all, who had taught Garibaldi patriotism—who had
kindled the poetry of the Nizzard's nature into flame. He it
was, too, who had nursed his protégé's reputation by publishing his American exploits far and wide in the revolutionary
press. But also their differences were rooted in their individual natures. Both were ardent, poetic, idealistic, but in
Mazzini the lyrical quality was under restraint to a studious
habit, a fixed faith, inflexible principle and a certain austere
pontifical egotism which was none the less uncompromising for
being founded upon religious self-renouncement. In Garibaldi,
on the other hand, it was all pure impulse, noble instinct,
quick, poetic intuition, a romantic passion for the chivalrous,
the heroic, and an unbounded self-confidence running into
innocent vanity which, again, under irritation, could turn into
suspicion and obstinate prejudice. Thus it was the antagonism
between a prophet-pedagogue and an ingenuous, wilful ward
who would now caress his mentor, now defy him, but never
accept his authority.

But in any case, circumstances being what they were, if
Mazzini elected to stand his ground in Milan, his decision was
not wildly unreasonable. He would show, at least, that he
was not to be driven out by intimidation. " I am here," he
wrote to the Ashursts, " disliked, dreaded, suspected, calum-
niated, threatened "; but he added, " I feel quite strong and
unmoveable and smiling . . . feeding my soul with its own
substance like the pelican with its little ones." To his anxious
parents he wrote beseeching them not to heed the idle gossip
of the Genoa cafés, where new rumours about him were in
circulation every day. As for his " sacrificing his private convictions to the good of Italy," let them observe the assumption
that those who gave that advice knew better than others wherein the good of Italy lay : " now as to that, I also ask permission
to have my own ideas." He was thinking, he declared, not of
Lombardy or Piedmont, but of Italy as a whole, and he was

persuaded it was necessary, whatever the immediate issue of events, for some few, at least, to "maintain the banner of the future unsullied by cowardly transactions."[6] For the rest, he drew courage from his few steadfast friends, particularly his English friends, of all classes. "Remember me as kindly as you can to *my* Mary," he writes to the Ashursts. "She is the very goodness." Mary was the kitchen help. "And you, my sweet friends, you all, my best of friends . . . I know that you are thinking of me often. I feel full with faith in you."[7]

And there were friends nearer to hand. He was now established in the Borgospesso, in the house of Rosales, and there the incorruptibles gathered around him. Even Agostino, *en route* for Genoa and Parliament, cheered him with a cordial visit; and Garibaldi, rejected of the King, sought him out. There was a prompt reconciliation, and the hero of Montevideo was consoled with a commission under the Provisional Government and a command on the Alpine front. And to add a touch of domestic diversion, ex-waif Susanna Tancioni reported herself. With her Perugian husband, Pio Tancioni, a "volunteer of Italy," she had packed her box and made her way to Milan. "It is probable," he writes to his mother, "that I shall send Susanna to Genoa. There is no need, in that event, to recommend her to you and the friends. . . . She looked after all my material interests in London, and I would not appear ungrateful for all the gold in the world." It was characteristic that he should feel the debt of gratitude was on his own side.

As for Maria herself, the Signora with the eyes of an aged Madonna and the tongue of a Deborah was content to concentrate upon her rôle as mother of Giuseppe Mazzini. Amid the intense political curiosity and the conflicting passions that agitated Genoa, she was now more than ever a centre of interest; but the political emissaries who cultivated her conversation for their own purposes found their match in this brusque old lady whose reserve was impenetrable and whose inquisition could be dangerous. Giovanni Ruffini, arrived from Paris, paid his dutiful respects and found her "self-contained, all reticence, all politics, and the negation of spontaneity."[8] Even Gioberti plied his arts and retired discomfited. "A Jesuit perfumed à *la* Parisienne " was the old dame's comment after he had bowed himself out. Her mother-heart was yearning to meet her son. She longed to pack her box and report herself, like Susanna, at Milan; but without a signal from him she would not stir. There was one God and Pippo was His prophet.

SPRING had passed into summer before Maria Mazzini took coach for Milan; and by that time the city was turning again to her son. For now the brief propitious gust that had fluttered Charles Albert's banners was dying down; and by the end of July the unhappy King was reeling back from Custoza across the rain-sodden plains, in full retreat on Milan. A dismayed Provisional Government hastily summoned Mazzini to its councils, and his advice was peremptory. There was no time for recrimination or debate, little for speech of any kind. Let government be vested at once in a Triumvirate of capable, energetic Milanese in the confidence of the people; let direct appeal be made to the citizenry; let there be a levy *en masse*, let earthworks be thrown up and the city equipped for defence; let provisions, munitions, funds be swiftly gathered. So he counselled: and he had his way. To support the appeal for military enrolment he himself headed the list of volunteers.

The transformation was immediate. In three days more was accomplished than, before, had been done in as many months. The streets were still tawdry with superabundance of weather-faded flags, and still variegated with the hues of diverse and often preposterous military uniforms; but the scene which, a while before, had suggested to young Dandolo the stage-embellishments of light opera was now vivid with swift and disciplined movement. The spirit of the Five Days was once more abroad. As for Mazzini himself, he was everywhere radiating electric energy, and on July 25—the anniversary of the death of the Bandieras—he released a characteristic appeal:

" We exist here below to labour fraternally to build up the unity of the human family so that the day may come when it shall represent *a single sheepfold with a single shepherd*—the Spirit of God, the Law. . . . Beyond the Alps, the sea, are other peoples striving by different routes to reach the same goal—betterment, association, the founding of an Authority which shall put an end to moral anarchy . . . an **Authority** which mankind may obey without remorse or shame. . . . Arise for the sake of these principles and not from impatience of suffering or dread of evil. Anger, pride, ambition and the desire for material prosperity—these are weapons common alike to the peoples and their oppressors, and even should you conquer with these to-day, you would fall again to-morrow. But principles belong to the peoples alone, and their oppressors can find no arms to oppose them."[1]

It was fitting that Maria Mazzini should witness at least the beginnings of this revival—fitting, says the Chronicler, that this long-deferred reunion should find her standing at last beside her son, with the Italian tricolour floating actually and symbolically above them. And did not the ladies of Milan honour the old Jansenist dame with what was for her the most appropriate of gifts—an illuminated Bible? No record has described for us the meeting of mother and son. For both it must have been charged with pathos no less than joy; it was a brief reunion, and it was fated to be the last.

But if only the Italian tricolour above their heads in those days had not borne also the cross of Savoy, Risorgimento history might have taken a different turn. Milan, dreading a return of the Croat butchers and women-floggers, was in the mood to offer desperate resistance; Venice, under Manin, was still at bay; Garibaldi and D'Apice were in Radetzky's rear with 30,000 men. Under the stimulus of Mazzinian direction the North might yet have roused the country. But after the vote of Fusion Milan was no longer mistress of her fate. She had placed herself under the protection of the House of Savoy, and now Charles Albert was to assume control. Too hesitant to achieve decisive victory in the field, he was able at least to prevent the political embarrassments of a Mazzinian ascendancy in the Lombard capital. Thus three days after Milan's Committee of Defence had been set up he deposed it in favour of a Military Commission of his own appointing. Came word also that His Majesty himself was on the way with a resolute army of 40,000 pledged to defend the city " to the last blood-drop." On August 5 the King, true to his word, entered the city at the head of his troops. On the same evening the incredible rumour was out that Milan, as fair bargain-price for the Piedmont army's safe withdrawal, was forthwith to be handed over to Radetzky. No doubt there was no Royal treachery.

It may have been true that the military situation was hopeless
—that the resources of the city were insufficient to maintain
the new army; and in any case the King was in the hands of
his Turin ministers. But that night at the Greppi Palace only
the bayonets of his soldiers saved a haggard and heart-broken
monarch from the fury of the people. For the rumour was
true, and Milan was to behold her King ride out with his
crestfallen 40,000 homeward. Before the catastrophe Maria
had returned to Genoa, and Mazzini, slinging his English
carbine (parting gift of gentle Mrs. Ashurst) over his shoulder,
had left for Garibaldi's camp.*

＊　　　＊　　　＊　　　＊　　　＊

By August 10 Mazzini was writing to the Ashursts: " After
having been a few days with Garibaldi, marched 22 miles a
day on foot, and reached Monza, near Milan, only to see it
fallen already in the hands of the enemy, here I am, safe
enough, as you see, for the present. What an overthrow!
What a bitter lesson to our monarchical people! What a sad
realisation of all my foreseeings! And how much more calculated than I myself was anticipating the betrayal has been!
And how beautiful again was Milan during the crisis! Had
not the King come there with his army the defence would
have been heroic."[2] The country was, in short, expiating " the
sin of having thrown at the feet, not of a principle, but of a
wretched man," the national flag.

His ire was at least understandable. The Turin Moderates
had forestalled him in the North; they had made use of all
their influence to thwart his national programme: and they
had made of their success only a demonstration of their utter
incapacity. The national movement which had begun with
so much promise had been diverted into a morass. As for himself, in the retreat from Monza he had left the ranks only
when it was evident that nothing more could be attempted for
Milan. At Lugano he had striven desperately with Colonel
Medici and Cattaneo to collect funds and forces to continue
the struggle in the mountains; but before reinforcements and
equipment were ready, Garibaldi, stricken with fever, had

* See Append. D.

retired to Nice, and Ramorino of " Savoy's expedition " had effectively foiled any further enterprise.

Henceforth, then, the struggle must be with Turin. From his hiding-place overlooking the Lugano lake he defined the issue in a series of articles in the London *Spectator*:

> " There are with us, as everywhere else, many shades of political opinion; but you will find, however thoroughly you search, but two parties—the *Moderate* and the *National* party; the party whose creed is the downward movement from the summit of society as it actually exists . . . to the people; and the party whose faith is in an upward movement and which seeks the formula of our progress, of our future life, from the very heart of the nation itself. The first party is represented by the notion, originating at Turin, of a Federative Diet; the other by the idea of an Italian Constituent Assembly."[3]

So he wrote, and in vigorous exposition enlarged upon the same theme in the columns of his newly-founded " *Italia del Popolo.*" And on the practical side, at least, he had fairly stated the issue. For whether with the Giobertian project of a Diet of loosely federated principalities under the Presidency of the Pope, or with the Cavourian policy of the gradual expansion of the kingdom of the House of Savoy, Turin was directly challenging the project of a Pan-Italian movement under the banner of the Italian people. And this challenge, as he understood it, struck down to the very roots of the Italian question. It meant, indeed, a conflict more fundamental than that with Vienna. For the struggle with Vienna was for the soil, while this with Turin was for the soul, of Italy. So, at least, he regarded it. For him the issue was whether Italy should be begotten and brought forth and baptised in the faith of the Italian Hetæria or should be conceived in compromise and shapen in diplomacy, and trained to an imitative, sterile career under the tutelage of the reactionary Powers.

So he braced himself anew for the struggle. Turin might be in opposition, Milan lost to the revolution, Naples likewise; but Venice and Tuscany and the Centre remained. And there was Rome. Always before him there was that last supreme resource. And his programme was plain. Let a Roman Constituent Assembly be convened and a Republican government established in the Papal States. From the Roman Assembly let it be proclaimed that a post-war National Assembly was the only legitimate organ for the settlement of the Italian question.   Meanwhile, and with all promptitude, let a Provisional Assembly be formed of representative groups from Sicily, Tuscany, Venice, Rome itself and all other accessible quarters.   The Turin Moderates would certainly override the Liberals and refuse to recognise the Roman Republic; but with Piedmont neutral the national struggle could be directed from Rome itself, under the people's banner and free from Moderate and dynastic complications.   Even so the issue was involved in desperate uncertainties.   To Mrs. Ashurst he wrote:

> "It would require a volume to tell you my life during the last five months—my feeling still an exile among my own countrymen—my foreseeing everything, but one, that has happened . . . the outburst of enthusiasm for the national creed . . . the threatenings and insults printed, placarded around me at a short interval . . . the elements of better things lost one by one through the infernal tactics of Ch. Albert and the Milanese Government—the hanging of all my hopes on a popular defence of Milan, from which a new life could have sprung, and my seeing the last hope vanishing . . . all these things, with all my internal life, I should wish . . . to tell you. . . . Still I do not despair, and it may be that I succeed in breaking up all these cobwebs. . . ."[4]

Some time in November the Roman web was "broken up" swiftly enough, and in a way not to be desired.   Thus, in the Government of Rome, Count Pellegrino Rossi had succeeded the metaphysical Mamiani as the last hope of the Papal intransigeants.   Cold, haughty, bureaucratic, unflinching, he had signalised his advent by surrendering to the tender mercies of the King of Naples the fugitive Liberals of the Southern revolution.   "You may tell the diplomatic corps," he declared to Count Spaur, "that the Pope's authority can be broken down only by passing over my body."   On the 15th of that month his lifeless body, lying across the steps of the Capitol, was duly passed over by a howling mob of expectorating, blue-bloused *Reduci* and Ciceroacchians.   Mazzinians were not implicated in the assassination, though Garibaldi openly extolled the deed, and even the gentle Margaret Fuller, friend of Emerson, in Rome at the time, condoned it.   "Had Rossi," she wrote, "lived to enter the Chamber he would have seen the most terrible and imposing mark of denunciation . . . the whole House, without a single exception, seated on the benches of

Opposition. . . . For me, I never thought to have heard of a violent death with satisfaction, but this act affected me as one of terrible justice."[5]

For the next two days there were monster demonstrations before the Papal Palace with ever-swelling vociferation, cheers for "Liberty" and cries of "Down with the Jesuits!" Conspicuous among the leaders were the shrill-voiced little Sterbini, the ever-irrepressible Ciceroacchio and the burly Prince of Canino, and around them by the tens of thousands were gathered a mixed multitude—citizens, Civic Guards, students, *Carabinieri,* club-men, Tiber-side ruffians—with flags bearing many devices. In the Palace grave-faced foreign ambassadors and pale priests surrounded the Holy Father, who sat as one astonished—bewildered shepherd whose sheep, by some black enchantment, had become wolves. Until at last, after twenty-four hours of demonstration, with futile parleys, and deputations coming and going, the incessant ominous roar without became more insistent, bullets scarred the Quirinal walls, and a priest, passing by an open window, fell dead. Within the Palace precincts the handful of Swiss halberdiers stood firm and barricaded the gates, but to what purpose now? This was no passing *fracas* or mob-riot, occasioned by Rossi's death. His death was an incident in the protest, and no more. Something was stirring in the heart of Rome. The pent-up passions of two years of delirious hope and tormenting dalliance and shameful disillusion were now uncontrollably finding vent.

Under protest the Pope submitted. A democratic Ministry was conceded (under Galletti, Sterbini and Muzzarelli) and jubilantly acclaimed. But a week later the Pontiff (disguised, it was said, as a coachman) emerged from the Palace and was whisked into a waiting conveyance and driven rapidly along the Appian Way and over the Alban hills to Gaeta. The Head of the Church on earth was an exile and Rome was without its Prince.

A quarter of a century later little Roma Lister, in her white frock and veil, knelt with her companions before the now aged Pontiff. "The Pope did not seem to be interested in anything but our names. When it came to my turn I answered 'Roma.' The Pope hesitated, and a slight chill seemed to fall."

" Brutto nome!" murmured the Holy Father. "*Ugly name!
Has she no other?*"[6]

Meanwhile the man sitting behind closed casements in the
little upper room in Lugano studied the chess-board of events.
He had accepted and countered the Turin gambit, and while
from the Watcher at Gaeta came murmurs of angry protest
("abominable, monstrous, illegal, impious, sacrilegious and
outrageous!") the thin hand stretched across the board and,
move by move, the pieces were advanced. On December 11
Galletti and two colleagues were nominated as Supreme Junta
to act in the regretted absence of the Pope, and announced the
early convocation of a Roman Constituent Assembly, to be
elected by manhood suffrage. On January 21, '49, the election
was held and a hundred and fifty Deputies were returned,
among them Deputies Garibaldi and Mazzini. On February 7
Deputy Filopanti of Bologna moved in the Assembly: " That
the Papacy had in fact and law ceased to exercise temporal
sovereignty over the Roman State; That the Pope be given
every guarantee necessary to the free exercise of his spiritual
authority; That the Government of the Roman State shall be
democratic and shall assume the name of the Roman Republic. . . ."

But a chess-game makes a poor figure. The man at Lugano
was no Mazarin or Richelieu, and this was no contest of nicely-
matched diplomacies; for him it was a struggle with principalities and powers for a kingdom of the spirit. "We have
in our hands the destinies of Italy, and the destinies of Italy
are the destinies of the world." " Think of me," he writes
to his English friends; "if in your most friendly mood, you
shall do me good. Whisper about me [together]. . . . I need
my guardian angels." And from Rome Goffredo Mameli,
Adele Zoagli's* son, sends him the message of destiny, com-
pressed into three words: " ROME REPUBLIC COME."

* See p. 32.

VIEWED as pure drama and with an eye for the bold external effect, Mazzini's journey Romeward was indeed strangely impressive. Eighteen years earlier, in his Savona cell, he had beheld his vision of a Republican Rome, centre of a new moral unity for Europe and mankind. Arrayed between that vision and its attainment had stood embattled tyrannies and entrenched traditions. Arrayed against it had stood the might of Imperial Austria, the anathemas of the Pope, a cordon of scaffolds, a barbed entanglement of intrigue and persecution. Yet, against the counsel of the wise and the broad derision of the mighty, he had hewn his way through. The Pope had fled, the princes likewise, and for the moment the puissance of Absolutism had been paralysed. The Republic of Rome was in being, and emblazoned upon its walls was the legend that proclaimed the dreamer citizen of the City of his dreams: " GIUSEPPE MAZZINI CITTADINO ROMANO."

Yet a closer view revealed how the purity of the Savona ideal was now dashed with dark confusions. The Republic of Rome was after all the republic of Ciceroacchio and Sterbini and Canino, of the Circolo Popolare and the secret societies, and the stain of Rossi's blood was still upon the steps of the Capitol. In the eyes of the Powers, the new republic was no messianic emergence but a bankrupt and ruffian government, indulging for the moment in an orgy of law-making, but likely at the first internal crisis to pass into anarchy and violence. So, indeed, Guerrazzi had warned him. " For the love of heaven," he had written, " beware of entangling yourself in the follies of men who, if they are not wholly scandalous, are without honour or reputation." Thus, now that the important hour had struck, he shrank from the challenge of it. Was it that he had something of the feeling that haunted Byron as he set out for Greece on the final enterprise—that what had lured him as the poetry of heroic action might just as well serve as a theme for a satirical lampoon?

At all events he had delayed his journey. "I ought to be there," he wrote in December, "but I feel worn out . . . quite unable to agitate personally and undergo the usual *procédé* of ovations and counter-manifestations." "Would to God I could do some good, still keeping shut in and invisible to every mortal creature." To Mrs. Ashurst he had written as early as September: "As far as I am concerned I am withered, lost: through my own or other people's fault, I was evidently not fit for living in this time of hours."[1] "God, I think, begins to forsake me. I feel disheartened, weak in soul, wavering, gloomy."[2]

At Lugano, in fact, the old fits of morose depression had threatened to return upon him. He wishes for Giuditta or some other sympathetic presence "with whom I might exchange a smile and forget this everlasting political business"; and then, in a curious confessional letter to his mother, he writes that so long as he is still subject to these "upsurgings of poesy" in his nature, the presence of any woman-friend would only beguile him "into dalliance with individual affections"; and he adds that he feels this danger so keenly that some mornings, in his cloistral hiding-place, when the sun shines brightly and he opens his casement window, the view across the lake affects him "like a temptation," and he is bound to shut the casements and blot the alluring picture from his mind.[3] For was he not "consecrated to a Duty"? "Joseph" must be reckoned as dead; only "Mazzini" remained, and Maria herself must be "a Roman mother" and urge him to his task. And when at the end of December he had left Lugano, passing through Switzerland to Marseilles (Grenchen re-visited *en route*), and from Marseilles by steamer southward, he was still shrinking from the ordeal. Thus to Emilie Ashurst Hawkes he had written from Marseilles (January 26): "I am still here trying to gather up and regain the moral strength that will be required by and by. It would appear ridiculous to anybody—not to you—but it is a fact that the landing at Leghorn, the sort of ovation that I shall have there, the speech *obligé* from a balcony, the unavoidable flood of *politiques de café*, and so forth, are now a perfect horror to me."[4]

It had to be endured. There was a poignant hour when the Marseilles steamer called at Genoa and the silent traveller on deck had seen the city lights twinkling through the dusk and heard the sound of the old familiar bells floating out over the waters; then a princely welcome at Leghorn with guards of honour, torchlight processions and pealing of bells more clamorous and less familiar; then on to Florence, where, after welcoming banquets and civic illuminations, he had made a vain attempt to bring Tuscany into union with the Republic of Rome. Guerrazzi was in control, and the "epigrammatic smile" was once more sadly in evidence, with other manifestations more choleric. Tuscany should not make common cause with the new masters of the Holy City.

Yet from February 9 to March 2 he had lingered on in Florence. There was, in fact, good reason. He was the guest of Giuditta Sidoli.

Strange how this one woman appears and reappears in the crises of his life! She it was who had helped him to found "Young Italy"; she it was who, in the hour of disaster, had protected him from himself and had been "the angel of his exile." And at least through all the intervening years no other woman had been able truthfully to say of him, "He is my lover." And now, with Rome and destiny beckoning him and his soul shaken anew with doubts and oppressed with forebodings, she it was who once more stood by him, understanding him, chiding him, heartening him, as in the olden days. "I am writing from Giuditta's house," he tells Lamberti. "To see her once more has given me more joy than I am able to express." And thus, in the decisive hour, she had crowned him with her faith, and, for the defence of his Republic, had given into his charge her only son. "Good, holy, constant Giuditta!"

So at last he had taken his reluctant leave and proceeded Romeward. Politically he was still depressed, and the sharp rebuffs from Guerrazzi, the failure to bring Tuscany into line with Rome, had further dispirited him. "I am leaving this very night [March 2] for Rome," he had written the Ashursts, ". . . rather gloomy, without any consciousness of power within me, wishing for physical action on a barricade or some other way more than for any other . . . mood [mode] of activity. . . . Did you see Gioberti's behaviour? . . . I do not like Guerrazzi at all."[5] In the same strain he writes to his mother: "I feel, not physically but morally, exhausted." What, after all, if Guerrazzi were right? What if the new republic should prove but a mockery of his dream? What if he were moving toward a vulgar farce inviting the coarse laughter of the world?

But in the mellow light of the March evening as, for the first time, he beheld the City, he knew himself matched to the fateful supreme task and was conscious of inward empowerment. "Go out of Rome," he wrote in after days to an English friend, "five or six miles in the direction of the Tuscan road, so as to get back to the City toward sunset, and feel, once at least . . . as I did." "I never did feel so much Immortality in Death as there—a secret of immense Life to come from there to us and others." Ten years later, in his manifesto "*Ai Giovani d' Italia,*"[6] he reviewed the scene. He had approached the City along the Tuscan road. The weather was peculiarly mild (roses had bloomed in the Roman gardens throughout the winter); the skies were soft and clear, and the sun was setting across the Campagna. Here in bygone ages the races of mankind had met and mingled; here had rolled the tides of the barbarian invasions; here the very dust beneath the wayfarer's feet was the dust of Peoples. Thus for the moment it seemed to him that the Campagna, with its vast, pensive solitude, its brooding silence, was a Campo Santo filled with immemorial graves. But yonder in the distance, islanded in that immensity, was that which witnessed, not to death, but to the life of the ages: yonder, solemn and majestic, stood the Eternal City itself. Twice within those walls had the world's life been organised; twice had Unity been elaborated for mankind. Yonder stood the Temple of the mediæval, the Christian, world: there, too, the Temple of the ancient Pagan world; and now these two worlds awaited a third, vaster and more sublime—the fulfilment of the trinity of history whose word was Rome!—And this had been the Savona dream; but now the Word proclaimed itself anew and with irresistible power to his own soul. "I did feel that power, I did feel the pulsations of the immense, eternal life of Rome through the enswathements with which priests and courtiers had covered the great

Sleeper as with a shroud."—And now the whole Campagna itself took on a different aspect. It was springtide, and he became conscious that the silence around him was pullulant, vibrant as with the stirring of new life. To him it seemed a portent of resurrection, the stirrings of reviving generations needing only the fiat that should call them forth. The Campagna was no field of Death; already it seemed multitudinous with the concourse of the united peoples of the future.

Thus in the gathering dusk he journeyed on. " I entered the City . . . with a deep sense of awe, almost of worship," feeling " as I passed through the Porta del Popolo . . . an electric thrill run through me—a spring of new life." Seeking to avoid a demonstration, he had entered alone and unannounced. Here and there, perhaps, as at Milan, a passer-by—some student or artisan or bare-footed friar—recognised the slight, sombre figure, and hurried to spread the news. The author of *The Disciples* has imagined that Friar Ugo Bassi was one of them :

> " And late one night, in the first days of March,
> When beds of violets scented all the air,
> And marigolds were in the springing grass,
> Came Ugo Bassi home, and, as he passed,
> Spake but these words, with radiant, awe-struck face
> That lighted all before him : ' I have seen
> Mazzini !' "

*　　*　　*　　*　　*

Some time in 1839, at a reunion of Polish exiles in Paris, an incident occurred which George Sand has related in detail. Mickiewicz, it seems, was present, and, in an informal discourse of a more or less literary character, dwelt upon great faith and great love as the essentials of great poetry. Then followed the incident which George Sand relates : " No one seems able to describe exactly what happened. Everyone present received a different impression and no two witnesses agree. Some declare he spoke for five minutes. Others insist he talked for an hour. The one thing certain is that he aroused so much emotion that the entire audience fell into a sort of delirium. All over the hall cries and sobs were heard. . . . Count Plater

returned home in such a state of exaltation that his wife . . .
concluded he had lost his mind. Then as soon as he related,
not the actual discourse (for no one has been able to repeat a
word of it), but its substance and effect . . . Countess Plater
fell into the same strange state"[7]—and so onward, the *furore*
spreading by contagion.

Madame Sand's comment is that there is in most men a
capacity for Ecstasy, active in the few, repressed in the many,
and always belonging to the perilous borderland of the mind.
Thus prophetic vision, illuminism, convulsionism, were all
manifestations of Ecstasy, varying according to the individual
bias and quality. Mickiewicz (declares Madame Sand) was an
Ecstatic, sharing to some degree the divine madness " con-
spicuously noticeable in many illustrious ascetics " from St. John
to St. Joan.

This theory, more novel then than now, may well have engaged the same gifted woman ten years later when both
Mickiewicz and Mazzini (whom she dubbed "her saint")
were at Rome. Others not remote from the ecstatic type were
either in, or hastening to, the City. Soon, for example, the
dark blue straggle of shaggy Garibaldians were to make picturesque entry, with the red-shirted Chief himself, leonine,
majestic, statuesque, sitting his white charger, his cloak flung
back over his shoulder. Riding close at hand, too, would be
Ugo Bassi, his brown hair curling down upon his shoulders,
his beard long and square-cut, his breast and right hand scarred
from the fighting at Treviso (but he bears no other weapons
than his crucifix and breviary); and in his saddle an English
Shakespeare, a *Byron* and the manuscript of his own unfinished poem. There was the boy-officer Morosini, too,
in his uniform of the *Bersaglieri,* his cock-feather plumes
curling gallantly over his hat, and Kosciuszko's pistols in his
belt. There was young Goffredo Mameli, the soldier-poet.
There were many more—Ecstatics all, if Madame Sand must
be believed.

And how, indeed, can one better explain the crowded events
and exploits of those brief months of the great Triumvirate
than as the contagion of a strange Ecstasy? How else could a
State, lately seething with faction and demoralised alike by
confusions at home and calamities abroad—how else could such

a State have been wrought into so potent a unity? How else could an isolated City have been persuaded to defy the menace of the advancing legions of Austria, Spain, the kingdom of Naples and the Republic of France, and withal to set its hand to the fashioning of domestic reforms which, for sobriety and courage of conception, have commanded the respect of posterity? And how, except for the contagion of Ecstasy, can one explain the thousand individual exploits that gather around such names as Garibaldi, Masina, Manara, of Giacomo Medici and Ugo Bassi, of Bixio and the boy Morosini?

It is true also that from the first Mazzini had around him his own personal devotees: faithful, self-abnegating Maurizio Quadrio; Aurelio Saffi, a young nobleman of Forli; Adriano Lemmi, whose wealth had financed the Lombard Volunteers; Carlo Pisacane, the fiery, free-thinking son of the Duke of San Giovanni; Goffredo Mameli, the young soldier-poet; Giuseppe Petroni, the Bolognese, deformed in body but indomitable in spirit; and with these a few old comrades of the Swiss exile like Scipione Pistrucci, La Cecilia, and Gustavo Modena and his noble wife. But the Rome of the clubs and cafés and even of the Assembly itself was, to say the least, problematical. The head of the Executive Council was the aged Carlo Armellini; and Armellini, though a lawyer of some erudition, was of only mediocre ability, and brought to the councils of State little more than a courtly, old-world dignity and a cultivated resemblance to the Emperor Napoleon. And for the rest, Ignazio Guiccioli, in charge of Finance, was honest and incapable; Aurelio Saffi, " all mildness and philosophy "—and courage— was still inexperienced; while the loudest voice was that of Pietro Sterbini, the club-politician and journalist. Farini with his anti-Radical prejudices, paints an unfavourable picture of the administration:

" Sterbini . . . brought into dependence upon himself the multitudes who were wont to get alms from the Municipality, and applied to Parliament for means of supporting them and even of finding work for such artisans as were without it. These crowds he distributed under chiefs whom he could trust so that by his agency and that of Ciceroacchio the school of revolt was brought under . . . thorough command. Knots of people might be seen prowling through the streets of Rome, furnished with hoes, and on their way towards *Tor di Quinto,* where they

made a show of working . . . who, on their way back, noisy and
touched with wine, made uproar according to orders . . . going round
at night with Cardinals' hats and one of the kind which the Pope uses.
. . . The police was in the hands or under the control of the mischief-
makers."[8]

On the whole it was a Government of well-meaning mediocrity
mixed with a wild and unprincipled element capable of bolting
the administration at any time of crisis. Vannucci, as envoy of
Guerrazzi's Government, studied the Assembly at its delibera-
tions and reported "many speeches and no decisions . . . good
intentions but neither discipline nor dignity . . . empty declamation and recrimination."[9] Moreover, the financial embarrassments inherited from the Papal administration were aggravated
by a declining revenue and increased public expenditure; and
if order was still being maintained in the city, plunder and
anarchy were running riot in the outlying towns. What chance
was there, then, to weld these elements into a unity and inspire
them with a worthy purpose? What chance to breathe a
Roman soul into this heterogeneous mass—the loungers of the
Pincio, the denizens of the underworld of political and ecclesiastical conspiracy, the wealthy and critical patricians, the
illiterates of the Trastevere, the light-hearted populace whose
enthusiasm was more easily vamped by a procession than
governed by a principle however sublime? Yet from the hour
of his entry into the Roman Assembly Mazzini dominated
Rome.

We are still able to picture the scene. The floor of the
Chamber was occupied by a full muster of deputies, the galleries
crowded by the general public. President of Assembly Galletti
was in the chair. Things were going none too well with the
Administration, and the deputies were in one of their frequent
recriminatory moods. The diminutive but turbulent Sterbini,
hotly criticised for incapacity in his Department, had resumed
his seat, breathless and dishevelled, after an angry harangue,
and the next victim, poor Guiccioli, had found his utterance
"choked by indignant emotion" and had sat down amid loud
uproar. It was one of those scenes of "disorder and empty
declamation" which Envoy Vannucci had described to his
Tuscan masters. And it was then that Deputy Mazzini,
member for Ferrara, was observed to enter the Chamber. At

his appearance, says Donaver, all the deputies rose to their feet, and Galletti, inviting him to a seat beside the Presidential chair, introduced him to the Assembly.

For most of those present this was their first sight of the man who had already become a mythic figure in the eyes of the nation. He was now in his forty-fifth year; his black hair, thin at the temples, was still innocent of grey; he wore a close-cut beard; his spare form was garbed, as always, in black; his manner, modest and composed, suggested an almost English reserve. Acknowledging the demonstration, he declared it ought rather to have been given by him to the Assembly, " for all the little good that I have, not done, but attempted to do, has come to me from Rome." The brief speech that followed, Farini gives in full,* but probably no verbal report could reproduce it. What men understood was that the speaker was pouring out the stored wine of his own innermost thought and faith, the vintage of the exile years.

Nor was the Mazzinian contagion confined to the Roman population. For example, there was Margaret Fuller, Countess Ossoli, then lodging in the Piazza Barbarini. " Last night" (March 8), she wrote, " Mazzini came. . . . He looks more divine than ever after his new, strange sufferings. . . . The crisis is tremendous, and all will come on him, since if anyone can save Italy . . . it will be he. But he is very doubtful if this be possible. . . . Freely would I give my life to aid him, only bargaining for a quick death." A few weeks later she wrote to Emerson in the same key. Mazzini was a great man, " in mind a great poetic statesman, in heart a lover, in action decisive and full of resource as Cæsar. Dearly I love Mazzini. . . . His soft, radiant look makes melancholy music in my soul; it consecrates my present life, that, like the Magdalen, I may, at the important hour, shed all the consecrated ointment on his head."[10] The Ecstasy had reached the Piazza Barbarini.

In one particular, certainly, Margaret Fuller had prophesied truly—all would come upon Mazzini. For within a month of his arrival the Assembly balloted for a new Triumvirate, and Mazzini headed the poll. With him were Armellini and

* It is faithfully interpreted in *The Disciples*, by Mrs. Hamilton King.

Aurelio Saffi. What was involved in that association was patent from the first: it was "Sieyès, Ducos and Napoleon." The tribute of Carlo Pisacane, an agnostic and a Socialist, was to the point: "Giuseppe Mazzini soared above the other two on the wings of genius, and his opinion prevailed in every department: his intelligence shone resplendent; an absolute element, this, of grand conceptions. No one contested his superiority"[11]—not even Sterbini, who preferred to resign.

Yet Mazzini's was not the ascendancy of the Demagogue nor even of the Hero. Both types were represented—in Ciceroacchio and Garibaldi—and they were definitely subordinate. Nor was his the pre-eminence of a *Tyrannus* exercising an iron authority with all the auxiliars of external magnificence, the pomp and parade of power. It was a spiritual ascendancy ruling by influence and weaving around the souls of men an other-worldly spell. And certainly no ruler was ever less given to ostentation. Installed in the Quirinal he demanded a room "small enough to feel at home in." His one solace was his guitar, his only luxury (apart from indispensable cigars) a bunch of flowers daily renewed. He lived on two francs a day, dining at a second-class restaurant and, during the siege, limiting himself to raisins and bread: his modest salary of 32 l. a month he gave to charity. And for the rest, he held himself accessible at all hours to the humblest citizen who might seek his counsel; indeed his rooms were so much at the mercy of the public that Arthur Clough, also in Rome at this time, continued to wonder that no spirited Jesuit had looked in with a pistol. Such a man ruled Rome less as a Duce than as a Saint.

Only in what affected his specific task was he arbitrary, and even here his character was complex. Thus Clough's impression was that of a certain subtlety. "I . . . paid my visit to Mazzini . . . he discoursed with me for half an hour. He is a less fanatical, fixed-idea sort of man than I had expected; he appeared shifty, and practical enough."[12] In office he was certainly capable of compromise and perhaps of tergiversation. The inveterate critic of ecclesiastical superstitions, he attended Mass as Triumvir and sanctioned State processions of the Bambino; and by recognising the distinction between Church and State, the religious and the secular, he lent countenance to a system which otherwise he was prepared to denounce as atheistical and immoral. Of the political wisdom of his attitude, as against Garibaldi's impulsive desire to " shut the Holy Shop," there has never been any question, and in compromising his private convictions he bowed to the necessities of his position; but withal he had, like Gladstone, the dangerous power of self-hypnotism, and one is left wondering how far a prolonged continuance in power would have affected him—how far his Italian subtlety would have carried him, and in what direction. What is not conceivable is that it would ever have diverted the main current of his purpose.

For in truth, whatever the complexities of his nature, the decisive hour had found him in harmony with his own spirit and raised to the highest elevation of his faith. It was not, indeed, that he moved in a region of exalted and extravagant hopes. On that score he had no illusions. As early as January he had outlined the general prospects with sufficient realism. "The Austrians *must* interfere. . . . The Pope is endeavouring to raise a reaction . . . the King of Naples is threatening Rome, the Grand Duke of Tuscany is preparing to run away and protest; Spain, Louis Napoleon, everybody, seem to be against us. We stand alone. . . . Shall we be able to resist? I do not know. . . . If there is any hope, it is in our position being very clear and well-defined, and in our Party having the leadership of the war. And even then——"[13] It was rather that he was living and moving in the white radiance of his dream, at once alive to the responsibilities and superior to the frustrations of the time. Even if the Republic were foredoomed to extinction, that was not the sovereign consideration. *That* was that the Republic should contribute itself to history as an Event whose significance no power could thereafter annihilate, and as a witness which no subsequent apostasy could destroy. Thus he beheld the city as if with a great shining about her, even as having the light of God, and he summoned men to walk in that light. *"Here in Rome we may not be moral mediocrities. We must act as men who have the enemy at their gates, and at the same time as men who are working for eternity."* So he declared in a Triumviral proclamation. One may apply to him, in those critical days and months, his own description of Schiller's Posa: " A breath of superhuman virtue

appears to diffuse itself around him, the sense of a solemn hope,
a calmness as of revelation." He had said, as Swinburne sang
of him,

> " When all Time's sea was foam,
> ' Let there be Rome,' and there was Rome."

THE man in the back room at the Quirinal had no cause to complain that events crawled on laggard feet. The month of March which saw the appointment of the new Triumvirate at Rome saw also Gioberti's fall from power in Turin, broken by his hostile policy to the new republic. It saw also a pallid and bodeful Charles Albert, mounted on sable steed and cloaked in ominous black, once more taking the field against Austria. It saw his final overthrow (after the inevitable Ramorino had ceded the pass) at Novara, and his mournful abdication and departure to a Portuguese monastery. It was the month in which Maria Mazzini heard a republic proclaimed once more in Genoa, and then (after vain hope of succour from the inevitable Ramorino) heard also the cannon of La Marmora reducing it to submission. Moreover, it was the month that saw Tuscany under Guerrazzi, after rejecting the Roman Republic's overtures, succumb ingloriously to a counter-revolution, leaving only Rome and heroic Venice, isolated in her lagoons, to continue the national resistance. It was, incidentally, the month that saw Ramorino's career terminated at last by a Piedmont firing-squad; and finally it was the month that found Paris resolving in its Republican Assembly to support the interests and honour of France if necessary by a partial occupation of Italian territory.

With such a month now behind them the Triumvirate had to look to the future. And besides the imperative question of defence, there were other difficult and urgent problems. Thus Finance, always disturbed in a time of revolution, was causing grave concern. The Papal Government had left in this department a legacy of embarrassments, and Sterbini's administration of the Public Works had increased the expenditure without improving the revenue. Even Triumvirs could not work miracles upon a depleted Treasury, and with gold at a premium and paper at 42 per cent. discount the situation was critical. Perhaps the most popular substitute for a miracle would have been the confiscation of the property of the Papalists who had retired with the Pope; but against this "most odious of revolutionary expedients"* Mazzini set his face. He ordered a new issue of Treasury bonds, and, reluctantly, repudiated interest payment on the issues of the late Papal Government.

But also it belonged to the honour of the Republic to deal without delay with the problem of poverty. As far as possible the unemployed were absorbed into the public services, but the Triumvirate turned its attention to bolder measures. A scheme was sanctioned for the withdrawal of necessitous families from overcrowded and insanitary areas and their settlement in specially selected localities in the city and provinces. As an earnest of this, " and in order to consecrate to benevolence what past tyranny had employed for torture," the Offices of the Holy Inquisition were taken over and equipped as model tenements at a nominal rental. A more far-reaching reform aimed at settling the peasantry on the land. The Triumvirate provided for the public administration of the mediæval estates of the Church and decreed that a large portion of the rural domains of religious corporations and other *main-mortes* should be farmed under a system of small-holdings. "All property was safe except the enormous estates of the Church, which the mildest reform could not have left untouched. In other countries, Catholic and Protestant alike, the wealth accumulated by the mediæval Church had undergone large curtailment by a process of which the propertied class had been the chief beneficiaries. But it was not for squires, courtiers or capitalists that Mazzini laid his hand on ecclesiastical property. It was for the benefit of the poorer peasants. . . ."[1]

Nor was ecclesiastical reform overlooked. The Triumvirate decreed the prohibition of fees for the performance of religious duties and provided for the "more fitting payment of the expenses of public worship" and for the readjustment of ecclesiastical emoluments in the interests of the poorer parish clergy. For the rest, taxes which fell heavily upon the poorer classes were removed, the tobacco and salt monopolies abolished, the death penalty cancelled, the liberty of the Press established and the electorate founded upon a basis of universal suffrage. Withal anti-clerical violence and vandalism were promptly

* Trevelyan.

suppressed. "Priests," reports Clough, "walk about in great comfort—arm-in-arm with a soldier perhaps; in cafés and legnos and all profane places they are seen circulating at least as freely as government paper . . . the Bambino also drives about to see the sick in infinite state and is knelt to and capped universally." The soldiers, he adds, were well-behaved, "far more seemly than our regulars"; "it is pleasant to my pastoral soul to see them sitting by market-women and shelling peas"; and ladies walked in the Corso till after 10 p.m. "Assure yourself," he writes to Palgrave, "that there is nothing to deserve the name of 'the Terror.' . . . One sees no intimidation. Since May 4 the worst thing I have witnessed has been a paper in MS., put up in two places in the Corso, pointing out seven or eight men for popular resentment. This had been done at night; before the next evening a proclamation was posted in all the streets from (I am sure) Mazzini's pen, severely and scornfully castigating such proceedings."[2] A typical instance of his moral authority over the populace is described by Mr. Bolton King: "Once in the fear of imminent attack upon the city the crowd fetched a few confessional boxes from the churches to make barricades. Mazzini reminded them that from those confessionals had come at all events words of comfort to their mothers. It is perhaps the most convincing proof of his grip on the people's hearts that the confessionals were taken back.[3]

Thus did the man in the Quirinal strive with prodigious energy to fashion his city after the pattern of his dream. "*Neither intolerance nor weakness. . . . Inexorable as to principles, tolerant and impartial as to persons. . . . Economy in the public offices, morality in the choice of officials. . . . Severe verification, order and control in finance. . . . No war of classes . . . no wanton or unjust violation of the rights of property, but a constant disposition to ameliorate the condition of the least favoured. . . . Frugality and caution in legislation, vigilance and firmness in administration*"—so he would have it. His energy was tireless; he seemed almost to have dispensed with sleep; men meeting him for the first time felt, like Saffi, that he had known them for a lifetime and needed no parley; they were surprised, like Clough, to find in him no sultanic pose, no arrogant dogmatism but only the anxiety to persuade and convince; they retired from his presence to speak of his fascination, his strange serenity. Thus the rumour of him spread and with it the infection of the Ecstasy. Only the incorrigibly prejudiced were repelled, and by these he was reviled with curious vehemence. And these revilings, except during the extremities of the siege, he made no effort to suppress. Anti-Government journals were freely published, and French agents plotted with Jesuit intriguers without hindrance. For he knew his strength. Thus, in the crisis of the French onslaught, Sterbini and his gang of clubmen, bent on an anti-Mazzinian *coup*, ride full cry through the streets, shouting for a Garibaldi Dictatorship. Suddenly out of the crowd a young artist, Egisto Bezzi, leaps at the bridle of the ex-minister, unhorses him, and dares him to trifle with the honour of Rome. And before this single-handed assailant the Sterbini gang, cowed and strangely powerless, fall back and vanish from the streets. Somehow it had smitten home to them that Bezzi was more than himself—was just then the embodiment of something abroad in Rome, viewless and intangible, but potent and not safely to be withstood.

Above all, the common people and the poorest of the poor were Mazzini's. They venerated him with that wistful and passionate Southern adoration which, when all was over and the ex-Triumvir still lingered among them, led them to bring their children to him that he might bless them. But even the wealthy and patrician classes, which had held coldly aloof, were touched to a new admiration for the strange being who governed without trials, without prisons, and had wrought a confused and leaderless State into a moral unity capable of heroic endurance. And presently, over in England, Lord Palmerston was to shock Tory sensibilities by declaring that " Mazzini's government of Rome was far better than any the Romans had had for centuries "; and *Punch* broke out into lyrical eulogy :[4]

> " Though brutish force the game has won,
> Triumvir, thou hast nobly done;
> Calm courage in a rightful cause
> Gains thee a loftier world's applause;
> And Rome's old heroes from their spheres
> Shout, chiming in with British cheers,
>   Bravo, Mazzini!"

Eleven years earlier, in his essay on Paolo Sarpi, Mazzini had predicted that "the first Italian revolution would make the Rome of the people a different thing from the Rome of the Pope." He was fulfilling his own prophecy. Only the Watcher at Gaeta would have none of it.

* * * * *

It would have been marvellous indeed if the Papacy had been lyrical in praise of the new and strange emergence at Rome. Repeated and solemn guarantees of the preservation of the spiritual independence of the Holy Church were, after all, a poor solatium for the repudiation of the Church's every title to temporal power. It was undeniable that the Triumvirs had heard Mass at St. Peter's and that the Sacro Bambino had been borne in solemn procession with full honours of State; but the administration of Church lands (in the interests of the peasantry) and the redistribution of clerical emoluments (in the interests of the poorer clergy), together with the shameless secularisation of the premises of the Holy Office, were hardly conclusive evidence of a proper submission to sacred authority. In order to regain his princely sovereignty the Vicar of Christ was resolved to turn the guns of Catholic Europe upon Rome, and the language of his appeals, if slightly rhetorical (and liberally edited by Antonelli), was at least unmistakable in its import. The States of the Church were now fallen into the hands of a "band of sectarians," a "faction of rogues," "roaring beasts," "apostates," "leaders of communism and socialism";[5] and the Holy Father trusted to the devout feelings of the Catholic Powers of Europe, that, as daughters of the Church, they would recognise their duty.

They did. Spain made ready to land an expeditionary force at the mouth of the Tiber; Austrian armies under Gorzowsky, Wimpffen and Lichtenstein advanced through Romagna, Tuscany and the Marches; and the King of Naples (by a happy inspiration conferring a Field-Marshal's baton upon the spirit of Ignatius Loyola) threatened a holy war from the Alban hills.

But, for energy and promptitude of filial response, the honours went to France. At Civita Vecchia on April 24 General

Oudinot, with a fleet of transports conveying Rome-ward a French expeditionary force, intercepted Colonel Manara with his Lombard volunteers, bound for the same destination. Oudinot was peremptory. "*What have you to do with Rome?*" he demanded. "*You are Lombards.*" The blue eyes of the young Lombard nobleman interrogated the Frenchman. "*And you,*" he inquired, "*do you not come from Lyons or Paris?*"

Clearly this was neither in the Savona dream nor in the Lugano programme; but France, marching behind an attenuated shadow of Napoleon toward the brief and dubious glories of the Second Empire, cared nothing for either.

*   *   *   *   *

Thus Mr. Arthur Hugh Clough, turning into the Caffè Nuovo with his *Murray* under his arm (it was April 30, and the day for the Campidoglio marbles)—Mr. Clough vividly records how, so doing, and ordering his usual morning cup of *caffè-latte,* he was served by a dilatory and preoccupied waiter with milkless *nero*—a sign, surely, that something was amiss. He records, also, how civilians and soldiers flung into the *Caffè* in evident haste, gulped their coffee standing, and departed in silence. And he records how, when he left (he was the last to leave), he found the flag-draped streets deserted; and how, about noon, in agreeable sunshine (but Mr. Clough was apprehensive of a probable shower) he sauntered up the Pincian hill and joined a mixed company of sight-seers, staring to the left of St. Peter's at certain white puffs of smoke, unmistakably cannon-smoke, and at the dark lines of infantry descending the vineyard slopes, with now and again the flash of bayonets as the sunshine caught the steel.

In fact, Oudinot, hopefully setting out in that propitious sunshine ("*Les Italiens ne se battent pas*"), and advancing up the Vatican and Corsini slopes and through the terraced vineyards and flowering rose-gardens and cypress-groves, musical that morning with singing birds—Oudinot thus advancing with his red-legged battalions, was met and fought to a standstill, and presently hurled back along the Palo road, hotly pursued. Leading the pursuit was a pack of raw youths cheered on by an apocalyptic horseman with flowing, tawny hair and white cloak streaming in the wind.

To this horseman, indeed, belongs in a sense the chief glory of the defence of Rome. Excepting, perhaps, Pisacane, he was the one leader of genius that Rome possessed on the military side. Was it, then, the cardinal error of Mazzini's administration that he withheld from him the supreme command? The leader himself was certainly disposed to believe so. As early as April 8 he had written to the Triumvir from Rieti:

"BROTHER MAZZINI:
"These lines bring you salutations. . . . May Providence sustain you in your brilliant but arduous career, and may you be enabled to carry out all the noble designs which you meditate. . . . Remember that Rieti is full of your brethren in the Faith and that immutably yours is
"G. GARIBALDI."[6]

Did this mean by any chance that Rome could best be made safe for the Faith by placing Brother Garibaldi in control? Two months earlier, indeed, Garibaldi had hinted as much. "I proposed a military dictatorship. . . . I could not use the argument further; modesty restrained me."[7] Instead, Mazzini appointed as Commander-in-Chief General Rosselli, a Roman officer whose principal claims to the appointment were his military rank and his conscientious fidelity.

But the fact was that Italy was not Uruguay, and in his own country Garibaldi had still to give full proof of his capacity. And there were other considerations. A steady flood of propagandist inaccuracies was pouring from Gaeta, and the Powers were being assured that Rome was now a den of thieves and adventurers. What chance was there of persuading a suspicious and critical Europe of the regular character of the Roman defence if its Dictator-Generalissimo were one who lent himself to the description of being a picturesque American filibuster? Moreover, in Rome itself such an appointment would have aroused military jealousy and dissatisfaction at a supremely critical time. For what hope was there of promoting the Nizzard *capitano* to supreme command over the heads of the regular staff, without dividing the councils of the defence with partisan animosities? Garibaldi was in due time called to

Rome, promoted General of Division and given command of the western ramparts, the position of supreme importance. All the same, the apparent slight rankled in the good Paladin's breast; with the Frenchmen storming the walls he would presently renew his request, and Sterbini and Co. would try to use him to raise a whirlwind revolution. And these things also belonged to the sorrows of a Triumvir "cursed with every granted prayer."

And at the present point, the personal relations between Triumvir and Paladin were not eased by Mazzini's calling off Garibaldi's headlong pursuit. It was exasperating. The battle had been hard-fought, the victory brilliant, and now, with the Frenchmen on the run, the glittering prize was to be snatched away by peremptory orders for the abandonment of the pursuit. It was hard for the victorious leader to avoid the feeling that he was the victim of malign antipathies. Yet Mazzini had again been forced to a difficult decision. A war with France was no conceivable part of the Roman programme, and there were hopes that, through liberal pressure in Paris, better counsels would yet prevail. De Lesseps, indeed, was shortly to be sent from Paris as Envoy Plenipotentiary to discuss a settlement. The one thing calculated to dash all hopes of such a settlement would have been a rout of Oudinot's men so complete and spectacular as to wound the pride of the French nation. So the Triumvir reasoned. Let Garibaldi's pursuit, then, be called off and let his five hundred red-legged prisoners (after prayers in St. Peter's for universal liberty and brotherhood) be sent back with monster gifts of cigars and snuff, wrapped round in tricoloured tracts! And while Generals Rosselli and Garibaldi led their brave troops southward to meet King *Bomba* and his Neapolitans (and the spirit of Field-Marshal Loyola), the Triumvirate would treat hopefully with Envoy De Lesseps.

Alas! the excellent De Lesseps, also hopeful, and bent upon engineering his diplomatic canal betwixt the Paris and Roman policies, was no more than an upright agent of a crooked Government, and had been sent only to parley until General Vaillant, with engineers, siege artillery and general reinforcements, could be hurried to Oudinot's assistance. The reinforcements duly arrived, and a day before the expiry of the armistice Oudinot renewed hostilities with a surprise attack.

Clearly there was nothing now to be done but defy the world. Once more Rosselli and Garibaldi were called back, this time from the pursuit of the routed Neapolitans, and while they took their posts on the ramparts of Rome the ever-vigilant *Punch* addressed a spirited Ode to Louis Napoleon.

> " The Romans may be right or wrong,
> I don't care which, in turning Pius out
> And sending all the Cardinals along
> With that good Pontiff to the right about;
> But let them choose their form of government,
> And what's the odds, so long as they're content?
> Are you to cram down their reluctant gullets
> The kind of Constitution you think best,
> By means of swords and bayonets and bullets?
> Against such tyranny I must protest."[8]

The English Court, however, felt differently, and Uncle Leopold was advising his dear Victoria that " the Pope ought to be replaced on his seat for the sake of everyone; and his ultra-liberal policy entitles him to be supported by all Governments and all right-minded people."[9] But in Chelsea Mrs. Carlyle discovered a new access of tenderness not unmixed with sterner passion: " Poor dear Mazzini—all my affection for him has waked up since I knew him in jeopardy and so gallantly fulfilling his destiny. . . . I sometimes feel myself *up to* wishing that the Romans, Mazzini included, may let themselves be all blown to atoms and their city made into a heap of ruins." Carlyle himself, recognising at last a contemporary Hero, and prepared to prescribe for him unflinchingly, was, indeed, altogether up to it. " Mazzini is busy at Rome . . . standing on his guard against all the world. . . . If he *could* stand there . . . and fight till Rome was ashes and ruin, and end by blowing himself and his assailants up in the last strong post. . . . Perhaps that is what he really was worth in this world. Strange, providential-looking, and leading to many thoughts." But Arthur Hugh Clough, tuning an improvised lyre in the actual roar of the guns and refusing ever " to incarnadine this inky pacifical finger," was prepared to be more easily satisfied[10] (and there were the Campidoglio marbles to be considered); and in

Florence Mrs. Browning, laying aside the cymbals, sang wistfully of the better time when earth should "disband her
captains and change her victories."

> " And soon we shall have thinkers in the place
> Of fighters, each found able as a man
> To strike electric influence through a race
> Unstayed by city-wall and barbican."[11]

And Margaret Fuller, exhausted after nursing the wounded at
the military hospital, writes to a distant friend in tamer prose:
" I know not how to bear the havoc and anguish. . . . I
rejoiced that it lay not with me to cut down the trees, to
destroy the Elysian gardens . . . and the sight of these far
nobler growths, the beautiful young men mown down. . . .
I forget the great ideas."[12]

Only, the man in the back room at the Quirinal would not
relent. " Mazzini has suffered millions more than I could . . .
in him I revered the hero and owned myself not of that
mould." In his leisure he visits with Saffi the zones of bombardment—the Via Gesù, the Piazza S. Apostoli and other
quarters where the " Papal benedictions " crash with destructive effect—or watches beside the dying in the wards, or, from
the Quirinal roof, looks across the Tiber to where, beyond
the barricades, the bastions spout flame around the Vatican
and the Janiculum, and where, amid the charred and crumbling
walls, the newly crimsoned rose-gardens of the villas Pamfili
and Spada and Corsini and the Vascello, the " red whirling
infernos " rage from day to day, from week to week. And
the boy Morosini is slain, refusing quarter, and Adele Zoagli's
poet-son receives his death wound, and young Masina, already
bleeding, leads his Lancers in a last wild charge through the
fire-swept Corsini gardens and—still mounted—storms up the
marble steps of the shattered villa, riding to his death. And
in the improvised hospital of S. Maria della Scala, on the right
of the high altar, Dr. Bertani bends over the lifeless body of
Manara. " I heard someone sobbing behind me. It was Ugo
Bassi "—brave Bassi who had courted death in vain and was
reserved for a crueller martyrdom. Only Garibaldi, singing
battle-songs in the heart of the carnage, his cloak and tunic
" slitten with ploughing ball and bayonet," his sword so bent

that it would not take the scabbard—only Garibaldi seems immortal. On guard on the Ramparts, the last night of the defence (it was June 29 and the Feast of St. Peter and St. Paul), he looks down upon the City, spreading out before him jewelled in light and strangely resplendent under the starless sky. For this strange Rome, its bastions breached, its meat and flour running short, and the bombardment in full play, must still observe the *festa*. There are lights gleaming in every window, there are rockets and bonfires and Roman candles, and St. Peter's dome itself, by Triumviral order, blazes and coruscates magnificently against the sultry blackness. So from the Ramparts he surveys the scene, watching this onslaught of a million blades of light that slash the invading darkness. Occasionally Garibaldi affects a romantic atheism, but just now the Ecstasy is still working and he beholds this Rome with the strange shining about her, challenging the night, and sees it all as fitting symbol of a more tremendous conflict—the battle now raging between spiritual Light and Darkness, "between (so he must express it) Arimanes and Oromanes," between religious despotism and a free faith, "between God and Satan."[18] Alas! a sudden thunderstorm crashes over the City and quenches the defiant fireworks in torrential rain; and when the storm is over, Rome is in darkness, with one only light remaining, conspicuous and portentous, in the surrounding gloom. It shines from the top of St. Peter's.[19]

*　　*　　*　　*　　*

And so what of it all?

One morning in July (the 13th) an aged man, unheeded by the French patrols, walks aboard the steamer *Corriere Corso* (Captain De Cristoferi) bound for Marseilles. He addresses the Captain: "I am Mazzini. I have no passport. Do you dare to take me?" Yes; Captain De Cristoferi would dare; but he must point out that he must call at Leghorn, where the Austrians are now in occupation and have a habit of searching vessels; and if . . . But the aged man waves the objection aside; he will take the risk and all responsibility. And at Leghorn the officials pass unnoticed the grey-bearded old steward sleepily washing the glasses and now and then staring idly at the white-coat sentries on the quay-side. And who, indeed, would have recognised him? In five months he had grown old. His hair was streaked with grey, his beard almost white; his eyes were bloodshot and famished of sleep; a slow fever had consumed the flesh from his bones and parched his skin; the clear olive of his complexion had become a jaundiced yellow. The Triumvir was well disguised.

But off Genoa it was more trying. "I was anchored off Genoa," he wrote to his mother, "but I did not let you know. You can imagine how I felt; but I thought it best for you." At Genoa, indeed, there were no Austrian officials to come aboard, but there were ghosts and olden dreams and voices in the wind; and in the dusk there were once again the twinkling lights of the Acquaverde; and yonder in the distance on the Sunset Shore, where the bluff headland curved outward and faded into sea and sky—yonder on the Riviera di Ponente was Savona.

And was it sunset now with the Savona dream? And from the Overworld did the Spirit of the Years borrow the tone of the Spirit Ironic and mock the vain illusions of youth? For once more in Europe the despots were creeping back and righting their tilted thrones; French Republic was passing once more into Napoleonic Empire; German democracies were in the dust; Russia, come to Austria's aid, had rolled her grey columns over a helpless Hungary; and Italy, unredeemed, was pledged again to her ancient servitude.

> "So hath the Urging Immanence used to-day
> Its inadvertent might to field this fray:
> And Europe's wormy dynasties re-robe
> Themselves in their old gilt to dazzle anew the globe."[13]

What of it all? He had held Rome to the limit of endurance and beyond; had protested to the last hour against surrender; had insisted—in vain—that either Triumvirate, Assembly and Army must march out to continue the struggle elsewhere ("where we are there is Rome"), or else arm the populace and fight from street to street. And after Garibaldi's little column had stolen out through the Porta San Giovanni and trailed off into the darkness to face "hunger, thirst, forced marches, battles and death," even then he had lingered on.

He must defy the French, defy arrest, defy the secret dagger of the Sanfedist, and wander among the ruins and the unburied dead, himself " like a walking corpse." Even at that hour he would rake together the embers of resistance if he could—did, in fact, attempt to plot a new rising to be led by himself.

But what of it all? Rome, touched now by the splendour of the old gods, now with a light divine and new—Rome in these last tremendous days had made immortal history. The Republic had been beaten, but it had been beaten as a gong is beaten. The blows that had fallen upon it had been resonant, sounding strange alarums which echoed through Europe and in the souls of men.

Yet, had this been in very truth the Rome of the New World, authentic oracle and herald of the age to come? Or had the prophet, entangled first to last in fatal fallacy, evoked a Rome still too deeply committed to the tradition of the Sword to stand as exemplar to future generations? " My theory, perhaps, runs the risk of sacrificing something of the purity of the *idea* in the pursuit of the means." Was that to remain the crucial confession? Knowing his touchiness on this side, his critics assail him with quotations from the Christian Scriptures, particularly the texts " *My Kingdom is not of this world, else would my servants fight* " and " *Render unto Cæsar the things that are Cæsar's.*" He stops to counter them with almost rabbinical zeal. The Divine Kingdom, he declares, is certainly to be established in this world, and the piety that reserves liberty and equality and unity for heaven is not encouraged in the Gospel: " Earth and heaven are continually brought together in the sacred volume." Did not Jesus come to destroy the castes and inequalities of nature admitted by Paganism? Did he not announce that the human family should form but one flock and should have but one shepherd, the interpreted law of God? Did he not proclaim here upon earth the superiority of the *idea* over the *fact*, of moral perfection over material good, and sanction a principle of Authority that disavowed the absolutism of Cæsar, even the Authority of the *spirit* of work, service and sacrifice, whose transmission also was spiritual and not according to the privilege of caste and birth? Did he not disavow the abject doctrine of absolute submission by giving his followers a rule for judging whether an authority be derived from God or contrary to His Law? As for the text "*My Kingdom is not of this world*" it is incorrectly rendered in the Vulgate; in its correct form it is "decisive in our favour": namely "*My Kingdom is not* NOW *of this world*" (Regnum meum non est NUNC de hoc mundo).* And so with "*Render unto Cæsar*," "a passage which is not a doctrinal one, but one in which Jesus by a simple exposition of a fact *then* existing, and which could only be changed . . . by the fulfilment of His mission, avoided the snare which the Pharisees had laid for Him." And for the rest, martyrdom and a heavenly triumph are not the final word of the Gospel. There is to be an earthly triumph too when the seed of sacrifice has fructified.[14]

So he argues, piling text upon text, somewhat evading the crucial issue of the legitimacy of the sword, but resolved that "in the name of Jesus and St. Paul" he would persist in his witness. Thanks to the power of foreign arms, the walls and stones of Rome might belong for a time to the Papal Cæsar, "but the soul of Rome is with us; the Thought of Rome is ours." Religion, he tells the Pope, save that which is a powerless bond, a dead letter, forsaken by the conscience of the people, and incapable of any future initiation—"religion is no longer in your camp; it is in ours." And then in his valedictory to the Roman people, as in his Bandiera oration at Milan, he propounds his own doctrine of *Ahimse*:

"Romans . . . your City has been overcome by brute force, but your rights are neither lessened nor changed. . . . By all you hold sacred, citizens, keep yourselves incontaminate. . . . Organise pacific demonstrations. Let your municipalities unceasingly declare with calm firmness that they voluntarily adhere to the Republican form of government and the abolition of the Temporal Power of the Pope; and that they regard as illegal whatever government be imposed without the free approval of the people. . . . In the streets, the theatres, in every place of meeting let the same cry be heard. . . . Thousands cannot be imprisoned. Men

* I am indebted to the Rev. Principal Wheeler Robinson for the probable explanation of Mazzini's curious error. The Vulgate passage in question, which begins "*Regnum meum non est de mundo hoc*," ends "*nunc autem regnum meum non est hinc.*" Mazzini apparently wrote with a confused mental impression of the two clauses and wrongly attributed a temporal sense to the *nunc* of the second clause.—G. O. G.

cannot be compelled to degrade themselves. . . . Your forefathers, Romans, were great not so much because they knew how to conquer as because they never despaired when overcome."[15]

* * * * *

And at least the recent armed conflict of the Republic had not been of his seeking. It was the Vicar of Christ who, to regain his temporal sovereignty, had appealed to the sword and had prevailed; and by July 14, Oudinot, reluctantly overriding the protest of 260 communes, had proclaimed the restoration of the Temporal Power. In Naples Mr. Gladstone was to become an eyewitness of the reaction and to describe it in a thunder of denunciation which should re-echo through Europe. It was the "violation of human and written law . . . carried on for the purpose of violating every other law, unwritten and eternal, human and divine . . . the awful profanation of public religion . . . 'the negation of God erected into a system of Government.'"[16] Thus Terror again stalked abroad through Italy, and while in Umbria and the Marches the Austrians were bloodily executing a Papal Purge, the "Red Triumvirate" of Cardinals was similarly expurgating Rome itself. Perhaps the new Triumvirs occasionally showed excess of zeal, but the Pope himself had already complained of "the inexplicable leniency of the French"; and thousands fled from the Holy City to escape the blessings of the Restoration. Nor were Garibaldi and his little army of the exodus overlooked. Over the Alban hills and northward across the Tiber and up beyond Arezzo and seaward to Cesenatico, pursued by the baffled legions of France, Spain and Austria, the defenders of Rome earned their promised reward—"hunger, thirst, forced marches . . . death." Ciceroacchio and his two sons, one a boy under sixteen, were taken and publicly shot. Ugo Bassi, betrayed by an informer whose life he had saved, was drawn in an open cart through the streets of Bologna, the scene of his supreme triumphs, to suffer the same fate. Awaiting death in his cell at Comacchio, he had time to draw a "Christus" on the wall and inscribe beneath it, "*Ugo Bassi here endured somewhat, glad of heart.*" . . . And in a lone farmhouse at Mandriole, on the edge of the marshes, with the blue waters of the Comacchio lagoons beyond, Garibaldi himself, lone fugitive in an Italy that could yield him no sanctuary, wept over the dead body of Anita, his wife.

Thus reaction had conquered. The forces of Radetzky, the troops of France, backed by King *Bomba's* mobile legions, with Gorzowsky's and Wimpffen's and Lichtenstein's columns, and Cordova's Spanish expeditionaries, had achieved their object; Vaillant's artillery had ploughed a fairway for the Pope's return; and while the Red Triumvirate and the Holy Office were preparing a wayward and still reluctant Rome for the Pontiff's welcome, Father Newman, in the chaste seclusion of Perry Bar, Birmingham, was celebrating the Papal triumph in noble prose. "In the very year of the Pope's return," says Ward, "Newman described with dramatic force the nature of the struggle between the armed soldiers of Mazzini and the spiritual power represented by the Papacy—a power whose peculiar strength lay in the intangible weapons by which it is enforced."[17]

Yet at least, on the other side also, there were forces viewless and intangible, memories which no artillery could demolish, a growing, deep distrust which not even the persuasions of the Holy Office could remove. It was difficult indeed (as Newman himself had eloquently argued) to rout an atmosphere, to exorcise a shadow. And now it was the rule of the people and a freer faith that was in the air; and upon Rome had fallen the shadow of its prophet. And even when an anxious and burdened Pope was found once more in his own place, saying Mass over the tomb of the Apostles, that shadow was still there, gigantesque and ominous, upon the sacred walls. It is there to-day.

AFTER NOON

MRS. CARLYLE, writing to Helen Welsh in 1850, reported the safe return of Mazzini. "I was immensely glad. . . . I did not think I *could* have felt so very glad."[1] She added that save for a greyish beard he had altered little; he was "the same affectionate, simple-hearted, high-souled creature—but immensely more agreeable—talks now as one who had the habit of being listened to." Thanks to Moritz Hartmann[2] we have a picture of the scene. Hartmann, seated by the Carlyles' drawing-room fire, was listening to a robustious monologue on German Parliaments and the futility of Democracy. Suddenly a voice was heard in the hall, a peculiarly musical, masculine voice which "stirred Mrs. Carlyle like an electric shock." She rushed to the door and "grasped the hands of the visitor in such a transport of joy that it seemed almost an embrace." Carlyle, too, was deeply moved. With his stork-like legs, says Hartmann, he reached his guest in one long stride. They recognised that the exile had suffered much, and Mrs. Carlyle was touched even to tears.

Yet Mazzini had certainly not returned a broken and humiliated man. "He looks," said Mrs. Carlyle, "much better than I expected," and his spirits were good. After all, he was no shamed and discredited leader. He had justified himself. He was ex-Triumvir of Rome. He had autographed an immortal page of history. For one splendid hour he had brought his dream to pass. And was not that enough? Ought he not now to accept the verdict of events and retire from active politics? Henceforth he could speak "as one who had the habit of being listened to." Ought he not to be content to occupy a detached position, resigning himself to literary and philosophic pursuits? Mrs. Carlyle thought so, and when the exile showed signs of persisting in his old ways her sympathies were strained. "Mazzini," she wrote, "is in hopes of kicking up another shine almost immediately. . . . I am out of all patience at his reckless folly. If one did not hear every day of new arrests and executions, one might let him scheme and talk, hoping it might all end in smoke: but it ends in blood, and that is horrible."[3]

There was truth in the criticism, and the criticism itself grew in area and volume in the succeeding years. Thus eleven years later Harriet Martineau, as oracle of the more advanced intelligentsia, delivered a final pronouncement. Mazzini, she declared, had lost as much by surviving the siege of Rome in '49 as O'Connell did by continuing to agitate after Catholic Emancipation. He could not, in fact, see facts as they were, could not willingly see his country saved in any way but his own, could not abstain from agitating a people who needed rest, and did not want his interference—could not, in short, acquiesce in the accomplishment by other means of a work to which he was inadequate.[4] In Miss Martineau's lengthy tirade there may have been passages which suggested personal virus (could it have been that the exile had belittled Mesmeric Atheism and Mr. Atkinson?), but the pronouncement fairly represents the criticism that gathered around Mazzini in this later phase. And even Mr. Bolton King inclines to the view that Mazzini should have retired after '49. "It is painful to turn from Mazzini in England, the great-hearted friend, the prophetic thinker . . . to his political action in Italy. Had he yielded to the advice of some of his friends and left politics at this time for literature his fame were brighter and his life more fruitful in pure good. His work for Italy was done."[5]

But was it? It would be easier to agree with this conclusion if Mazzini's career had ended with the Milan fiasco of 1853 or the Genoa tragedy of 1857. Thanks to Thayer and Trevelyan the English-reading public has long been familiar with the work of Cavour and Garibaldi in the later stages of the Italian struggle, but the biographer-historian has yet to appear who shall give us, from a close examination of the facts now available, and with ampler detail than the limits of Mr. King's biography would allow, the Mazzinian side of the story. No doubt such a study would show that Mazzini's judgment was often at fault and his methods as often deplorable. Like some mediæval monk, as Herzen says, he understood deeply one side of life, and invented the rest. Perhaps he never fully understood the promptings, and above all the limitations, of his Italians. Moreover, he was more and more closely surrounded by cosmopolitan conspirators who increased his isolation and flattered his prejudices. All this may be conceded, and more; but it may still be questioned whether, in his lifetime, Italian Unity would have been achieved at all, if, after '49, he had retired from the struggle. But for him the movement might will have halted somewhere between Turin and Naples.

For no reading of Risorgimento history can miss the fact that in the end, and again and again before the end, it was Mazzini who forced Cavour's hand. Not that, even so, the Italy of the Savona ideal was ever brought to pass, but at least the political unity which might have become—and may yet become—its medium was achieved. Thus in the inevitable reactions and confusions, the shifts and expediencies, the bewildering and bewildered policies, which followed upon the debacle of '48 and '49, it was Mazzini's contribution not only that he held before his Italians the single idea of an Italy one and indivisible with Rome for its capital, but also that he maintained that idea in the sphere of political action, and in the end forced it into recognition. For if Cavour, true to his own genius, was always aiming at the ever-varying *possible,* as distinct from the merely desirable, Mazzini was always concentrating upon the desirable, as distinct from the merely possible. But also he had the faith, the vision, the tenacity and tensity of will which went far toward converting the desirable into the possible. Mazzini's was the creative, Cavour's the manipulative, genius of the Risorgimento. And if, in the Apostle's case, there was too often a touch of antinomianism about his methods, as, in Cavour's, there was always the cheerful unscrupulosity of the man of the world, nevertheless the combination-in-opposition of the two minds was the one effective instrument of national unity. For the curious comment of history is that even the antagonism of the two was somehow co-operant to the one result. It was the Apostle who created the situation which the diplomatist would never himself have brought about, which again and again he definitely sought to prevent, but which, with his adroit and tactile genius, he was well able to exploit, once it was in being. It was Mazzini's iron obstinacy of purpose which was the anvil upon which Cavour beat out his national policy; and when that policy was finally shaped it was seen that something, at least, of the design of " Young Italy " had hardened into fact.

Something else should be noted. In spite of tragic failures the revolution of '48 had not been fruitless. It had brought forth one liberal State, Piedmont, capable of preserving its free institutions, and in Victor Emmanuel II. the House of Savoy had at last contributed a monarch with an honest and undissuadable devotion to constitutional government. No doubt it was one of the errors of Mazzini's career that he was slow to recognise the full significance of this emergence. He predicted the early vanishing of Piedmont's " vain shadow of a constitution " and the reversion of the new King to the old despotism; and the falsifying of this forecast did not work in him a corresponding change of attitude. Nor was it likely that this should escape the notice and censure of historians who have reviewed the period from the Cavourian standpoint; and no doubt there was arrogance in Mazzini's hostility. But at least it was not a blind arrogance. For the fact that under Cavour Piedmont was remodelling its institutions, secularising its courts, modernising its industries, multiplying its commercial contacts abroad and as profitably reducing its Clerical connections at home—all this conveyed no assurance to Mazzini's mind that a new avatar of Italy had emerged. How could it have done so? The truth was that the sum and substance, the spirit and policy of the new régime in Piedmont, were the direct negation of what he conceived to be the fundaments of the Italian apostolate. Turin had no " national programme," no Pan-Italian policy, no declared " mission," no " faith," no inviolable " formula." On the contrary, it was frankly opportunist. It honestly believed that more could be accomplished by patient intrigue and the maturing of foreign alliances than by any succession of desperate insurrections. If ever the time were propitious for

pronouncing for a United Italy, then Turin would pronounce
for it; not before. It was a policy calculated certainly to appeal
to an Italy morally exhausted after the high hopes, the bitter
disappointments, and the heavy sacrifices of '48, and particularly to a middle class anxious above all things for the recovery
and extension of trade, and persuaded that commercial edifica-
tion must be based upon political stability: but it was as much
anathema to Mazzini as the policy of By-ends to Bunyan's
Pilgrim.

And at least the consistency of his opposition was never in
dispute. His protest was precisely that of the puritan Pilgrim
against the prudentialism of the worldly-wise. And by the
same token Cavour could have arraigned the Mazzinian irreconcilables in the language of By-ends' indictment: "Why,
they, after their headstrong manner, conclude that it is their
duty to rush on their journey all weathers; and I am for waiting for wind and tide." The statesmanship of By-ends was
beyond question, but it was always left to the Pilgrims to point
out that the difference between them was not simply in the
method employed but in the end proposed. The Turin method
of piecemeal unification through the expansion of the Sardinian Kingdom, through diplomatic intrigue, through barter
and treaty and foreign alliance—such a policy might achieve
in the long run a united Kingdom of Italy; it could never
achieve the Italy of the Mazzinian dream, "initiatrix of a new
epoch of European progress." *That* could be achieved only
through a moral Risorgimento, through a nationhood created
by the mind and will and soul of the Italian people themselves. Thus it was almost as if the antagonism between Turin
and Savona were the antagonism between the flesh and the
spirit. At all events, it was not strange if Mazzini did not feel
that the emergence of the Turin Policy argued that his work
was done—that having conquered Italy for half his ideas he
might safely leave the other half to the stewardship of the
Moderates.

And no doubt an antagonism so fundamental was beyond
reconciliation. Yet, if the two leaders had found themselves
exchanging views in private across the table instead of in public
across the Continent, they might at times have understood each
other better. And for this aloofness Mazzini was not wholly

to blame. Thus, in the summer of '52, Cavour re-visited Paris and London. In Paris he sought out Daniele Manin, ex-President of the Venetian Republic, in his humble lodging; and their conference bore fruit in Manin's manifesto of the following year. In London it would have been no more difficult for Cavour to have sought out the ex-Triumvir of the Roman Republic in his equally humble lodging at Chelsea. Instead, he preferred to linger at Kensington Gate, cultivating the society of the paper-knife Procida, "Mariotti" Gallenga. "He came in (says Gallenga) all fresh and brisk and bustling, as was his wont, sat down with us *en famille,* plying us with questions . . . and at last, coming to the point, he told me that Italy was in need of all well-thinking Italians, and that I . . . was bound to bear a hand. . . . He went on naming Bezzi,* Radice, Ruffini, and other old exiles."[6] Kensington Gate was not so far from Chelsea that Cavour could not have spent an hour with yet another "old exile" as "well-thinking" in his way as Bezzi or Ruffini or even Gallenga. But Mazzini was passed over and the two men never looked into each other's eyes—unless, indeed, the story is to be credited that Mazzini once interviewed the Minister, in disguise.

Withal, so long as Austria and her underlings in Italy pursued their policy of terror and butchery, so long were violent outbreaks unavoidable. For the crime of possessing arms men were shot in batches; for trifling offences women were publicly stripped and flogged or had their hair torn out by the roots; flogging was employed alike for punishment and for extracting "evidence," and the official flogger was remunerated at the stimulating rate of one lira per stroke. At Milan the ice and vinegar used as restoratives for the bastinadoed victims were included in the charges extorted from the municipality; it was the same with the screws, timber and shears used at public executions; and in the same spirit mothers were charged for the rope used in the hanging of their sons. Thus, while Lombardy-Venetia staggered under an intolerable load of punitive taxation, there were (according to Tiverone's estimate) 961 political executions in twelve months. It appeared to be true, as Palmerston declared, that the Austrian ruling-class were

---

* The artist who had unhorsed Sterbini in the streets of Rome. (See p. 220.)

"the greatest brutes that ever called themselves by the un-deserved name of civilised men ";[8] true also, as he added, that they understood no argument but force.

In any case it was hardly in human nature, certainly not in Italian nature, to submit to the organised diabolism that now ruled over Lombardy and the South. Nor was it convincing to exhort the suffering populations to be calm and await the slow result of Turin diplomacy—a diplomacy whose methods were dubious, whose success was uncertain, and whose very aims were obscure. Mazzini was not open to contradiction when he claimed that plots and uprisings were inevitable—that in such populations, however cowed and terrorised, there would always be bolder spirits who would find relief in desperate action. As he saw it, the only question was whether these out-bursts should be left to spend themselves in anarchic frenzies or be controlled and developed, as far as possible, into insur-rectionary movements under the national banner.

And for the rest, if the struggle was ever morally justifiable (and the conscience of liberal Europe and America had sus-tained it) its continuance was justifiable now. No doubt it is possible to observe to-day that after the fall of Rome and Venice, the republican revolutionary initiative was virtually exhausted: but the lines of demarcation between one period and another, so apparent and diagrammatic to the historian, are usually less clearly defined in the eyes of the actual makers of history, living within the horizon of their events. To Lamberti Mazzini wrote hopefully: "I firmly believe that we have presented the prologue of our Drama and no more ";[7] and at the despots and reactionaries themselves he flung his defiance: "What matters the triumph of an hour? What matters it that you have restored the former order of things? Can you restore men's faith in it?" Nor could he who, for two decades, had sedulously preached revolt, disclaim further responsibility and choose the hour of darkness and defeat as the convenient time for retirement into literary seclusion. "Young Italy" was in covenant not only with the living but with the dead, and all the graves of the patriots, the scaffolds of the martyrs, barred the way to withdrawal. Even had he desired to withdraw he was too deeply committed to do so; and he had no such desire.

With these considerations in mind, then, we may turn back to the events which immediately followed the fall of Rome.

*   *   *   *   *

Father Newman in his celebration of the fall of the Mazzinian Republic had painted an engaging picture. He had represented a meek hierarchy—" a few old men with red hats and stockings "—" a hundred pale students with eyes on the ground and beads in their girdle "—confronting the haughty clarion and black artillery of the embattled Mazzinian hosts and at last overcoming them by the patience of faith and the intangible forces of the spirit. And if to the eye of the profane the picture seemed a trifle highly coloured, at least there was no denying the Papal restoration, nor the fact that it marked the definite repulse of revolutionary democracy. Nor was it any the less definite because the restoration was dictated, not by the impulse of a penitent people, but by a system of civil and military coercion which filled the gaols with political prisoners and the seaports with terrorised fugitives, and left a trail of blood from Naples to the Tyrol.

Yet in the nature of things the restoration was menaced from the first. For if it was true that the Pope and the Princes had returned, and were being maintained, through foreign intervention, it was also true that the powers that had secured their return were themselves involved in insecurity. The Austrian throne had emerged (with a new tenant) from the Viennese confusions, but Austria had retained Hungary only with the aid of two hundred thousand Russian bayonets, and her tenure of Italy was dependent upon the goodwill of France. And while the methods of terrorism employed by the Empire had lowered Austria's prestige in the eyes of the civilised world, the French Republic had emerged from the Roman *fracas* with diminished reputation and was threatened with domestic crises of its own.

Thus when Mazzini, first at Pâquis, Geneva, and then at Lausanne, flung himself into new and strange enterprises, his activity was no mere agony of persistent purpose. " Our victory," he wrote, " is certain. I declare it with the profoundest conviction, here in exile, and precisely when Monarchical reaction appears most insolently secure." So through the autumn and winter he multiplied his activities. He founded a publishing society, revived and edited his monthly review, the *Italia del Popolo,* flung a flaming *J'accuse* at the heads of recalcitrant French liberals, attacked the Papalism of Montalembert, began (but never completed) a popular translation of the Gospels, with an introduction addressed to the Italian people, indicted the Papacy in a lengthy essay, and organised a relief fund for Republican refugees. There were more grandiose projects. There was a design for an Encyclopædia dealing with " the true sources of the religious and civil life of Humanity," and a plan for an International Council (with federated national councils and a Democratic Tax) to establish relations " between the democracies of all parts of Europe and America." This was to be a sort of League of Nations, " not a temporary agitation which will have to be reproduced everlastingly, but something permanent, a great Association of Nationalities, a constant machinery, *fonctionnant toujours et regulièrement."* With Ledru Rollin, Arnold Ruge and others he succeeded in founding a Central Democratic Committee for Europe; and while the multi-lingual Maurizio Quadrio, hiding in Geneva, circulated appeals in all the European languages, and Adriano Lemmi recruited Louis Kossuth at Kutajah, other emissaries organised groups of Slavs, Poles, Roumanians, Hungarians, Bohemians, Germans and French.

Withal he refused to be stampeded by his own extremists into an exclusively Republican campaign in Italy. Cattaneo argued for a group of Italian republics, Roman, Sicilian, Cis-Alpine; Ferrari pressed a similar programme; Mazzini set them aside and founded with Saffi, Saliceti and Montecchi his Italian National Committee with a non-party programme of Independence, Liberty and Unity. " We, even though we had the power to do it, would not impose a republic or any other form of government. The nation must declare, freely, universally, legally, what it desires." Cattaneo protested; the policy " left the door open to the House of Savoy ": Cernuschi declared it necessary to " republicanise Mazzini afresh "; but he stood his ground. It was, indeed, a piquant situation. The man whom Turin beheld as the Mullah of Republicanism, reciting his narrow creed with a dervish fanaticism and incapable of compromise, was prepared to risk schism in his own party rather than force the republican issue prematurely. No doubt he was governed for once by tactical considerations. By broadening his platform he would draw away, if possible, the more vigorous elements from the Moderate Party.

And so the winter passed, and even Farini, in a passage of slightly choleric purple, was moved to a reluctant admiration for a tenacity so invincible, a resiliency so inexhaustible. "Mazzini, who fancied himself Dictator by the grace of God, resumed his rank and power in exile with the consent of the fugitive Deputies. Nor was he content to lord it secretly over his own party, but he assumed the manners and bearing of a Roman autocrat, or rather of an Italian Emperor, for he created offices of State . . . published his *Motu proprio* to the Romans and his Manifesto to the Italians"[9]—and much else, to the horror of the good Farini and of Turin.

The truth was that his survival filled Moderates and re-actionaries alike with a curious alarm. In the troubled imagina-tion of men he was now the terror that walked in darkness, and the myth of a Mazzini brooding dark designs of retribution and wrath assumed gigantic proportions and fantastic shapes. There was, indeed, a pleasant rumour that he had embarked for America to found a Utopian colony called the New Rome; but there were more disquieting reports which placed him in Spain, in Malta, in London, in Switzerland, or somewhere in German territory; and henceforth not a bomb would explode in Paris nor a dagger flash in Ancona but the hidden hand of the arch-conspirator would be suspected. Mazzini had some-how got on the nerves of Europe. Concerning all of which the poet Dall' Ongaro was moved to write his much-quoted *stornello,* which may be roughly rendered thus:

> "Mazzini is in Germany, some explain:
> Some say to England he has fled:
> Some say Geneva, others Spain,
> And some would have him worshipped, others—dead.
> Expound to me, ye braided fools and vain,
> This hundredfold Mazzini whom ye dread!
>   Yet, would ye of his circuits read the signs?
>   Inquire, then, of the Alps and Apennines!
>   He is where'er pale fear doth quaking dwell
>   Because the hour hath struck the traitor's knell:
>   He is where'er hope's kindling eyes foresee
>   Italia ransomed, blood-bought, whole, and free."*

* See Appendix E.

Meanwhile, the object of universal alarm was living with Saffi and a small group of fellow-exiles in the Villa Montallegro, which they had rented, on the lake-shore outside Lausanne. They lived frugally, ate twice a day at a common table, separated for their individual labours, and assembled in the evening for an interval of conversation, cards and chess. Mazzini was, in fact, breathing once more the atmosphere he found most congenial—the atmosphere of faith and affection, slightly perfumed, perhaps, with the odour of incense. "Only those who knew my friend intimately," wrote the adoring Saffi in the later years, "can form any conception of the intellectuality and charm of those Montallegro evenings." What depths of sad serenity (as Saffi recalls) in those eyes! and yet what a gay companion he made himself, how brilliant his conversation, how droll and affectionate his badinage, how kind his treatment of the servants, how deep and broad his sympathies! Occasionally the old "black fits" would return, and then the Chief would lock himself in his room and see no one, but only to re-appear next day and become once more the life and soul of the party. No hint, says Saffi, would he give, in word or manner, of the nature of those secret conflicts; but in his letters to Emilie Hawkes he confesses to "emotions of rage" and the temptation to "make myself what they [the reactionaries] assert me to be" and organise a vast vendetta. "To have to struggle against feelings of hatred, for which we have not been born, is very sad."[10]

       *   *   *   *   *

So the early months of 1850 still found him in the Villa Montallegro, a sort of benign Superior in a community of minor brothers. And now as always it was the Religious Question that dominated him. Who could doubt (he wrote) that, right or wrong, the human mind now believed it caught glimpses of new destinies, and that it claimed its independence to pass under revision the standards and conventions which had hitherto governed its life—a revision which ecclesiastical authority forbade in vain? Who could fail to see that the Past and the Future were now contending for the conscience of mankind? Who could deny that the authoritarianism of an ecclesiastical and social caste was now morally obsolete, and that the authority of the future must be found, not simply in the voice of tradition, but also in the leadership of genius and virtue ratified by the conscience of the peoples? And therefore who could question that the Papal system, committed to immobility and the despotic principle, had no living future? Plainly the time was at hand for the establishment "between the Capitol and the Vatican" of the Church which should rescue Europe from moral anarchy—the Church of the future, identifying itself with the life of Humanity and blessing all progress led by the Spirit of Truth—"the Church which shall have neither Pope nor Laity, but wherein all shall be believers, all priests." But why, he asks, do not the priests of Italy see this? Why do not they see that their Church has become Cæsar's and must be restored to God? "In the name of God, are you Christians? Do you understand the Evangel? . . . Between Humanity and the Pope place the open Gospel, then search your consciences and judge."[11]

But the alternative was not contemporary Protestantism. Protestantism, by separating the national and political from the religious sphere, was denying the unity of life. Catholicism, after all, had a comprehensive outlook, a conception of corporate life, but the Protestant peoples, individualistic and divided, were too apt to reserve Fraternity for the ideal sphere. In world politics they were inclined to oppose to the Papal cry of "Authority for all" the self-protecting policy of "Liberty for those who possess it." "England, the United States, Switzerland, fold their arms and tacitly aid the triumph, which they believe to be iniquitous, of old authority over liberty. Like Pilate, they wash their hands of the blood of the just." So he argued, and he was frankly antagonised by the narrowness of British Dissent, which, in his own bitter phrase, prated of brotherhood in its chapels, and, in the same breath, extolled Britain's "Providential isolation." It was hardly an unfounded complaint. "If tyrants fight," exclaims young Mr. Spurgeon of the Italian struggle of '59, "let them fight; let free men stand aloof. Why should England have aught to do with all the coming battles? As God has cut us off from Europe by a boisterous sea, so let us be kept apart from all the broils and turmoils into which tyrants and their slaves may fall."[12] "Tyrants and their slaves!" It was as if the one contemptuous gesture sufficed to dismiss alike the Italians and their oppressors. What claim had either upon the political interest of God's Englishmen? There was, indeed, no question of the great-heartedness of Mr. Spurgeon; it was his conventions that cramped him. But the Church of the future must strike another note than this—" the new Catholicism of Humanity," the solidarity of mankind!

Thus the winter passed, and in the spring of the year, after a secret visit to Paris, Mazzini was once more in England, surprising as we have seen, the Carlyles, re-illumining the Ashurst circle, and playing the part of earthly providence to a mixed and increasing company of refugees.

IN the reminiscences of Herzen and Pulszky we have occasional, and not always favourable, glimpses of the exiles of '48 and the later years. They were certainly a mixed and numerous class. There were fugitive insurrectionaries from Baden and Vienna, from Posen and Galicia, from Paris and from all parts of Italy—men and women of every rank and calling—students, artists, lawyers, aristocrats, artisans. Too often the excitements of conspiracy and revolution had unfitted them for ordinary life. There were wild and irresponsible spirits like the poet Herweg, coarse violentists like Heinzen, erratic egotists like Gallenga and Orsini, benevolent cranks like Gustav Struve; and the best of them were apt to be restless, irritable and garrulous, talking interminably of "delivering Europe" and "hurling the tyrants from their thrones." All the same, the majority were sincere and self-sacrificing. They haunted the cafés of Pâquis, the eating-houses of Soho, and congregated according to their elective affinities. Their world was the smoke-laden atmosphere of dingy committee-rooms; they declaimed or applauded furious harangues; they read letters from all quarters of the Continent protesting that Europe was once more "ready to rise." As time passed, the more adaptable were absorbed into the commercial, literary or academic worlds; the rest hovered around their chosen haunts, living precariously and mysteriously. Often they became crabbed and embittered, and quarrelled among themselves. Like bigoted sectarians, they split upon minor differences and glided down side-streets to assemble with their exclusive coteries and listen to arguments as threadbare as their own faded garments. But always the old formulas lingered on their lips, always they exchanged the old conspiratorial signs and passwords. Like dispossessed nobility, they were proud of their class, looked with antipathy upon the vulgar world, and still dreamed of a time when they should claim their inheritance. Their watches had stopped in '48.

Among this mixed company Mazzini and Worcell moved with something of that unconfessed embarrassment which afflicted Maurice and Kingsley when they fraternised with the cruder and more blatant of the early Socialists. But masters of conspiracy must not be ruled by their personal tastes. Moreover, they had a certain responsibility. These men and women were their chorus; they were more: they were their spiritual children or stepchildren, and must be fathered and cared for. And since the saintly, devoted Worcell was visibly wasting away, it was left more and more to Mazzini, in Mrs. Carlyle's phrase, to make mincemeat of himself for his numerous and difficult family.

Fortunately there were now two valuable coadjutors. There were Ledru Rollin, gigantic embodiment of the (authentic) French Republic, and Louis Kossuth, no less imposing Paladin of Hungary. It was, indeed, a little regrettable that neither M. Rollin nor M. Kossuth were all that the Prophet could have desired. Thus he was constrained to confide to a sympathetic Herzen that M. Rollin, though an excellent man, was unhappily governed by a curious misconception. He believed that the French (and not the Italians) were the *initiator-people,* an error which vitiated his entire political philosophy. Of Kossuth, Mazzini wrote to his mother: "I will tell you, mother, just what he is: the incarnation of Hungary. He really loves his country and would sacrifice everything for it. In this . . . he will always be great. For the rest, he will be what circumstances may dictate. . . . Gastaldi is right, not in exaggerating my merits, but in recognising that I work through faith in a general principle, while Kossuth works exclusively for his country."[1] Conceivably, the great Hungarian, too, may have had his embarrassments. Was it not enough that one should seek to liberate Hungary? Why must one be expected to pledge oneself in addition to the Universal Principle of Nationality, the Divine Law of Progress, the Oneness of Humanity, the Democratic Fraternity of the Peoples? What, for example, would a free Hungary think of the idea of an independent Transylvania? And if one crossed the Atlantic to set before the great American people the wrongs and aspirations of Hungary, why should one be expected to divide his public by pronouncing against African slavery? This excellent

Mazzini was really a trifle unreasonable. Still, there were possibilities of fruitful co-operation, and the Hungarian had already signed, and left with a Mazzinian agent, an undated proclamation for combined Hungarian and Italian action, to be used should occasion arise.

Affairs, then, were not unhopeful, and after a clandestine visit to the Continent, Mazzini was back in London in '51, founding a new Society of the Friends of Italy, flinging himself into new journalistic enterprises (including the Paris *Proscrit* and the Genoese *Italia e Popolo*), taking the platform at rousing meetings in the Provinces, castigating Louis Blanc and the Continental Socialists (for demoralising the proletariat), and hurling a final doom at the nocent head of the French Republic. *"Impotent to repeat the rôle of Napoleon, you have burlesqued his conceptions . . . with pigmy travesties of his gigantic ambitions. . . . You are now reduced to playing the immoral, atheistic part of Louis Philippe, and above your head hangs, fatal and inevitable, his self-same doom. . . . And in that day, Sire, abandoned, scorned and vilified by those who to-day degrade themselves most with lying flatteries before your face, you will pass . . . to die in exile."*[2] Meanwhile, in the charmed circle of the Ashursts and Stansfelds, the prophet of doom laid aside his thunder and occasionally took up his guitar.

*   *   *   *   *

With the Ashursts, in truth, the family chronology might have been dated as Before and After Mazzini; for the history of their inward, and to some extent their outward, lives took direction from his advent. Besides a son, William, who practised law in his father's office in Old Jewry, there were four daughters. They were Eliza Ashurst, who read George Sand and cultivated the friendship of the daring Miss Jewsbury; Matilda, married to Joseph Biggs, a manufacturer; Caroline, wife of James Stansfeld, M.P.; and Emilie, who studied art and read Bentham, and whose husband, Sidney Hawkes, was Stansfeld's partner in the Swan Brewery, Fulham. As long as their parents lived, the sisters spent their Sundays together in the Ashurst home. They were Radical and " emancipated " women, and shocked Victorian sensibilities by smoking—except Eliza, who asserted her emancipation in other ways and contracted an undesirable marriage with a Frenchman named Bardonneau. But at heart they were nonconformist Romantics in quest of a Cause, and the advent of the Italian exile with the aura of a conspirator, the bearing of a poet-scholar and the face of a messiah, was electrical. They had gained an introduction to him through Thomas Duncombe, the Radical M.P.; and Duncombe had warned them that they would find him preoccupied, if not inaccessible. Instead, after the first shy exchanges in French (it was in 1844), he had walked into their lives and taken possession. It was incredibly delightful, as if they had suddenly turned a corner and found themselves in an enchanted country. For their new friend was not like others; his designs were so vast, his devotion to his poor organ-grinder boys was so noble, his helplessness in worldly affairs so appealing; he was withal so wise and yet so childlike, so good and yet so excitingly and almost perilously human! Nor were their men-folk less enthusiastic: and once, in the exile's presence, Mr. Ashurst senior (looking sternly round upon Eliza and Emilie and Matilda and Caroline) took occasion to deliver a parlour-carpet homily, concluding, "And if I could think my daughters capable of shrinking from *you* for what the world might say, I should disown them." On that score, certainly, they were never in the slightest danger of being disowned. "The dear Angel," wrote Emilie, "took possession of us once and for ever."

And if he was their Angel before he left in '48 he was their demi-god now. But also he was something dearer and more intimate. Perhaps it was Eliza Bardonneau's death in Paris that drew him closer into the circle. It was in the winter of 1850, at a time when he was in hiding near Grenchen. To him the news had come first, and it had fallen to him to break it to the family. How tenderly and delicately he had performed the office! How manifestly he had suffered with them! How constant had been his letters and how full of outpourings of affection! "My dear, dear friend," he had written to Mrs. Ashurst, "how I should wish to be able to take on my own poor, doomed life all your sorrows!" and how gladly he would give his life itself to be able to infuse into them his own faith! "If ever (he writes to William

Ashurst) I felt the wretchedness of my belief not being shared by all of you whom I love it has been now." "I have been suffering with you all, and longing to be near you all, and to . . . endeavour, not to console you, but to make your grief less dry, less despairing, less rebellious against mysteries that we cannot fathom. . . . I cannot plunge into the depths of the Infinite; my soul is a man's and not an angel's and I shrank from such suffering inflicted upon one we love; and I feel with you and almost love you better for the words I blame. Still, there have been moments in my life in which I had a glimpse of the knowledge [meaning] of suffering . . . [and] I do firmly believe in immortality. . . ." "Death would only spread her icy wings between us if we ceased to love. And this faith of mine, which I would give my actual life gladly for feeling able to infuse in you all—and my grieving with you over our actual loss—and my loving you all more dearly than before—is all the consolation that I can give to you."[3] It would have been strange if they had failed to prize a friendship so self-devoting.

And as usual his mother shared in these intimacies.

* * * * *

For Maria Mazzini, indeed, these last years had been full of difficulty and disappointment. After the bright hopes of '48 the gates of exile had once more closed between mother and son. All that was left was the solace of his letters and those of his friends; and certainly no other Mazzinian plot was so completely successful as this filial conspiracy of love by which he engaged his friends to cheer her loneliness. How numerous were her correspondents, and how well they understood what themes lay nearest her heart!

Thus just now (1852) Emilie Hawkes describes to her Pippo at work, "grave, preoccupied, almost severe," in his Radnor Street den, his "everlasting cigar" in his mouth, a litter of papers and a bunch of fresh flowers beside him, and "the sweetest of sad smiles" for friendly interruptions; or Pippo at a family party, transformed into a social being, joking and quizzing and indulging in a thousand mock-impertinences, "the life and soul of all our circle"; or Pippo sitting at Caroline's bedside, interesting himself in the least little details about the new baby; or Pippo explaining foreign politics to Papa, or listening for the hundredth time to the history of dear Mamma's cough, "and speaking so lovingly of you, who have made all mothers sacred in his eyes."[4] And Caroline Stansfeld writes to her as "mia madre d' elezione," and longs "for the hour when, at your knee, I shall be permitted to call you by that name." And is not Maria's portrait to be given the place of honour at Pippo's next dinner party, when, says Caroline, "we shall drink your dear health and to the time when we shall all be together in his Italy."[5] And then faithful, devoted Maurizio Quadrio, also in England, and not to be outdone in this filial ministry, must write to her long and lyrical descriptions of the sublime effects of Pippo's speeches at English public meetings—"great tears rolling down the cheeks of white-haired old men and fair-haired maidens," applause passing into a solemn hush—the entire assembly rising at last to attest its faith, "like the early Christians."[6] And Aurelio Saffi (just now completely captivating Carlyle) solaces her with his own gentle epistles. All of which *Scià* Maria can readily accept and believe, for is not Pippo the Lord's elect? And all her correspondence is methodically docketed and dated, and trusted friend Napoleone Ferrari, of the old-time brotherhood of the balcony, is told where, after her death, he shall find it (for Antonietta's Jesuits must not lay hands on it): and Ferrari must also see to it that her annuity for Pippo is so fixed that he can never give away the principal. And then, to please Pippo, does she not sit for her photograph in her best silks? Thus we behold her with patterned shawl and white frilled cap, and cap-strings tied with ample bow-and-ends—a dour *Calvinistic* face with dark, troubled eyes set wide apart, and long, aquiline nose, and deep lines from the nostrils to the drooping, reticent mouth: a face that somehow brings to mind an Auld Licht Sabbath.

But in Genoa who did not know that that austere figure, wrapped in impenetrable reserve, represented an Idea that might one day explode the city and the kingdom? Not a day but she was on some Mazzinian errand or other, and just now, with Pippo making secret trips to the Continent, she must address him once more as "niece Emily," and direct her letters to Quadrio. (And it is childlike Quadrio's irritating little way to *read* them and pass them on to Pippo with the comment, "Very moving.") And for the rest, it is very lonely in Genoa: for she must treat as reprobate all who fall away from the one infallible Mazzinian faith, and the elect are few. This long while the Ruffinis have been excommunicated, and most of Maria's own kinsfolk; and even daughter Antonietta, since her marriage, is too much under the thumb of the Jesuits to be trusted. Only, for Maria's comfort, there are always her Jansenists and a little group of Genoese incorruptibles, and poor wandering Giuditta, and the incomparable English sisters. "A kiss and my blessing for your little one," she writes to Caroline Stansfeld in August; "and, when I am no more, tell him of your 'Madre d' amore.'" And next day, as the noon sunshine kindles over the Bisagno valley, she returns from Mass (it is Sunday) with her friend Isabella Zerbini. On the way home she takes from her bosom Pippo's latest letter and begins to read from it: then suddenly cries, "*My son! My son!*" and sinks unconscious into the arms of her friend.

How quickly (notes Pietro Cironi) the house fills with priests—Antonietta's priests—with poor Antonietta herself lamenting that her mother can neither confess nor receive the sacrament! But it is her son's devotees—Ferrari, Gastaldi, Giacomo Medici, old bookseller Doria, Alberto Mario—who guard her bedside, and it is one of her Jansenists who, with threefold solemn invocation of *Gesù, Giuseppe* and *Maria,* recites the last offices. And when the end comes, and the Press of Genoa unites in respectful tribute, it is left for a Turin "Moderate" journal (the *Opinione*) to assail her in death as a bigot and a nullity.

But behind the flower-heaped catafalque of this nullity follow fifteen thousand mourners—Lombard émigrés, gentlefolk, Working Men's Associations, English and American seacaptains, Deputies, artisans. It is a political, a Mazzinian demonstration, surely; but how decisively the old lady would have approved! And as the cortège passes with bands and banners in ominous slow procession, Genoa, looking on from its crowded streets and balconies, understands. It is Maria Mazzini's final gesture: "My son! My son!" And in the harbour the foreign ships, English, American, Danish, Dutch, Swedish, fly their flags at half-mast; and at nightfall every cottage in the Bisagno valley burns candles in its windows to shine upon the road that leads to Maria's last resting place beneath the willows and cypresses on the Staglieno hill.

In London Mrs. Carlyle hastened to Mazzini, but he would see no one. "Do not come," he wrote to the Ashursts; "I want to be alone for one day. But write, each of you, one word of blessing. . . ." "I am strong and calm and believing . . . only I feel as if they had taken away some vital, essential part of me, and I was groping for it."[7] There was nothing left for him now in Genoa but graves.

* * * * *

Before the summer was out he was concentrating upon a new insurrectionary project. He felt "more and more the sacredness of a mission which she approved," he was now, thanks to Maria's foresight, free from the irksome necessity for hack-writing, and able to concentrate upon his Italian schemes. To the one-time waif, Susan Tancioni, whom he was supporting at Lugano, and whose children he was educating, he wrote in difficult English that his mother had " set on his head," he thought, the sum of £120 a year. "I think that on the whole I am not very rich, but quite enough . . . taking away [i.e., allowing for] your pension, I should have still for my own expenses some fifty shillings a week. . . . Saffi is here, but with nothing, and living at this time at my own expense. . . . Mention in your first the banknote."[8] He added that his mother's old servants were provided for, and that he had sent £40 to two cousins, "old girls, very poor "; and for the rest he must devote himself more than ever to the liberation of Italy.

And if he had needed an additional goad, it had been supplied by the imprisonment of Giuditta on his account. Mazzini was, in fact, in touch with Giuditta through Lamberti, and in 1851 she had returned to active propaganda. Radetzky had learned of this and had pressed the ducal police of Parma to order "an energetic inquisition" in the hope of obtaining " clearer traces of the Mazzinian designs." Late in 1851 her house had been raided at a time when she and her daughters were entertaining a company of friends, but on the instant of the alarm her family contrived to dispose of much incriminating material by the simple process of swallowing it. Del-Cerro relates how Giuditta, detecting a letter of Mazzini's under the Police Commissioner's hand, had detached the little document with a disarming smile and the excuse that as the Commissioner must be tired, she would read it to him; which she proceeded to do, inventing the contents and beginning "Dear Sister." It is hard not to believe that here, too, there was a predisposition of the officer in charge to assist the victim. This, indeed, was one of the besetting difficulties of the despotic governments in Italy. Radetzky's pressure, however, was insistent and a little later Giuditta was imprisoned in the ducal gaol and then removed to the ill-famed prison of Santa Margherita, Milan—the prison described by Pellico. Her letters to her daughters during her imprisonment, quoted by Del Cerro, reveal her character. "First of all I bid you good morning, my dear Elvira and my dear Corinna, embracing you with all the tenderness of my heart. Do, I beg of you, keep up your usual occupations, just as if I were away on a visit to Achille. . . . Pat poor Trenmor [her dog] for me, and don't forget the little birds at my window." She asks them to send her books and mentions Thiers' *Histoire du Consulat et de l'Empire.* Later she writes: "The good Father Christopher says somewhere that the Lord is the friend of the afflicted who trust in Him, and that is what I repeat to you now. Sorrow sanctifies and reinvigorates the soul. In the name of all the love you have for me, endure this hard ordeal, I beg of you, with resignation and calmness. The only thing that troubles me is the thought that you .are suffering, and I assure you that when it seems to me that I see you calm and tranquil, I am so cheerful that I almost forget my surroundings."

Radetzky's suspicions of new Mazzinian designs were not unfounded. Mazzini was, in fact, in touch with a secret organisation at Milan. The organisation was not of his founding nor was the design of his conceiving, but the leaders were republican and the plot was, as usual, simple. Goaded to fury by the hangings and woman-floggings under Radetzky, the Milanese conspirators had resolved upon a new rising. February 6 (1853) was fixed for the attempt—a Carnival Sunday when, it was known, the Austrian Staff would be dining at the Palace. A Garibaldian sergeant named Fanfulla and a hundred picked men were to rush the Palace guard and capture the staff. The Guards' quarters were to be similarly seized and the Castle with its arsenal and magazine was to be stormed by two insurgent columns after the sentries had been overpowered. At a given sign the city lights were to be cut off (the head of the gasworks was in the plot), but from the top of the Cathedral a signal was to flash out to the armed bands secretly posted outside the city, who were then to pour into Milan.

Mazzini hesitated. The risks were great and a failure would be catastrophic. But the Milanese were undissuadable. The attempt would be made with or without his co-operation; on the other hand, his aid might turn the balance and ensure success. It was true. The insurgents were short of funds, and in addition to his annuity had not his mother left him £2,000 of free capital? Moreover, his emissaries could be supremely serviceable in recruiting the auxiliary forces outside Milan. He resolved (Giuditta was now released and far from the danger-zone) to support the attempt. "I have never," he confessed to his English friends, "felt my own moral responsibility so highly involved."[9] At least he was under no fantastic delusion. The plot, he explained, rested upon a foundation that might at any moment collapse: moreover, it was evident that the upper and middle classes were holding aloof; they would come in only after the first round had been won. "The first step, through the popular element alone, *must* be a victory, and a brilliant one; if not I shall be accursed—that is not much—and the cause will be lost, ruined." But he had given his word.

The Genoa group—Dr. Bertani, Giacomo Medici, Cosenz, and others—disapproved; but it was too late, and he was impatient. Genoa, he declared, had not the data for a sound judgment: Genoa knew only Genoa; he knew the whole situation "from the Abruzzi to Vorarlberg." And by December, clean shaven and "looking like a Jesuit," he had crossed the Swiss frontier and was extracting grim amusement from travelling by train with a company of Austrian whitecoats.[10] To secure a leader for the auxiliary insurgent forces was difficult. For immediate purposes Garibaldi, selling tallow-candles in New York, was out of the question; instead he sent for Klapka, a Hungarian Generalissimo. Saffi, meanwhile, was secretly co-operating in Piedmont and the Centre; Lemmi and Quadrio at Genoa. By February 5 Saffi with 3,000 volunteers was at Bologna, another column was at Pavia, Acerbi was posted near by; Klapka was at Lugano, Mazzini himself at Chiasso. He, at least, had done his part; everything now depended upon the Milanese. At the important hour he released a final manifesto. Let insurrection transform martyrdom into victory! "Be it tremendous as the tempest that sweeps our seas, steadfast as the Alps above us. Between these Alps and the Sicilian Sea are twenty-five million of our kinsmen. The struggle will be brief if only you will it!" Also he released Kossuth's proclamation. It had been given in general terms long before the Milan project was thought of. In the circumstances it was straining good faith to use it without Kossuth's specific approval, especially as the Magyar chief was in London in constant touch with Mazzinian agents. At the last moment Mazzini sought to withdraw it, but it was too late.

For at the decisive hour Milan, quiet and passive under the stars, gave no sign of tempestuous outburst, and no signal flashed among the Duomo spires. Instead Sergeant Fanfulla left town secretly and in haste; other key-men were as mysteriously missing; the leaderless bands, waiting in vain, melted away into the darkness of the deserted streets, and the insurrection that was to be tremendous as a southern hurricane sputtered out in a few street-corner scuffles and a skirmish over a barricade. Next morning seven Italian corpses swung in Austrian gibbets under a winter sky; nine more three days later. The "revolution" was over.

*   *   *   *   *

Forecasting the sure consequences of failure, Mazzini had well said "I shall be accursed." He was. What a travesty of National Insurrection had been this *fracas* of bombs and daggers and sharpened nails—this marshalling of poor heroic or half-heroic milkmen, coalmen, porters, errand-boys, for desperate, cut-throat escapades—a score of youths running amok through the streets and stabbing bewildered white-coats tumbling out of taverns and cafés! And truly, the Apostle, more and more entangled in dubious methods, was being thrown out of his true rhythm and posture. Yet, at least, this had been no sudden apostasy. He had grown up with this method and idea from the days of Jacopo Ruffini. The projected rising in which Jacopo lost his life was to have been a "street-movement" of this character. And whatever material advance had been registered in the Italian struggle had been initiated by these same reprehensible "street-movements"—movements which the Moderates had habitually condemned, but whose successes they had punctually appropriated. It was the "street-movements" in Sicily which had given the first impetus to Constitutionalism; the "street-movements" in Milan in '48 which had led to Charles Albert's campaign, and the Turin move to annex Lombardy; the "street-movements" in Rome which had begun that campaign against the secular power of the Church which Piedmont was now following up in its own interests. So he was able to argue.

And what if this latest "street-movement" had succeeded? What if Radetzky and his Croat butchers and women-floggers and hangmen had been driven out once more? What if the bells of Milan had once more clashed a triumph and the volunteers of Italy had again poured through the gates and along the tumultuous, roaring Corso? Would the Moderates have registered their solemn protest, or Risorgimento historians have recorded their grave reproof? It was failure that was unpardonable, and that failure was immediately due, not to Mazzini's intervention, but to last-moment, unpredictable defections among the Milanese.

None the less, a hurricane of accusation and malediction blew down upon him. The fiasco was yet another "Mazzinian dream," and its victims were the dupes of his fantastic folly. Nor was it only from hostile quarters that the storm proceeded. "Give Mazzini," said Dr. Bertani bitterly, "three men and four stones and he will announce a national revolution"; and at Bertani's instigation Mazzini was deposed from the head of the National Committee. In Paris Manin sorrowfully agreed, criticised the (so-called) Mazzinian Theory of the Dagger in the London *Times*, and came out with a new national society. And while Kossuth, first through Mayne Reid and then over his own signature, repudiated the Milan proclamation as a forgery, and Agostini, secretary of the National Committee, added his own repudiation, English and Continental critics hastened to swell the chorus of abuse. No charge was too paltry, none too grave, to bring forward now. Even Emilie Hawkes, after a private visit to Genoa and conferences with Bertani and Medici, seems to have felt the situation hopeless and advised him to "give it up," and thereafter he played with the phrase in his letters.

But that, at least, he would never do. "I am dead at heart, Emilio," he wrote to Venosta.[11] The cowardice, the baseness, the heartlessness which he saw and felt had surpassed all that in his blackest moments he could have conceived. So he declared. And his intimates found him repeating oftener than usual, and with sadder intonation, Mr. Browning's lines:

> " One task more declined, one more footpath untrod,
> One more devils'-triumph and sorrow for angels,
> One wrong more to man, one more insult to God!"

But all his emotions were in leash to the one fixed determination to go forward. Nothing should change him. If Bertani and Medici and Manin were moving perceptibly to the Right; if, as he had reason to believe, Garibaldi had accepted a pension from Victor Emmanuel's private purse, then the necessity was all the greater for his remaining in the field. He would not pretend to act with these men, but he would act.

He did so. He excommunicated Bertani and Medici, declared the National Committee dissolved, assailed Manin in a long and devastating rejoinder, effectively refuted Kossuth, flung at the Italian public a defiant *apologia*, and founded a new organisation bearing the ominous title "National Junta of Action." He still had hopes of a following; in Rome particularly, where there were Liberal incorruptibles who had not yielded to the enchantments of Turin. "Rome," he wrote a week after the Milan fiasco, "will go on organising." Alas, "Rome" would not—Cardinal Antonelli looking well to that. But in any case he himself would go on organising. Passing from hiding-place to hiding-place among the Alpine snows, with an Austrian gallows, perhaps, awaiting his capture, he could still found his Junta of Action and leap defiant out of mortal disaster, to challenge the world. Herzen, with his Russian insight, had read him aright: "Such men do not give in . . . the worse things go with them, the higher they hold the flag. If Mazzini loses friends and money and barely escapes one day from chains and the gallows, on the next he takes his stand more obstinately and resolutely than ever . . . denies himself everything, even sleep and food, ponders whole nights over new plans, and every time actually creates them; flings himself again into the conflict, and again beaten, sets to work once more."[12] In this unyielding steadiness, as Herzen adds—this faith which ran far ahead of facts—there was something of grandeur and something, perhaps, of madness. Herzen was prepared to accept the less welcome hypothesis and to defend it. A great man acting directly was bound to be a great madman. "Often it is just that grain of madness which is the essential condition of success. It acts on the people's nerves and carries them away."

Meanwhile, by May (1853) the madman was safely back in England, and Emilie thought the time had arrived for writing his life. But he would not have it. "My life! Ah me! . . . a title and no book at all." Besides, dear Emilie could not possibly write it impartially—could not, he was convinced, supply "the shadow-side" which ought also to be given.[13] But others, at least, were ready enough to supply the shadow-side, and Turin found the opportunity too good to be lost. The myth of Mazzini as the terrorist of Europe was inflated to monstrous proportions, and Farini, as literary exponent of enlightened Moderation, was inditing purple passages on Mazzinian fanaticism—"a Druidic piety, immolating its victims to its own idol."[14] Yet Turin, if slightly more eclectic, and worshipping at various shrines at sundry times—Turin also had its idols, its priests, its sacrifices, and was just now preparing, on strange altars reared upon the pestilential mud of the Crimea, to "immolate" many more "victims" than were claimed by the gibbets of Milan.

TURIN'S interest in the Crimea was due to a new crisis in European affairs. For in 1853-54 the French Empire, needing a brilliant war, was standing hopefully with Great Britain in defence of a high-minded Turkish Sultan menaced by a brutal Russian Czar. In England itself political and patriotic feeling was steadily rising; for if direct intervention against Austria in Italy was outside the ethics of international diplomacy, the menace of Russia on the Indian frontier justified a vigorous policy in the Near East. Thus, while a Franco-British fleet was demonstrating hopefully in Besika Bay, Lord Palmerston at the Carlton was toasting the Turkish Sultan as a great reformer and the French Emperor as a paragon of most single-minded sincerity. The music halls and the churches vied in support of a firm policy; and even Dissent—so often, as Palmerston admitted, in advance of the general conscience—was aroused to martial ardour. Thus through their eloquent mouthpiece, young Mr. Dale of Birmingham, the Nonconformist manufacturers of the Midlands expressed their ability to rejoice in a war waged, " not for commerce nor for territory, but for justice, mercy and truth."

The sentiment was sincere. Palmerston's Liberalism in all matters relating to the government of foreign States was unimpeachable, and under his guidance a war begun for the protection of Turkey-in-Europe might end with the liberation of Poland and Hungary. In this connection Palmerston himself was indulging in private fantastications of an apocalyptic character. Lombardy and Venice might possibly be turned over to Piedmont, Poland made a buffer-State, and in a general re-shuffle of territories from the Aaland Isles to the Crimea, Prussia might advantageously be enriched with certain Baltic provinces, Turkey with Georgia and perhaps Circassia, and Austria with Wallachia and Moldavia.[1]

The main possibilities were attractive to Turin, and Cavour hastened to offer the Allies a neat auxiliary force of Piedmont regulars for the furtherance of the Crimean crusade. It might be difficult to explain to Valerio, Brofferio and the incorrigibles of the Left how the fortunes of Italy, lost among the vineyards of Novara, could be recovered in the mud of the Crimea; and still more difficult to expound the moral connection between the cause of Italian Liberalism and the defence of the Moslem Sultanate; but otherwise the way was clear. Victor Emmanuel as ally of Victoria and Napoleon was good business, and Piedmont would book a through passage to the Paris Congress by way of Balaklava, Tchernaja and Sebastopol. There was even the remote but fascinating possibility of Austria's being drawn into the war on the side of Russia, in which case Piedmont would annex Lombardy with the Allies' support. "Your friends the doctrinaires and Liberals," wrote Cavour to Madame de Circourt, "will perhaps find our policy absurd and romantic"; but he was prepared with his defence.

But it was characteristic of the exasperating irrelevancy of the republican prophet that Mazzini should assail the policy as neither absurd nor romantic, but wicked. In London, in the midst of the rising war-fever, he privately and publicly criticised the Palmerston policy. He bowed before "the quiet, silent devotedness" with which the British people accepted all the sacrifices inseparable from the war; but such devotion, he declared, deserved a better cause. The British policy was "irreligious," and not less so because it had received the blessing of the Churches. "Irreligious . . . I maintain the word. I know the protest which, should what I write be deemed in any way important, would rise from your thousand sects now swarming on the corpse of Faith. It does not move me."[2]

For on what principle did England, inert respecting the rights of Poland, Hungary and Italy, intervene to defend the claims of the Ottoman Empire to its European outpost? Or was it supposed that Turkey was a valuable barrier to the encroachments of a despotic Russia? The only true barrier would be a living wall of young, free, associated peoples— Polish, Serbian, Albanian, Moldavian, Wallachian, Hungarian —nationalities which "must soon or late form themselves into a great confederation." Such a policy would have been " truly great and beautiful " and would have endowed England with a European initiative and made her " the focus of civilising power for centuries." But for this the necessary moral enterprise was lacking. Englishmen, rich in individual piety, lacked a collective faith. " A certain half-despairing, half-selfish moral inertness has grown parasitically on your souls and cramped your old Saxon vigour; a cowardice of the intellect, which *sees* the aim in a merely contemplative way . . . a sort of morally sleepy, lazy, self-benumbing disposition, the incipient lethargy of dying collective bodies, and the unavoidable characteristic of all irreligious epochs . . . each man . . . left to wander about cloaked and muffled in his own individuality, conscious, however he may parade, of his own weakness."

But it was for Turin that he reserved his wrath—Turin that was degrading Italian soldiers to the level of mercenaries, hired for an unprincipled foreign war; Turin that was spilling Italian blood to secure a Moslem ascendancy over Christian populations; Turin that was in open alliance with Napoleon III., betrayer of the Republic of France, assassin of the Republic of Rome. In an Open Letter the Prophet accused Cavour of a perfidious, diplomatic gamble, and did not hesitate to incite the soldiers of Piedmont to desertion. Who could look any longer for the salvation of Italy from this cabal of conscienceless intriguers? And in softer tones Manin and Kossuth half-agreed.

Mazzini went further. With poor, death-struck but indomitable Count Worcell, he sought to fan the smouldering embers of revolt. Now or never was the time to act, if Italy was to be snatched from the abyss. With Austria—courted alike by the Allies and by Russia—doubly preoccupied upon her Eastern frontiers, with France deeply engaged and obliged to call off even the Roman garrison, what was to hinder an Italian rising? And who could fail to see that the hard-pressed Crimean Allies, finding Austrian attention once more diverted to Italy, would cease wooing her and turn, *bon gré, mal gré*, for a new anti-Russian ally, to Poland? A liberated Poland would kindle Hungary, a Polish-Hungarian explosion would ignite Bohemia. . . . . In short, let Italy but strike the spark, and the flame must spread and the despots be ringed round once more with insurrectionary fires. . . . And Garibaldi was providentially in England!

It was a desperate project, and Garibaldi, in spite of martial encouragements at Newcastle and dinners at the Stansfelds', was non-committal. He must first confer with the brethren at Genoa. And at Genoa, in Brother Giacomo Medici's business office, after due conference with the Bertani group, he published (in Mazzini's own journal) his answer. Let "our young men" beware of being drawn into insurrectionary movements of which he, Garibaldi, had not approved. Let them beware of being drawn away "by the misleading insinuations of men who were either deceived or deceivers." Perhaps the allusion was to Orsini's mad scheme for a rising in Massa and Carrara, but the reference was ambiguous enough to wound the Chief. "'Ingannati o ingannatori,'" he repeats to Emilie. "And we taught him patriotism!" Thus threatening—incredibly—to write his "last words of truth to the Patriots" and retire forever, he confessed to feeling himself deserted "in a world of fallen souls." Only Worcell was left,—bed-ridden now, in that sunless basement lodging. He sat beside the old man, pen in hand, taking down his last messages. When Worcell and Lamennais died it was like the passing of an era. The age of Messianism, of mystical revolutionism, of the Hetæria, was no more; the age of subtlety and craft and patient intrigue had arrived. Calvin was exchanged for Richelieu, Dante for Macchiavelli.

*   *   *   *   *

Meanwhile Victor Emmanuel's Crimean forces, gallantly routing 50,000 grey-coats at Tchernaja, covered themselves with glory. Patriots wept proud tears over the latest despatches; Turin, gay with flags and vibrant with martial music, rejoiced in its streets and theatres; and amid the general darkness of Italian affairs, Cavour's Crimean policy flamed up in dazzling coruscation. The little Minister had gambled and won.

And after all, was it not possible to misjudge this Cavour, as if he were merely high-priest of the great god Sly? What if he had a purpose greater than he would acknowledge? What if he also had some unconfessed, unsuspected *Savona*? To

Madame de Circourt the little Minister wrote with strange fervour about "calling back to life a nation shut up for centuries in a frightful tomb"—wrote of Piedmont's providential mission to use her opportunities to plead before Europe the Italian cause. "We shall not," he declared, "draw back." Onward, rather—when once this Eastern Question is lifted out of the Sebastopol trenches on to the green tables of diplomacy—onward to the Paris Congress! And for a preliminary tuning-up of public opinion abroad, King Victor Emmanuel (in the charge of a responsible Minister) should visit Paris and London.

What, indeed, could have been happier? Napoleon received him as a brother, and Paris, recalling Novara, acclaimed him as every inch a soldier. Victoria received him as a typical mediæval knight-errant, and London, recalling his defiance of certain Papal bulls, hailed him as a courageous Constitutional sovereign. The Duchess of Sutherland likened him to St. George, and Protestant societies made associative mention of Martin Luther and (a happier reference) Henry of Navarre. The *Re galantuomo* had, indeed, been admirably coached and had as admirably responded; and Cavour, who had been slightly apprehensive of an occasional royal lapse from a difficult and exacting rôle, was able to write delightedly (in private) that the King had behaved himself like a perfect gentleman.

But Cavour, too, had won golden opinions. There may have been fastidious folk who could deplore a certain lack of ministerial distinction, and Grant Duff achieved an apt quotation from Mr. Tennyson:[3]

> "I see the wealthy miller yet,
>   His double chin and portly size,
> And who that knew him could forget
>   The busy wrinkles round his eyes;"

but there was no escaping the geniality of the fair, fat and florid little man with the twinkling spectacles and brisk address and clothes that looked as if he had slept in them; and even the blended suggestion of farmer and country attorney disarmed a too ready suspicion of diplomatic subtlety. He was able to convey to the Third Napoleon a happy sense of Italian devotion to the Napoleonic dynasty as the predestined arbiter of Europe, and he had found the arbiter responsive. ("Write confidentially to Walewski and state what you think I ought to do for Piedmont and Italy "); and a moving description of the Piedmont Monarchy as the spiritual offspring of British Constitutionalism, and of its filial dependence upon the British Throne as the moral arbiter of the world, was not less successful. The Queen was cordial, conferred the Garter upon Piedmont's Constitutional monarch, and admitted that there was much truth in what Cavour had said. (" It must ever be an object of our interest to see Sardinia independent and strong.") Thus Piedmont, having proved victorious at Tchernaja, had extended its operations and captured Windsor and St. Cloud.

And at the Paris Congress the victory was consolidated and developed. Throughout the session the bucolic little man in spectacles and a crumpled frock-coat was a model of rustic good sense, keeping in the background, assiduous in private conferences, and observing on all public occasions a seemly and deferential discretion; but somehow a Congress of European plenipotentiaries convened to settle the Eastern Question found itself (to the angry astonishment of Buol and his Austrians) detained to discuss the condition of Naples, the Austrian occupation of the Roman States and the general Italian situation. The hint was thrown out (through Walewski) that certain Grand Dukes would be well advised to abandon their methods of repressive absolutism, and (through Clarendon) that the Papal Government, " the shame of Europe," needed wholesale reformation. The King of Naples received a Congressional admonition " in the name of justice and humanity," and Austrian policy in Lombardy and Romagna was reviewed in relation to the Vienna Treaty.

It was fitting that at this stage the Sardinian Minister should be heard. And as the little man rose and faced the Austrian representatives across the table, it may be true that those who observed him remarked a subtle change of demeanour. It suddenly became evident, in fact, that this man was no mere bucolic, pitchforked into the politics of a petty State; he was an aristocrat; he was a lawyer; he was an Italian, facing the representatives of his country's oppressors and conscious that he had Europe for his audience. But he was also a statesman. He was neither violent nor effusive, neither mellifluous nor rhetorical;

his delivery was artless, jerky, direct, the delivery of one who is in command of his facts and is more concerned to present those facts than to achieve a speech. He spoke with deadly composure, moderation and logical precision, and when he sat down the business was over. Slowly the truth dawned upon an august assemblage of the political intellects of Europe. It had been Cavour's Congress. He had not put Italy on the map, but he had made out her case before the assembled representatives of the Powers, and he had put the Italian Question in the Protocol.

How far was Cavour now prepared to go, and in what direction? He was a political realist, and therefore he did not know. There were many possibilities—a Kingdom of Northern Italy, a Federation of Italian States under a Sardinian hegemony, a division of Italy between Naples and Piedmont. Who could tell? And there might be possibilities still more engaging. But in Paris he took the opportunity of renewing his intercourse with Manin. Since Mazzini's deposition in '53 Manin had been more active than usual. He had lately addressed the House of Savoy in almost Mazzinian style: "Make Italy, and I am with you; if not, not." To Luigi Cibrario, a ministerial colleague, Cavour reported his impressions of the visit: "I have had a long conference with Manin. He is still somewhat Utopian, has not dismissed the idea of a strictly popular war . . . . [and] urges the unity of Italy and further rubbish of that sort."* "Rubbish of that sort!" Yet he himself had now brought Unity appreciably nearer.

But the man who, yesterday and through many a dark day gone by, had made Italian Unity a creative conception, a living idea, was now isolated and hostile. He was ready enough to recognise a master-stroke of statecraft, but what evidence was there that the policy behind it put Italy, rather than a favoured province of Italy, first, or proceeded by any other method than the shifts and hazards of a chancy diplomacy toward any other result than that of a gambler's luck? In his paper-littered den in Cedar Road, where his pet canaries flitted uncaged in a

---

* The last clause is omitted by Chiala, but appears in Ollivier (*Empire Libéral*, iv. 596), whose source was Rattazzi. (See Crispi: *Memoirs*, i. 71, where the letter is quoted as to Rattazzi; Thayer, i. 428; Cesaresco: *Ital. Charact.*, ch. on Mameli, etc.

perpetual fog of tobacco, Mazzini was, in fact, planning desperately to recapture a lost initiative and embarking upon the forlornest of all his enterprises.

*   *   *   *   *

A deplorable, marplot Mazzini now (says the Chronicler), solving no Italian problem whatsoever, but in himself constituting one problem the more! Yet what should we expect of him? That he should hasten to proclaim the salvation of Italy through the new Dynasts? That he should dance before the ark of a new, potential Napoleonic covenant? That he should announce (with the excellent Master of Balliol and Mrs. Browning) that Louis Napoleon's was the one living head in sight with European Ideas? As for Turin, poor heroic Poerio might gasp from his pestilential Montefusco dungeon "*Let our pole-star be always and only Piedmont*," but what was Piedmont's own orientation? Even Manin, with all his Cavourian sympathies, had been exercised concerning this problem. The exclusively Piedmontese party, he declared, was saying in effect, "*The Savoy dynasty is more to us than Italy*." For when had Piedmont shown any belief in United Italy, or looked beyond the annexation of Lombardy and certain of the Duchies? By 1857, it is true, Cavour was secretly conniving at the establishment of a new National Association—with ex-republican Pallavicino for President, and ex-republican Garibaldi for Vice-President, and ex-republican La Farina for Secretary, and with poor Manin to give it his dying blessing. Cavour would even assure La Farina in strictest secrecy, like one confessing a mortal sin, that he privately accepted the formula of "Italy One and Independent with Rome for her capital"; "*but remember*," he added, "*that among my political friends no one believes the enterprise possible*." And to confer upon this so shameful theme at all, La Farina must visit his Premier by stealth at daybreak by a secret stairway. "If I am questioned in Parliament or by diplomats," adds Cavour, "I shall deny you like Peter. . . ."[4]

As for Napoleon, Jowett of Balliol was hopefully observing of his hero that the Emperor followed the best of plans— namely, the plan to have no plan. But the Exile, whose secret information was often uncannily accurate, was otherwise persuaded. By '58 he had grounds for suspecting that, in all matters pertaining to Italy, the Napoleonic Plan hardly conformed to the Balliol formula. It was specific and detailed and had been discussed in secret conference with Cavour. It included the possible restoration of the Muratist dynasty in Naples (in the person of kinsman Lucien Murat), the restoration of the Napoleonic dynasty in Tuscany (in the person of kinsman " *Plon-Plon* " Napoleon), and the territorial expansion of Piedmont in return for the cession to France of Nice and Savoy. Later there was a confirmatory portent. It was the betrothal, with Cavour in the rôle of Cupid, of Princess Clothilde of Piedmont to Prince Napoleon (*Plon-Plon*). The auguries were propitious. The preliminary course of the Royal romance had not run too smooth, paternal opposition had been heavy and obstinate, and the union had the desired quality of surprise. Princess Clothilde was a slip of a girl, the Prince was middle-aged, experienced and dissolute.

But at least it was hardly to be expected that this programme would evoke from Mazzini a *Nunc dimittis*. To such programmes prophets rarely kindle with approving zeal. Nor, indeed, was it easy to perceive how such jobbery could issue in national deliverance, or further the European movement. By convenient Royal marriages, and Royal wars, and accommodating territorial exchanges, a " Kingdom of Italy," or group of kingdoms, might be joinered piece by piece; but not by such methods could a Nation be brought forth; not by such methods could " the new Word " become " incarnate " and " the new era of a United Europe " be proclaimed. If the Prophet, feeling himself deserted in a world of fallen spirits, resolved upon fierce and desperate protest, it was not surprising. An absurd rumour, released in Turin, and pursued with shrill hue and cry by Disraelian Mr. Urquhart in the British provincial Press, accused him of being an agent of the Czar. In Carlylean vein he commented upon it to the Ashursts: " I would if I could. *He* is true and straightforward, a mighty despotic Fact, going through the world undisguised, to ruin or conquest. *They* are tyrants with a liberty-cap on their head; a new un-Holy Alliance."[5]

At all costs, then, Italy must be saved from the machinations of this crew. There was no doubting the moral mandate.

The Italy that had risen in '48 had not risen for "Etrurian Kingdoms," Muratist dynasties and an aggrandised Piedmont; and the heart of the people was still sound. If in their political ignorance they were led away by Turin, it was because they did not know, could not know, and could not be persuaded to believe, the facts. They could be educated only by Action. The flag of Italian Unity must be kept in the field.

But in 1856 the Napoleon-Cavour pact had not developed; and when young and ardent Jessie Merington White visited him at Cedar Road, she found him far enough removed from being the republican monomaniac and sinister *Carbonaro* of hostile caricature. He admitted that the Italian people were not troubling about the future form of government: that question would be decided "according to circumstances," when the proper time arrived. What had actually taken root in Italy was the idea of Unity, of a National State. As for Piedmont, her assistance was essential, and sooner or later she would certainly take over Lombardy and Venice. Only, circumstanced as she was, as an independent State, pledged to the ruling House and tethered by diplomatic relations with the Powers, she could not *initiate*. The United Italy initiative must be created by popular movements, by risings in Lombardy, the Centre and the South. And these risings were inevitable. The people in the oppressed areas were suffering too terribly to submit. All that leadership could aim at was to co-ordinate the risings and save them from being mere frenzied blows struck in the dark—save them from the demoralisation that waited upon local and sectarian revolts. And even so, failures and setbacks were probable. Only, once Garibaldi became convinced that nothing would come of the Paris Congress, the prospect would be more hopeful. He would return to his true rôle as revolutionary leader. "You are prepared," asked Miss White, "if a revolution brings Piedmont into the field, to let its King have the crown of United Italy?" "I am prepared to acknowledge the sovereignty of the people, whether they decide on a United Republic or a United Monarchy."[6] It was not, on the face of it, a fanatical programme.

Indeed, as the weeks passed, ardent Miss White and Emilie Hawkes were slightly perplexed by little homilies from the same quarter on the ethics of toleration. Would they be so good as to repeat, morning and night, That people in this actual mortal world are neither angels nor devils; That our present task is not that of the Last Judgment, but of saving from the Devil those who have a leaning for him, and of helping upward those who aspire toward the Angel; That, in any case, we must make the best of the former sort for the good of the latter; and, That we must look less to the keeping of ourselves proudly unblameable as independent individuals, and more to the Aim to be reached for all?[7] Miss White didn't know, but thought it sounded a little jesuitical. But who that had met him could entertain an unworthy doubt? Certainly not Miss White.

" My first visit to his tiny room . . . remains ever present. . . . Birds were flying about the apartment, a few lilies of the valley stood in a vase on the mantelpiece, books and papers were scattered everywhere, and there, writing on his knee, on the smallest fragment of the thinnest imaginable paper, sat Mazzini. He rose at once; his hand-grasp and luminous eyes fascinated and encouraged you, yet filled you with momentary awe. . . . Soon I was listening as a student to a master anxious to convince, but not in the least desirous of *imposing* his convictions."[8]

It was clear, however, that something was in the wind.

What was in the wind was, in fact, an unexpected Cavourian kite. For at this period the wizard of Turin was making secret overtures to the Reds. He was, it appeared, prepared to wink at revolutionary movements in Modena and elsewhere; just now they would not be inconvenient demonstrations. Mazzini was advised of the *bouleversement*. Could even Cavour, then, be " made the best of," for the good of the cause? Could action be organised with the tacit acquiescence of Piedmont? Then he, for one, would support any overtures that held out a fair promise of co-operation. " My position," he wrote privately, " is extremely delicate and difficult between . . . [the Cavourian party] and the extreme men of our own ": but he would strive for a working agreement. Cavour was certainly in indirect contact with the revolutionary groups at Genoa. Mazzini himself would risk a stolen visit. Once on the spot, even though in hiding, he could superintend negotiations. Bertani and Medici had deposed him, but he still had his own influential men. There was Carlo Pisacane, there was the Marquis Pareto, there were others. And if all failed and negotiations with Turin broke down, he would rally his own group and act in his own way. But it was strange to be going back to Genoa at last in this fashion—by stealth, like a thief in the night.

THE negotiations failed. In the nature of things, Cavour was primarily fore-pledged not to Italy but to the interests of Piedmont and the House of Savoy. For Mazzini to propose the fusion of all patriot-elements by means of a politically neutral formula, for him to propose the postponement of the issue of King or Republic until the Nation should be free to make its sovereign choice—this was only to exacerbate their fundamental antagonism. It only exposed and advertised Cavour's embarrassments without removing them, exasperating him as a litigant is exasperated who is forced into damaging admissions under cross-examination. There was another element in the antagonism. In Cavour's detestation of Mazzini's attitude there was something of the gambler's dislike for the obtrusive moralist, something of that sustained aversion which a Cavalier (with Roundhead repressions) must have felt for a Puritan gospeller. Cavour had come to hate not simply Mazzinianism but Mazzini.

Yet Cavour had won over Mazzini's former following. He had won over Garibaldi, Dr. Bertani, Medici, Cosenz, Sirtori, Pallavicino, Fanti, La Farina. It was galling. In Genoa Mazzini had met Bertani and Medici, a few others. They showed themselves respectful, cordial, even affectionate, but they declined to be magnetised: they were, he felt, "meditating something apart," and he was no longer to share their confidences. In the columns of his *Italia del Popolo* of Genoa he opened a "Thousand Muskets Fund" for the aid of "the first province to rise in the name of Italy." It was designed to test the actual temper of Turin and to chime—or clash— with Cavour's "Hundred Cannon Fund," ostensibly for home-defence. Medici consented to act as treasurer of the Muskets Fund, and then, on his own authority, altered the character of the appeal and destroyed its significance by inviting subscriptions for the first province that would rise "in the name of the King." Mazzini excused the recalcitrants naïvely. It was " weakness rather than wickedness." They were creatures of enchantment. Faced with the Austrian white-coats they were giants, capable of prodigies of valour; but before the political black-coats of Turin they contracted into infants. They would fight for Italy, die for her; they could not *believe* for her. They could not believe with a faith which held by the impalpable, incalculable elements in a nation's soul, by its volcanic passions, by its electrical enthusiasms. They were governed instead by accomplished facts, by the consideration of analysable resources—the Piedmont monarchy, the French Empire, regular armies, military alliances. They had forgotten the lessons of Milan and Rome. Well, they must be taught again. As for the Turin Moderates, he had exhausted upon them the last degree of long-suffering patience. He would " hoist the old flag and send them to the Devil."

It was an angry Prophet once more. It was endurable to see Italy in her chains; in her chains he had first loved her. What was unendurable was to see profane hands strike off her chains in order to bind upon her what he conceived to be a new and inglorious servitude. It was unendurable to imagine her deceived and degraded into accepting her " liberty " as the gift of kings, at the hands of " the French Pretender."

So he would " hoist the old flag." If an audacious popular movement could be launched, in Lombardy or the South, the situation might yet be saved.

*   *   *   *   *

The South was undeniably the field. Mr. Gladstone's thundering letter upon Neapolitan misrule had turned the eyes of Europe upon Naples and the foul dungeons of the Vicaria. The sleep of Englishmen was broken by nightmare dreams of those infernos, lit

> " By such faint daylight shadowy
> As down four hundred steps is poured,"

where men, for the high crime of loving Italy, languished " in their long dying," dragging their coupling-shackles in the thick, perpetual, pestilential darkness of their tomb. Even British Ministers and members of Parliament were lending their private aid to Panizzi for his mild plot to rescue victims interned on the convict-islands. And the South itself was preparing. Mazzini was in touch with Fabrizi and Rosalino Pilo, who assured him that the country was honeycombed with insurgent-societies; La Farina was reporting similarly to his own group. News came of mysterious explosions in *Bomba's* powder-magazines, of a rising under Baron Bentivegna (organised by Fabrizi and Pilo) in Sicily; of the blowing-up of a troopship on the way with Government reinforcements; and an attempt on the life of Ferdinand by a soldier, Agesilao Milano, was only another indication that the southern revolutionary volcano was not quiescent. The Court was panic-stricken, and Milano's execution was a scene of mediæval ferocity. At a sign from the executioner, " the *tirapiedi* [*lit.*, pull-feet] suddenly pushed the prisoner off the ladder, adroitly catching him by the feet as he fell, and swinging with him into space. At the same time the hangman scrambled down and seated himself astraddle on the shoulders of the victim, and the three swung to and fro in sight of the immense multitude, jamming, struggling and pulling."[1] King *Bomba* well understood how to vary the monotony of executions by means of circus-diversions. Yet perhaps the gratitude of the public was dashed with other sentiments; the crowds carried in their ears poor Milano's dying cry : " *O God! I die like a thief for Italy!*" In *Bomba's* realm there was one spot, as Thayer comments, where the word *Italy* could not be suppressed—the scaffold.

By the summer of '57 Mazzini was in hiding once more in Genoa, with his plans formed. He believed it possible, by a bold and swift movement, to overrun the South; believed that a spark struck in Naples would find tinder enough to burn out the Bourbonic plague and kindle a beacon for an All-Italy rising : believed, too, that British indignation at the Neapolitan horrors supported the hope that England would keep the ring against foreign intervention. Jessie White and Aurelio Saffi had toured Scotland, where sentiment was warmly Mazzinian, and subscriptions were pouring in for his Muskets Fund. He consulted his group. The Marquis Pareto, Count Pasi, Count Rosalino Pilo, Alberto Mario (soon to marry Jessie White) and

Carlo Pisacane, were all for action, and Adriano Lemmi was prepared to supplement the expeditionary funds out of his seemingly bottomless purse. Above all, Carlo Pisacane, blue-eye and tawny-headed, a born leader for such an enterprise, and trained to the profession of arms, was eager and insistent, and would brook no delay. Indeed, the instinctive sympathy between Mazzini and Pisacane was peculiar. In religion the younger man was a freethinker with no other faith than that of an idealised Italy; in social and political theory he belonged to the Socialistic school which aroused the Chief's vehement antagonism; yet the two understood one another and were drawn together. Pisacane had served under Mazzini at Rome, standing with him in the difficult controversies with Garibaldi. He stood with him now. Garibaldi was offered the leadership and declined point-blank: Pisacane accepted.

In June Pisacane proceeded to Naples in disguise to satisfy himself at first hand of the prospects of a rising. He met the insurgent leaders in secret council and returned with his resolution fixed. The continuous repressions and butcheries in Naples since '48 had prepared the field: the revolution was in the hearts of the educated classes: *Bomba's* army was largely officered by liberals, and the rank-and-file had no stomach for a fight. As for a Muratist counter-plot, Pisacane held it to be a chimera. The masses, once they had been given an insurgent victory, would rally to the National flag. Mazzini's plan therefore was sound. The expeditionaries, landing on the southern coast at a point arranged with the insurgents, would raise the country in conjunction with the local bands and *squadre*, and march on Naples. Sympathetic risings could be organised at Leghorn and elsewhere. If the plan worked, Piedmont would certainly be drawn in and the movement would spread to Lombardy. And for the rest, at the worst he and his men could go the way of the Bandieras. Better a fruitful death than a sterile life!

The crux of the problem was Genoa. No expedition could succeed without a base, and the natural base for an expedition sailing south was Genoa; but the city was under the Piedmontese Government. Piedmont had refused to co-operate in a programme of action: would it remain neutral? Cavour, vaguely advised of vague possibilities, was inclined to be favourable, then reversed his decision. The risks were too complicated.

If Mazzini, says Thayer, had eaten hasheesh he could not, in the circumstances, have dreamed a wilder dream than that of defying Piedmont from Genoa. Garibaldi, Bertani, Medici and Cosenz anticipated Thayer's judgment, and even the loyal Saffi shook his head. Yet Pisacane and Rosalino Pilo and young Baron Nicotera were pledged to the enterprise, and Mazzini cast the die. He would risk all. He himself would assume control in Genoa with a *coup-de-surprise*, and hold the base, if possible, until Pisacane had succeeded in raising the South. Then Piedmont, presented with a new situation, would possibly withdraw her veto. It was a mad decision; so mad that when a nervous French Emperor notified the Piedmont Government of a probable Mazzinian plot in Genoa, Cavour was pardonably incredulous. "So long," he retorted, "as the Emperor shall live and keep down the revolution in France, we can sleep on both our ears without fearing that our sleep will be disturbed by Mazzini."[2]

The Genoa plot failed. Jessie White Mario, who was present and was arrested five days later, has summarised the facts. "The organisation to seize the arms was perfect; up to the evening of the 29th (June) there was not the slightest sign of alarm. But shortly before midnight Mazzini received warning that the Government had been advised. . . . In a moment messengers were despatched with orders to suspend all operations, and save for one mishap all would have gone off quietly. At the Fort Diamante, where the order did not arrive in time, the troop of young men who were spending the evening with the soldiers, had succeeded in shutting up the entire garrison in a casemate when a soldier discharged his musket at the insurgents, and one of them, returning the fire, killed a sergeant of the 7th Regiment of Infantry. That was the only blood shed in Genoa."[3] It was more than enough to condemn the whole sorry scheme. Mazzinians had turned their weapons against the one liberal and constitutional State in all Italy.

Cavour's rage was understandable. This incredible plot had all but succeeded. Had it done so, would Napoleon have believed that he, Cavour, was not privy to it? It was not simply that the conspiracy had touched the raw nerve of the little

Minister's personal and political pride; it had threatened the policy upon which he was labouring and over which he was watching with the jealous devotion of an artist for a still unfinished masterpiece, of a father for a child who was to perpetuate his name and honour. In Genoa, where the wildest rumours of Mazzinian incendiarism and pillage were now circulating, and where all was pandemonium hue-and-cry, he ordered the strictest search to be concentrated upon Mazzini. Six of the leaders, including Mazzini, were sentenced to death in contumacy, six to twenty years' hard labour, one to thirteen years, three to ten years. Impatient at the failure of the police to land "the chief of assassins," Cavour appealed from Turin to the French Emperor for the services of the renowned detective, Vidocq. "If we catch him [Mazzini]," he promised, "he will, I hope, be hanged," and he indicated the prospective site for the execution: "*il sera pendu sur la Place de l'Acquasola.*"

The whole sorry venture had indeed been nerve-racking for the chief conspirator. He was now fifty-two and physically unfit for the undertaking. In Genoa most of all it was intolerable to him to live in concealment, yet his capture, until Pisacane had embarked, would have involved the entire expedition. "Non son chi fui," he wrote sadly; he was not the Mazzini of old. The close confinement in uncouth hiding-places had palled upon him, the stifling summer-heat had debilitated him, the midnight conclaves had been exhausting, even the clangour of the city bells had frayed his nerves. He had felt the strain, too, of the very devotion of his " sublime children " of the working classes, who had concealed him in their homes, passed him on from house to house, decked his bed with flowers, denied themselves sleep to guard his door, removed the rings from their fingers and bestowed them upon him. Nor had his own stoical contempt of danger and his deeper contempt for the detective powers of the police, relieved the tension. He had chafed under what he had conceived to be the unnecessary precautions imposed upon him by his own followers. He had been a conspirator before some of them were born, and he knew his business. Surely he could find his way about in his own city. There was another vexation which he mentioned to his intimates—the coarse manners of some of the confederates—their "spitting about" and other "inharmonious little things." It was a pity.

But now his answer to Cavour was to defy Vidocq and remain in Genoa, smuggling across the border one by one, and with astonishing success, the more deeply implicated of his colleagues, and occasionally varying his venue with a visit to Turin. Thrice, indeed, a body of riflemen and police had descended upon the Marquis Pareto's house, overlooking the Piazza Corvetto, while the Chief was in hiding there. Twice the Marquis's Irish wife had baffled them by hiding her (protesting) guest in a mattress of maize-leaves beneath an ironing-board on which a servant was ironing the household linen, and twice the maize-leaves were probed to within an inch of his body. The third time he himself, wearing a suit of the Marquis's (Pareto was already under arrest), and otherwise disguised, opened the door to the search-party, walked out with a *signorina* on his arm, obtained a light for his cigar from a member of the posse, and proceeded across the Acquasola Place, "where (notes the chronicler) the band was playing."*

He was, indeed, still hopeful. If only Pisacane succeeded in raising the South all might yet be well. There had even been musical evenings between the house-raids at the Paretos', and he could write chattily to Emilie Hawkes about Ruskin and her statuette of Dante. If only the South were "up"! . . . But Pisacane, his little force outnumbered, his ammunition spent, was lying dead in the stained and lead-ploughed dust besie the orange-groves of Paula, his comrades fallen around him.

*   *   *   *   *

Mazzini's leadership was now shattered more completely than by the Milan fiasco, and the Moderate journals of Turin were vying with the reactionary Press of Europe in exploiting his failure. The wildest calumnies were abroad. Had he not laid mines under Genoa? Had he not intended to blow up the city? Had he not plotted to open the gaols and turn the convicts loose? Had he not given express orders to loot? No

---

* No explanation of Mazzini's escape seems sufficient, apart from the supposition that in the higher ranks of the Genoese police there were some who were secretly disposed to let him slip through their fingers.

lie was too extravagant for ready circulation. If Pisacane's memory was assailed as that of a reckless filibuster who had disgraced the Italian cause, the chief conspirator was reviled as a coward who, having laid his dastard plot, had retired to a safe distance and left his dupes to their fate. Motived by revenge and lust for power, and blinded by malignity to the mad folly of his schemes, he had sent them to their death but taken care to save his own skin. It was about this time, too, that Gallenga, now prospering as a Cavourian Deputy, thought it opportune to revive (with convenient omissions) the story of the Chief's Genevan plot against the life of Charles Albert.

Thus the skies were darkened with clouds of venomed shafts, and if he affected to despise them, there were some that pierced through the joints of his armour and rankled. From his place of concealment at Quarto, within sight of the sea and of his boyhood rambles with Jacopo, he hurled at his accusers a violent and bitter reply, and Thayer, who, in his massive biography of Cavour, records his hero's ethical ambidexterities with a certain fond indulgence, yields to the temptation to annotate Mazzini's tirade with censorious moralisings. "Every line of the Mazzinian apologia," he declares, "is written in gall. The pent-up hate, distilling itself into venom, the Lucifer pride . . . the delight in imputing baseness, reveal a sorely wounded moral nature." Mazzini, in fact, "had reached that final stage in the evolution of a fanatic where he could no longer discriminate between the goodness or badness of his planas on the moral side."[4]

Much must be admitted. It is true that from first to last Mazzini was committed to his insurrectionary theory, and too ready to believe that any spark struck on the anvil of revolutionary action, if only it were in the name of Italian Unity, was holy fire. In this his zeal could be at least as fanatical as John Brown's or Garrison's for Abolition and as Calvinistically high-handed and Government-defying as Gordon's for a British theocracy in the Sudan. It is true, also, that his plot for the seizure of the forts and armoury in Genoa was indefensible, provoked though it may have been by Cavour's vacillation, and encouraged though it certainly was by the belief that a success in the South would alter Piedmont's attitude. For the rest, he was under sentence of death. For three months he had lived, whether in cellars or in coal-heavers' kitchens or in the *palazzi* of the rich, under the pressure of the severest mental and nervous strain conceivable. His own fate and that of his friends, including Giuditta, the success of the entire enterprise, had been hourly at the mercy of an informer's whisper, the chance indiscretion of a friend, an intercepted letter, the detective glance of a spy. His nights had been sleepless, his days consumed with labour or harassed with anxiety. He had passed through the fevers of hope, of suspense, the shocks of cumulative disaster. He had suffered physically under the close confinement and the exhausting heat. His health was broken, and a painful and disfiguring eruption on hands and face, which incapacitated him on his return to England, was probably already afflicting him. Amid all this, he had steeled his will and rallied his powers for a supreme effort to save his friends, condemned, like himself, to the gallows. Withal, having witnessed the chance of Union dashed, as he believed, by the refusal of Turin to rally to a politically neutral, national banner, he had seen the crowning tragedy of Pisacane's failure and death abetted by the limitations imposed upon the expedition through Piedmont's attitude. To be assailed, then, at such a time by the Gallengas of the day, by tepid patriots and esurient scribblers, by politicians whom, however mistakenly, he despised for turning the Italian movement into a backstairs intrigue with the crowned Liberticide of France; and with it all, to be accused, not simply of a fatally mistaken policy, but of arson, anarchy, revenge, ambition, cowardice and whatever other base and wicked motive was within the invention of malicious minds—this, after all, was perhaps calculated to excite in him those not inconsiderable powers of invective which his critics resented with such indignant horror and to which Thayer devotes his deploring passage. Mazzini had dipped his pen in gall. It would have been strange had he dipped it in honey.

But it is history itself which supplies the curious comment. For, as Saffi was entitled to point out in his introduction to the *Scritti*,[5] scarcely more than two years had passed before the " crime " of '57 had become a peculiar virtue, a heroic incentive, a " national glory."

For within that brief passage of months Cavour himself,

yielding to insistent pressure from the Left, was secretly conniving at a repetition of the Pisacane enterprise. Cavour's
position, it is true, was in important respects different from
Mazzini's in '57—different even "on the moral side." For
Cavour's word was still pledged to Napoleon; Cavour's diplomatic relations with the Naples Court and Government were
still cordial; the Piedmont Embassy was still assiduously cultivating the confidence and goodwill of the new occupant of the
Neapolitan throne: and Cavour's sovereign was sketching for
the young monarch's approval an attractive scheme for the
division of Italy, North and South, between the Bourbon House
and the House of Savoy. Nevertheless, Cavour, without revealing to his Right hand the deft operations of his Left, was
prepared to appease the Patriots with a repetition of Pisacane's
plot against the Bourbon oppression. And this time, at all
events, Turin was to turn a blind eye to Genoa as the base of
operations. Arms might be smuggled through, volunteers
mustered by the hundred, and transports secretly engaged. The
liberation of the South by means of an expedition from Genoa
was no longer a hasheesh dream. Cavour's change of attitude,
if it had not moralised that project, had rationalised it.

Thus the expedition of '57 had not only pointed the way to
be taken, it had also shown the pitfalls to be avoided, and
where Pisacane had failed, Garibaldi was to triumph gloriously.
Thus, too, in the blaze of the Garibaldian victories, the deeds of
'57 discovered a new and luminous significance; the criminal
Mazzinian folly became a magnificent and prophetic episode;
North and South united in hymning the fallen heroes of Sapri;
and presently Victor Hugo, in a curious parallel, was to pronounce Pisacane greater than Garibaldi, "as John Brown was
greater than Lincoln." For a truer exposition of the parallel
we may turn to Trevelyan:

"Pisacane's expedition against the Bourbons is related to Garibaldi's
successful expedition three years later, exactly as John Brown's raid on
Harper's Ferry is related to the American Civil War. Pisacane was at
the time condemned by almost all the friends of freedom as having
brought discredit on the cause, but a few years later his name was the
watchword of that cause in the hour of its triumph, when the ghosts of
the forerunners seemed to be marching in front of the triumphant
columns of liberation. Like John Brown, he had exacerbated the feud
and made compromise impossible, and so helped to bring on the final

struggle. . . . The Genoese part of the plot . . . had scarcely the shadow of an excuse, but its failure served at least to show that without the secret connivance of the Piedmontese authorities no effective expedition could sail from Genoa against the Bourbons. In 1860 this lesson was not forgotten by Garibaldi—nor by Cavour."[6]

Thus is history made. Thus, says the poet of the Overworld, do the mortal minions of the Great Enchantment serve " a Will that wills above the will of each." And thus at last the " negation of God, erected into a system of Government," was to be swept from the earth.

Meanwhile, broken in health and hope and grieving for his dead, an aged Chief continued to elude the vigilance of Cavour. And there was still solace of a kind. There was always the faithful circle in England, and it was consoling to think of them. Just now it was pleasant to reflect, for example, that the Stansfelds would be at Eastbourne—far-off, tranquil Eastbourne, untroubled by despots, revolutions or *'sbirri*. James would be relaxing after his Parliamentary fatigues, and dear Caroline— he could picture her with bonnet and crinoline and parasol— would be watching the gulls, with little namesake Joseph busy with bucket and spade beside her. From his Quarto attic it was pleasant to smuggle a note to them into the post. " I am in such a place ! . . . The more I feel inclined to despair . . . the more I feel anxious about those I love. I too am looking at the waves of the sea. I have a dog here, the most selfish of dogs, still a most affectionate one. Kiss little Joe most fondly for me."[7]

EVENING STAR

1848 was a dream of the past. A decade had gone by and remitted it to history. The faded *grands seigneurs* of the revolution still haunted the backstairs committee-rooms of Soho, still conspired to " deliver Europe " and " hurl the tyrants from their thrones "; but Europe was no longer dreaming the Republican dream. The time was past when every sunrise hung a revolutionary cockade on the breast of the morning; and republican messianism, like its one-time poet Heine, was dying of slow paralysis and disillusion. Meanwhile, in a modest apartment, somewhere near Portman Square, an elderly gentleman in black—known to his neighbours as " Mr. Flower "—was seated among his books and papers. His hair, still dark but streaked with grey, was growing thin, his moustache whitening at the corners, his rather close-cut beard was white; his cheeks were sunken and of clay-like pallor; his face was deeply lined; his movements were stiff with rheumatism. As usual he was smoking and writing.

"Mr. Flower" was, in fact, engaged upon a book on Religion. He would never really write it. He had turned to the task as a serious diversion from other enterprises, not in the strictly literary line. Had the book been completed it might have been a contribution of some pith and moment, but he was complaining of enfeebled powers. The public would demand of such a book, he complained, that it should be long, learned, logical and exact, and three out of those four demands were now sadly beyond him. He was too weak and unsettled for concentrated study, for the elaboration of a thesis, for repeated journeys to the Museum library.

We know, however, the form the book would have taken.

283

There would have been a lengthy symposium of the various historical faiths and of " their resultant civilisations "; a section on " the great monumental works which are landmarks in the series of religious syntheses "; following this there would have been a series of interlinking studies showing the line of " the development of the religious principle," and chapters dealing with the analogous heresies issuing from each faith and the various summarising philosophies elaborated within each religious period; the entire treatise aiming at offering a review of " the operation of the Law of Progress " in relation to " the general tendency of the religious synthesis of the future." Alas! such a work would require much "looking through books difficult to have." Something less ambitious " Mr. Flower " thought he might possibly achieve—a little volume of disconnected Reflections; but this, also, remained a project unfulfilled. What he did actually accomplish was the completion of a series of essays, already published in part, on the Duties of Man.

For indeed just now, as always, he had much to distract him. He must find English employment for the latest batch of Italian refugees—Profumo, Felice Orsini and many others; he must supervise the writing of Italian biographical sketches for Professor Nichol's Biographical Dictionary; he must arrange for the issue of an appropriate medal for the lamented Pisacane expedition (it was sad that there were so few to wear it; but Cavour was striking medals for all sorts of things, and this was so much worthier); and he must continue to badger the British Foreign Office over the scandalous detention of Miss Jessie Merington White in a Piedmont gaol. Felice Orsini, too, was very much of a distraction; of late, indeed, he had become quite impossible. Vain, valiant, handsome, impetuous, he had in him the makings of a hero, a criminal, or a martyr: and just now, smarting under the censure of his Chief for having outrageously insulted Emilie Hawkes, he had taken himself off to act on his own account. Apparently he had crossed to the Continent to court death—or Madame Herweg. It was all very trying. Then there was also the sad distraction of Carlyle's *Frederick*. Alas, Carlyle! all feudalism and the immoral worship of Force! as if the People counted for nothing, but only Kings, Kaisers, Margraffs, Burgraffs, drill-sergeants! " Bad, unredeemably bad."[1]

Meanwhile the explosive Felice Orsini (under the unexceptionable disguise of "Mr. Allsop of England") was in Paris with a new (and explosive) Programme of Action concocted by a few of the revolutionary *grands seigneurs* of Soho. The Programme, it seemed, outlined a Franco-Italian alliance, preceded by a French Revolution, preceded by . . .? Orsini, lurking in the shadow of the Paris Opera House (*William Tell* was on the boards), supplied the lacuna by flinging his Birmingham bombs at the royal carriage and turning Rue Lepelletier into a shambles. The trial of the would-be tyrannicide and actual slaughterer of innocents became the fashionable event of the season, and while all Paris applauded the exemplary coolness of the Emperor and his consort, Society found a new diversion in discussing the fascinating criminal. "All the Russian and Polish great ladies," wrote Hübner, "go crazy over him. They admire his beauty, his courage, his heroism. The Empress, too, is infatuated." Orsini, in fact, became the most prominent of European publicists; even the London *Times* opened its columns to engaging accounts of his romantic personality; and while English pamphleteers rushed into print—and gaol—with eager pamphlets on the Ethics of Tyrannicide, an enterprising Regent Street shopkeeper reaped a silver fortune with an exhibition of Orsini (in oils) at one shilling. It appears to have been a reproduction of this work of art which young Mr. Algernon Charles Swinburne of Balliol hung on his wall (facing a portrait of Mazzini), and before which he performed his corybantic rites; and a young English girl, later to achieve deserving celebrity as a religious poet, made her first literary flight with an impassioned poem on the same subject.[2] In Paris, too, under the stimulating eloquence of defending counsel, the Orsini *furore* spread, and while the Empress interceded in vain for his reprieve, Orsini himself touched new springs of emotion by impressively repudiating assassination as contrary to his life-long principles, and by appealing to Italians to rely for national redemption upon their own self-sacrifice, the constant unity of their efforts and the practice of true virtue. There was also a political repercussion in London. For while French colonels blustered angrily against England as a plotters' den, and Palmerston, for the Government, offered a conciliatory sop in the form of a new Conspiracy Bill, Mr.

Milner Gibson, an impenitent Mazzinian, shepherded Glad-stone, Disraeli, Lord John Russell and John Bright into the Opposition lobby, and the Government was out. Orsini had certainly had his fling, and his death, wrote Herzen, smote Europe like a thunder-clap. It was a strange world.

Moreover, if Orsini's bombs had missed the Emperor, they had been effective against " Mr. Flower." The facts of the case have been put succinctly by Holyoake, who knew both Orsini and his former Chief, and sympathised with the Paris attempt: " Orsini concealed his plot from Mazzini, who never incited it, never approved, never justified it—he deplored it."[3] There was, in fact, never any shadow of collusion. But Turin was capable of creating indictments out of less than shadows, and the opportunity was too good to be missed. Cavour inveighed against the infamous " Chief of Assassins " and informed a horrified Chamber that the next Mazzinian attempt would be upon the person of Victor Emmanuel. The charge marked a new phase in the Mazzini-Cavour war, and a Mazzinian counter-attack was promptly released.

Mazzini to Cavour.

June, 1858.

" Sir,

" I have long known you to be an upholder of the Piedmontese Monarchy rather than of our common country; a materialistic worshipper of facts rather than of any sacred, eternal principle; a man of astute rather than powerful intellect; an exponent of tortuous tactics, opposed to liberty alike by patrician pride and innate tendency. But I did not think you a calumniator. Now you are become such. . . . Therefore, if heretofore I have not liked you, now I despise you. Before you were simply an enemy; now you are basely, indecently an enemy."

For who (he continues) should know better than Cavour that regicide had no place in the programme of a party whose first act, when it came into power in the Roman Republic, was to abolish capital punishment throughout the State, and thus prohibit even legitimised killing? Who should know better that, in the eyes of all who held by the democratic faith, the liberal Constitution of Piedmont (however mutilated by its chief Minister) was sufficient in itself to outlaw any suggestion of violence against its sovereign? It was, in fact, Cavour him-self whose policy was provocative of dispeace. It was Cavour whose policy was creating in Italy a fatal schism and corrupting the youth of the country by substituting diplomatic artifice for national action. And whither was this substitute-policy leading? Had not Cavour, choosing between the friendship of constitutional England and despotic France, engaged himself to the French despot? And at what cost? At the cost of presently handing over the South to Murat as prefect of the Emperor, and of pledging Italy to a further perpetuation of disunion! And who could reasonably suppose that Napoleon would outrage French sentiment by allowing Murat to concede a greater liberty to Naples and Sicily than was allowed in France itself? or that the Emperor, without other support henceforth than that of his reactionaries and Clericals, would fling mortal defiance at Rome by going counter to the Papal policy? or that he would willingly bid against his own interests by helping to found in the North of Italy an independent Italian Kingdom large and powerful enough to menace, next day, his own vassal dominions in the South? What, then, was this Cavourian policy but a violation not only of Italy but of logic and of elementary political sense?

" Between ourselves and you, sir, yawns an abyss. . . . We desire above all things National Unity: you seek nothing if not territorial aggrandisement for your Royal Master. . . . We believe in the initiative of the Italian people; you fear it, seek to thwart it, and put your hope in Diplomacy and the favour of foreign Governments. We desire that the country should freely choose its form of government: you deny the national sovereignty and make Monarchy the prepotent condition of any assistance of the national cause. We seek support from the peoples that commune with us in a common aim, in sufferings and in struggles: you seek support from the oppressors, from those deliberately and necessarily opposed to our unity. We adore a Faith, a Principle: you bow the knee to Force, to the Treaties of 1815, to Despotism. Between ourselves and you, sir, Italy shall judge."[4]

It was all very distracting, and the book on Religion had to be set aside.

The next move was with Cavour.

* * * * *

Cavour promptly suppressed the *Italia del Popolo*—the longest-lived of all the Mazzinian periodicals—in which Mazzini's letter was published, and some months later the

Piedmont Government sequestrated the Italian properties from which the Exile derived his annuity under his mother's will.[5] The menace of Mazzini's criticism, however, was not met by such methods; and however much the Chief Minister might affect to despise it, that criticism, relentless and insistent, was a goad that forced his pace. For fluctuant as the Exile's influence might be, it needed, and Cavour understood that it needed, only a prolongation of existing conditions in Italy to bring about a Mazzinian revival. Moreover, he understood that the same consideration weighed with the French Emperor. Napoleon might bitterly reproach Piedmont for harbouring a nest of Mazzinians at Genoa, but Cavour was able to retort that there were more Mazzinian agents in Marseilles and Paris than in the whole of Piedmont. "*I repeat to you,*" Cavour had written to Paris as early as February, "*that I took the portfolio of the Interior in order to combat Mazzini. . . . It may happen that the French Government will oblige me to quit office: but let it think of the consequences. . . . The prestige of the Moderate Party will be destroyed and the influence of Mazzini will be augmented to an immense degree. If that is what the Emperor desires . . .*"[6]

It was not what the Emperor desired, and it was not what Cavour desired. He had taken office "*in order to combat Mazzini*"; but there was no real escape from him except by means of a vigorous Italian policy. To the insistent Mazzinian demand for a popular initiative there was no effective reply but a Royal initiative; to the Mazzinian charge of Moderatist inertia there was no convincing answer but Moderatist activity. Apart from Cavour's own sincere Italianism, Mazzini's opposition was the supreme compelling force that drove Piedmont forward.

The next move, then, was still with Cavour. He made it when, a month after the publication of Mazzini's attack, he travelled to Plombières on a false passport for a secret meeting with the French Emperor, to arrange a "war of Italian liberation." It was an engaging picture. The little sun-parlour looking out upon the Vosges—the lean, sallow man with the beak-like nose and the drooping dark moustaches—his frock-coated, florid little visitor with gleaming spectacles and the air of a rural attorney called in about the family will. The scene, the actors, the plot! The plot, indeed, was difficult. It premised a war calculated to appeal to France, to Piedmont, and to the sympathies of Liberal Europe, without at the same time antagonising Russia or irritating Prussia. Thus, the candid avowal of a desire to terminate the Austrian occupation of Italian territory was not to be thought of; clearly, it was open to the awkward retort that a French garrison was in occupation at Rome. Yet, on the other hand, no other pretext seemed discoverable; and while Fashion sipped the Plombières waters in the morning sunshine two perplexed heads, charged with European ideas, bent over a map of Italy in vain search for an acceptable war. It was not until, by happy inspiration, their attention wandered upon the lamented Orsini's late field of revolutionary activity—the region of Massa and Carrara—that they knew themselves saved. "There," declared Cavour, in genial reminiscence, "we discovered what we were hunting for with so much ardour."

And the plan, once hit upon, was simple. Nothing, in fact, could be easier than to secure from the long-suffering populace of that region a spontaneous and urgent petition for annexation to Piedmont; nothing more proper than for the Piedmont sovereign to decline the prayer, but at the same time take occasion to warn the Duke of Modena that he must reform his government; nothing more certain than that the Duke would reject the advice; nothing more natural than that Victor Emmanuel should thereupon occupy Massa. The rest was plain. Austria would rush to the defence of the Duke, France to the defence of the King. The war was found.

The terms of the alliance presented less difficulty, and between breakfast and luncheon Italy was carved into a Four-State Federation. Thus the territorial expansion of Piedmont was to take in Lombardy-Venetia and the Legations; Tuscany was to go to *Plon-Plon*; the Pope was to retain his territories except the Legations, and preside over the Federation; and Lucien Murat might be awarded the Two Sicilies. Between luncheon and dinner (it was in the course of an invigorating drive in the imperial phaeton) little Princess Clothilde, who was fifteen in March, was conveyanced to elderly and dissipated Cousin *Plon-Plon*, and Nice and Savoy were tentatively ceded to France. It was a fair day's work, and a rejuvenated

Cavour was able to return to Turin with the French Pact and a National War in his pocket. The tonic qualities of the Plombières waters were excellent.

The secret visit was, indeed, a triumph of realist diplomacy. Cavour, as Thayer observes, " understood the terms on which Italy could be redeemed. Mazzini did not; that was the real abyss that yawned between them." Without disputing the judgment, it might conceivably be maintained that a further and equally real abyss yawned between their respective conceptions of redemption. According to the Plombières pact, Italy, deprived of Nice and Savoy, was to be divided into four loosely-federated States, three of them despotic, all four of them under the protection of Imperial France, and under the presidency of the most absolute Prince in Europe—the Pope. This was Italian " redemption." Nevertheless, it would be unfair to interpret the pact as a reflection of Cavour's Italian programme. For in fact the little Minister had no intention of abiding by the terms of his bond. He was gambling upon the turning up of new shifts and chances in the general whirligig of events. For Cavour, in spite of the immense passion of his Italian patriotism, was fast advancing to that last stage in the evolution of a diplomatist—the stage wherein, when the fortune of State are at stake, politics become a gamble in which marked cards and loaded dice are permissible.

By the end of April (1859), after a whirl of crises, a tangle of frustrations and a plague of delays, the consummation was in sight. Austria, adroitly manœuvred into declaring war, was once more lumbering across the Ticino with horse, foot and artillery; Massa and Carrara, jubilantly tearing down the ducal ensigns, had acclaimed the Cross of Savoy; Parma and Tuscany were following the exciting example; and while Bologna and Ferrara, moved by the general insurgency, flung off the rule of the Pope, Lombard and Venetian volunteers poured over the border into Piedmont to enlist under the Crusader-King. Nor were there Republican elements lacking to complete the martial and patriotic pageant. Thus by a bold stroke Cavour conciliated the Left and popularised the campaign by bestowing military rank upon the guerrilla chieftains of '48. The sight of Garibaldi in the dapper uniform of a Piedmont General (commanding the " Hunters of the Alps "), with Giacomo

Medici, Cosenz and Bixio riding at his side, was worth an army corps. Was it not truly the romance of war—D'Artagnan and his Musketeers in a new and breathless serial, " *Ten Years After* "? And if the sight of the Garibaldians was like a waft of '48, the spectacle of a French Army of Italy, with a Ney and a Murat on its staff and a Napoleon in command, was like a pageant of Resurrection. It was as if once more the banners of '96, of 1800, of 1805, were in the wind: Lodi, Milan, Mantua, Marengo, Austerlitz! It was a delirious hour.

Only Mazzini remained implacable, a Daniel at the feast, a Jeremiah preaching defeat to a nation at war. " Pippo," wrote James Stansfeld to Jessie White Mario, " adheres to his first strong conviction that Venice will not be liberated, and that peace will be concluded on the Mincio."[7] He hurled a too loftily-flighted homily at the head of Napoleon (" *There is something above success, something stronger than Fact, something higher than idolatry—God, right, time* "), then, aiming lower, staggered Cavour with an explicit prediction: " *You will be in the camp in some corner of Lombardy when the peace which betrays Venice will be signed without your knowledge.*"

It was execrable: it was also persistent. For out of the ashes of the *Italia del Popolo* now arose a new Mazzinian organ, *Pensiero e Azione*, to circulate dreary repetitions and variations of this same jeremiad. If (declared the new journal) the war were actually prosecuted to a victorious conclusion, it would mean only the vassalage of Piedmont, and of Italy—and the conversion of the Mediterranean into a French lake. But there would be no such conclusion. There would be a sudden, ruinous peace before the war was half-won. The Emperor would compel the King of Piedmont to desist, conceding to him the *solatium* of a certain portion of territory, and abandoning the Venetian provinces to their fate. Turin was justly enraged. Surely thwarted ambition and the writhings of a Lucifer-pride had at last accomplished Mazzini's madness. How otherwise would the insensate Prophet invite the just abhorrence of a nation at war and weave the black strands of his prophesyings into a noose for his own neck in the hour of victory?

But the war was less than two months old, with the defeated

Austrians retiring once more upon the Quadrilateral, when the announcement of the Peace of Villafranca burst like a thunder-clap over Italy. Mazzini's prediction had been fulfilled to the letter, and the French Emperor, riding that July morning down the dusty highway beyond the Mincio and revolving the terms of his so sudden peace—the Emperor had, in fact, played his predicted rôle as exactly as if he had learned it, line by line, out of the Mazzinian oracles. Nor was it simply the fact of the peace that vindicated the Prophet; the reasons that lay behind it, so far as they could be adduced, confirmed his analysis.

For beyond question, and apart from those humane compunctions which may move the heart of even a successful commander confronted with the awful price of victory—beyond question Napoleon was alarmed. He distrusted Cavour, who had failed him in his attempt to foist *Plon-Plon* upon Tuscany. And now, thanks to Cavourian machinations, he beheld the Duchy moving, with Parma, Modena and the Romagna, toward union with Piedmont. Thus within two short months the Sardinian kingdom, from being a subordinate ally, had come to assume the position of a dangerous rival. And there were other considerations. The risings in the Roman States had embarrassed the Emperor's relations with the Pope, and a rupture with Rome, with its disturbing effect upon the Clericals in France, was not to be risked. Moreover, even Garibaldi's success in the field was unwelcome; and here again the Emperor suspected Cavour, who had over-ridden his protest against the employment of the revolutionary chieftain. For now, while Napoleon and his staff were conducting their military operations with a slow, stiff and somewhat costly correctitude, Garibaldi was waging war as a revivalist campaign, and with astonishing results. In truth, his passage through the Alpine villages had been less a military march than a crusade; youths had flocked by the hundred to his banner, and there were strange stories of peasants bringing their babies that the great chief might bless—and even baptise —them. Nor did his military operation fall below his evangelistic success. With 3,000 ill-armed recruits he had held rather more than the entire First Army Corps of the Austrians and won spectacular victories at Varese and Como. And what was all this if not a gratuitous demonstration of the validity of the Mazzinian argument that miracles were latent in the unreleased forces of popular enthusiasm? The war, in fact, was assuming the character of a popular revolution. Russia, observing as much, was withdrawing her sympathy; Prussia (with Bismarck at St. Petersburg) was massing on the Rhine; and the British Queen and her Consort were deploring in dolorous duet the woes of the " poor dear Duchess of Parma " and Austria's unhappy reverses. Clearly it was time to make peace.

It was made. In an upper room in a little house on the Villafranca road, while French Guards and Austrian Uhlans fraternised in the July sunshine outside, the French Emperor and the young Kaiser discussed their terms. Austria was to retain Venetia and the Quadrilateral; Tuscany and Modena were to be returned to their ducal rulers; Romagna was to be restored to the Pope; Piedmont was to receive the gift of Lombardy at the hands of the French Emperor; the Pope was to be made honorary President of the motley Federation. At one item the young Kaiser boggled. It was hard to give up Lombardy. There were urgent ministerial conclaves, even imperial tears; but the treaty was signed. " One little thought," wrote Mr. Gladstone to Poerio, " to have lived to see the day when the conclusion of a peace should create in one's mind a feeling of disgust ";[8] but so it was. *The Times* in an acid editorial dissertated upon the latest riddle of the great modern Sphinx, whose very existence depended upon his not being found out;[9] and Mrs. Browning, hard put to it to defend her paragon, presented him as the idealist-victim of an un-believing world.

> " But HE stood sad before the sun
> (The people felt their fate).
> ' The world is many, I am one;
> My great Deed was too great.' "[10]

* * * * *

The people, as Mrs. Browning remarked, felt their fate. They felt it deeply. And at the Royal camp, near Desenzano, a frantic Cavour, unconsulted and unadvised, sought the presence of his sovereign. For a while, awaiting the arrival of horses for the final stretch of the journey, he tarried in a village café and listened, unrecognised, to the noisy discussion at the tables. There were angry voices denouncing Napoleon, others freely cursing Cavour: was there one voice more penetrating than the rest, to recite above the angry din the appropriate prophecy: "*You will be in the camp in some corner of Lombardy when the peace which betrays Venice will be signed without your knowledge*"? There was no need. The event itself was reciting it.

When, a little later, the Minister burst into the presence of his King, it was not as Count Cavour, but as something more elemental. And in that hour, his voice hoarse, his gesticulation violent, his lips quivering, it was left to him to take up one by one every plea, every argument, every consideration, advanced by the man whom, above all others, he had abhorred. The pleas, the policy which he, Cavour, had held up to odium as the vain imaginings of fanaticism, the unconscionable conceptions of a dreamer whose pride had assumed a sovereignty above the lordship of Kings—to these it was now left to him to turn and urge them upon his King as the one sure course of honour and, perhaps, of salvation. Let the King refuse to receive Lombardy as a gift at the hand of a foreign patron. Sooner let His Majesty abdicate and wander homeless through Europe than submit, and cause the nation to submit, to that ignominy. Rather, let the King dare to trust the voice of his own heart and the voice of the people. Let him heed the bitter cry of the South, of Romagna, of the betrayed Duchies, of Venice. Let him place himself at the head of his Italians and continue the war in the name of a United Italy. Let him show the people that henceforth he had no other future than the future of the nation.

The voice was the voice of Cavour, but the language was the language of Mazzini, and Majesty may well have surveyed his exhorter with surprise. Reckless in love and in battle, Victor Emmanuel could, indeed, be admirably self-contained in crises of state; and now, though perturbed, he was able to view the situation more calmly than Cavour. The King, in fact, had less to burden him. He had not concocted the war; he had only fought in it—admittedly with credit: nor had he con-

cocted the peace nor so much as signed it: he had only been
informed of it. And, after all, the terms might have been
worse. In two months he had seen his dominions doubled;
Milan was free and Lombardy was once more under the Cross
of Savoy. These were material considerations; and that night
he was to dine with the French Emperor.

But not Cavour. He, the man of Paris and of Plombières,
he who had conceived the war, plotted it, arranged it down to
its last political detail—he was now ignored, thrust aside,
treated as if he had no existence. The Emperor, having made
peace with the Kaiser, would dine with the King. *Voilà tout!*
Before his sovereign the terrible little figure lingered, pleading,
expostulating, commanding, until a not impatient monarch was
constrained to indicate that, after all, the King and not his
Minister was the head of the State. Then with lamentable cry
the last, uttermost protest escaped from his Minister's tortured
soul: "*I, Cavour, am the real King! It is I whom the people
acknowledge first of all!*" Could the arch-enemy, could Mazzini himself, have defied the Crown in terms more arrogant?
It was intolerable, and Majesty, not without ire, turned upon
the apparition: "*You, King? You are a little rogue!*" And
the apparition, thus exorcised, remained a moment with
clenched fists upraised, then vanished as in sulphurous smoke-
cloud.

Yet the poor Cavour, beside himself, was in a deeper sense
more truly and freely himself than at any previous moment of
his astonishing career. His fury was far more than the rage
of an unscrupulous gambler who had lost to a cheat whom he
had reckoned upon outwitting, more even than the wrath of a
statesman of supreme ambition who had found the labour of
years, the dreams of a lifetime, dashed in a single hour by a
treacherous hand; it was the passion of an outraged patriot.
In this earthquake of events the exterior façade of Cavour's
official reputation and diplomatic make-believe had been torn
away; what remained, what for the moment was exposed, was
the throbbing enginery and furnace-glare of the man's innermost passionate purpose, a purpose which, with all its com-
plexity, its wheels within wheels, was pounding steadily onward
for Italy, supremely.

Thus it became manifest that, after all, Cavour's antagonism to the Mazzinian policy had belonged more to the Minister of the Crown than to the patriot and the man. And now, thrust by strange events into that position of detachment which, of necessity, his rival had always occupied, and taught like him to distrust the favour of princes, Cavour's mind arrived at a single desperate leap at those conclusions which he had made it his life-work to resist. It was not simply that he was now advocating a National War unaided by a foreign alliance; the logic of that acceptance had thrust him still further along the Mazzinian road. He was prepared to consider " the arming of the Revolution " and to admit the necessity for methods of conspiracy. To Louis Kossuth, who had hastened to Italy, he turned as to a fellow-revolutionary; his utterance was vehement, he smote his breast: " *I say to you, M. Kossuth, this peace will never be made, this treaty will never be executed! If necessary I will take Solaro della Margherita* [leader of the Piedmont Clericals] *by one hand and Mazzini by the other. I will turn conspirator. I will become a revolutionist. But this treaty shall not be carried out. No! A thousand times no! Never! Never!*"[11] Yet even in his extremest revulsion Cavour remained Cavour. He would beckon the Blacks with one hand, the Reds with the other. In his fierce determination to nullify the scheme of the royal twister who had fooled him he would embrace the Revolution, he would conspire with Kossuth in Hungary, with Mazzinian agents in the South; but only in order to make the treaty inoperative. The question of any distinctive political faith was irrelevant. For him by this time it had no existence.

Yet, in this hour of disillusionment, the people at least vaguely divined that the little Minister was greater than the disaster that had overwhelmed him. His policy had crashed, his war had failed, his power was gone; but they dimly understood that the fallen leader was still at bay and waging a desperate struggle. At Milan, as his train passed through, *en route* for Turin, a great crowd assembled to cheer him; then, gathering about his private carriage and beholding a haggard man, aged beyond belief, huddled in the corner, sleeping the sleep of utter exhaustion, they hushed their voices into whispers and turned silently away. It was a tribute more impressive than thundering *evvivas*.

Meanwhile, the man to whom these strange events had brought so signal a vindication was once more hastening to Italy. He had been expressly excluded from the wartime amnesty. He made the journey in disguise and found concealment in the back room of a baker's house in Florence.

ONCE more under Italian skies, Mazzini was renewing his youthful fire and feeling the thrill of resurgent life. To his English friends he wrote of the enchantment of Florence—the fascination of the Arno by moonlight, the beauty of the city itself with its reverend monuments of a past that was truly great. And if, in sad contrast (and hurried English), he pictured a " superficial, light-minded generation walking about in crinolines " or idling outside the innumerable cafés, he was none the less able to believe that the great past was now making a new appeal.

Italy was, in fact, faced with a new and high decision. The Cavourian debacle had justified Mazzini's own long-derided opposition to the Bonapartist alliance, and while Cavour himself, in temporary retirement on his broad acres at Leri, was rumoured to be favourable to a Southern expedition, with Genoa for its base, even the Tuscan Government, under the Cromwellian leadership of its iron Baron, Ricasoli, was disposed to consider the Exile's programme. Thus the ducal despots were warned that, treaty or no treaty, their return would be resisted by the Duchies, and to support their resistance (and offset the threat of a Papal expedition against Romagna) an Army of Central Italy was being formed by the league of insurgent States. Its Commander-in-Chief was an ex-Mazzinian, Fanti, who had been one of the Savoy expeditionaries in the early days of Young Italy; second in command was Garibaldi; under him were Cosenz, Bixio and Medici. Napoleon, alarmed by these unauthorised developments, intervened to veto any union between Tuscany and Piedmont; but the country was in no mood to heed the prohibition now, and Liberal sentiment abroad was excited against France. In England in particular the pro-Austrian sympathies of the Court were now countered by a Liberal Cabinet, and Palmerston was once more inscribing the copy-books of the Powers with enlightened maxims. He went further. Adopting a much-abused Mazzinian formula, he roundly declared that the Italian people "must be allowed to elect their representatives to a National Assembly, empowered to decide on their future destinies, of which the people are, undoubtedly, the only arbiters."

There could hardly have been a more sudden or spectacular vindication of the Mazzinian policy, and in private letters to his English friends he allowed himself an occasional flourish. "There has been an explosion in my favour in Garibaldi's camp," he wrote, "which made him ill for three days. 'Viva Mazzini' was written everywhere. But this is subsiding."[1] It was subsiding, for the Monarchist defection among the former Republicans was still immense and obstinate, and even Jessie Merington White's husband, Alberto Mario, was offending the Chief with hectic articles extolling "our leader, the King." "I am rather annoyed with Mario," Mazzini confessed. Mario was "evidently wanting to play a part of his own"; and this was always annoying. And why could not these men see that between saying to the King, "*Declare for Unity, and we will follow*," and saying to the people, "*Declare for the King, and Unity will follow*," there was a difference wide as the poles asunder? The people, too, were still sadly astray, morally good but politically ignorant and exploitable. "I feel an immense pity for the deluded mass of the people. Do you remember John Huss saying to the peasant who was casting new fuel on the burning pile: 'O sancta simplicitas!'? I really feel something akin."[2] Moreover, just now the Tuscan Government vexed him by issuing at the public expense a special edition of—Macchiavelli. Macchiavelli and not Dante! Scepticism and tactics instead of truth and the poetry of truth! A saddening portent!

As for the Monarchist issue, he cleared the air with a direct appeal to Victor Emmanuel (September, 1859). It was an appeal with an occasional inflection of the old "Olympian tone," and delivered *de haut en bas*, as his manner was when addressing Kings; but at least there was no question of its sincerity. Would Victor Emmanuel (he inquired), dinned as he was by the servile adulation of place-hunters and time-servers, give heed to the word of a free man who cherished

toward him neither fear nor private expectation nor any ambition save to live and die at peace with his own conscience?
Then let him be assured that what Italy was seeking was
Unity. Let him act upon that conviction with the faith which
begets faith. Let him fling aside prudence, the virtue of normal
times, and gird himself with that audacity which, in the difficult, supreme hour, belongs to the genius of the strong. Let
him make common cause with the people and fraternise without fear with the National Revolution. " You spoke of Independence, and Italy gave you 50,000 volunteers. Speak of
Liberty and Unity, and she will give you 500,000. . . . The
People and You!"

" I call you to place yourself at the head of a National Revolution
with an initiative that may become European in its scope. . . . Be great
as the Purpose which God has placed before you—sublime as Duty—
bold as Faith. You shall have all, and ourselves first of all. . . . And
I, republican, soon to return to exile to preserve inviolate even to the
grave the faith of my youth—I will nevertheless cry with my brothers
of the common fatherland, ' President or King, God's blessing be upon
you, and upon the Nation for which you have dared and conquered !' "[3]

" And conquered!" For what was to be feared? Austria—
with all Italy rallying to one crusading banner and Hungary
prompt to rise in Austria's rear? France—with Prussia already
massing on the Rhine, and with Napoleon manifestly unable
to face Europe with *two* Italian wars within a year—the one
for Italy's " liberation," the second for her return to bondage?
England—with every disposition on that country's part to
favour Italian aspirations the moment those aspirations ceased
to interpret themselves as truckling to Napoleon? The field
was never so clear ! But then, was it not always apt to be clear
to Mazzini?

And for the rest, no doubt his inveterate suspicion of Turin
led him to exaggerate the evil possibilities of the governing
party. He could discern no suggestion of response to his appeal
for a National programme. At first he looked with disfavour
even upon the union of Piedmont and Tuscany. It seemed a
piecemeal project which simply brought Tuscany under the
thumb of the Moderates. He suspected the King of being
secretly pledged to Napoleon. He could not believe that Piedmont was secretly but sincerely supporting the union of all the

liberated provinces. In general, he was bitter and intransigent, and the Tuscan Government was antagonised. " The calumnies they broadcast about me," he wrote to Saffi, " are shameful. . . . In Florence those who are suspected of siding with me are persecuted worse than in the days of the Duke. . . . I am being hunted like a mad dog."[4] Towards the end of September he left Florence, travelling through " the most beautiful part of the Apennines, with a few rare villages where the peasants speak like Dante in his love-poems," and settled once more at Lugano. He was still hopeful. The leaders, he felt, might be wrong-headed or faint-hearted, dizzied by the vertiginous whirl of events, but the youth of Italy might yet save the day. A Pauline text was much in his mind: "*Predica verbum: insta opportune; importune; argue, observa, impera.*" He would obey it. What emerged was an appeal amazing in its sweep and energy, coming as it did from the stricken man who, a while before, was complaining of enfeebled powers. It was, in fact, a return to the style of the '30's, with all the old-time panoramic dogmatism and rainbowed rhetoric—such an appeal as Giuditta, leaning over his shoulder, might have read and praised in the far-off youthful days. And as usual the final dehortation was against Turin. Let the youth of Italy beware of turning from the living God to serve idols—Force, Tactics, Mammon. What would it profit to raise the cry " *Out with the foreigner!*" only to be enslaved under tyrannies of their own? Let them beware, then, of the Subalpine locust-plague now stripping Italy bare of all the flowers and fruits of enthusiasm and faith. Let them beware of the *Moderates* who extolled the happy mean and whose political course was a faltering passage between truth and falsehood. Let them beware of the political *realists*, barren of principle, destitute of all initiative, and prompt to act only after others had achieved the event. Let them denounce the seducers who taught that the people might redeem themselves by shouting now for Barabbas, now for Christ, as circumstances might dictate.[5] . . . And so onward in inexhaustible polemic.

Then through the autumn he was straining every nerve to bring about united action. There was, it was known, the possibility of a joint-invasion of the insurgent territories by the combined armies of the Pope and the King of Naples.

Mazzini urged that this should be anticipated by the united forces of Tuscany, Parma, Modena and Romagna. The advance, he argued, should be through Umbria and the Marches, culminating in the invasion of Naples and Sicily. It was a bold project, and he was compelled to work behind the scenes, recognising sadly enough that his personal association with it would only arouse prejudice (" my name would not please Garibaldi "). Even so, the prospects were good. Cavour was in aggressive mood; General Fanti at the head of the united forces of the League, Ricasoli at the head of Tuscany, Farini at the head of Emilia, and Garibaldi himself and his lieutenants, were all disposed to favour a modified form of the project. But there were the usual exasperating delays, and with the New Year (1860) Cavour, returning to power and reassuming the official mind, promptly quashed the movement at the moment when Garibaldi was on the march.

Cavour's change of front was understandable. The angry Minister who in July was appealing to his sovereign to defy France, tear up the Villafranca terms, and continue the war, was now once more the responsible and wary negotiator. Five French Army Corps were still on Italian soil; the union of Tuscany and Piedmont was still awaiting Napoleon's approval. Moreover, the terms of the Villafranca treaty had committed the Emperor to support the restoration to the Pope of the insurgent Papal territories. It was evident, then, that prudence forbade the hazards of a campaign of liberation which would certainly embarrass negotiations and might lead to an open clash with France. Cavour preferred to wait. But easy as it was to lampoon the project as a wild Mazzinian dream, it was none the less true that the actual situation in Italy called for something other than a waiting policy. No power on earth could conserve the impetus of national enthusiasm through month after month of inaction, and only a bold programme could save the cause from settling into muddy stagnation in the squalid puddles of local politics. Moreover, when Mazzini claimed that to allow action to be paralysed by the bogey of French intervention was to surrender to a shadow, he was justified. Within twelve months Sicily, Naples and the Centre had been overrun without either France or Austria daring to oppose the march of the liberators.

And in fact Cavour's advantage was brief. His primary aim was to consolidate the kingdom of Upper Italy, and his immediate concern to drive a bargain with a reluctant Napoleon for the union of Piedmont and the Duchies. He achieved it, as Mazzini had foreseen, by ceding Savoy and Nice to France. But this act exposed him once more to the full blast of the Mazzinian attack, and lost to him the one popular leader whose support was politically invaluable and whose antagonism was a first-class disaster. For, as Thayer naïvely records, " to the immense injury of United Italy, it happened that Nice was the birthplace of Garibaldi."[6] Clearly, if the Cavourian policy proved unpopular and divisive, the cause was traceable to this regrettable lapse of Providence in the selection of the Paladin's birthplace. There were, as Mr. Thayer suggests, so many other possible birthplaces—" Savona or any other town on the western Riviera," any one of which would have served quite admirably. But Nice . . . ! It was deplorable. Perhaps, too, it was only less unfortunate that Savoy happened to be the cradle of the Piedmont kings. But at least Victor Emmanuel was reasonable, whereas Garibaldi, livid with fury over the vendue of his own particular corner of Italy, turned up in the Turin Chamber of Deputies and led a lamentable outcry, supported, as might have been expected, by such shameless irreconcilables as Pareto, Valerio and Bertani. Thayer is specially severe upon these recalcitrants, so manifestly motived by " the hope of winning a cheap popularity by their spurious patriotism," and adds: " Such buncombe deceives nobody. When amputation is necessary, how stands the surgeon who, in order not to risk his reputation, refuses to perform it?" Yet in this instance the " surgeon " (the Turin Chamber) was not consulted until the amputation was virtually effected—was indeed called in only to lend an appearance of competency and regularity to the operation; and the operation itself was " necessary " not in the sense that the severed members were diseased and were endangering the life of a languishing patient, but in the sense that the mutilation was dictated by a third party, alarmed by the patient's rapid increase in weight and vigour. In short, the excision of Nice and Savoy was to safeguard France on its Alpine frontiers against the menace of a too powerful Piedmont.

In any case the storm of protest increased in violence, and
Garibaldi (supported now by an enthusiastic Laurence
Oliphant) projected a descent upon Nice, to prevent the
plebiscite by the simple process of smashing the ballot-boxes.
No Ministry could have survived without the relief of a prompt
and engaging diversion; but once more the Wizard was equal
to the emergency. Cavour, that is to say, turned to the Reds,
appropriated Mazzini's policy, and secretly connived at sending
the enraged Paladin upon a campaign of liberation in the
South. Certainly it was a desperate course, and Cavour, filled
with justifiable misgiving, blew hot and cold; but what else
could be done? To Villamarina he opened his mind: "*You
know that I do not desire to push the Neapolitan question. . . .
On the contrary, I think it would be to our interest if the
present state of things* [the Bourbon rule in the South] *continued for some years longer. But . . . I believe we shall
soon be forced to form a plan.*"[7]

It was too true. In Sicily for some time past Mazzini's
agents—Fabrizi, Crispi and Count Rosalino Pilo—had been
forcing the pace. Early in March Mazzini himself had
released his famous appeal to the South: "*It is no longer* (he
wrote) *a question of Republic or Monarchy, it is a question of
National Unity, to be or not to be. . . . Garibaldi is bound
to aid you. Dare, and you will be followed. Only dare in
the name of National Unity.*" And five days before Cavour's
letter to Villamarina, Rosalino Pilo had crept out of Genoa
harbour in a fishing-boat, bound for Messina. Before he
reached Sicily the insurgents were up. In Palermo the insurrection sputtered out, but in the mountain regions the insurgent
squadre were capable of indefinite resistance. Pilo took over
the leadership and, with a slight excess of hope over definite
information, spread the electrifying word that *Piddu* (Garibaldi)
was coming. And now the Mazzinians, negligible enough in
normal times, were prospering by the Government's fallen
prestige, and Garibaldi, dragged back from his march on
Imola, and infuriated over his beloved Nice, was rushing hither
and thither like a raging lion, rending the air with continuous
and minatory roarings. Thus there was no help for it.
Cavour was forced to the conclusion that the Reds must be
placated and Garibaldi ordered south. No doubt Mazzini's

hand might be behind it all. It was behind almost everything, these days. But just now that hand, in Herzen's phrase, was "inexorable as the finger of fate." It was, in fact, pointing Cavour forward to a line of policy which, in spite of himself, he had to follow: and if he adopted it, it was not because he loved it, it was because he could neither destroy it nor avoid destruction if he ignored it.

And at Quarto, on the clear, starry night of the 5th of May, little groups of men gathered in the grounds of the Villa Spinola, presently to follow their leader along the leafy avenue and across the open road, where a double line of onlookers murmured their Godspeed, and so down the steep, broken pathway to the shore; then into open boats, to steer, after racking delay, toward distant signal-flares flashing fitfully in the dawn; and at last to scramble up the side of their two belated ships and put to sea. The Thousand had embarked. And in that dawn Garibaldi, statuesque in his vessel's prow, sailed forth into his Dream.

How like poor Pisacane's setting off on that starlit summer evening three years ago—and how unlike! And southward, in the convict-island of Favignana young Baron Nicotera, who had sailed with Pisacane, was still dragging his chain. For in Pisacane's last stand on the Padula road young Nicotera, shot in the head and fallen beside his captain, had somehow escaped the general shambles; instead he had been shut up to die in the scorpion-infested dungeons of Santa Caterina; yet had not died, but lived on, month after month, until, a thunderbolt smashing his cell, he had been brought to light and urged to petition His Most Christian Majesty of Naples for pardon. "Show me the petition-form," demanded the pale ghost; then, with his left hand (his right wrist was broken), wrote across it: "*To the Wild Beast Ferdinand, not yet satiated with human blood.*" And just now, in his island-prison, this young Nicotera, looking seaward, beholds two vessels steaming south and flying no flag. What ships they are, or what their errand, he cannot tell; but somehow he feels a strange, unaccountable gladness at the sight of them. It was a true inspiration. They were carrying as their impalpable contraband his own and his comrades' liberty and the freedom of the South.

SINCE 1852, following her imprisonment as a Mazzinian suspect, Giuditta Sidoli had resided in Turin, where her influence among the liberal intellectuals was soon established. Unflinching in her political convictions, but with a flexibility of sympathy greater than the Exile's, she gathered around her representatives of every grade of liberal opinion. Nor was it merely that a legend had grown around her as the one-time lover of the great Agitator and *fondatrice* with him of Young Italy; there was about her a fascination and a nobility which were hers in her own right. Thus Cabinet Ministers, senators, prefects, revolutionary patriots from the provinces, all sought her unpretentious *salotto* in the Piazza Bodoni, and her genius as hostess was admirable. She possessed culture and charm; her speech was in purest Italian, still " perfumed," as Giurati remembered, with the " slightly exotic quality "; her tact was dexterous and unfailing; she knew how to launch a discussion, and then, with a glance, a smile, a punctual jest, steer it off the floating mines of explosive antagonisms. Like Mazzini, she dressed always in black; her hair, ringleted at the temples, was now prematurely white (she was fifty-six), but her " great velvet eyes " retained their lustre, and her presence was distinguished. And now her activities were less restricted than formerly. Her daughters Elvira and Corinna were married, her income was modest but sufficient, and the recent revolutions had removed the ban placed upon her communication with political friends in Tuscany and Modena. Her influence was far-reaching, and it was no secret that her word had weight with Mazzini. Thus, for example, she had privately intervened during the Gallenga controversy and restrained Mazzini from pressing the exposure to a point which would have convicted Melegari of complicity. What few suspected, however, was that now and then her house sheltered the Chief himself. Its windows, however, looked upon an eminence known as the Ramparts. On the highest and least frequented ridge Mazzini, with a trusty friend, would watch, at times for hours, for the given signal from the Piazza Bodoni; then for a while the Sidoli *salotto* would be closed to all visitors.[1] And just now there were many excuses for secret consultation. History, in fact, was being made very rapidly.

For if, in season and out of season, Mazzini had proclaimed the miraculous possibilities of a popular apostolate of action, Garibaldi was now to demonstrate that the doctrine was no mad, fanatic heresy. On the May morning that saw the Thousand take the road on Sicilian soil no one, indeed, would have viewed them as a Homeric host. The straggling column that trudged through the beanfields of Marsala, between the mountains and the sea, was simply an ill-armed, ill-equipped straggle of men and youths, mostly in civilian clothes, with here and there the gleam of a red shirt or green tunic to accentuate the general drabness. They were, in truth, a ragged regiment, and more so after a week's forced marches through cane-brakes and cactus-thickets, over sun-seared, blistering ridges and across parched or rain-drenched plains: thus young Mr. Algernon Bicknell, very English, and with contrastive recollections of Whitehall and the Guards, surveyed them with amazement and wrote home about "Garibaldi's ruffians." Before them, withal, was a country of two million inhabitants, garrisoned by 24,000 well-equipped regular troops, supported on the coast by naval armaments. Yet morning by morning in those following weeks it seemed as if the astonished public of Europe and America were fated to shake some new Garibaldian miracle out of the folds of its newspapers. For in a brief month the Thousand, with irresistible *élan,* had routed the enemy in successive engagements, captured Palermo, and swept the island clean of the Bourbon hosts. It was a "fantastic Mazzinian dream," but it had come true. Sicily was won.

For whom and for what? That was the question which agitated the Powers. The Pope was alarmed, Naples distraught, and while Vienna administered sedative sympathy, Napoleon concealed an impotent exasperation behind a mask of omniscient reserve. It was certainly embarrassing for the Sphinx of Europe to be confronted with a riddle not of his own propounding. As for Cavour, he was in the position of the luckless mountaineer whose shack, caught in a sudden blizzard, has been swept bodily to the edge of a crevasse and stands balanced and precariously rocking on a jutting snag. For from the storm that had blown up over the Alpine frontiers of Savoy and Nice, Cavour had sought shelter in his Southern makeshift, only to find himself and his policy perched on the perilous edge of a Mazzinian revolution.

Indeed, from the first, as we have noted, Cavour had distrusted the Sicilian venture. It was a policy of necessity, not choice, and was full of awkward possibilities. Thus the Thousand had no sooner embarked than official telegrams from Turin were instructing the fleet to arrest the transports should they touch at Sardinia or veer towards the Papal dominions. Conceivably it would have been less embarrassing from the diplomatic point of view if the expedition had faded into pathetic history among the orange-groves and cypresses of Calatafimi, or degenerated into bandit-forays among the stark mountains of the interior. But now Garibaldi's triumph was assuming menacing proportions. It was a triumph won not by Piedmont but by the volunteers of Italy; their captains and organisers were all of them old Mazzinian cadets; their very names—Garibaldi, Bixio, Crispi, Quadrio, Fabrizi, Mario, Sirtori—sent shudders down the sinuous spines of the Moderates; and these veteran revolutionaries were now brought together, flushed with success and remote from Turin. Worst of all, Mazzini himself was said to be already at Palermo. Moreover, although the island had been taken in the name of Victor Emmanuel, the Paladin and his group were in reality holding it under their own hand, and *Punch* pictured a suppliant monarch knocking at a door on the inner side of which leaned an unresponsive Garibaldi with folded arms. Thus, with Sicily for a base, what was there to prevent the movement's crossing to the mainland, overrunning the entire Neapolitan territory and precipitating a new international crisis? And Cavour's apprehensions were reasonable. By the very success of his political achievements for Piedmont he had placed that State in a position in which it was answerable to the Powers for Italian developments. But by the same token it was equally true that its initiative was paralysed: for a leadership which reacted nervously to every foreign protocol and ambassadorial hint was incapable of directing a National revolution.

In any case Cavour acted promptly. To the admiral of the fleet he gave instructions for the arrest of Mazzini and his conveyance by warship from Palermo to Genoa. "*Envoyez La Farina à Garibaldi pour qu'il l'invite au nom du Roi à faire arrêter Mazzini et à vous le remettre. . . . Vous enverrez Mazzini à Gênes sur le ' Carlo Alberto.'*"[2] It was unfortunate, however, that Mazzini was not, and had never been, at Palermo. He had, indeed, anticipated Cavour's wishes. For just now at Genoa an elderly and clean-shaven gentleman, his *capote* drawn low about his eyes, was beguiling a scant leisure by accosting Cavourian agents and police and requesting to be directed to streets and places familiar to him since the days of his boyhood. He had forced Cavour's hand over Sicily; he must now force it over Naples and the Centre. "We must confront monarchical Piedmont with the alternative of throwing off the mask and acting *against* Unity, or of breaking openly with Imperial France."[3]

It was a Herculean task, and there were hours when the black moods returned upon him. "Italy," he wrote to young Nicotera, "is convulsed; she is drunk with materialism. . . . Neither I nor anyone else can change her now. Only events, adversities and disillusionments will do that. . . . Even should her Union be proclaimed from Rome to-morrow, I should take no delight in it; for the country, with its contempt for every ideal, has chilled my soul." Still, he added, they must "stand by the invalid" and try to restore her to consciousness. And for this there must be concentration upon the one issue—the development of the Southern movement under the banner of National Unity. Republicanism must no longer be made an issue, and Republican diehards must think again and be willing if necessary to act under the monarchist flag. "To march behind a column of men who, even though it be the banner of monarchy that waves above them, are advancing to do battle with Papal or Bourbon despotism, does not trouble my conscience sufficiently to induce me to withdraw, especially when I consider the immense good that must result."[1] With Piedmont, then, or without it, the movement now localised in Sicily must be extended to Naples and the Centre, then on with united forces to Venetia, and finally to Rome!

Yet the obstacles were all but insuperable. His movements were circumscribed; he was in hiding under the usual sentence of death; Cavour was demanding his arrest; his correspondence was being watched; his health was enfeebled by a painful spinal attack; the summer heat was exhausting him. As for organisation, he had none, nor adequate independent funds. Garibaldi had swept the field; even Saffi, raising money in England for the cause, was pledged to place it under Garibaldian control; and save for a Republican rump, who reproached the Exile for deserting the flag, his principal followers were almost all under the sway of the victorious General. Thus even devotees like Jessie White Mario and her husband, invaluable as agents in Genoa, had overridden his appeal and left for the Garibaldian camp. And as for Garibaldi himself, flushed with victory and courted by the King's men, he was hopelessly undependable. Superb in action, he was a child in council; his will was the wind's will, and his judgment was apt to reflect the views of the last man he conversed with. Meanwhile the reactionaries were working with frantic desperation, and the wildest schemes were afoot for isolating Sicily and preserving the existing régime on the mainland. Sicily should be converted into a separate kingdom, or given Home Rule and a model Constitution, or, finally, Naples and Piedmont should negotiate a formal alliance, dividing the peninsula into two separate kingdoms, North and South. This last was a return to Victor Emmanuel's proposal of '59; Napoleon urged it, Lord John Russell bestowed a tepid approval, and Cavour was disposed to accept it as the basis of a new policy: "*Nous sommes disposés à le seconder s'il adopte une politique vraiment nationale.*" Withal there were wild rumours, probably baseless, but disquieting even to the British Foreign Office, that, as the bargain-price for Piedmont's annexation of Sicily, the island of Sardinia, and even Genoa, were to go the same way as Nice and Savoy. Truly the hour was critical, the most critical since '48.

Mazzini braced himself for the struggle. The Garibaldian agent at Genoa was Dr. Bertani. To approach Bertani was repugnant. He and the Doctor had been colleagues and they had quarrelled. It was Bertani who had moved his deposition from the head of the National Association after the Milan fiasco; it was Bertani who had invented the famous gibe that, given three men and four stones, Mazzini was prepared to announce the liberation of Italy; it was Bertani who had consistently influenced the Genoa group against him. To go to Bertani now, uninvited and undesired, to risk a rebuff, to be forced into the position of an applicant in reduced circumstances, offering his services *en amateur* and for what he could get— against this his pride rebelled. Nevertheless, Bertani was the key-man and must be won over—" created." " The great thing is not my position, it is the birth of a People "; " the *individual* is dead within me; nothing but the aim survives." Bertani, he heard, was now a sick man, conducting his Garibaldian operations with prodigious energy and irascibility from his bed. He would go to him, offer to fetch and carry for him, be his subaltern. . . . And at least the scene was piquant —the grey-haired visitor at the paper-littered bedside of the sick man, and the disquieted invalid himself, propped with pillows, on guard against the occult, hypnotic compulsion of that mild but strangely dominating presence. Nor was the experiment a failure. The visits became frequent and the Mazzinian bulletins more hopeful: " I see him, concealed in a little room, people belonging to the Moderates being in the other "; " he begins to show me a little affection." Bertani was, in fact, " created." With Crispi at Palermo and Bertani at Genoa the *liaison* was established.

Thenceforward Mazzini's communications with the leaders in Sicily became increasingly urgent and imperative. Cavour's policy of the immediate annexation of Sicily, he declared, must be held up: for the moment that the island came under Piedmont it would cease to be a base for future operations on the mainland. On the other hand, annexation must be rushed through if the danger of Sicily's being turned into a separate kingdom became imminent. Above all, the Cavourian scheme for partitioning North and South between the two Crowns must be cut short by a Garibaldian invasion of Naples and an overland expedition through the Roman States and the Abruzzi. "*Let nothing dismay you. Neither L. N.* [Napoleon] *nor anyone else can move against you without provoking a European war.*" So he exhorted.

Yet the struggle was disheartening. Through June and July he was working feverishly to fit out an overland expedition, only to find each successive attempt deflected to meet Garibaldi's needs in Sicily itself. In July Cavour, suspecting mischief, stopped supplies between Genoa and Garibaldi's headquarters. "The Government," he declared angrily, "is holding its peace, but it will not long put up with being played with." Bertani grew irritable, Nicotera morose, Crispi silent, Mazzini desperate. "For the love of God," he wrote to Crispi, "send us word—to go to the Devil, if you like—but only let us act." Swift action was, indeed, the only weapon against Cavour, and delay would ruin all. But now more than ever Cavourian agents were swarming around Bertani, and it seemed as if the task were too heavy for mortal strength. Moreover, there were distractions. Emilie Hawkes was in Italy. Her marriage with Sidney Hawkes had been conjugally a failure and was in process of annulment. In Italy she had formed an almost clairvoyant attachment with a patriot named Carlo Venturi whom she had scarcely met, and she was now hovering about Genoa with exacting demands upon the Chief's interest and counsel. He wrote to her pathetic notes from his place of concealment ("I feel somehow as though you were angry with me"), met her for secret conferences by night at the Acquasola, discussed the virtues of Venturi in detail, but finally rebelled when Emilie urged that he and her lover should lodge together. "Dear, I must be sincere with you. Do not forget my crotchets. . . . I am not happy. I have often soul-cramps and long moments of moral weariness. . . . I must be alone, consuming my own smoke."[5] To the Ashursts and Stansfelds he wrote wistfully. He was longing for a last "dumb" holiday at Eastbourne with plenty of gulls and sad dozing, and the novels of Miss Burney and Miss Edgeworth and *The Castle of Otranto* for the beguiling of a gentle descent into idiocy. "If I stop here I shall evidently sink into that state, but not gently. . . . Dearest William and dearest Bessie, I am getting dreadfully old." For diversion he had a tame

Genoese sparrow or two ("one especially, my favourite, because he is deprived of his tail"); and for heart's ease there was always the chance of a stolen visit to Turin and a signal from the window in the Piazza Bodoni. But the end of the tribulation was in sight.

* * * * *

For by the beginning of September D'Artagnan Garibaldi, having presented an astonished Europe with a fresh series of military miracles—and just now sped forward by an urgent letter from the distinguished author of *The Three Musketeers* himself—was driving through clouds of dust along the great trunk road to Naples. The Bourbon kingdom had fallen, and while *Bomba's* son was fleeing to the classic refuge of Gaeta, Cavour's nightmare-vision of the rolling tide of a Franco-Austrian invasion remained unverified.

Clearly the time had come for a final effort, and Dr. Bertani, resuscitated from his "death-bed" and charged with Mazzinian electricity, hastened south to intercept the Conqueror. He succeeded. In a wayside tavern on the Naples road he and Garibaldi met, and the Doctor promptly switched on the Mazzinian current. It was true (he admitted) that Piedmont was now impatient for annexation. Well, let it wait. Let it wait until Italian liberation should be completed—the Papal States, Venetia, Rome! It was extravagant advice, but they were moving in the midst of extravagant events. The counsel was accepted, and in a proclamation published at Palermo (Sept. 17) Garibaldi underscored the moral: "*Annexation was desired* [by Cavour] *at Palermo in order that I might be prevented from crossing the Strait. Annexation is desired* [by Cavour] *at Naples in order that I may be prevented from crossing the Volturno. But as long as there are chains to be rent asunder in Italy I will hold on my way, or I will lay my bones by the roadside.*" As a rebuff to Piedmont it had its uses. It impressed Turin with the persistent tendency of the Unity movement to force its own channel; clearly, it was becoming doubtful if its course could be effectively dammed even by Cavourian engineering.

On the day of the proclamation Mazzini arrived at Naples— a Naples free at last of the Bourbons. How moving the sight of it! how dreamlike its loveliness! how sacred the assurance that its martyrs—the Bandieras, Pisacane, Bentivegna, Milano, Pilo—had not died in vain! He found time to describe to the Stansfelds the view from Megellina: "The sunset was enchanting; then the full moon arose, still more so. There is a sweetness in the outlines, in the lake-like sea, in the blue sky, in the semicircular spreading of the town, in the lights of the boats, in the murmur of the waves, even in the surrounding Roman ruins. . . . which can only be felt, the sombre reddish light of Vesuvius . . . gliding in with a note of fatality. . . ."[6]

There were, indeed, other notes of fatality. With doubtful wisdom he plunged into the old life, founding yet another journal and submitting to the usual exhausting round of conferences, discussions, and interviews with everybody—friars, priests, journalists, pamphleteers and every variety of political crank. He was still urgent, insistent, "inexorable as fate." The South was free. Now for the Centre! But perhaps he had been wiser to stay away, for his influence through Crispi and Bertani was at this stage more effective than his personal presence. He might, indeed, avow his intention of suspending all partisan agitation, but, do what he would, his presence was a symbol, a flag, a proclamation of the Republican idea. Pallavicino as Vice-Dictator called upon him to leave the city, and a torchlight demonstration organised against him by the local Cavourians brought a suborned mob howling to his door with shouts of "*Death to Mazzini!*" He shrugged his shoulders and took no notice. "They have amused themselves with shouting *Morte!* (he wrote to his English friends), . . . nevertheless I am living and loving."

And in any case the long fight was all but won. He had forced Cavour's hand in the South: he was now forcing it in the Centre: and Turin, compelled to watch the ominous shadow of the Revolution creeping steadily up over Sicily and across to Naples, was once more driven to adopt his programme in self-defence. For with Garibaldi still defiant and the South still unannexed, what was to prevent the shadow lengthening over the Abruzzi into the Papal States, and from the Papal States to Venetia? To M. de Talleyrand Cavour put the case succinctly: "*If we are not at Cattolica before Garibaldi, we are lost.*" The Revolution, he added, would otherwise invade all

Italy. They were "forced to act." "*Nous sommes forcés d'agir.*" Once more it was too true. But was the little Minister as distressed as he appeared to be? M. de Talleyrand could not be expected to know. At all events, within a week Turin had flung an ultimatum at the Papal Government, and a week later the King's troops were swinging down the Umbrian highways and through the Marches, " taking in the Papal fortresses at the rate of one a day."[7] It was strange, almost dreamlike. The net that had hung limp so long was now being cast wide and drawn up, hand over hand, with astonishing rapidity. Hand over hand! Hand of Mazzini over hand of Cavour!

And in the chill damp of an October dawn Garibaldi and his Red-Shirt staff sat their horses under the poplars on the Vagrano road and waited to welcome the victorious monarch. The Paladin looked rather more brigand-like than usual: his red shirt was the worse for wear, his *poncho*-cloak was soiled, and because the morning was inclement he had bound his head with a coloured kerchief beneath his black Spanish hat. Presently from the near distance came the sound of cheering and the blare of bands, and marching up through the valley in full panoply of war (these Garibaldians must be shown how the thing can be done!) came the Royal Army of the North. The question might indeed have been raised by the churlishly disposed: " Why had it come?" But the answer was plain. It had come to relieve the Dictator, assuredly overburdened, of his irksome responsibilities; to take the place of his gallant but slightly irregular forces, assuredly eager to be disbanded; and to escort His Majesty on his first visit to receive the homage, assuredly long overdue, of his loyal South. Dr. Bertani, it is true, would have had the King's troops detained at the frontier pending a fuller statement of the Dictator's own mind in the matter; but the natural eagerness of the Royal Staff to hasten to the relief of their Red-Shirt brothers was well understood; under restraint it might even have become violent.

And save for the rain, nothing could have been more impressive than Naples' welcome. In open carriage King and Paladin rode together along roaring streets, through triumphal arches, under festooned tricolours, and amid a pink avalanche of rose-petals flung from crowded balconies. The drenching rain, it is true, had somewhat marred the colossal allegorical creations, erected for the occasion, in lath-and-plaster; they flapped and sagged in the downpour; but a moving representation of Venice, widowed and mournful in her weedy lagoons, lost nothing of its effect. Nor was the emblem wholly melancholy. In a startling fashion it brought home the magnitude of the results of the recent campaign. Save for Venice and Rome, Italy was One; the national flag floated over her hundred cities from the Alps to the sea; and Mrs. Browning, striking her punctual lyre, invited the nation to "swear by Cavour" that the liberation should be completed and that Victor Emmanuel should be "true King of us all."

"*Swear by Cavour!*" It was even so. For was not the triumph his? Lombardy, Tuscany, Parma, Modena, Romagna, Sicily, Naples, the Papal States—were they not the fruits of his diplomacy, the trophies of his genius? Patiently, cunningly, stone upon stone, he had reared the edifice which was to be the monument of his enduring fame as the master-builder of United Italy : and beside him upon the stage of history, crowned and laurelled with a nation's gratitude, would stand the glorious Paladin and the *galantuomo* King. Cavour, Garibaldi, Victor Emmanuel! Victor Emmanuel, Garibaldi, Cavour! "Swear by Cavour!"

Meanwhile, disguised in the red shirt of a Legionary, a frail and elderly figure passed unnoticed out of Naples and fared northward across the sea to London and to a little room in a back street in Fulham.

MAZZINI returned to his one-roomed lodgings in London, Garibaldi, with his bag of seed-beans, to his island-farm at Caprera. And the retirement of the Paladin, like that of the Apostle, was not without its pathos. At the end the King dismissed Garibaldi, says Herzen, as a man dismisses the driver who has brought him to his destination; nor was the suggestion of a parting tip lacking to bear out the comparison. There was the offer of a castle and a steamboat (respectfully declined) and of roses from the Palace gardens (gratefully accepted). And so, at all events, the island-adventure was over; it was time for the Admirable Crichton to return to his former humble rank; and *Punch* illustrated the year of wonders with the representation of a slightly pompous Victor Emmanuel, with Garibaldi as his kneeling valet, putting on the top-boot (which was Italy) with the royal foot well home in the heel and toe (which were Naples and Sicily).

But the happiest of metaphors must break down at some point, and no cartoonist's ingenuity could have added Francis Joseph's leg still lodged in the upper part of the boot (which was Venetia) and the Pope's foot uncomfortably bulging in the region of the knee (which was Rome). And for the moment there was a disposition even among patriots to overlook the anomaly. There was, indeed, a comforting proclamation from Turin that " the era of revolutions was ended "; Italy had been achieved, and now the reorganisation of the provinces was the signal for a multitudinous and exciting scramble for lucrative civil appointments. It was at this time that Giuditta Sidoli, in her *salon* at Turin, let fall the cruel *mot* which became proverbial: " They have created Italy, and now they are eating her." But while from afar a " thin melancholy hand " was still pointing Italians forward to duties not yet achieved, and while on the festive streets of Turin Giuditta continued to appear in symbolic black—" for Rome and Venice," Count

Cavour, taking a final leaf from his rival's book, conferred with Kossuth for a Magyar revolution to assist a projected Venetian campaign, and expounded to an approving Chamber the idea of a free Rome as capital of a united Italy.

But in truth the little Minister had brought off his last *coup*. He was overwrought and threatened with apoplexy; and a violent scene in the Chamber with Garibaldi agitated him and hastened a collapse. To the end his wandering mind was full of thoughts of his country; he had Italy on his hands and on his heart, and he recollected that he must inspect the Mt. Cenis tunnel; and when his King entered by the much-used secret staircase and stood at his bedside, the sick man spoke earnestly of Neapolitan reforms. "The bad must be cleansed; yes, yes, Sire, cleansed, cleansed." But a more pressing crisis had to be met—perhaps this, too, not without a touch of diplomacy. " I must prepare for the great passage. . . . I have confessed and received absolution; later I shall take Communion "; and, a statesman to the last, the little Minister gave instructions that the public should be informed of this. The future of his Church policy should not be prejudiced by the popular suspicion that its author had died outside the Faith. It was in the early hours of a June morning that Fra Giacomo hastened with the holy oil in answer to an urgent summons, and it is said that the sick man rallied to utter two words: " *Friar, Friar, a Free Church in a Free State!* " and " *Italy is made—all is safe.*" It was still early morning, and the little Minister had made his last pronouncement.

By a curious reaction Cavour's death was the signal in England for a new maledictory outburst against Mazzini. The *Morning Chronicle* commented upon the inscrutable providence which had removed the statesman and spared the agitator; *The Times* assailed the Exile as the curse of Italy; and Miss Martineau, deploring his survival of the siege of Rome, announced (in *Once a Week*) that events had exposed his political ignorance and futility. He was incapable, she had discovered, of meeting other men's intellects or putting anyone in possession of a clear idea. He was, in short, an enemy of his country " more dangerous than any in the past."

Still, the Execrated continued to possess his charmed circle, with new and select circlets always forming around it. There were admiring overtures from Mr. Ruskin (who contemplated contributing an introduction to the Exile's *Duties of Man*), cordial correspondence with Grote and Mrs. Gaskell, stimulating intercourse with Masson and the Amberleys and young Mr. John Morley; there were dinner-parties at the Seeleys' to meet John Bright and others (with "servants dressed in a way that made me feel inclined to bow to them"), and friendly visits from exiles like Herzen and Ledru Rollin and, above all, the Saffis; and now and then there was a box at the Opera for a Meyerbeer performance. The Carlyles, too, were within call, with the unfailing Nathans, Rossellis, Shaens, the Mallesons, and Milner Gibsons, the Taylors and Craufords and Rabbi Morais, and many more; and the "Muswell Hill brigade," though sadly scattered, was still unswerving in its devotion.

Thus the days passed, and the American Civil War dragged through its second year—its third; Windsor became a house of mourning in which a widowed Queen sat inconsolable; and while the Reverend Mr. Baxter was agitating the faithful with predictions—from David and the Book of Revelation—of the coming World Monarchy of Louis Napoleon (and the rapture of 144,000 virgins), and Archbishop Manning was alarming his Catholic flock with predictions of similar convulsions, the French imperial Sphinx himself was propounding a new riddle whose answer had something to do with Mexico and Maximilian; meanwhile, also, Prussia was shaping to become "the Piedmont of the North," and Bismarck was ingenuously endeavouring to correct an unfortunate phrase about "blood and iron" by explaining that by "blood" he meant only "soldiers." As for Mazzini, he remained restless with repressed activity and plagued with ill-health. There were times, indeed, when he kindled to the romance of Italian achievement. Thus after the Sicilian-Neapolitan campaign Herzen called upon him. "With both hands stretched out, as his habit was, he rushed toward me with the words 'And so at last it is coming true!' There was a look of delight in his eyes and his voice trembled. . . . As I listened to him I tried to catch a single note, a single sound of wounded pride, and I could not catch it."[1] For the rest, his talk ran upon what he occasionally called Negro Abolitionism, upon Women's Suffrage, upon Garibaldi's exploits, upon poor Poland butchered by Cossacks and Tartars,

upon the French Empire as "an immorality and a lie."
He addressed a private appeal to Lincoln on the Mexican situation and revolved a project for a united Greek, Serbian, Bul-
garian and Rumanian rising to "generalise" the Polish
struggle; but the apathy of Europe was invincible. "The
egotistical indifference," he wrote, "which pervades the whole
of Europe to sufferings of men whom we write down as
brothers whenever we amuse ourselves about philosophy or
religion is, to me, appalling and sickening. It takes, and has
taken, away from me long ago every possible pleasure in life.
There ought to be an expiation to teach mankind that they
have been made One, and that they are every day sinning
against God." And borrowing a figure which Carlyle had
once put to memorable use, he hinted at a future European
cataclysm. "As filthiness, allowed to go on in the streets and
dwellings of a town, teaches physical oneness by spreading con-
tagious diseases to the neighbouring towns, so something ought
to teach—will perhaps teach—egotistical countries that there is
a law of moral oneness."

Meanwhile, Italy, having funeralled Cavour and failed to
respond to Ricasoli, was leaderless; and with Rome still fenced
off and hostile, the lack of a unifying national centre was every
day becoming more menacing. The rival claims of Turin,
Florence and Milan were exacerbating provincial jealousies, and
from Rome itself the ex-King of Naples, under Papal protection, was abetting anarchy and brigandage in his late dominions.
Thus at last the mystical Mazzinian dogma, long gibed at by
realist wiseacres, that a free Rome held the secret of national
unity—that dogma was now developing into a political truism;
and Garibaldi, leaving his goats and beanfields, appeared
suddenly on a Palermo balcony with the cry of "Rome or
death!" The crusade was unauthorised, and Turin launched
its punctual veto; but so it had done before, to transform it in
due time into royal recognition; and Europe once more awaited
a Garibaldian miracle. But this time the red-shirt columns,
winding Romeward over the hills of Aspromonte under the
blaze of an August sun, were met with a volley from Victor
Emmanuel's Bersaglieri, and the Liberator pitched from his
saddle, wounded by a richocheting ball. The wounded chief
was promptly placed under arrest, and his troops (he had for-

bidden them to resist the King's forces) were flung into convict prisons. The episode filled the public mind with a sense of outrage, and the royal volley echoed round the world. No government worthy the name could permit unauthorised campaigns led by private citizens at their pleasure, but in the circumstances to check the *Garibaldini* by a discharge of ball-cartridge could have been justified only if it had been the evident intention of the red-shirts to attack. The King's "*caro Garibaldi*," who only yesterday had presented his sovereign with two kingdoms, Italy with her liberty, and the world with an immortal exploit, deserved better handling than to be shot down like a brigand.

What was evident to the country was that Victor Emmanuel had acted under pressure from Napoleon, and even Moderates began to grow restive. Later, when a Garibaldian volunteer named Greco confessed in Paris to a plot to assassinate the Emperor, it was easy to revive old calumnies and invent new ones by connecting Mazzini and James Stansfeld with the conspiracy. The time was unfortunate. It was when Victor Emmanuel, eager for Venetia, and despairing of his Ministers, was turning secretly to Mazzini and complotting with him for an insurgent attempt. That Greco was a police agent, that his "confession" was a fiction, and that Mazzini had had no dealings with him, was afterwards established; but the outcry, in spite of Palmerston's and Gladstone's intervention, obliged Stansfeld (then Junior Lord of the Admiralty) to resign from the Ministry. But with a wholesome Radical reaction yielding Stansfeld a triumphal progress through the North, and with Garibaldi arriving in England (March, 1864) to collect funds for a new Venetian venture, the stage was set for a popular demonstration of protest.

And for this, certainly, Garibaldi was a gift from the gods. For if Mazzini was never a figure to arouse Londoners to a delirium of enthusiasm; if he passed unnoticed on the streets and aroused little public interest with his Italian lectures on Sunday evenings at St. Martin's Hall, with Garibaldi it was otherwise. His *flair* was irresistible. Who could resist the red shirt, the *poncho*, the tawny mane? Who could withstand the benignity, the child-like simplicity, the strength and sweetness, the rugged power, the gentle grace, of so Homeric a being? The nation rose to roar its welcome to the hero of Rome and Sicily, the martyr of Aspromonte. But a Government with a *penchant* for embarrassment intervened. Ministers developed a tender concern for the visitor's health, and while they insisted that a protracted sojourn in so ungenial a climate would be undesirable for the distinguished guest, they saw to it that meanwhile he should be politically quarantined in the isolative purlieus of Mayfair. Thus while the Hero was being rescued from the embraces of the nation and caged behind the golden bars of ducal hospitality at Stafford House, English dailies publicly assured themselves in prim editorials that the great Italian would not so disregard the obligations of his position as to have any intercourse with his former associate, Mr. Mazzini. It was a gratuitous insult, and the thought of the opprobrium heaped, in the hour of his protégé's apotheosis, upon "the noble, emaciated figure of the old man with the flashing eyes" aroused Herzen's Russian soul to vehement protest. But in any case the Garibaldian *furore* was not to be stayed. D'Artagnan had come to town, and who should not know it? Even a resourceful Government had no means of conveying its guest through London in a vacuum, and the Liberator's passage from Nine Elms to the Duke of Sutherland's house was a triumphal progress almost unparalleled in the annals of royalty. At Stafford House, where the guardians of privilege closed jealously around him, the scene was somewhat different but no less impressive. Palmerston, Russell, Derby, Shaftesbury, Dufferin, Argyll, waited upon him; Mr. Gladstone engaged him in Italian conversation, and while carriages streamed up in never-ending procession, the nobility and gentry pressed forward for the honour of shaking the Hero's hand. Herzen was a sardonic observer: "The men shook his hand with the vigour with which a man shakes his own when he has put his finger in boiling water; some said something as they did so; the majority grunted . . . the ladies, too, were mute, but they gazed . . . long and passionately."[2] It was a worse ordeal than Calatafimi—Milazzo—the Volturno; and Mr. Gladstone lost a night's sleep through nervous excitement.

Twice the Hero escaped. At the Crystal Palace, where he was presented with a sword, he astonished the public with the confession, "I am not a soldier, and I do not like the soldier's trade." The second escapade (it was three days after President Lincoln's assassination) took him to Teddington for a friendly luncheon-party at Herzen's house. It was a day of pleasant April sunshine. Saffi and other exiles, Russian, Polish, French, Italian, were among the guests, and James and Caroline Stansfeld were also present. The poorer classes of Teddington gathered at the gates and had their moment of beatitude when the Hero drove up and passed into the house. A little later a second carriage arrived and an old, black-garbed gentleman with a white, close-cut beard stepped out. Garibaldi and all the house-party came out to greet him at the gate, and the little crowd at the railings, catching his name, gave him, too, a generous cheer. And the luncheon found the Hero himself in expansive mood. He had escaped for a while from the powdered flunkeys of Stafford House, and once more—a stolen visit but none the less sweet—he was among his own people. His eyes rested upon the pallid old gentleman in black, and he rose, glass in hand, to make his memorable speech:

"I want to-day to do a duty which I ought to have done long ago. Among us here is a man who has performed the greatest services both to my native land and to freedom. . . . When I was a lad and was full of vague longings, I sought a man to be my guide, the counsellor of my youth. I sought him as a thirsty man seeks water. . . . I found him. He alone was awake when all around were slumbering; he became my friend and has remained my friend. . . . In him the holy fire of love for fatherland and freedom has never dimmed. That man is Giuseppe Mazzini. I drink to him, to my friend, to my teacher."

The toast was drunk in silence, and, because exiles are usually sensitive souls, in tears. Even the servants, says Herzen, were deeply moved. It was a moment of exaltation, quietly solemn, in which old hurts were healed, old misunderstandings dissolved: it was the summing-up of the hopes, the struggles, the aspirations, of a life-time.

But clearly, a nervous and always-embarrassed Government could not have digested another such Garibaldian luncheon: Mr. Gladstone read the report of the Liberator's speech "with surprise and concern,"* and the Duke of Sutherland's yacht

* (See Morley, *Life of Gladstone*, bk. v., ch. viii.) Morley has a foot-note: "Speech not discoverable by me;" but Gladstone's reference was clearly to the Teddington tribute to Mazzini.

was kept under steam; the Liberator's health became more
than ever a matter of Ministerial concern, and while Palmerston
explained to a deeply moved House of Lords that for a person
of General Garibaldi's simple and exemplary habits, dining
late and retiring after midnight, must necessarily be injurious,
Mr. Gladstone, in a more critical Lower House, explained that
even apart from the Hero's health (admittedly a matter of deep
and world-wide solicitude) any repetition in the provinces of
the national reception in the metropolis might impair a unique
historical event.　There was a final rally (at Prince's Gate) and
a private visit from the Prince of Wales; the Hero was once
more charged by the flower of the British aristocracy in crinolines or swallow-tails, the band of the Horse Guards played
" *Non curiamo l'incerto domani* " and other appropriate Italian
airs, and in forty-eight hours the Duke of Sutherland's yacht
was steaming South, and from the deck a robust invalid in a
red shirt and *poncho* was waving his farewell to England.

*　　　*　　　*　　　*　　　*

The *incerto domani* arrived in due course to present Europe
and the world with new complications, and anxious Governments with new embarrassments.　At St. Martin's Hall, instead
of Mr. Mazzini's Italian addresses on the Duties of Man and
the spiritual function of Nationality, a German Jew named
Karl Marx, with a massive head and a slightly Fijian mop of
hair, expounded his Socialistic International Working Men's
Association to a select representation of the Proletariat.　Also
a Russian gentleman of the old nobility, named Bakounin, and
variously suspected of being in league with the Czarist police
and with Satan, was meditating his terrorist International for
the abolition of Religion and the Political State.　And even in
America proletarian idealists were making play with a disturbing quotation from the speeches of the late President Lincoln
to the effect that " the strongest bond of human sympathy outside of the family relation should be one uniting all working
people of all nations and tongues and kindreds."[3]　Meanwhile,
the political States had their own preoccupations.　Palmerston
was in his grave, and Napoleon III. was mourning a short-lived
Mexican Empire; Prussia and Austria were eyeing each other
suspiciously over the spoils of a defeated Denmark, and the

German Bund was discussing the significance of a reorganised Prussian army and a new instrument of Bismarckian diplomacy called the needle-gun. Victor Emmanuel shifted his national Capital from Turin to Florence and his political interest from Paris to Potsdam; and at Biarritz (instead of Plombières) and with an ebullient Count Bismarck (instead of a rubicund Count Cavour), an ageing Emperor of the French exchanged difficult insincerities about France's benevolent interest in the rise of " a greater Prussia " (instead of a greater Piedmont). Then finally (July, 1866) Bismarck flung his Prussians into Austria and the battle-flags of Italy were once more in the wind. Mazzini hastened across the Channel and pressed for a bold strategy, the masking of the Quadrilateral and a forward thrust at Vienna: Napoleon, antagonised by an unauthorised campaign, urged a war of extreme moderation; and while bitter political rivalries divided the Italian councils and equally bitter jealousies divided the military command, the King's army was rolled back at Custoza and the King's navy defeated at Lissa. Only Garibaldi in the Trentino, with Medici at his side, pressed forward, and his furious efforts were negatived by the main army's reverses. But while Vienna and Rome were taking new heart, Bismarck, in grey cloak and steel helmet (and as if posed for a Guedalla panel), was sitting his horse on a hill-top near Sadowa, watching his Prussian hussars go in to complete the work of *zundnadel* and rout the Austrians off the field. The Vatican received the news and understood: " Il mondo casca "; and Napoleon stepped in to convey Venetia to Victor Emmanuel. In Italy Austria was left with no more than " the pleasures of memory, the charms of reminiscence "—and the Tyrol. Only Rome, fenced off by foreign bayonets, still remained outside the Union: and in four more years that fence— Paris having more desperate need of it—would be removed, and the Eternal City would be acclaimed as the Capital of a United Italy.

But to the man who had toiled while others slumbered the fulfilment brought no satisfaction. For him the Risorgimento had somehow fallen away into a sad mockery—the galvanising of a corpse. The elements of true life had indeed been abundantly manifest; they had inspired the souls of the faithful, they had approved themselves in a hundred exploits and upon a thousand scaffolds; they had flamed forth in Milan, Bologna, Sicily, Rome; they had added immortal names to the scroll of the heroes of Italy: but a movement begun in faith and enthusiasm had continued through artifice and calculation, and in the end the " first King of Italy " had collected his provinces by permission of a foreign despot, and the last remaining portion of unredeemed territory had been " liberated " by Prussian bayonets on the plains of Königgrätz. The Italian peninsula was now, indeed, a political as well as a geographical expression; but to the Prophet the tragedy was that it was nothing more. He had proclaimed, it is true, that Unity was the great thing, but the Unity actually achieved was, not even the ghost, but only the soulless body of his ideal. " Little it matters to me," he wrote to his English friends, " that Italy, a territory of so many square leagues, eats its corn and cabbages cheaper; little I care for Rome if a great European initiative is not to issue from it "; and it seemed that it must now be his lot to consume his last days " in the grief, supreme to one who really loves, of seeing the thing one loves most inferior to its mission." The Pities, watching from the Overworld, may well have spared a sigh for one dreamer whose dream had touched the earth only to materialise into something profane and undesired.

CURFEW DEFIED

CHAPTER I FAREWELL TO ENGLAND

UNTIL the autumn of 1868 the inhabitants of Fulham Road continued to observe the coming and going of the old gentleman at number 18, who was Mrs. France's lodger. His name was said to be "Mr. Ernesti," but he was very retiring, rarely conversed with his neighbours except the children in the street, and for weeks together he would be out of town. Mrs. France was not communicative about these disappearances nor about her lodger himself, but it was plain that he was very genteel, that she thought highly of him, and that he made no trouble except for the tame birds flying about his room.

The fact was that the manners and habits of a conspirator had rather grown upon "Mr. Ernesti." Thus he would rarely admit a visitor to his private lodgings; instead, callers were usually directed to the address of a third party, where he would see them only when satisfied of their identity and good faith. There were even stories of the *cachette* in the wall, through which "Mr. Ernesti" would make a preliminary survey of his visitors. If later he entered into correspondence with them his letters were usually written in invisible ink upon commercial note-paper closely inscribed with records of business transactions, and he was pleased to supply his correspondents with the chemical preparation for removing the superficial text. When he went to the City he carried a sword-stick for a cane, and in general lived in an atmosphere of mystery.

This, at all events, was the way of "Mr. Ernesti"; but "yours affectionately, Joseph," was, as always, a different

327

being. Even so, there were no doubt certain characteristics that had grown upon him with the passing years; and, in due time, in a lengthy obituary, the London *Times* (coached, perhaps, by Gallenga) was able to supply its public with a generous exposition of them. He was "a solitary man incapable of looking out of himself," and sure only of one thing—"that he could be no man's fellow-worker either in thought or action. Men might learn from him, sacrifice themselves for him, but they could have nothing in common with him."

"If we could except a few devoted English women, there is hardly a human being whom long familiarity had not estranged from him. With manners consummately affable and courteous he combined an overweening conceit and a narrowness and bigotry of view which hardly tolerated independent minds. . . . . He was never very warm in his praise of living friends, and he was apt to denounce as adversaries all who were so unfortunate as to differ from him. . . . He was a lonely genius . . . spurning the suggestions of the plainest common sense, professing to do all for his fellow-beings, yet nothing with them or by their aid."[1]

There was sufficient of truth in all this to embalm its falsity. With all his personal self-abnegation there was a dominant self-righteousness about his public avowals, and when his methods were most questionable his sense of impeccability was most militant. In his relations with his colleagues he could be exacting and occasionally splenetic; a north-easterly wind could blow through his warmest appreciations of his political contemporaries, and sometimes the wind was due east. He was certainly not free from the intolerance which usually besets the apostle. He abhorred Cavour as St. John abhorred Cerinthus; he hated the Moderates as St. Paul hated the Judaizers; and he could be as exacting with his own fraternity as St. Francis with his Little Brothers. Nevertheless there never was a leader who evoked from his colleagues a greater personal devotion or whose affection for them was warmer, more generous or more constant; and to declare that there was hardly a human being whom long familiarity had not estranged from him was a curious perversion of the facts. Estrangements are inevitable in public life; they are apt to increase in proportion to the tension of the times, the gravity of the issues of the day; but neither Cavour nor Bismarck, Palmerston nor Lincoln, retained through all estrangements an inner circle of colleagues more loyal, more deeply devoted in their personal attachment to their leader, than the exiled Chief. When *The Times* pictured him as though he were more isolated than Arnold's forsaken merman, solitary in his weedy cave, it had forgotten Saffi, Quadrio, Bertani, Campanella, Cironi, Varé, Lemmi, the Nathans, the Rossellis—so many more—whom "long familiarity had not estranged," as well as English and Continental colleagues out of number.

In England, indeed, his friendships multiplied, and Professor Masson has left a happy picture of the social life of this forsaken *solitaire*:

"In private society Mazzini's habits were simple, kindly, affectionate, and sometimes even playful. He had a good deal of humour and could tell a story or hit off a character very shrewdly and graphically, not omitting the grotesque points. . . . In a varied group round a fireside, or joining in a game at cards . . . or else more apart and smoking a cigar with one or two selected for that companionship, he was very ready to talk. The talk . . . was good, utterly unpedantic, . . . and often with whim and laughter. Inevitably, however, some topic would be started on which Mazzini would show his *tenacity*. . . . Whatever it was, if Mazzini had an opinion, he would fight for it, insist upon it, make al ittle uproar about it, abuse you with mock earnestness for believing the contrary. That would not last long; a laugh would end it; we knew Mazzini's way. But sometimes the difference would go deeper. . . . You might unawares assault one of his principles. Then he was down upon you . . . there was a touch of *Matérrialism** in you, though you did not know it; you were at all events an Individualist or . . . a Classicist. Then Mazzini broke out and he grappled you with the yearning of an apostle, yet with a vigour of reasoning and an acuteness of analysis which you were hardly prepared to expect. . . ."[2]

It was not, perhaps, surprising that there were others besides the "few devoted English women" who sought and continued to seek his society. Henry Sidgwick succumbed to his fascination and wrote of being "quite overwhelmed"; John Morley found him "the most morally impressive man he had ever known, or that his age knew"; George Meredith, completing his *Vittoria* in '66, paid his tribute with a portrayal of Mazzini in the person of "the Chief"; Jowett of Balliol found him "very noble," and (though overmuch preoccupied

* "His favourite word for all mere acquiescence in customary Religion without real belief was Materialism. This word . . . he pronounced in a cutting Italian way (*Matérrialism*)."—Masson.

with "two abstract ideas—God and Nationality") a man of
genius whose reputation would probably increase with the passing of time. The Whistlers pleased him, especially "dear,
good, believing Mrs. Whistler." He discussed religion with
Edwin Arnold and found him "good, I think," and "very
intelligent within a certain phase." Ruskin was for him "the
highest critic, in the best philosophical and artistical sense, in
Europe" and "thoroughly conscientious." His prejudice
against the Evangelicals was perhaps mollified by his intercourse with some of the militant Dissenting leaders, among
them the Welsh poet-preacher, "Gwilym Hiraethog":
William Lloyd Garrison renewed his contact with him and (in
spite of the Exile's deplorable addiction to tobacco) found
himself attracted "by an irresistible magnetism"; "his soul
was full-orbed." Young Carl Schurz, later to attain to eminence in America, visited him and came to rank him with
Bismarck and Wendell Holmes as one of the three greatest
conversationalists he had ever met. Holmes was "more
spirited," Bismarck more imposing, "but in Mazzini's words
there breathed such a warmth and depth of conviction, such
enthusiasm of faith . . . that it was difficult to resist such a
power of fascination." Felix Moscheles found him a poet
and prophet. "He would penetrate into some innermost recess
of your conscience and kindle a spark where all had been darkness. Whilst under the influence of that eye, that voice, you
felt as if you could leave father and mother and follow him,
the Elect of Providence." George Jacob Holyoake,* Freethinker and Co-operator, worked for him and revered him as
the one living leader with a truly European mind. "Kossuth
astonished us by his knowledge of English, but he knew little
of the English people. Louis Blanc knew much; but Mazzini
knew more. . . . He understood the English better than they
understood themselves. . . . No man of a nature so intense
had so vigilant an outside mind." Miss Blind sought his
counsel and recorded an impression that ranked Mazzini with

---

* In his *Bygones Worth Remembering* Holyoake writes: "Mazzini did me
the honour of presenting to me his volume on the *Duties of Man*, with this
inscription of reserve: 'To my friend G. J. Holyoake, with a very faint hope.'
Words delicate, self-respecting and suggestive. It was hard for me, with my
convictions, to accept his great formula, 'God and the People.' It was a great
regret to me that I could not use the words" (i. 206).

the mythic figures of history "from Moses and the Buddha to Savonarola." Harriet Eleanor Hamilton King came to know him and found "a sort of living flame" surrounding him. "His lodging was poor and small, but there was no ostentation of poverty. . . . In his presence one could hardly think of material things: wherever he was, there was a palace."[3] And Jessie White Mario joined the chorus: "Anyone may write of what Mazzini *did*, but what he *was* none can know save those whose supreme privilege it was to have lived in close association with him."

But strangest and most extravagant of all his later devotees was Swinburne. Already in his Oxford days he had come indirectly under the Exile's influence, mainly through Prof. Nichol, and through Saffi, whose Italian lectures Swinburne attended at the University. By 1867 the young poet's vagaries were alarming his friends, and Jowett, acting with Purnell of the *Athenæum*, and Karl Blind, privately appealed to Mazzini to take intellectual charge of him. The conspiracy succeeded, and presently Swinburne was writing: "I, unworthy, spent much of last night sitting at my beloved Chief's feet. He was angelically good to me. I read him my Italian poem all through. To-day I am rather exhausted."[4] It must have been no mean ordeal. For a Swinburne recital was apt to take on exciting accompaniments of a slightly Dervish character—"convulsive jiggings" round the room, with "red hair flying" and "arms flapping." In this instance the poem —"*A Song of Italy*"—ran into some two thousand lines and included a pæan to the "crownless chief"—"Mazzini, O our prophet, O our priest!" In the prophet-priest's account of the proceedings there are likewise hints of slight exhaustion, particularly as the rhapsodic utterance of the corybant became "almost unintelligible for me." But at least Mazzini read his man. To Emilie Venturi he confessed to a fear that his own influence over his ward would "vanish before unfolding." "Swinburne is, I fear, in one respect unredeemable. . . ." "He might be transformed as far as direction goes, but only by some man or woman—better a woman, of course—who would love him very much and assert at the same time a moral superiority on him."[5]

Nevertheless, he took his elusive charge in hand and laboured to win him from his "absurd, immoral, French 'art for art's sake'" heresies. He succeeded. The fantastic being with the brow of a young god and the body of a gnome became something of a political philosopher: so much so that the Reform League came forward with the offer of a safe Parliamentary seat. It was an engaging prospect, and Parliament was within sight of a bizarre acquisition; but the Chief discouraged the project. Let the poet follow his true vocation, translate his new impulse into poetic expression, and help to "re-link Art with Heaven!" The counsel was obeyed, and *Songs before Sunrise* was written, and dedicated to Mazzini. One day before its publication the poet, caught by the tide while bathing, and nigh to drowning, reflected with great comfort that the book was completed and that "'the Master' would be pleased." He was: and the volume was at least an impressive tribute to his influence. Gosse's judgment may be cited: "In other times and cases we find Swinburne the slave of his own splendours, carried whither he would not by the Pythian intoxication of words. But this is not the case in the finest passages of *Songs before Sunrise*. . . . We are surprised to discover the most rapturous of troubadours transformed into one of the great poetic intelligences of the modern world."[6] Nor did the extravagance of the poet's hero-worship abate with the passing of time. Five years after "the Master's" death he wrote of him to Watts-Dunton in the old style of hierurgic rhapsody. The "very highest honour, privilege and happiness" of his "whole life" had been "that of being presented to the man who was to me (I should think) what Christ Himself must have seemed to the very first disciples, and for whom I would very gladly have given all the blood of my body and all the power of my heart and mind and soul and spirit."[7] Perhaps, too, something of the Mazzinian dogma remained with him. He was no Theist, but he liked to consider himself "a kind of Christian, of the Church of Blake and Shelley," regarding "the semi-legendary Christ as the type of human aspiration and perfection."

For the rest, Mazzini found solace chiefly with the "Muswell Hill brigade," as of old, and spent his free evenings at the Stansfelds' in Thurlow Square. Emilie (Hawkes) Venturi, plunged early into widowhood, found comfort in his friendship and gradually grew into his faith; and Matilda (Ashurst) Biggs, stricken with mortal illness, turned to him for " conversations on immortality and divine things." There was another friend of bygone days who turned to him for comfort, as to " the most pious man he now knew ": for at Cheyne Row a lonely Carlyle was brooding sadly over faded letters and diaries, " summoning out again into clearness old scenes now closed " on him " without return."

*   *   *   *   *

Time now, his friends thought, for the Chief to turn to the writing of that long-deferred book on Religion. Alas! it could not be done now. " How tired and morally worn out I do feel!" And, after all, he must believe that the best contribution, and the kind most needed, was a man faithful to the end to the ideal purposes that held the reverence and fired the passion of his youth. Besides, was there not news of a republican revival in Italy and some faint hope of unfurling the old flag and dying " like Cooper's Corsair," in the act? Yet in his private reading he turned with strange zest to the writings of the Mystics—to Eckhart and others—and would have liked well enough to " drag himself from library to library," unearthing their neglected lore. Also he became curiously interested in the history of the Anabaptist movement, and Weill's " *Peasants' War* " excited him. Did it not point the lesson that it was the religious movement among the sixteenth-century German peasants (and not the later French Revolution) which communicated the social-democratic impetus to Europe? And had not this aspect of Reformation-history been too much neglected? For these peasants, in spite of their fanaticism, went beyond Luther in their insistence upon a new earth as well as a new heaven; and in following up the rejection of Papal absolutism with an examination into the claims of their economic masters they proved their instinctive logic. Altogether the early Anabaptist emphasis upon an earthly theocracy kindled him as " one of the most eloquent proofs that religion is at the head of the whole movement of mankind." He persuaded Emilie Venturi to translate the work and Holyoake to publish it.

As for Mysticism, he could at least follow the mystical

emphasis upon the oneness of Life, and this oneness, he recognised, could lend value to contemplation and prayer.
Thought itself, in a spiritual universe, was "a sort of action,"
and the "strong, silent, unheard belief" of the prisoner, the
secret aspirations of the sufferer, could weigh with God and
influence the destinies of Humanity. In this sense he thought
he recognised a general principle underlying the Christian
doctrine of redemption. "Even now I have somewhat strange
ideas of what Martyrdom and Love in a Just Man can achieve
for all." "There have been moments in my life in which I
had a glimpse of the . . . [meaning] of suffering, and I
felt that Jesus' sufferings—they only—achieved in mankind
what his intellectual belief, the same that philosophy had before
him, would never have achieved."[8] But the mystical doctrine
of absorption in the Divine, lending itself to a strained effort
after a high experience, was not for him. Was it not, he
asks, a vain attempt to deny time and space and the necessary
limitations of earth? From initiation to initiation, from sphere
to sphere man must ascend Godward through faith and duty,
and this progressive order could not be cancelled, nor could
there be any true salvation which did not recognise the social
aim. To Mrs. Hamilton King,* troubled in her own inner
life, he writes:

"I fear, dear friend, that you are bent too much on self-analysing, on
thinking too much of your salvation. Let God think of it; your task is
to act for the fulfilment of His Law whenever and as much as you can;
to pray and wish fervently for it whenever action is forbidden, and to
trust Him without any terms. Actions, sufferings, victory, martyrdom
have been decreed and weighed by Him long before you seek for the
formula which will best act on Him. Love Him in a simple, unexacting,
unscrutinising way as a child his mother, and remember that self-
torturing has in itself a hidden taint of egotism."[9]

Thus, too, the influence of his Calvinistic Jansenism never
left him. All things had been "weighed and decreed" by

* Mrs. Hamilton King (best known by her volume of poems *The Disciples*)
embraced the Roman Catholic faith after Mazzini's death. To the present
writer, in her later years, she deplored the general decay of religious belief.
"I should welcome any sign of it, even if it were Brahmin or Buddhist." She
held that Mazzini, though opposed to Papal absolutism, was Catholic in sentiment and much less heterodox than many Catholic Modernists of that time
(1911).

God from eternity. But he would have nothing to do with what he liked to term the orthodox "aristocratic dogma of Grace" as an arbitrary and selective favour bestowed upon a limited number of the race. Grace was a universal baptism and "God called us by creating us" and endowing us with the power "gradually to incarnate the Ideal." Withal, while Personal Immortality remained a fixed article in his creed, he had nothing but repugnance for the increasing vogue of Spiritualism:

> "When men no longer believe in God, God revenges Himself by making them believe in Cagliostro, in the Comte de St. Germains, and in table-turning. All this rubbish of tables in convulsions, of *mediums* who traffic in souls, of spirits stammering alphabetically I know not what stupid answers to stupid questions, irritates me like a profanation of the sanctity of death. When I think that if it occurred to me to ask these people for a conversation with my mother they would make her appear amongst a circle of sceptics, *blasé* men in yellow gloves and ladies in crinolines . . . to divulge . . . the commonplaces limited to the questions put to her, I am seized with disgust. . . . In a *séance* at a fixed hour, in the midst of vicious men and frivolous women, that an abject creature, often less than mediocre, and frequently hired for a fee, should have the power of evoking Jacob's ladder ! . . ."[10]

His faith in personal immortality grows out of his faith in God and in man's spiritual affinity with Him. Mortality, he argues, is a universal law; and does not the very word "law" suggest the idea of an ultimate good? It must mean more than a principle of Irony or of Tyranny, else from whence could have come to us, "particles of the universe" as we are, our own consciousness of the Good, our aspirations toward a higher life, our capacity for love, for holiness, for martyrdom? Is it not impossible even to frame a conception of Tyranny, Irony, or Evil, save as the reverse of Goodness? And would not even the existence of a Tyrant God imply a Good God "elsewhere above"? But in these matters, he declares, more truth is revealed in "the flashes of the virgin soul" than by all "the dim lanterns of analysis and reasoning." And so with immortality itself. As our sense of the infinite, of duty, of a transcendent ideal, should teach us God, so it should teach us human survival. "Life cannot die; it would be God dying"; and for us survival would be a lie if it did not mean consciousness of identity. Thus "love is the vouchsafer of

immortality." "I believe in the progressive development of
our affections when we live and die in them; they are the best
part of our life . . . and I live and walk, sad but composed
and firm, as if I was surrounded by the dead I love, and as if
any change in me, any withering, barren, egotistical grief
would not only grieve them, but prolong the separation." "I
would not for all the world that you should fall into the depths
of inert despair if I died. If love is not an empty word . . .
but rather a state of progression for the soul, you would feel
yourself bound to worship with a renewed enthusiasm all that
you found good in me, and all that I loved . . . the Beautiful,
the Grand, the True."[11] It is for us to "make life valuable."

So at one time or another he declares himself to his friends
and would "give his heart's blood" to have them all share
his faith. Only he is no proselyter nor founder of a new cult,
and when Emilie Venturi suggests that he should attempt the
conversion of orthodox Bessie Ashurst he demurs. Bessie, he
replies, is "quiet in her own creed" and would never attach
herself to the new with a faith which would make her "more
active for good" than she is already. She would only be unsettled, nothing more.

*　　*　　*　　*　　*

And now it was time for the Exile to turn again home. He
had refused an amnesty, but the old sentence of death had
at last been revoked. But these days a new and irrevocable
death-sentence was being plainly inscribed upon him. His
health was perceptibly failing; he had serious pulmonary
attacks; his colour had changed to a waxen pallor; his beard
was white, his hair streaked with grey. Even the beloved
guitar had been reluctantly set aside this long while. "For
the first time yesterday night," he had written to Caroline
Stansfeld in '62, "I took up the guitar and *hummed* the
Russian tune and the 'non ti scordar di me' of Campana.
The result was a quarter of an hour of pains. There is an end
of *that* too." And now, in Paris, the Emperor Napoleon informed Lord Lyons that Mazzini was seriously ill, and did not
(Lord Lyons observed) express any wish for his recovery.

All the same, there might yet be time for a last effort, and
the longing for action became at times tormenting. "I know

I shall not live long and I hate the thought of dying in bed
. . . *di peso ad altri, grave a me stesso.*" And perhaps at
Lugano health and strength would revive a little—enough for
a last effort. So he must pack his few books and belongings
and bid farewell to dear friends.* Sad to leave them! "In
England friendships are slow and difficult to make; but they
are more sincere and durable than elsewhere . . . and proved
in action rather than in words. . . . Nor shall I ever forget
it while I live, nor ever proffer without a throb of gratitude
the name of the land . . . which became to me almost as a
second country."[12] Sad to leave this London itself! Only
as yesterday seems that murky January day when we arrived
in the great city—Giovanni, Agostino, Angelo—the four of us
—and made our way through mud and rain to the *Sablonnière,*
and wrote hopefully to our mothers! . . . One-and-thirty
years ago! But now it is time to bid farewell. And Onslow
Terrace, looking behind its curtains, sees Mrs. France's elderly
lodger, with trunk and portmanteau, drive finally away—a
weeping Mrs. France, we may be sure, in the doorway.

* He did not, however, formally break up his residence until February, 1871.

UNDER the more genial skies of Lugano Mazzini did in some measure revive. And with the Italian Monarchy arresting the development of the national revolution, and Marxian Socialism and Bakounin Anarchism bidding for the soul of his Italian working class, what was he to do but take up the challenge and fling himself into one last struggle? It was curfew-time, but the fires should flame out defiantly yet once more.

As for the Economic Question, it was no new engrossment for him. "It is the Riddle of the Sphinx," he warned the upper classes. "You must solve it or run the risk of being devoured." The supreme danger, as he saw it, lay in the alienation of labour through the apathy or hostility of the already emancipated classes. Remember, he wrote, that "if the people, called irrevocably to rise, should receive from those who have already risen nothing more than checks, fierce repressions and injustice on the one hand, and neglect, scorn and antipathy on the other . . . they will advance, not as a fertilising river but as a devastating flood; they will rally to watchwords of wrath and revenge and to the purely negative and subversive ideas already rampant in Europe."[1] There was a deep and radical vice, he declared, in the present organisation of society, and it was sheer irony to take a gospel of Progress to men and women condemned to a life-and-death struggle for bare animal existence.

His own economic ideas may have owed something to Lasalle. He looked for a gradual and peaceful economic revolution based upon popular suffrage and the development of co-operative associations. First slaves, then serfs, and now hirelings, the working classes must gradually free themselves from the final yoke by uniting Labour and Capital in the same hands. This, he declared, was the Cause of the future; and the abolition of all arbitrary class-distinctions, the establishment of labour as the commercial basis of society, would be the "most beautiful" of all conceivable revolutions. But this could be done by peaceful methods and must be brought about by the industry and initiative of the workers themselves. They must mount upward by their own efforts, by a ladder, not a lift. Thus he differed from Louis Blanc (and favoured Lasalle) in contending that the Working Men's Associations must be based on the voluntary principle. Land, railways, mines and certain key-industries, he agreed, should be under State control; the Banking system should be reorganised, and the incidence of taxation lifted from industry and the necessities of life; but the reorganisation of labour, the gradual elimination of the middleman-class, and the consequent reform of production and distribution, should depend upon the initiative and energy of the workers themselves. The State could encourage the movement by advancing capital to the Co-operative Associations at low interest; it ought not to enforce the revolution. The workers had no reason to expect to induce society to look favourably upon the substitution of the co-operative system for a system of salary and wages save as the Workers' Associations supplied valid evidence of efficiency.

Nevertheless, as early as 1862, he was seeking a working-agreement with the Socialists. Political Democrats were condemning Socialism in the name of liberty; Socialists were condemning Political Democracy in the name of collectivism: but was there not, he asked, common ground upon which both sections could unite, leaving secondary issues for later decision? "For us no revolution exists that is purely political. Every revolution must be social in the sense that its aim is the realisation in society of moral, intellectual and economic progress. But neither can there be a revolution that is purely social. The political system—that is, *the organisation of power* in a way favourable to the progress of the people—is a necessary condition for the social revolution." This much at least they held in common; and they agreed, further, that the economic problem was essentially international and must be approached accordingly. Thus the one reasonable method was for the artisan classes of Europe to establish a common centre of organisation which, while allowing freedom to the various national groups of Friendly Societies, should seek to maintain a har-

mony of movement towards the general end. "I believe in
association as the sole means we possess of realising progress
. . . and I know that association will never be fruitful of good
except among free men and free peoples, conscious and capable
of their mission."

But this Karl Marx was impossible. Mazzini found him
"a man of acute but *dissolvent* genius, domineering in temper,
jealous of the influence of others, without strong philosophic
or religious beliefs, and, I fear, with more of anger in his
heart, albeit righteous anger, than of love."[2] And if Marx
was bad, Bakounin, with his doctrinaire anarchism and his
cheerful advocacy of bloodshed as a social *tonic*, was worse.
From these sheep-dogs turned rabid the flock must be protected. And alas! even among good Italian democrats there
were also a rabid few who needed to be dealt with: for even
the good Cattaneo himself and Alberto Mario had been bitten.
They had gone over to the "Materialists." Strange, he thinks,
that these good men should succumb! In their hearts they
worship the Ideal—and they proclaim a creed that is the end
of all idealism. They earnestly desire the ennoblement of the
people, and they teach them that the thought of a Kepler, a
Dante, the genius of the fire-bringers from Prometheus to
Jesus, were no more than the secretion of material substance.
Strange that they do not see that the logic of their doctrine is
the rule of Force and must lead either to anarchy or tyranny!
So he pours into the columns of his own weekly press endless
exhortations, warnings and prophesyings. "All the materialist
young men are separating themselves [from me], Bakounin
is denouncing me . . . others are attributing what they call
[my] *recrudescence* of religious feeling to the fears arising
in old age." Be it so. A coming generation would know
better. And he believed he was already visibly gaining
ground.

To some extent it was true. He succeeded in organising a
separate Working Men's Federation, presently founded yet
another propagandist journal, his *Roma del Popolo*, and projected a Roman Congress of Workers' Associations to serve as
a counterblast to the Marxian International. But when the
time came he would not go up to it. "I hate meetings and
applause, meaningless *vivas*—everything," and he could not

endure to return to a Rome "profaned by monarchy." "I can be a voluntary prisoner or conceal myself like an animal anywhere—not in Rome."

*   *   *   *   *

Meanwhile, amid wars and revolutions, strikes and Socialist Internationals and the general commotion of Governments, the Catholic Church moved to the aid of a shaken world. Pius IX. had already established the dogma of the Immaculate Conception, and in the *Syllabus Errorum* the destructive heresies of Democracy and Science had been faithfully exposed. And now, after a lapse of three centuries, a new Œcumenical Council was called to provide "an adequate remedy to the disorders of Christendom." It was indeed an impressive moment. There was no denying the gravity of the disorders nor the vehement desire of Christendom for their settlement; and in the eyes even of the unbelieving there was something august and deeply moving in the spectacle of the great Church, mighty in her ancient traditions and mightier in her claim to supernatural authority, turning to confront a challenge that was baffling the wisdom of the world. "I am awaiting your Council," said Guizot to Manning. ". . . It is the last great moral power and may restore peace to Europe." Even the deliberateness of the movement added to its impressiveness. The Council was not suddenly decided upon and hastily convened, as if under pressure of a desperate urgency long neglected or even denied. It was planned with deliberation and ordered with unhurried precision. Nor did the peculiar circumstances at this time surrounding the Papacy itself fail to contribute an additional significance to the event. For of late the Papal Court, as centre of a temporal sovereignty, had been abased in the eyes of men. Twenty years earlier the Holy Father himself had stolen out of the Eternal City, a fugitive dispossessed of his title as the Prince of Rome; and though that title had been restored, his dominions had been ruthlessly diminished. Of a kingdom that had once extended northward from the borders of the Neapolitan State to the frontiers of Lombardy-Venetia, little more than Rome itself now remained. The Pope was a Prince whose capital was all that was left of his State, and that itself was manifestly foredoomed to pass from his keeping. In so far, then, as the deprivation of earthly dignities could affect her, the Church had suffered extreme adversity and humiliation. Yet it seemed as if Europe, which had stood by and witnessed her abasement, was seeking once more her wisdom and her authority. How strange if at such an hour, when the wit of earthly senates had failed, she should take up, one by one, the problems that vexed a bewildered world and approve her majestic claims by solving them! It seemed as if she proposed to do no less; and by December (1869)—it was on a day when Rome and St. Peter's were swept and deluged by a torrential storm—the six hundred Fathers assembled in Council, gathered from the ends of the earth.

Their labours were long and arduous. They had gathered in December: it was in the midsummer heat of the following year that they reached their final session. Some of the Council, broken in health, had been obliged to relinquish their task: some had died; but 533 remained, and the consummation was observed with appropriate solemnity. There were processions, solemn Masses, choral litanies, and the Fathers, mitred and venerable, passed into the Council Hall through a reverent assemblage of the laity and a double line of troops. To add to the solemnities a terrific thunder-storm broke over St. Peter's and continued its uproar for an hour and a half. In the gloom that descended upon the sanctuary a taper had to be lighted before the aged Pope could read his proclamation. The noise of thunder-claps drowned the *Placets* of the voting Bishops, and lightning darted about the dome and cupolas and stabbed the thick shadows around the baldacchino. It was thus, amid Sinaitic accompaniments, that the work was done, the votes cast and the labours of the historic Council consummated. Then the venerable Fathers clapped their hands, the dense crowd waiting in silence at the great door took up the signal, a cloud of white handkerchiefs waved in the dusk, and a storm of exultant voices swelled and echoed through the sanctuary. The "remedy to the disorders of Christendom" had been pronounced. The world had been given a final definition of the dogma of Papal Infallibility.

Yet perhaps, among unbelievers in an unquiet and afflicted

Christendom, there was some excuse for a feeling of disappointment. The disorders were actual and indisputable, the remedy seemed remote and unconvincing. There had, indeed, been rumours of dissension among the Fathers themselves, and the hostility had spread among the faithful far beyond the limits of the Council. Thus even Dr. Newman had spoken with asperity of certain "brand-new views imported from Rome," and of the latest "move in ecclesiastical politics," and had been driven to re-read Cowper on Needless Alarm. "I certainly think," he had confessed privately, before the Council was concluded, "this agitation of the Pope's Infallibility most unfortunate and ill-advised, and I shall think so even if the Council decrees it, unless I am obliged to believe that the Holy Ghost protects the Fathers from all inexpedient acts (which I do not see anywhere promised) as well as guides them into all truth, as He certainly does. There are truths which are inexpedient. . . . For myself, I refuse to believe that it can be carried till it actually is."[3] Lord Acton was not less disturbed. It was certainly distressing to be obliged to reflect that a supernatural guidance which operated to the point of inerrancy still allowed so large a latitude to human indiscretion, and that an infallibly inspired definition of Infallibility might yet be ill-advised.

As for Mazzini, he took up his pen and wrote his last fiery protest and apologia—"*From the Council to God.*" He painted a highly coloured contrast between the First General Council at Nicæa and its latest successor. "I accuse you," he wrote, "of living no real life." Life was love, and they knew no longer how to love. Life was movement, unfoldment, and they were seeking to petrify the Living Word, binding the idea to its transient symbol. Life was communion, and they denied the universal diffusion of the Spirit. Life was production, and they struggled simply to conserve. Science went forward regardless alike of their dogma and their anathema. Art wandered in the void, now returning to pagan ideals, now pursuing religious aspirations other than the Church's. Two nations, the Greek and the Italian, had burst asunder the walls of their tomb without asking or receiving of the Church "one holy word of baptism" or of consecration; and thanks to no Papal crusade, four millions of black slaves had been emancipated across the Atlantic. Let the hierarchy know, then, that the appeal was now from the Council to God, " the destroyer of all idols." The true Council of Rome was yet to be convoked. It would one day be summoned by a free people united in the worship of the ideal. It would be composed of " the worthiest in intellect and virtue among the believers in things eternal "; it would assemble to interrogate the heart and conscience of Humanity and " demand of that prophetic but uncertain instinct of the future which exists in the peoples: *What portions of the old faith are dead within you? What portions of the new are wakening within you into life?*"

The essay appeared in the *Fortnightly Review*. Carlyle read it and approved, and Emilie wrote to Lugano to communicate the pleasant news. It moved him. "You want evidently to excite me. . . . I wish you could. However . . . I would feel rather glad of Carlyle's praise." Meanwhile the sultry July days wore on, and ominous tidings were flashed from Paris and Berlin; the venerable Fathers hastened back to attend to the urgent necessities of their dioceses; von Moltke's troops massed on the Rhine frontier; and an ailing and dispirited Emperor of the French left Paris for Metz, Châlons and Sedan. One more Mazzinian prophecy was on the eve of fulfilment. And while the Pope, from behind the defences of a newly defined Infallibility, became a powerless spectator of the march of unwelcome events, and while King Victor Emmanuel was lending colour to the suspicion that he desired to range Italy on the side of the French Empire, the sick man at Lugano roused himself for one last, desperate and reprehensible fling.

* * * * *

Ever since the King's troops had failed Garibaldi, in his second attempt upon Rome, the popularity of the House of Savoy had been clouded. Republican sentiment had revived in the cafés and in the press, the army was disaffected, and in the provinces volunteer bands were drilling in secret. What was to hinder a popular rising, the overthrow of the Government, the liberation of Rome, and the proclamation at last of the Republic of Italy?

There was, in fact, much to hinder it.   Insurrection under a coercive dictatorship or foreign oppression was one thing; under a democratic constitution it was another.   Under such conditions to turn from the ballot-box to methods of conspiracy and to run the risk of civil war was sheer outlawry.   Saffi mildly hinted as much, but the aged Chief was not to be turned aside.   Saffi had really been behaving very well, but he had his limitations.   "Now listen and don't get angry. You have no intuition of the state of the Monarchy and the Italian situation: and you haven't it because, though superior to the majority in most things, you lack the *initiating* faculty. . . .   You are waiting for the Monarchy to proclaim the Republic."[4]   Mazzini, in short, was able to persuade himself that the situation was exceptional.   The National Revolution had been checked half-way in its course.   The Monarchy did not represent the sovereign choice of the nation; it had been foisted upon the people by Cavourian intrigue and French diplomacy and the force of circumstance.   And the consequences had been disastrous.   Already there were signs that the Crown might revert at any moment to the old despotic tradition, and in any case the Monarchy had turned the popular movement back upon itself and stabilised a *bourgeois* régime.   Aristocratic and middle-class interests had entrenched themselves under Government protection, and henceforth their policy would be defensive and repressive.   The economic emancipation of the working classes, the elevation of the Italian people as a whole, the development of a truly national commonwealth—these were no longer to be expected, but instead a growing schism in the nation between the privileged and the unprivileged.   The result he believed he could foresee. The schism would fling the working classes back upon the gospel of materialist agitators and would lead in the end to anarchy and " a revolution of hate " and to the emergence of a new order based upon the dictatorship of force.   What chance was there of breaking this sequence save by carrying the National Revolution through to its logical republican conclusion, and doing so before the state of government had hardened into a fixed tradition?   It was not a party question, it was a National issue.   And the country, he was persuaded, would respond to a truly National Programme.   But a

National Programme demanded a National Government, and a National Government was precisely what did not exist. Therefore it must be created. But in the nature of things the Monarchy and the forces of privilege would never proclaim it, would never sanction it, would only resist it. Therefore the Monarchy must be overthrown.

So he argued. Insurrection under a constitutional government was indeed deplorable; but the case was peculiar. Writing to Caroline Stansfeld, he unburdened himself: "Yes, dear, I love more deeply than I thought my poor dream of Italy, my old vision of Savona." He confessed himself impatient. The sands were running out. He wanted "to see before dying . . . the ideal of my soul and life." And for the rest he was frequently ill, which was "very annoying," and conscious of the increasing infirmities of age. "Take me at once as doomed," he writes to Emilie Venturi, "as a phantom of the past, or rather as a dear—if you can—loved remembrance. . . . 'Finis Joseph.'"

Once more, then, he flogged his energies to the task. There were secret journeys to Genoa and elsewhere and midnight conspiratorial conclaves. At such times "the great magician" (with shorter steps now, but with the old "divine smile") would appear from nowhere and salute each comrade with a personal word of greeting, "as if (said one of them) our names were written on our foreheads." And when Bismarck, suspecting a French-Italian alliance, cast his mind upon a possible republican diversion in Italy, the Chief was prepared to do business. "We desire German Unity. We hate the French Empire. We want Rome and Nice. Aid us and reckon upon us," and send us "muskets and money like lightning." Muskets and money from Prussia! He would stop at nothing now. The only thing he marvelled at was the indifference of the Government. "They have in their hands proofs entitling them to shoot me twice [over]." Why did not they at least try to catch him?

He had not long to wait. On August 14 (1870), by good, providential hap, the passenger steamer *Florio* was boarded by a gunboat crew off Palermo, and an aged gentleman whose passport proved unsatisfactory was respectfully escorted to a vessel of His Italian Majesty's Mediterranean Squadron.

Treated as a distinguished guest rather than as prisoner, he dined with the ship's officers, sitting next the Captain; and at Gaeta, whither he was conducted, he was received "with every kind of respect." The commanding officer of the local garrison took charge of him, and he was lodged in comfortable quarters in the fortress-tower. The prisoner was indeed very weak and "rather sad," but uncomplaining. "I have the wide sea before me and the Italian sky above me. It is quite enough." He had also a Byron, a Dante, a Shakespeare, and Tasso's *Jerusalem*. How like Savona!

So the weeks passed. His guards were changed with unusual frequency, because a few conversations with their prisoner turned them into his worshippers. The turnkey spent minutes over the opening and closing of the doors, because he would not have his charge fretted by the gaol-like clanking of heavy locks. And for a touch of irony, the local Military Governor was General Giacomo Medici. Peter Taylor plotted a daring rescue which somehow fell through; Emilie Venturi journeyed post-haste from London to Gaeta; and for the rest, he found diversion enough in the study of passing events. Was not Garibaldi—strangest of men!—in France, fighting for the French Emperor, in the vain hope of securing for reward the return to Italy of his beloved Nice? He followed Garibaldi's fortunes, and in the newspapers he read of Gravelotte and Sedan, the fall of the Second Empire and the exile of Napoleon III. The "crime of '49" had at last been expiated. And then in September there was a brief burst of gunfire outside the gates of Rome, and through a breach near the Porta Pia the King's troops poured into the city. A formal plebiscite yielded 40,788 votes for union with the Kingdom of Italy, 46 votes for the continuation of the Papal Government. Italy was One. And in October the prisoner at Gaeta, once more declining a royal amnesty, was unconditionally released, and left the fortress. There were reverent and affectionate ovations, and a guard of honour attended him as he inspected the sights of the city and visited Cicero's tomb. Then, with Emilie Venturi, there was a journey by train to Leghorn to visit the Nathans and Rossellis. Sad and memorable journey! For did it not mean crossing the Campagna and beholding Rome once more? That weary, jolting ride through the dust and

heat! Emilie could never forget it. Somehow for the silent
old man beside her it seemed like a slow dying, a last
sacrament, a summing up of the past, a farewell to all earthly
hope. "Rome was the dream of my young years; the
generating idea of my mental conception; the keystone of my
intellectual edifice; the religion of my soul." So he had
written years before. "Rome was to me, as in spite of her
present degradation she still is, the temple of Humanity.
From Rome will one day spring the religious transformation
destined for the third time to bestow moral unity on Europe.
I shall never see her more; but the memory of her will mingle
with my dying thought of God and my best beloved." Yet,
once more, he was beholding her. To a sympathetic friend
Emilie wrote of it all: "He was very still. I could not have
spoken for my life." And now she beheld him with "a
reverence newly mixed with awe." He turned, she remembered, as St. Peter's came into view, and gave her "one look,
with a smile." His countenance, she thought, wore a look of
faith in renunciation which recalled "the solemn image of
'the eternal type of all martyrs of genius and of love.' . . .
'Nevertheless, not my will but Thine be done.'"[5]

Thereafter there was a journey alone to Genoa, and a last
visit to his mother's grave in the Staglieno cemetery. A keeper
recognised him, and as, in the gathering dusk, the bent figure
of the old man passed slowly down the hill, a little company,
a priest among them, drew up in silence outside the cemetery
gates, "bowing and almost touching the ground." "They
felt my sadness and contrived to show they were sharing it."

And then there was a last visit to England for friendship's
sake—a pathetically feeble Mazzini now, but still capable of
electrical intervals in congenial company, the inner flame
shining through a thin transparency. Let anyone, for instance,
mention the suppression of the Byron memoirs. . . . Was
there no one to protest? Would not the voice of poor accused
Byron cry from the grave some word of explanation, extenua-
tion, remorse? Was it justice to suppress the memoirs and
stifle if only a cry of anguish, and leave the soul of a great
poet under a stigma of unrelieved, unextenuated shame?
"Can a man like Dr. Lushington persist in stealing the
defence, in gagging a soul when the accusation is hurled

against the silent, defenceless tomb? . . . Monstrous! . . . If only I was young . . .!"[6] He lodged at Mrs. France's at the old address, and gaunt, broken old Carlyle called to spend a farewell hour of sad reminiscence, and felt as he bade him good-bye that he would never see him again.

VIEWED from Hardy's Overworld, or from the elevation of history, the years 1871-72 marked the end of a European epoch. How different, the Europe of '72 from the Europe of '05! The last of the Napoleons had vanished, the Second Empire had dissolved, United Germany had emerged in the North, in the South, United Italy. And with a resetting of the stage came a new turn in the drama and new figures in the cast. Marx had already written the first volume of *Das Kapital,* Tolstoy had written his *War and Peace* and was dreaming of a World Religion, Edison was at work upon his novel experiments. A young Junker, Paul von Hindenberg, was already a veteran of two wars. Behind the scenes other players were making-up. In America a promising youth named Tom (Woodrow) Wilson was preparing for an academic career; in Wales a small boy named David Lloyd (George) was cutting his autograph here and there on the stones of Llanystumdwy; in South China a smaller boy named Sun-Yat-Sen was learning his letters; in Russia Vladimir Ilitch Ulianoff (Lenin) was cutting his first teeth; at Porbandar, in North-Western India, little Mohandas Karamchand Gandhi was learning to lisp his Vishnu texts.

As for Mazzini, by February, 1871, he was back at Lugano, plunging into new and endless labours. He was busy with his Working Men's Associations, his Friendly Societies; he had founded his Roman periodical; he was hurrying forward— against Garibaldi's strange and bitter opposition—his Working Men's Congress, and pouring out incessant articles, letters, and appeals. He had no longer the strength for the task. Asthma whistled in his throat, numbness, dizziness and cramp debilitated him, and an anxious Dr. Bertani called in a specialist from Milan. But the work went on. To glance over his contributions to the *Roma del Popolo* alone is to appreciate something of the miracle of will daily repeated during those last months. Week by week, with scarcely a break, his articles and reviews appeared and his correspondence was maintained. There were contributions on the Franco-German War, on the French Commune, on International Politics, on M. Renan and France, on much besides : and always their burden was the same. Europe was in dire peril, and there could be no salvation except through the making of a new European mind, the quickening of a vital and social faith, the recognition of a Sovereignty that transcended material interests. As it was, " destitute of any common faith, of any conception of a common aim capable of uniting nations and assigning to each its special task for the good of all, destitute, too, of all unity of law to direct its moral, political and economic life, the European mind lies at the mercy of each new dynasty or popular interest or caprice." He mourned over France. " A nation alternating between an indifference which allows her inertly to contemplate the dismemberment of her soil, and a vandalism which transforms the sanctity of the republican faith into a passion of hatred and vengeance, and the divine aim of life into an idolatry of the senses and greed of material good— is irrevocably lost if some immense effort be not made to restore her to the sphere of high thoughts, the adoration of the ideal, the lost religion of duty and sacrifice, and recall all her children to communion in love and works." But it was his Italians who lay nearest his heart. " I am bent now " (he wrote to his English friends) " upon two things : conquering a large portion of the middle class to my own ideas, and saving our working classes from the [Marxian] *International* and other evil influences." So he preaches to them week by week in his *Roma del Popolo*.

" Many among those to whom our words are more expressly addressed believe in God or profess to do so. Have they never thought—if this belief is within them as a profound reality and not a mere lip-avowal— of the logical consequences involved? Have they considered that if God is, there necessarily exists between Him and His creation a Thought, a Providential design?—that there exists alike for the individual life and for Humanity, a plan, a purpose, an end?—that there exists for us all, individuals and society, a holy, absolute duty to co-operate for its fulfilment?—that an *end*, whatever it be, assigned to Humanity, has need, for its attainment, of the united energies of all the faculties and powers, active or latent, in Humanity itself?—that gradually to achieve and constitute through Association the moral unity of the human family is the indispensable means of ascending to that end?—that hence the progressive elimination of all caste, of all artificial distinctions, and—within the limits of the possible—all the inequalities which tend to separate men from one another and hinder their concordant activity—is part of the Providential design?   Herein . . . exists the reason for our movement, its justification, the certainty of its victory.   And herein should also exist for us all, Catholic or Protestant, Christian or non-Christian—for all of us who believe in God—that sense of reverence and love for the unemancipated classes which to-day are knocking at the portals of the civilised world."[1]

So the torch lighted at Savona and rekindled at Solothern must be held aloft to the end.

But the Prophet was not heeded. His prophesyings had become trite. Throughout Italy the subscribing constituency of his *Roma del Popolo* did not exceed 2,000 readers; and while the old irksome problems of journalistic finance and subscription-hunting returned upon him his Congress met at Rome and talked itself out. There were other troubles. Garibaldi was growing more and more petulant and suspicious. He had had ill-success in his French campaign, and (as Deputy for Nice) had been ungratefully howled down in the French Chamber. He returned to Italy in a bitter mood, and the persecuting hostility of Mazzini and the Mazzinians became his fixed idea. Crispi, too, developed political ambitions of his own and was permanently alienated; and Mario came out in open opposition as a *doctrinaire* materialist: and when a harassed Chief sought solace in family affection the response was chilling. His one surviving sister would admit him beneath her roof only on condition that he would abandon political agitation. Nor was there any comfort to be got from Italy itself. He wrote privately of his supreme disappointment.   " *This* is only the phantom, the mockery, of Italy, and the thought haunts me like the incomplete man in *Frankenstein*, seeking a soul from his maker."   " My day is spent in writing," he wrote to Emilie, " only getting up every quarter of an hour and walking up and down the rooms during three minutes. I smoke perennially, I am sorry to say; but what can I do?   I write unwillingly, through a sense of mere duty, without a spark of enthusiasm, and smoking is a mere diversion to the soul's fog which is coming heavy on my head, like a leaden cap."   So the *tinta grigia* overspread his world, and there were times when he felt "out of place on earth" as if he had "no longer any business here." "It is ungrateful, and I feel really remorseful for it, but I sink under a sense of loneliness." "Strange," he wrote to Varé, "that I should see all those I have loved disappear one by one, while I remain, I know not why." And at times he lingered over this lengthening rosary of bereavement—his father, his mother, his two sisters, Jacopo, Mameli, Pisacane, Agostino Ruffini, Scipione Pistrucci, Lamberti, the Modenas, Jane Welsh Carlyle, the Ashursts, Cironi, Grillenzoni—so many more. And now one more was to be added—Giuditta. She died as she had lived, in the Mazzinian faith, and a letter in a well-known but sadly shaken hand consoled her last hours.

"*Amica*, you are suffering and are gravely ill. I know you are brave, resigned and believing. All the same, the knowledge that an old friend is watching in spirit at your bedside may be dear to you and give you a moment's solace. If that is so, be assured of it. I have never ceased to think of you, esteem you, love you as one of the best souls I have ever met in my journey through life. You will, I hope, be spared to us: but even if you should be taken from us, you must not fear what men call death, but which is no more than transformation. One day you will meet those who love you and whom you love.

"Trust in God, in His law and in your own pure conscience. Give a thought to me, too, and bless me. I dare not bless you, but my heart is with you.

"Your friend,
"Giuseppe."[2]

If the familiar *tu* of the Grenchen letters was now exchanged for *voi*, the *mia cara* for *amica*, the restraint was not that of outworn affection but of tender and reverent valediction: moreover, the letter might be opened by other hands than hers. "Good, holy, constant Giuditta!" he writes to Varé. "Did she die a Christian? I do not belong to that faith, but any faith, however imperfect and marred by false dogma, comforts and consecrates the pillow of the dying better than the barren, meagre, wretched delusion of Science called nowadays Freethought and Rationalism." And to Caroline Stansfeld he writes pathetically: "I have had so many dying this last year, and I am always repeating to myself the lines of Goethe—

'Die Vögelein schweizen im Walde.
Warte nur, balde
Ruhest du anch.'"
["The little birds are silent in the forest.
Bide awhile; soon thou too shalt rest."]

But until *then,* on with the work! Even writing now brought on attacks of giddiness, the asthma returned, the slightest exertion became a labour of Hercules. "The asthma will pass," he remarks to Georgina Saffi, "or I shall pass. With this dilemma I console myself."

In February (1872) he moved from Lugano to Pisa to the home of his friends Pellegrino and Janet (Nathan) Rosselli, in the Via Maddalena. Neighbours understood that the aged visitor was an English friend—"Mr. George R. Braun," but when the old attacks returned with pleuritic complications, the local physician found his English patient well able to converse in Italian. (And did not the doctor remark that Mr. Braun appeared to love Italy? And did not the patient in half-soliloquy take up the phrase and murmur: "*Love Italy ... Love Italy. . . . No one has ever loved Italy more!*"? And late in February he was still at work. "Sometimes" (he writes to the Saffis) "I think I am destined to do a little *mischief* even yet, before I vanish"; and to best-loved Caroline he writes on March 4 that he is still working "and smoking, too, though moderately," though the bronchitis is rather worse. On the whole "we are marching on and conquering ground." Still, he can do little except write a few articles, "weak, shattered, breathless as I am—*nominis umbra.* . . . Write, dear, and tell me of yourself and of Joe and James."[3]

Then on the morning of March 10, in the white-walled bedroom with its simple furnishings and its table strewn with unopened letters and uncorrected proofs, an emaciated old man talked ramblingly of Italy and his Working Men, of the future and of times gone by. Janet Rosselli was at the bedside, and Sarina Nathan, and Felice Dagnino from Genoa and Adriano Lemmi. Quadrio and Saffi, Campanella and Dr. Bertani were hastening from Rome, but they would arrive too late. To the watchers the dying man's wandering speech was hard to follow. Was he once more with Jacopo rambling over the green fields and hills of Bavari, or with the "Pleiads," discussing the

Hetæria on the Acquaverde balcony? Once it seemed, indeed, as if some tremendous conflict engaged him, so that his utterance became rapid, agitated, imperative. Was it that he was labouring in one last desperate struggle to force the hand of Cavour? Then suddenly he sat up and spoke with clarity and decision: "*Si! Si! Credo in Dio!*" ("Yes! Yes! I believe in God!"). And with one look of recognition and farewell he fell back. His eyes closed as if in sleep. It was the end.

*　　　*　　　*　　　*　　　*

In Genoa the sunshine bathed the Staglieno hill and lingered upon a new-made tomb. Above it no Chorus of the Years or the Pities recited a final threnody, and the eighty thousand mourners assembled upon the hillside beheld no sign and heard no voice. But at last the Exile had been welcomed home, and at last the Prophet had received honour in his own country and in his own town.

And across the sea, in a house in Cheyne Row, Chelsea, a lonely old man sat at his fireside and communed with the past. "I remember well when *he* sat for the first time in the seat there, thirty-six years ago. A more beautiful person I never beheld. . . . He might have taken a high place in literature, but he gave himself up as a sacrifice . . . for Italy . . . lived almost in squalor. . . . His mother used to send him money, but he gave it away . . . used to come here and talk of 'the solidarity of the peoples' . . . much sought after and invited to dinners and all that. But he didn't want the dinners. . . . At last it has come to an end, and the papers and people have gone blubbering away. . . . Poor Mazzini! After all he succeeded. . . . Italy united, with Rome for her capital. . . . Well, one may be glad. . . . We wait to see whether Italy will make anything great out of what she has got."

We wait.

Meanwhile, in Genoa, in the Piazza Acquasola, stands a statue of the Great Exile. By a curious irony it has been erected in the place where Cavour once threatened to have him hanged. It represents an austere and pensive figure, standing with folded arms and gaze bent downward in an attitude of fixed and brooding reflection. It is a noble conception. But sometimes, to the solitary watcher, when the great Piazza is deserted and the twilight of a new day steals over the city—sometimes it seems as if the posture of that silent figure changed—as if the head were no longer bowed, as if a hand were half-raised in signal of attention, as if the gaze became forward-looking and expectant—the attitude of one intently watching and listening.

APPENDIX A

" LORENZO BENONI "

IN 1853 Mazzini writes to Caroline Stansfeld from Switzerland:
"What you tell me about the Edinburgh novel [*Lorenzo Benoni*] is
very interesting, I could say important, to me. Of the two Ruffini one
[Agostino] is ill at Genoa, and I thought he was, through his physical
condition, unable to write a novel. The other is in Paris, and he is
inferior in capacity to his brother, and of rather lazy mental habits.
Who is the writer, of the two? Agostino is the younger of the Ruffini.
I think he had in him all that Masson says: only marred, checked by an
exaggerated tendency to analysis and by want of faith in himself and
others. The name Benoni is, strange to say, of my creation. It means
in Hebrew ' the son of my grief'; and I mentioned it to them some
fifteen years ago as the title of a hypothetical novel I was proposing to
write. The subject I do not like to see treated in a novel; the memory
of the martyrs is too solemn, too sacred to me for my possibly liking
fancies and unrealities to be put round it. But I feel nervously impatient of seeing the book as a revelation of feelings, past and actual,
in the writer." (*Mazzini's Letters to an Eng. Family*, i. 266.)

The book, *Lorenzo Benoni: Passages in the Life of an Italian: Edited
by a Friend*, was published anonymously by Constable (Edinburgh) in
1853. Agostino, prior to 1848, had resided in Edinburgh for some years
and was supposed, as Masson tells us, to be at work on a novel. " It
was always spoken of, with utter confusion of tenses, as an achieved
reality which had yet to come into existence. . . . Did some discussion
arise which it was desirable to stop, ' Ah! you should see,' would be
Ruffini's way of stopping it, ' how wonderfully that is all settled in my
novel . . . which I am going to write.' " (*Memories of Two Cities*,
pp. 140, 141.) *Benoni*, however, was written by Giovanni Ruffini,
though it is possible he had access to Agostino's MS., if indeed it
existed. In July, 1853, Giovanni writes to his mother that he is sending
to Agostino a review of *Benoni* from *Tait's Magazine*, and adds that
a review in the *Quarterly* is entitled " Autobiography of Signor Ruffini."
He objects to this. " No one, it seems to me, has the right to violate
my individuality, as Mazzini would say, and substitute me, the real
entity, for a fictitious one [Lorenzo]." (Cagnacci: *Mazzini e i Fratelli
Ruffini*, pp. 383, 384.) All the same, the book is virtually an autobiography interwoven with a very slight thread of romance. It deals
with the Genoa of the '20s and '30s, the home life of the Ruffinis, school
and university life, the initiation of Mazzini and the Ruffini brothers as
Carbonari, Mazzini's exile, and the founding of " Young Italy," ending

357

with Jacopo's death. The names are, of course, fictitious. Giovanni is "Lorenzo," Jacopo "Cæsar," Mazzini "Fantasio," Andrea Gambini "Uncle John," Passano "Nasi." Altogether the book very vividly reflects middle-class life in Genoa in that stirring period, and is of unique interest and value for the study of Mazzini in the first phase of his career. Although written after their estrangement, Giovanni's delineation of Mazzini is exceedingly sympathetic. The book, hailed at the time as a second *Gil Blas*, had an immense popularity and ran through several English editions. It is still read in Italy, and deserves to be read in England. It was followed in 1855 by another romance, *Dr. Antonio*, in which once more the hero bears marked resemblance to Mazzini, though with little attempt at historical fidelity. In this romance the portrait of Eleonora Ruffini (as "the Signora Eleonora"), living in retirement in Taggia while her two surviving sons are in exile, is faithfully painted.

APPENDIX B

MAZZINI'S BETRAYAL AND ARREST IN 1830

THE story of the betrayal is told in full detail, and fully documented, in Signor Luzio's *Mazzini Carbonaro*. Doria, it seems, approached Governor Venanson with the suggestion that he (Venanson) himself should secure first-hand evidence against Mazzini by disguising himself as a Carbonaro desiring initiation into the second rank of the Order— Doria offering to give Mazzini the necessary instructions in advance. The Governor, however, demurred. Although a comparative stranger in Genoa he was known to the Mazzinis and his disguise might be penetrated. A local coffee-house keeper who was an ex-soldier and a police-agent took his place and masqueraded as an army officer. Mazzini relates the facts in his Autobiographical Notes. "I received an order to go at a certain hour to the *Lion Rouge*, an hotel then existing in the Salita S. Siro, where I should find a certain Major Cottin, either of Nice or Savoy . . . whom I was to affiliate. We young men were treated by our leaders like mere machines, and it would have been quite useless to ask why I was selected for this office rather than some member personally known to the Major. I therefore accepted the commission. However, before I went—impressed by I know not what presentiment— I agreed upon a method of secret correspondence with the Ruffinis, who were intimate with my mother, through the medium of the family letters, in case of possible imprisonment." (*Works*, vol. i., pp. 25, 26.) The date of this appointment, inaccurately recollected in the Autobiographical Notes, was October 21, 1830. His arrest was not made until November 13. Mazzini thus describes it: "At the moment when the *Sbirri* seized me, I had matter enough for three condemnations upon me: rifle-bullets; a letter in cipher from Bini; a history of the three days of July, printed on tricoloured paper; the formula for the oath for the *second rank* of Carbonari; and moreover (for I was arrested in the act of leaving the house) a sword-stick. I succeeded in getting rid of everything." (*Ibid., p. 27.*) He leaves us to wonder how.

According to the police report, Mazzini was arrested at 7.30 a.m. as he was entering the house on his return from a visit to Chiavari. This slight conflict of testimony may be explained. Mazzini was, it seems, challenged by a Carabineer as he entered the house. Passing himself off as a patient with an urgent call for Dr. Mazzini, he was allowed to enter the house (where Dr. Mazzini was obstinately declining to answer the police inquisition concerning the whereabouts of other members of the family); then, apparently, Mazzini was arrested as he attempted to pass out, having in the interval got rid of the incriminating material.

But there is a further explanation of his success in doing so. Orders were issued at this time for the arrest (as well as Mazzini) of Passano, Antonio Doria, the Liberal bookseller, and four young lawyers—Pietro Torre, Nicola Gervasone, Gaetano Morelli, and Cesare Bixio. All these arrests and perquisitions were carried out with such laxity as to call forth angry complaints from Venanson. (See Correspondence of Piedmont Police Dept. with Austrian authorities, 1830. Cited by J. W. Mario: *Vita*, p. 83, *ediz. econom.*) Thus Gervasone's papers were allowed mysteriously to vanish from the room during the search, and bookseller Antonio Doria's premises were entered only after the police had announced themselves and waited for admittance long enough to allow of the destruction of incriminating matter. Only the town house of the Mazzinis was searched, and literary papers were left undisturbed. In short, Carbonarist influence was secretly at work in the higher ranks of the police and the Government. "It was generally believed," says Ruffini in *Benoni*, "that one of the [three] eminent magistrates forming the commission [appointed to investigate the charges against the accused] was a Carbonaro." There appears to be some evidence for this.

Two years later some of the "Young Italy" arrests at Genoa were characterised by the same intentional laxity. In the case of Giovanni Ruffini, the name of an elder brother (not implicated) was substituted for his own on the summons-form. Giovanni, observing the error as the Commissioner read out the formula of arrest, made to interrupt the speaker. "I had already stepped forward . . . when the younger of the police officers passed quickly behind me and said in so low and rapid a whisper that I rather guessed than heard the words: '*Tacete, ne va la vita!*'—'Hush! your life is at stake!'" (*Benoni*, ch. xxxiii.)

APPENDIX C

MAZZINI AND "LA CUGINA"

IN his interpretation of certain pseudonymous allusions in the Ruffini letters of the Swiss exile (1833-1837) Professor Cagnacci, the able editor of the correspondence (*Gius. Mazzini e i Fratelli Ruffini*, 1892), tripped into a curious error. It calls for notice here because the blunder has flung a fantastic shadow upon Mazzini's conduct during the period in question.

The facts are simple. In their letters to their parents both the Ruffini brothers and Mazzini, fearing postal espionage, masked their own identity and that of their colleagues behind fictitious names. Thus Mazzini is referred to as "Emily" (Emilia) and so subscribes himself, addressing his mother as "Aunt." In the same way he refers to the brothers as "the cousins." Agostino signs himself "Paul" (Paolo) and Giovanni "Francis" (Francesco). But in the Ruffini letters there are also frequent references to "La Cugina" (*i.e.*, "the cousin"—feminine) and to "Antonietta." Professor Cagnacci is clearly right in deciding that "La Cugina" and "Antonietta" are one and the same person. A very cursory examination of the correspondence is sufficient to make this plain. Usually Agostino writes of "La Cugina" and Giovanni of "Antonietta." But who is this Cousin (*cugina*) Antonietta? Professor Cagnacci came to the conclusion that "she" was Mazzini himself, and thus by identifying "La Gugina," "Antonietta" and "Emilia" as Mazzini he was able to develop a strange Mazzinian apocrypha. For it is not simply that by this identification we are presented in the Ruffini letters with a Mazzini who is the author of historical dramas unknown to fame, and who is the hero of arrests in Paris and an adventurous journey to Italy (disguised as a Capuchin) at a time when his friends were daily conversing with him elsewhere, but also we are invited to behold him philandering with some half-dozen successive women at a time when he was vowing eternal constancy to Giuditta. Thus in 1834 Agostino writes from Bienne: "The good *Cugina* is ill [with inflammation of the jaw—a malady which was also attacking Mazzini at Lausanne] . . . tormented not only in body but also in mind. Her dear friend Giuseppina Yanch died in childbirth at Milan some days ago." Two years later (June 16, 1836) he writes: "Truly I don't know what to think of *La Cugina*. This new attachment of hers is not the first— I believe it is the fourth or fifth—since the death of La Yanch." And in August of the same year Giovanni writes of "Antonietta's" "new [literary?] passion," while Agostino (August 19) writes: "*La Cugina* sees nothing, listens to nothing, is interested in nothing but the creations of her imagination. It is a genuine artistic egoism. Just now she is jubilant, expecting funds from the publication of her first book." Who, inquires Donaver in his *Vita di Mazzini,* is this Giuseppina Yanch? and observes, following Cagnacci, that we must regard her as one more woman who figures in "the Mazzinian psychopathy." Strange psychopathy, indeed, if at this period we must add La Yanch and her four (or five) successors, together with Francesca Girard of Grenchen, to the swelling litany of Mazzinian lovers!

But a study of the whole Ruffini correspondence together with the extracts from Agostino's private journal supplied by Cagnacci and with Mazzini's letters to his mother, to Giuditta Sidoli and to Rosales, as given in the *Epistolario*, completely explodes the identification. It is enough to note here the following. Agreeing with his letter of May, 1834, referring to " La Cugina's " torments of mind and body, Agostino enters in his journal: " Separated from Giovanni and Mazzini.—Very strange conduct of Ghiglione. Half-mad." In 1834-35 we find by the correspondence that " La Cugina " accompanies Agostino to Paris, where " she " works on a drama entitled *Alessandro de' Medici*. In Agostino's journal we read: " In Paris with Ghiglione. . . . Ghiglione madder and madder." In the summer of 1835, after the return of Agostino, and, later, of his companion, to Switzerland, Agostino writes (August 26) from Grenchen: " *La Cugina* left to-day for Bienne to publish her *Alessandro de' Medici*." Giovanni writes (July 30): " I have read and re-read Antonietta's drama." On September 22 Mazzini writes from Grenchen to Giuditta: " An historical drama is in the press—*Alessandro de' Medici*. The author is a young Genoese." On November 6 he writes to Maria Mazzini: " I have finished my *brochure* [*i.e., Faith and the Future*]. . . . A drama by a Genoese named Ghiglione is being issued from the same press." On July 15, 1836, Agostino writes from Soleure: " *La Cugina* is arrested in Paris." On the same date, also from Soleure, Mazzini writes to his mother: " Persecutions have begun in Paris. They have arrested the author of that play, *Alessandro de' Medici*."

It appears to be clear, then, that " La Cugina " and " Antonietta " are to be identified as the young Genoese dramatist Antonio Ghiglione, whose drama, *Alessandro de' Medici*, was published at Bienne in 1835 and was favourably noticed by Mazzini in an essay on the Modern Drama written at this time. It follows that Giuseppina Yanch of Milan and her numerous successors have nothing to do with " the Mazzinian psychopathy," that of Antonio Ghiglione appropriating them all. And when, later, " La Cugina " makes perilous journey to Italy in Capuchin disguise, it is still Ghiglione and not Mazzini. (But cf. Bolton King: *Mazzini*, p. 82 and foot-note. Dent's *Everyman* edn.)

APPENDIX D

MAZZINI IN THE RETREAT FROM MONZA

COLONEL MEDICI, commanding the column which Mazzini joined after leaving Milan, August, 1848, described the episode in a letter to the English Press in 1861 :

"A general acclamation saluted the great Italian, and the legion unanimously confided its banner . . . to his charge. . . . The march was very fatiguing—rain fell in torrents—we were drenched to the skin. Although . . . little fit for the violent exertion . . . his constancy and serenity never forsook him for an instant, and notwithstanding our counsels—for we feared for his physical strength— . . . he would not leave the column. It even happened that, seeing one of our youngest volunteers . . . with no protection against the rain and sudden cold, he forced him to accept and wear his own cloak. Arrived at Monza, we heard the fatal news of the capitulation of Milan, and learned that a numerous body of Austrian cavalry had been sent against us. . . . Garibaldi . . . gave orders to fall back and placed me with my column as rearguard to cover the retreat. . . . My column, always pursued by the enemy, menaced with destruction at every moment by a very superior force, never wavered . . . but kept the enemy in check to the last. In this march . . . the intrepidity and decision which Mazzini possesses in such a high degree . . . were the admiration of the bravest amongst us. His presence, his words, the example of his courage, animated our young soldiers, who were, besides, proud of partaking such dangers with him." (See E. A. Venturi : *Joseph Mazzini: A Memoir*, pp. 87, 88.)

The episode was brief, hardly more than three days, but the picture is engaging. We behold him—muddied, rain-soaked and unshaven—marching in civilian garb save for bandolier and cockade, the Colours (bearing his motto, *God and the People*) attached to his rifle. We get a nearer glimpse of him in the diary of one of the volunteers quoted by Cironi. Near Monza, says the diarist, the enemy suddenly threatened a charge. "It was one of those moments in which one can read in men's faces all that is passing in their hearts." He glanced, he says, at Mazzini. "His look was animated, his bearing erect, almost he seemed reinvigorated at the approach of danger." So the scene passes and the picture fades! At Como, since nothing more could be attempted, Mazzini left the column and endeavoured, as has been noted, to collect funds and reorganise resistance.

APPENDIX E

DALL' ONGARO'S " STORNELLO "

See p. 242.

CHI dice che Mazzini è in Allemagna,
Chi dice ch' è tornato in Inghilterra
Chi lo pone a Ginevra, e chi in Ispagna,
Chi lo pone a Ginevra, e chi in Ispagna,
Ditemi un po', grulloni in cappa magna,
Quanti Mazzini c' è sopra la terra?
    Se volete saper dov' è Mazzini
    Domandatelo all' Alpi e agli Appennini.
    Mazzini è in ogni loco ove si trema
    Che giunga a' traditor, l' ora suprema.
    Mazzini è in ogni loco ove si spera
    Versare il sangue per l' Italia intera!

APPENDIX F

MAZZINI AND GARIBALDI'S SOUTHERN EXPEDITION

IN the *Contemporary Review*, March, 1888, Karl Blind contributes his personal recollections of Mazzini's relation to the Expedition of the Thousand:

" The version of Mazzini as given to me is that Garibaldi, thinking himself sure of the king [Victor Emmanuel II.], broached the matter [of the projected expedition of '59] to him, contrary to the original agreement, [made] . . . lest the secret should find its way to Paris. . . . [As a result] A thundering despatch came from Napoleon, and Garibaldi had to resign. The secret in this instance not having been kept—Mazzini further explained—the first confidential understandings in regard to the campaign to be begun in Sicily (1860) were not communicated to Garibaldi. In that case, too, Mazzini and his friends were the initiators. Having been present at some of the preparations, I can vouch for what was then being done."

NOTES

References to *Epistolario* volumes are to those of the National Edition.

B.M.I.   =J. W. Mario: *Birth of Modern Italy.*

Cagnacci=Cagnacci: *Mazzini e i Fratelli Ruffini.*

E.F.R.   =E. F. Richards: *Mazzini's Letters to an English Family* (3 vols.).

La Madre =Luzio: *La Madre di G. Mazzini.*

Maz. Carb.=Luzio: *Mazzini Carbonaro.*

Works   =*Life and Writings of Jos. Mazzini:* English edn. (6 vols.).

BOOK I

CHAPTER I.

[1] J. T. Bent: *Genoa*, p. 405.
[2] Letter to Lord Hobart, March 30, 1802; E. S. Wortley: *Highcliffe and the Stuarts.*
[3] Luzio: *La Madre.*
[4] J. W. Mario: *Vita;* Donaver: *Vita;* Bolton King: *Life.*
[5] Luzio: *Ibid.*
[6] Morley: *Gladstone*, bk. v. vii.

CHAPTER II.

[1] Giov. Ruffini: *Lorenzo Benoni*, ch. ix.
[2] Donaver: *Vita*, p. 4.
[3] Codignola: *La Giovinezza di G. M.*
[4] Luzio: *Maz. Carb.*
[5] Salucci: *Amori Mazziniani.*
[6] M.'s letter to his mother, August 2, 1844.
[7] *Works*, i., Autob. Notes.
[8] *Benoni.*
[9] Salvemini: *Ricerche*, p. 76; Codignola: *La Giov. di G. M.*
[10] *Zibaldoni.* See Salvemini, Codignola: *Ibid.*; Salucci: *G. M.: Poesie Giocanili.*
[11] Matthew Arnold: Lines " To Marguerite."
[12] See M.'s evidence after arrest; Luzio: *Maz. Carb.*
[13] *Ai Giovani d' Italia,* sec. xvi.

CHAPTER III.

[1] *Benoni.*
[2] *Ibid.*
[3] R. L. Stevenson: *Memories and Portraits*, iii.
[4] Luzio: *Maz. Carb.*

CHAPTER IV.

[1] Luzio: *Maz. Carb.*
[2] Luzio: *Ibid.*
[3] Thayer: *Cavour*, i. 20.

BOOK II

CHAPTER I.

[1] *Epistolario,* v. 260.
[2] Swinburne: Poem " Sestima."
[3] *Ai Giovani d' Italia,* 1859 (*Scritti Polit. ed. Econ.,* vol. ii.).
[4] Autob. Notes (*Works,* vol. i.).
[5] Dora Melegari: *Lettres Intime.*
[6] F. W. H. Myers: *Essays Classical and Modern.*
[7] Thomas Cooper: *Autobiography* (edn. 1872), pp. 300-301.
[8] M.'s essay, *Faith and the Future* (1835).
[9] *Al Conte Cavour,* June, 1858.
[10] E.F.R., vol. i.
[11] Luzio: *Maz. Carb.,* pp. 105-106.

CHAPTER II.

[1] Luzio: *Maz. Carb.,* p. 100.
[2] See Bolton King: *Life.*
[3] *Benoni.*
[4] See letter to Palmieri, *Epistol.,* i. 6.
[5] *Benoni,* ch. xxx.
[6] Garibaldi: Memoirs (Dumas edn. 1861), ch. iv.
[7] *Catechismo Filosofico,* 1832. (See Thayer: *Cavour,* i. 195 ff.)
[8] *Politica,* vol. ii.
[9] Del Cerro: *G. Mazzini e G. Sidoli.*
[10] *Lettere d' Amore di G. M.* (and see A. De R. Jervis: *Mazzini's Letters*).
[11] D. Melegari: *Lettres Intime.*
[12] See Salucci: *Amori Mazziniani* and *Lettere d' Amore di G. M.* The passages are Mazzini's references in his letters to Giuditta to a certain " A." February, 1834: "Do not, I beg of you, send money for A. . . . Leave it to me. Oh, if only you knew how your words . . . 'I wish I had him with me' burn into my brain."—May 21: "No bad news of A. Don't imagine I am trying to prepare you for evil tidings."—October: "I have written with some heat to Démosthène. . . . I have to beg for news of A. as a favour," etc.

CHAPTER III.

[1] *Lettere d' Amore di G. M.*
[2] J. W. Mario: *B.M.I.*
[3] Autobiog. Notes.
[4] *Ibid.*
[5] Related to David Masson by Agostino Ruffini. See Masson's *Memories of Two Cities.*
[6] See Letters to Giannone, Rosales and Melegari, 1834. (*Epistolario.*)
[7] See J. W. Mario: *Vita.*
[8] W. M. Thackeray: *Paris Sketch Book.*
[9] Luzio: *La Madre.*

CHAPTER IV.

[1] Cagnacci.
[2] G. B. Shaw: Preface to *Methuselah.*
[3] Letter, September, 1836; *Epistolario* v.

[4] *Epistol.*, iii., p. 78; Jervis: *M.'s Letters*, p. 18; W. M. Rossetti: *Gabriele Rossetti*, pp. 168-173.
[5] Cagnacci.

CHAPTER V.

[1] *Epistol.*, iii., p. 322.
[2] Grant Duff: *Notes from My Diary.*
[3] Autob. Notes.
[4] Luzio: *La Madre.*
[5] *Epistol.*, v. 91.
[6] *Epistol.*, xii. 108.
[7] E.F.R., i., p. 140.
[8] Alex. Herzen: *Memoirs*, iv. 165.
[9] Cagnacci.
[10] Luzio: *La Madre*, p. 106; cf. *Epistol.*, iv. 373, 375.
[11] *Scritti*, iv. 353.

BOOK III

CHAPTER I.

[1] *Epistolario*, iv. 393.
[2] *Epistol.*, v. 339, 342, etc.
[3] *Epistol.*, v. 323.
[4] *Epistol.*, v. 298.
[5] Cagnacci: Letter, February 26, 1837, *et seq.*
[6] Masson: *Memories of Two Cities*, p. 125.
[7] Cagnacci.
[8] Autob. of Mrs. Fletcher (private edn.), pp. 230-234. [Note: The Ruffini referred to by Mrs. Fletcher was probably G. B. Ruffini of Modena.]
[9] D. Melegari: *Lettres Intime.*
[10] Luzio: *La Madre.*
[11] *Contemporary Review*, May, 1895; Melegari: *Ibid.;* Salucci: *Amori Mazziniani.*
[12] Letter, January 21, 1837.
[13] Mrs. Fletcher's Autob. Cf. Donaver: *Vita.*

CHAPTER II.

[1] M.'s letters to his mother, November 1-11, 1837. Cf. Carlyle: *Reminiscences.*
[2] Margaret Fuller Ossoli: *Works*, ii. 189.
[3] Cagnacci.
[4] Cf. Marg. Fuller Ossoli: *Ibid.*, and J. W. Mario: *B.M.I.*
[5] Luzio: *La Madre.*
[6] W. J. Linton: *Memories*, p. 50.
[7] Jane Welsh Carlyle: *Letters*, 1839-63 (Huxley).
[8] *I.e., lapidavano.*
[9] E.F.R., i. 40, 41.
[10] Jane Welsh Carlyle: *Ibid.*

CHAPTER III.

[1] Cagnacci.
[2] Giurati: *Duecento Lettere*, p. 67.

[3] A. De R. Jervis: *Mazzini's Letters*, p. 46.
[4] J. W. Carlyle: *Letters; Ibid.*, p. 210.
[5] *Epistolario*, xii.; Letter, May 21, 1843.
[6] J. W. Carlyle: *Letters; Ibid.*

CHAPTER IV.

[1] *Epistolario*, xii. 377.
[2] Letter, June 16, 1843.
[3] *Epistol.*, x. 341.
[4] Salvemini: *Mazzini*, ch. vii. See Mario: *Vita*, ch. xiii.
[5] *Libro di ricordi.* See Mario: *Vita*, ch. xiii.
[6] *Politica*, ix., p. 306.
[7] Letter to Sir James Graham: *Works*.
[8] Duffy: *Conversations with Carlyle*, p. 109.

CHAPTER V.

[1] *Hist. de la Renaiss. Polit. de l'Italie*, p. 192; R. M. Johnston: *Roman. Theoc.*, p. 60.
[2] Farini.
[3] Charles Dickens: *Roman Candles*.
[4] Masson: *Ibid.*
[5] Thomas Cooper: *Autobiog.*, p. 299.
[6] E.F.R., vol. i.
[7] A. Lumbrosa: *Scaramuccie;* Donaver: *Vita*.
[8] Cagnacci: Letter, November 15, 1847.
[9] *Letters of Lord Beaconsfield*, p. 210.
[10] *Correspond. of Carlyle and Emerson*, ii. 163.

BOOK IV

CHAPTER I.

[1] E.F.R., i. 83.
[2] Cagnacci.
[3] *Epistol.*, xix. 159.
[4] *Works*, v. 97, 98.
[5] *Allocution*, April 29, 1848.
[6] *Epistol.*, xix.; *Letters*, April 23, May 5.
[7] E.F.R., i. 84.
[8] Cagnacci.

CHAPTER II.

[1] *Works*, v.
[2] E.F.R., i. 91.
[3] See *Spectator:* articles December 2, 1848; February 17, March 3, 1849.
[4] E.F.R., i. 93.
[5] Margaret Fuller Ossoli, ii. 247.
[6] Roma Lister: *Reminiscences Social and Political*, 2nd edition, p. 29.

CHAPTER III.

[1] E.F.R., i. 93.
[2] E.F.R., i. 109.
[3] *Epistol.*, xx; Letter, September 26, 1848.

[4] E.F.R., i. 107.
[5] E.F.R., i. iii.
[6] *Scritti Polit. ed. Econ.*, ii. 206, 207.
[7] M. J. Howe: *Intimate Journal of George Sand.*
[8] Farini: *Rome*, iv. 3.
[9] N. Bianchi: *Diplom. Europ.*, vi. 451; Johnston: *Rom. Theoc.*, p. 245.
[10] Marg. Fuller Ossoli: *Works*, ii.
[11] J. W. Mario: *B.M.I.*, p. 198.
[12] A. H. Clough: *Prose Remains*, p. 147.
[13] Letter to Caroline Stansfeld, January 26, 1849; E.F.R., i.

CHAPTER IV.

[1] G. M. Trevelyan: *Garib.'s Def. of Rome*, pp. 101, 102. (And see Maz.: *Works*, v.; Official Acts of the Rom. Repub.; B. King: *Ital. Unity*, i. 328.)
[2] A. H. Clough: *Ibid.*, p. 154, etc.
[3] B. King: *Life of M.*, Everyman edn., p. 131.
[4] *Punch*, vol. xvii., p. 35.
[5] *Allocut.*, February 18, April 20, 1849.
[6] See J. W. Mario: *B.M.I.*
[7] *Garib. Mem.*, 1860 edn.
[8] *Punch*, vol. xvi., p. 215.
[9] *Letters of Q. Victoria*, 1837-61, vol. ii., p. 213.
[10] A. H. Clough: *Amours de Voyage.*
[11] Mrs. Browning: *Casa Guidi Windows.*
[12] Marg. Fuller Ossoli; *Ibid.*, ii. See letters, July 8, August 28.
[13] Thomas Hardy: *Dynasts.*
[14] On the Encyc. of Pope Pius, December, 1844; *Works*, v. 343 ff.
[15] *Works*, v.
[16] Gladstone: *Two Letters to Lord Aberdeen*, 1851.
[17] W. G. Ward: *Newman*, i. 195.
[18] *Garib. Mem.*
[19] Trevelyan: *Ibid.*

BOOK V

CHAPTER I.

[1] Jane W. Carlyle: *Letters* (Huxley), pp. 344, 345.
[2] See J. W. Mario: *B.M.I.*, pp. 219, 220.
[3] J. W. Carlyle: *New Letters and Memorials*, ii. 68, 69.
[4] *Once a Week*, December 14, 1861.
[5] B. King: *Life*, ch. ix.
[6] Gallenga: *My Second Life.*
[7] Giurati: *Duecento Lettere*, p. 311.
[8] Letter, September 9, 1849.
[9] Farini: *Rome*, vii. 4.
[10] E.F.R., i. 132.
[11] *Works*, v. 331 ff.
[12] C. H. Spurgeon: Sermon in Surrey Gardens Music Hall, May 1, 1859; *Met. Tab. Pulpit*, i.

CHAPTER II.

[1] Letter, November 14, 1851; *Epistol.*
[2] Letter to L. Napol.; *Scritti Pol. ed. Econ.*

[3] E.F.R., i. 170, 171.
[4] Cozzolino: *Maria Mazzini.*
[5] *Ibid.*
[6] *Ibid.*
[7] E.F.R. See Letters, August, 1852; *Epistolario,* xxv.; *B.M.I.,* ch. xvi.
[8] *Epistol.,* xxx. 397.
[9] E.F.R., i. 237.
[10] *Lettere di G. M. ad A. Saffi,* p. 60.
[11] Donaver: *Vita,* p. 329.
[12] Herzen: *Memoirs,* iii., p. 72.
[13] E.F.R., i. 298.
[14] Farini, v. 4.

CHAPTER III.

[1] Letter to Lord John Russell, 1854. See Guedalla: *Palmerston,* p. 360.
[2] *Works,* vi., Append.
[3] Cf. Grant Duff: *Notes from My Diary,* 1911 ed., p. 61.
[4] Trevelyan: *Garib. and Thousand,* Nelson ed., p. 74.
[5] E.F.R., i. 296.
[6] Mario: *B.M.I.*
[7] E.F.R., ii. 58.
[8] Mario: *Ibid.*

CHAPTER IV.

[1] Giglioli: *Naples,* p. 320.
[2] Letter to Villamarina, June 17, 1857.
[3] Mario: *B.M.I.*
[4] Thayer: *Cavour,* i., pp. 455, 462.
[5] Saffi: *Scritti Mazzini,* vol. ix.
[6] Trevelyan: *Garib. and Thous.*
[7] E.F.R., ii.

BOOK VI
CHAPTER I.

[1] E.F.R., ii.; Letter, November 3, 1858.
[2] Mrs. H. E. Hamilton King: *Recollections of Mazzini,* p. 6.
[3] G. J. Holyoake: *Bygones Worth Remembering,* i. 227.
[4] *Al Conte di Cavour,* June, 1858 (*Scritti Pol. ed. Econ.,* vol. ii.).
[5] See E.F.R., ii. 128. The confiscation was revoked later.
[6] Cavour: *Lettere;* Letter, February 15, 1858. See Thayer, ii. 513.
[7] J. W. Mario: *B.M.I.,* p. 278.
[8] Cadogan: *Cavour,* p. 251.
[9] *The Times,* July 15, 1859.
[10] E. B. Browning: *A Tale of Villafranca.*
[11] Cesaresco Martinengo: *Cavour;* Thayer: *Cavour,* ii. 114.

CHAPTER II.

[1] E.F.R., ii. 133.
[2] E.F.R., ii. 147.
[3] *Scritti Pol. ed. Econ.,* ii.
[4] Saffi: *Lettere,* p. 181; Letter, August 22, 1859.

[5] *Ai Giovani d' Italia: Scritti Pol. ed. Econ.*, ii. 195 ff.
[6] Thayer: *Cavour*, ii. 218.
[7] Letter, March 30, 1860.

CHAPTER III.

[1] See Del Cerro: *Mazzini e Giud. Sidoli.*
[2] Crispi: *Memoirs*, i. 251.
[3] Crispi: *Ibid.*, p. 272.
[4] Letter to Nicotera; Crispi: *Ibid.*, i. 272.
[5] E.F.R., ii. 184.
[6] E.F.R., ii.
[7] Trevelyan: *Garib. and the Making of Italy*, p. 215.

CHAPTER IV.

[1] Herzen: *Memoirs*, iv. 166.
[2] Herzen: *Ibid.*
[3] Nicolay and Hay: *Lincoln*, x. 53.

BOOK VII

CHAPTER I.

[1] *The Times*, March 12, 1872.
[2] David Masson: *Memories of London*, pp. 205-209.
[3] H. E. Hamilton King: *Recollections of Mazzini.*
[4] Gosse: *Swinburne*, p. 154.
[5] E.F.R., iii. 154.
[6] Gosse: *Ibid.*, p. 163.
[7] Hake and Compton-Rickett: *Letters of Swinburne*, p. 152.
[8] E.F.R., i. 174.
[9] H. E. Hamilton King: *Ibid.*
[10] A. De R. Jervis: *Mazzini's Letters.*
[11] E.F.R., ii.
[12] *Works*, iii., pp. 179, 180.

CHAPTER II.

[1] *Scritti Pol. ed. Econ.*, ii.
[2] *Agli Operai Italiani:* article in the *Roma del Popolo*, July 13, 1871.
[3] W. G. Ward: *Newman.*
[4] Saffi: *Lettere.*
[5] E.A.V., *Joseph Mazzini*, Memoir and Essays.
[6] E.F.R., iii. 214.

CHAPTER III.

[1] *Questione Sociale:* article in the *Roma del Popolo*, No. 40, 1871.
[2] *Lettere d'Amore di G. M.*
[3] E.F.R., iii.

SUPPLEMENTARY BIBLIOGRAPHY

A representative bibliography is appended to Bolton King's *Life of Mazzini* (Dent's Everyman edn., pp. 370-373). The following is a (by no means exhaustive) supplement:

BIOGRAPHIES, BIOGRAPHICAL STUDIES AND LETTERS

ENGLISH

Hinkler, Mrs.: *Life of Mazzini*. (London, 19—.)
Jervis, Alice De Rosen: *Mazzini's Letters*. (London, 1931.)
King, H. E. Hamilton: *Recollections of Mazzini*. (London, 1912.)
Richards, E. F.: *Mazzini's Letters to an English Family* (3 vols.). (London, 1920.)
Richards, E. F.: *Foreshadowings of the Future Faith.*

ITALIAN

Berretta, E. and P.: *Lettere d' Amore di G. Mazzini*. Introd. by A. Salucci. (Genoa, 1924.)
Cantimori: *Saggio nell'idealismo di G. Mazzini*. (Florence, 1904.)
Codignola, A.: *La Giovinezza di G. Mazzini*. (Florence, 1926.)
Cozzolino, I. C.: *Maria Mazzini ed il suo ultimo carteggio*. (Genoa, 1927.)
Levi, A.: *La filosofia politica di G. Mazzini*. (Bologna, 1917.)
Luzio, A.: *La madre di G. Mazzini*. (Turin, 1919.)
Luzio, A.: *Mazzini Carbonaro*. (Turin, 1920.)
Luzio, A.: *Carlo Alberto e Mazzini*. (Turin, 1923.)
Mondolfo, R.: *Mazzini e Marx*. (1924.)
Rosselli, Nello: *Mazzini e Bakounine*. (Turin, 1927.)
Salucci, A.: *G. Mazzini: Poesie Giovanili*. (Milan, 1926.)
Salucci, A.: *Amori Mazziniani*. (Florence, 1928.)
Salvemini, Gaetano: *Nuovi documenti nella giovinezza di G. Mazzini e dei fratelli Ruffini*. (*Studii Storici* Review, Pisa, 1911.)
Salvemini, Gaetano: *Mazzini*. (Florence, 1925.)
De Sanctis, Francesco: *Mazzini*. (Bari, 1920.)
There is a concise summary of Mazzini's life and thought by Giulio del Sillaro (*Vita di G. Mazzini*. Milan, n.d.).
An interesting souvenir publication, *Genova a Giuseppe Mazzini*, was issued by the *Rivista Popolare*, Rome, in 1905, the centenary of Mazzini's birth; and the *Musée Neuchatelois* for January-February, 1929, contains Mazzini's letters to the Courvoisiers (Marguerite Mauerhofer). The *Revue d'Histoire Suisse*, No. XII., 1932, has a further contribution by Mlle. Mauerhofer on Mazzini's Swiss exile. Prof. S. M. Brown, of Lehigh University, has written a useful monograph on *Mazzini and Dante* (Academy of Polit. Science, N.Y., 1927). For a discussion of Mazzini's political ideas see C. E. Vaughan: *Studies in the Hist. of Polit. Philos.* (Manchester University Press, 1925).

The National Italian edition of Mazzini's writings, still in process of publication, now (1932) numbers some 55 vols.

Among Memoirs containing recollections of the Ruffinis and Mazzini, Masson's *Memories of London in the Forties* (Blackwood, 1908) and *Memories of Two Cities* (Oliphant, 1911) are valuable, and the *Memoirs of Alexander Herzen* (Chatto and Windus, 1927) are of particular value for the later years of the exile.

There is interesting Mazzinian material in the (American) *Democratic Review* for 1852 (*Mazzini—Young Europe,* with portrait, p. 41; *Campaigns of Chas. Albert and the Republicans,* p. 193, etc.; *Republican Sketches; Ciceroacchio,* p. 167, etc.; and an article by Victor Hugo on *Napoleon the Little,* p. 369). In *Once a Week* (London) for December 14, 1861, George Meredith sums up against Austria in a poem *The Patriot Engineer,* and Harriet Martineau against Mazzini in an article on *Political Agitators.* Karl Blind has an informing article on Garibaldi and Mazzini in the *Contemporary Review,* March, 1888. In an article in the *Dublin Review* (1913?), Mrs. H. E. Hamilton King claims Mazzini, in spite of his anti-Papalism, as a Catholic believer more orthodox than many Catholic modernists. An excellent popular study of Mazzini and his Italian contemporaries is that by Rupert S. Holland: *Builders of United Italy* (Henry Holt and Co., N.Y., 1908). Perhaps the noblest of all appreciations of Mazzini is that by F. W. H. Myers, republished in 1921 in his *Essays Classical and Modern* (Macmillan). See, also, G. W. E. Russell in *A Pocketful of Sixpences* (Thos. Nelson and Sons) for a neat and sympathetic prose-portrait in miniature. Two leading articles on Mazzini in *The Times* are reprinted in *Eminent Persons* (*The Times* Office, London, 1880).

Among the works of fiction in which Mazzini figures may be mentioned George Meredith's *Vittoria,* G. Ruffini's *Dr. Antonio* (and, of course, *Benoni*), Warwick Deeping's *The Lame Englishman* (a sympathetic portrayal where, however, the description of Mazzini as "tall" is hardly accurate; he was 5 feet 8 inches), and Richard Huch's *Defeat.* In English poetry he appears in Mrs. Browning's *Casa Guidi Windows,* Arthur Hugh Clough's *Amours de Voyage,* Swinburne's *Songs Before Sunrise,* and Mrs. Hamilton King's *The Disciples.* Mazzini is said to have inspired Browning's *Italian in England.*

INDEX

376 INDEX